Diagonal-banded Sweetlips

Did You Know?

- **Diagonal-banded sweetlips are tropical fish found throughout the western Pacific, including the northern part of the Great Barrier Reef.**

- **Adult diagonal-banded sweetlips have blue-black stripes on their bodies and spots on their yellow fins and tails.**

- **Diagonal-banded sweetlips swarm together over coral reefs in large groups, or schools.**

CALIFORNIA
Science

Macmillan
McGraw-Hill

Program Authors

Dr. Jay K. Hackett
Professor Emeritus of Earth Sciences
University of Northern Colorado

Dr. Richard H. Moyer
Professor of Science Education
  and Natural Sciences
University of Michigan–Dearborn

Dr. JoAnne Vasquez
Elementary Science Education Consultant
NSTA Past President
Member, National Science Board
  and NASA Education Board

Mulugheta Teferi, M.A.
Principal, Gateway Middle School
St. Louis Public Schools
St. Louis, MO

Dinah Zike, M.Ed.
Dinah Might Adventures LP
San Antonio, TX

Kathryn LeRoy, M.S.
Executive Director
Division of Mathematics and Science Education
Miami-Dade County Public Schools, FL

Dr. Dorothy J. T. Terman
Science Curriculum Development Consultant
Former K–12 Science and Mathematics Coordinator
Irvine Unified School District, CA

Dr. Gerald F. Wheeler
Executive Director
National Science Teachers Association

Bank Street College of Education
New York, NY

Contributing Authors

Dr. Sally Ride
Sally Ride Science
San Diego, CA

Lucille Villegas Barrera, M.Ed.
Elementary Science Supervisor
Houston Independent School District
Houston, TX

Dr. Stephen F. Cunha
Professor of Geography
Humboldt State University
Arcata, CA

American Museum of Natural History
New York, NY

Contributing Writer

Ellen Grace
Albuquerque, NM

 The American Museum of Natural History in New York City is one of the world's preeminent scientific, educational, and cultural institutions, with a global mission to explore and interpret human cultures and the natural world through scientific research, education, and exhibitions. Each year the Museum welcomes around four million visitors, including 500,000 schoolchildren in organized field trips. It provides professional development activities for thousands of teachers; hundreds of public programs that serve audiences ranging from preschoolers to seniors; and an array of learning and teaching resources for use in homes, schools, and community-based settings. Visit www.amnh.org for online resources.

RFB&D
learning through listening. Students with print disabilities may be eligible to obtain an accessible, audio version of the pupil edition of this textbook. Please call Recording for the Blind & Dyslexic at 1-800-221-4792 for complete information.

D

The McGraw·Hill Companies

Macmillan/McGraw-Hill

Send all inquiries to:
Macmillan/McGraw-Hill
8787 Orion Place
Columbus, OH 43240-4027

ISBN 978-0-02-284379-3
MHID 0-02-284379-5

FOLDABLES™ is a trademark of The McGraw-Hill Companies, Inc.

Printed in the United States of America.

5 6 7 8 9 (058/055) 11 10 09 08

Scientific Method

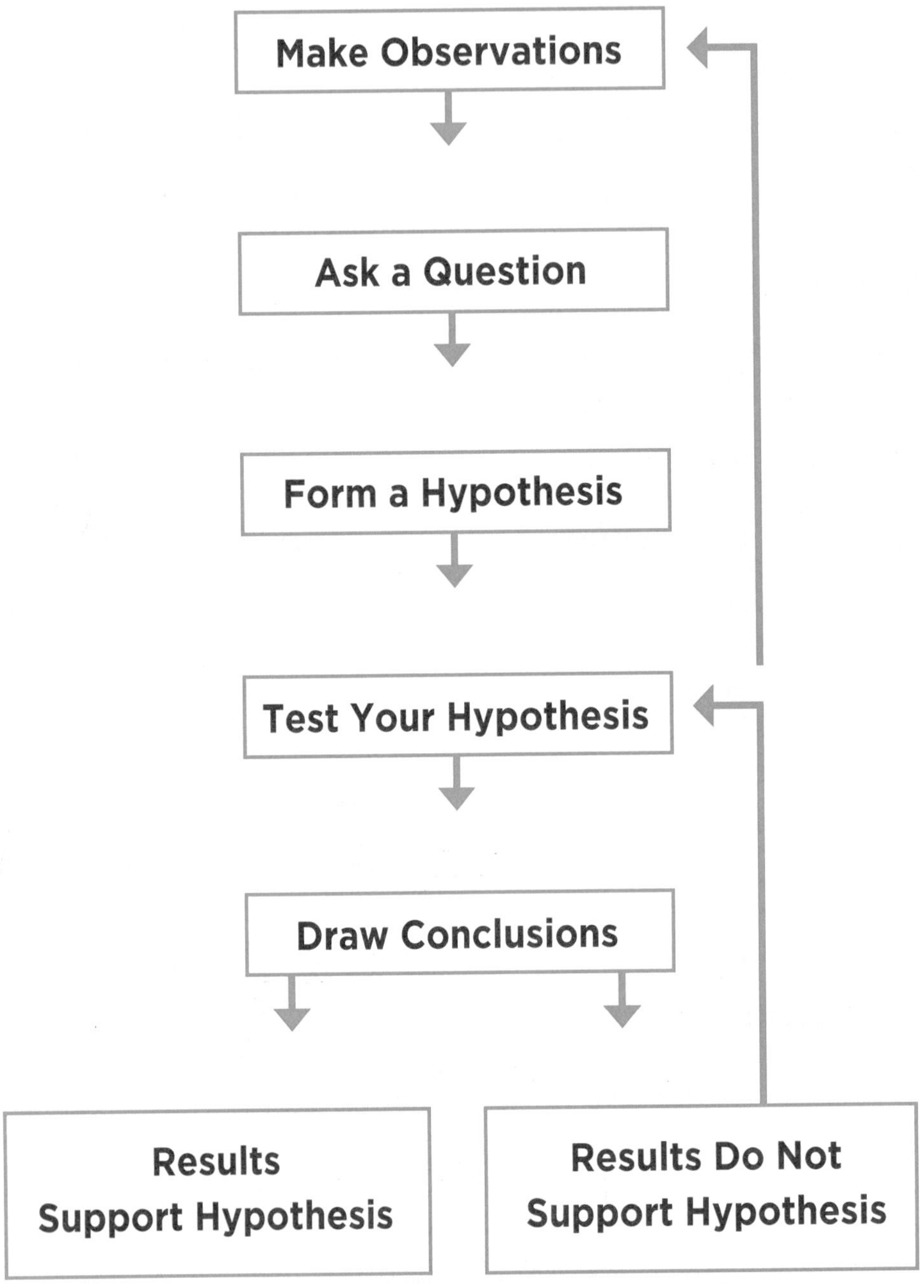

Make Observations

↓

Ask a Question

↓

Form a Hypothesis

↓

Test Your Hypothesis

↓

Draw Conclusions

Results Support Hypothesis

Results Do Not Support Hypothesis

Be a Scientist

Students make measurements and record data. ▶

Life Science

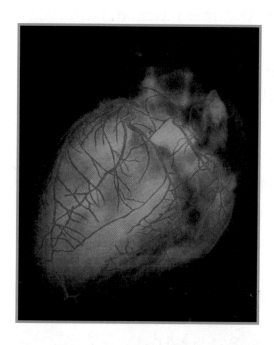

▶ **The human heart beats about 70 to 90 times a minute.**

Earth Science

▼ **This astronaut catches floating candy
   while in a space vehicle orbiting Earth.**

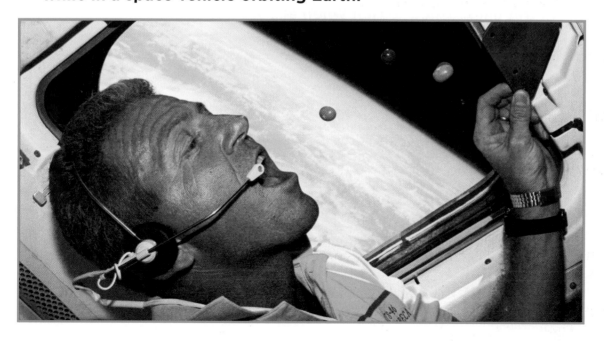

Physical Science

▼ **The iron in this ship turned to rust when exposed to air.**

▼ Crystals of salt have a cubic shape.

Activities

Life Science

Earth Science

Activities

Physical Science

Reference

◀ **This student is using a thermometer.**

Safety Tips

In the Classroom

- Read all of the directions. Make sure you understand them. When you see "⚠ **Be Careful,**" follow the safety rules.

- Listen to your teacher for special safety directions. If you do not understand something, ask for help.

- Wash your hands with soap and water before an activity.

- Be careful around a hot plate. Know when it is on and when it is off. Remember that the plate stays hot for a few minutes after it is turned off.

- Wear a safety apron if you work with anything messy or anything that might spill.

- Clean up a spill right away, or ask your teacher for help.

- Tell your teacher if something breaks. If glass breaks, do not clean it up yourself.

- Wear safety goggles when your teacher tells you to wear them. Wear them when working with anything that can fly into your eyes or when working with liquids.

- Keep your hair and clothes away from open flames. Tie back long hair, and roll up long sleeves.

- Keep your hands dry around electrical equipment.

- Do not eat or drink anything during an experiment.

- Put equipment back the way your teacher tells you to.

- Dispose of things the way your teacher tells you to.

- Clean up your work area after an activity, and wash your hands with soap and water.

In the Field

- Go with a trusted adult—such as your teacher, or a parent or guardian.

- Do not touch animals or plants without an adult's approval. The animal might bite. The plant might be poison ivy or another dangerous plant.

Responsibility

- Treat living things, the environment, and one another with respect.

Be a Scientist

Scientists found evidence that water used to flow on the surface of Mars.

What Is
Science?

Science is a way of understanding the world around us. The work of scientists often begins when scientists ask questions about something they observe. Asking and answering questions is the basis of inquiry.

In this section, you will see how scientists use inquiry skills as they study the planet Mars.

Investigation and Experimentation

6. Scientific progress is made by asking meaningful questions and conducting careful investigations. As a basis for understanding this concept and addressing the content in the other three strands, students should develop their own questions and perform investigations. Students will:

a. Classify objects (e.g., rocks, plants, leaves) in accordance with appropriate criteria.

b. Develop a testable question.

c. Plan and conduct a simple investigation based on a student-developed question and write instructions others can follow to carry out the procedure.

d. Identify the dependent and controlled variables in an investigation.

e. Identify a single independent variable in a scientific investigation and explain how this variable can be used to collect information to answer a question about the results of the experiment.

f. Select appropriate tools (e.g., thermometers, meter sticks, balances, and graduated cylinders) and make quantitative observations.

g. Record data by using appropriate graphic representations (including charts, graphs, and labeled diagrams) and make inferences based on those data.

h. Draw conclusions from scientific evidence and indicate whether further information is needed to support a specific conclusion.

i. Write a report of an investigation that includes conducting tests, collecting data or examining evidence, and drawing conclusions.

Inquiry Skills

These are the inquiry skills scientists use. You can use these skills, too.

Observe

Compare

Infer

Classify

Measure

Use Numbers

Communicate

Predict

Record Data

Analyze Data

Sequence

Form a Hypothesis

Use Variables

Experiment

Make a Model

Draw Conclusions

The diagram on this page shows what is usually called the scientific method. Think of a scientific method as a plan of inquiry that uses science process skills as tools to gather, organize, analyze, and communicate information. Scientists don't always follow all these steps in the same order, but they often start with an observation about the world around us.

You, too, are constantly making observations every moment you are awake. You might look out the window to see if it is raining. You might listen for the sound of thunder to find out if a storm is coming.

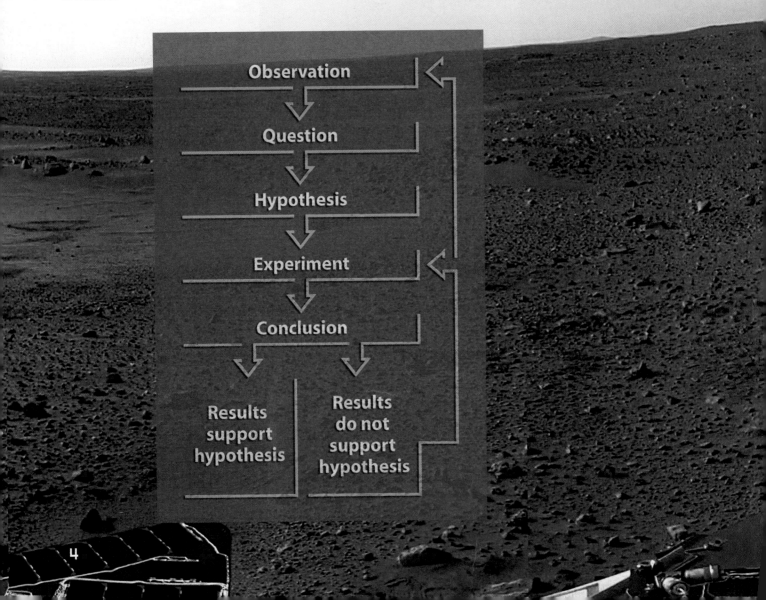

Observation

Question

Hypothesis

Experiment

Conclusion

Results support hypothesis

Results do not support hypothesis

Scientists observe the world around them. To observe means to use your senses to learn about something. Scientists ask questions based on the observations that they have made.

Do you think this photograph was taken on Earth or on Mars? Look for clues in the photo that might help you answer this question. What is the color of the sky and the ground? Do you see any objects that look like they are artificial? How do you think the photograph was taken?

Inquiry Skills

When you make observations, you use these skills.

Observe Use your senses to learn about an object or event.

Classify Place things that share properties together in groups.

Measure Find the size, distance, time, volume, area, mass, weight, or temperature of an object or an event.

Compare Note similarities and differences between objects.

Scientific investigations often start with an unanswered question. If scientists cannot find an answer to a question, they go one step further. They propose a possible answer that can be tested. This is known as forming a hypothesis. A good hypothesis must

- be based on what you observe.
- be testable by performing an investigation or experiment.
- be useful in predicting new findings.

When scientists looked at this photo of the surface of Mars (inset), they wondered if the channel might have been formed by running water, similar to a stream on Earth. How do you think scientists might find the answer to this question?

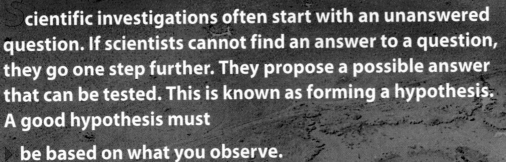

After they come up with a question, scientists do research to find out what is already known about the question and what others have learned from their experiments. Scientists may use books, scientific journals, or Internet resources to find out what other scientists know. When they find information, scientists use it only if it is supported by observations.

In this case, scientists found previous observations of the hardness of rocks near streams. The observations indicated that water wears away at softer types of rock to form streams.

Scientists used that knowledge as they formed a hypothesis about their question about whether or not the channel on Mars was formed by water. A hypothesis is a testable question. That means you must be able to make observations that support or disprove your hypothesis. Scientists formed a hypothesis that said "If the rock on the sides of the channel is a harder type of rock, then there was once water on the surface of Mars."

Inquiry Skills

When you ask questions and form hypotheses, you use these skills.

Infer Form an idea from facts or observations.

Form a Hypothesis Make a statement that can be tested to answer a question.

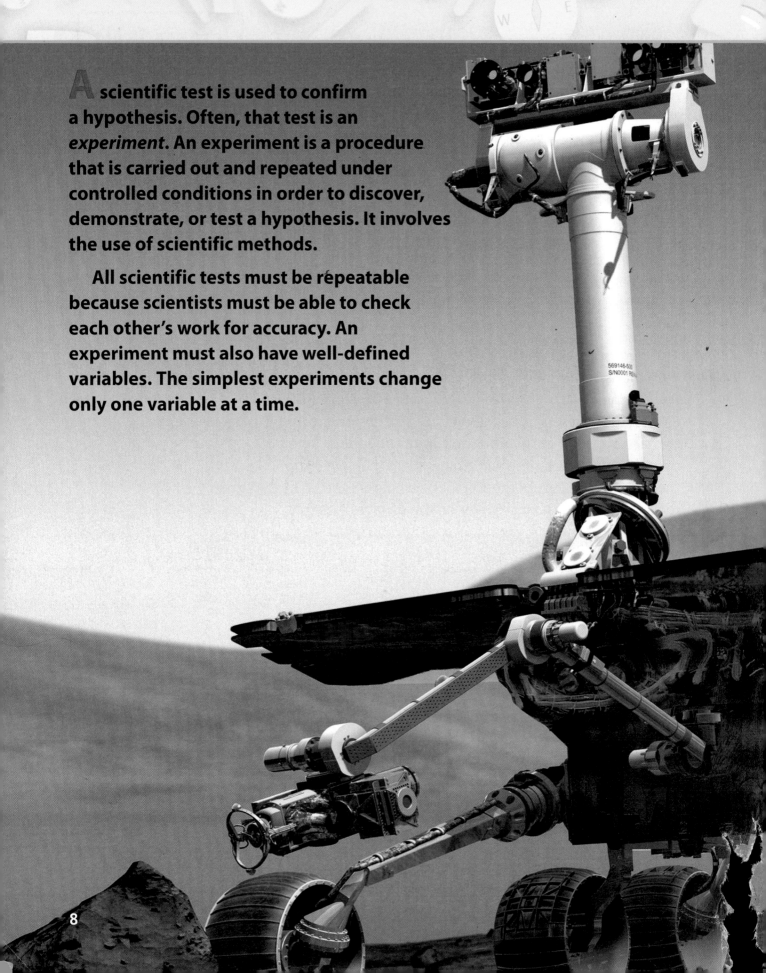

A scientific test is used to confirm a hypothesis. Often, that test is an *experiment*. An experiment is a procedure that is carried out and repeated under controlled conditions in order to discover, demonstrate, or test a hypothesis. It involves the use of scientific methods.

All scientific tests must be repeatable because scientists must be able to check each other's work for accuracy. An experiment must also have well-defined variables. The simplest experiments change only one variable at a time.

Sometimes, scientists cannot conduct a direct experiment to test their hypothesis. For example, scientists cannot go to Mars themselves to search for evidence of water. In 2004, they sent two robots, Spirit and Opportunity, to perform experiments and send data back to Earth.

During their first mission in 2004, the robots took samples of Martian soil. They took the samples from different locations on the planet and at different depths beneath the surface.

Inquiry Skills

When you experiment, you use these skills.

Experiment Perform a test to support or disprove a hypothesis.

Use Variables Identify things in an experiment that can be changed or controlled.

Predict State possible results of an event or experiment.

Make a Model Make something to represent an object or event.

5 IE 6.c. Plan and conduct a simple investigation based on a student-developed question and write instructions others can follow to carry out the procedure. • **5 IE 6.d.** Identify the dependent and controlled variables in an investigation. • **5 IE 6.e.** Identify a single independent variable in a scientific investigation and explain how this variable can be used to collect information to answer a question about the results of the experiment.

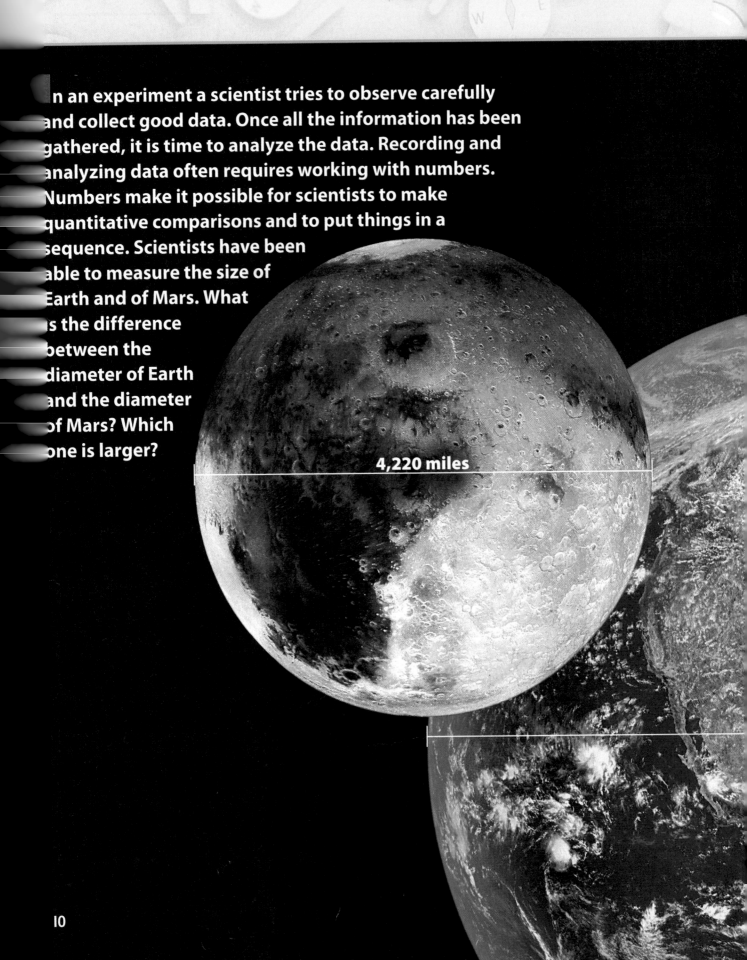

In an experiment a scientist tries to observe carefully and collect good data. Once all the information has been gathered, it is time to analyze the data. Recording and analyzing data often requires working with numbers. Numbers make it possible for scientists to make quantitative comparisons and to put things in a sequence. Scientists have been able to measure the size of Earth and of Mars. What is the difference between the diameter of Earth and the diameter of Mars? Which one is larger?

4,220 miles

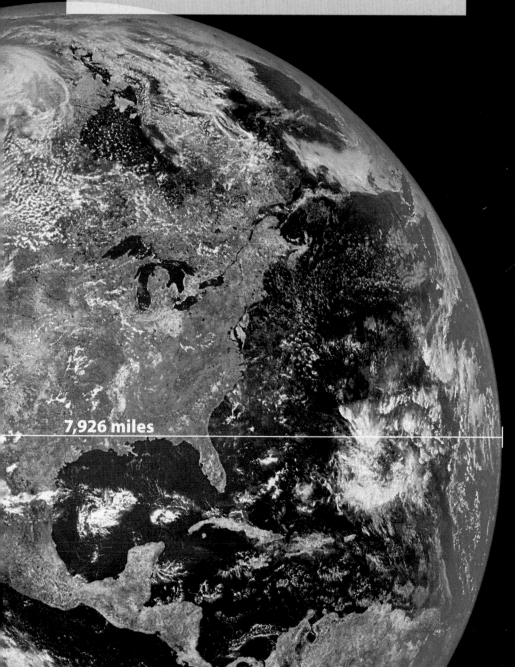

Spirit and Opportunity performed many tests on the samples that they gathered and sent the data back to Earth. This data included information about the hardness of the rocks, the types of rocks, the materials that the rocks were made of, and how deep they were found. Scientists analyzed that data, looking for patterns in the hardness of the rock that were similar to those seen where streams formed on Earth. The data showed that the rock along the sides of the channel was a harder type of rock.

7,926 miles

Inquiry Skills

When you collect and interpret data, you use these skills.

Use Numbers Order, count, add, subtract, multiply, and divide to explain data.

Measure Find the size, distance, time, volume, area, mass, weight, or temperature of an object or an event.

Record Data Gather information in notes, drawings, pictures, charts, tables, or diagrams.

Analyze Data Use the information that has been gathered to answer questions or solve a problem.

Sequence Arrange objects or events in a well-defined order.

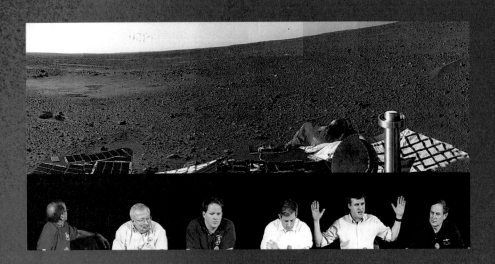

After analyzing the data, scientists are ready to draw conclusions. A conclusion is a statement about whether or not a hypothesis is valid, or supported by the evidence. Sometimes the data do not support the hypothesis. When that happens, and if they have kept careful records, scientists can search for any mistakes. If no mistakes are found, the hypothesis must be rejected. Perhaps different methods or observations are needed.

Why is it important for scientists to communicate about their research? One reason is to give other scientists the opportunity to comment on their work. After all, it takes many repeated experiments yielding consistent results before those results are accepted as "good science."

 5 IE 6.h. Draw conclusions from scientific evidence and indicate whether further information is needed to support a specific conclusion. • **5 IE 6.i.** Write a report of an investigation that includes conducting tests, collecting data or examining evidence, and drawing conclusions.

NASA scientists analyzed the data from the Mars robots' first mission. After several months of data analysis of the rock samples, they concluded that the evidence about the hardness of the rocks on Mars supported their hypothesis that there was once water on the surface of Mars. They announced their initial results in a press conference. They then published their data and their results in scientific journals.

Inquiry Skills

When you draw conclusions and communicate results, you use these skills.

Draw Conclusions Decide how the results relate to the hypothesis.

Communicate Share information.

13

Asking Questions and Forming a Hypothesis

Now that you have read about methods in science, you can put them to use. Experiments start with an unanswered question. Students wondered about the craters on Mars. Here is a question they wanted to explore.

Question

Does the distance an object drops affect the size of the crater it forms?

They turned the question into a **hypothesis**. A hypothesis is an "if ... then ..." statement. You can test a hypothesis and observe results of the test. Here is their hypothesis:

Hypothesis

If we change the distance an object is dropped onto a soft surface, then the crater formed will be larger with the greater distance.

5 IE 6.b. Develop a testable question.

Defining Variables

Once you have a hypothesis that you can test, then you can set up a plan to test it. The test for your hypothesis is your *experiment*. You must identify what you are testing and what you are not testing. These factors are called *variables*.

The factors you are not testing are controls or *controlled variables*. In this experiment the controlled variables will be:

- the weight of the object dropped.
- the substance the object falls into.
- the depth of the substance the object falls into.

The only factor that will change is what you are testing. This is the *independent variable*. The best experiments test only one independent variable at a time.

In this experiment the independent variable will be:

- the distance the object is dropped.

In an experiment, the factors you measure or count are called the *dependent variables*. They depend on what you chose for the independent variable. You will be measuring the width of the crater in centimeters.

What other variables can you identify?

 5 IE 6.d. Identify the dependent and controlled variables in an investigation. • **5 IE 6.e.** Identify a single independent variable in a scientific investigation and explain how this variable can be used to collect information to answer a question about the results of the experiment.

Once you've decided on a hypothesis and identified your variables, you can design your experiment. Here's a procedure the students planned.

Procedure

1. Fill a large rectangular aluminum foil pan with two 5-pound bags of flour. Distribute the flour evenly across the pan.

2. Use a golf ball as the object to drop. With a meterstick, measure lengths of string in 10 cm, 20 cm, and 30 cm segments.

3. Have one partner hold the string. The second partner holds the golf ball at that height and drops it onto the flour. Measure the size of the crater for each drop. Smooth out the surface after each drop. Repeat for each length of string. Repeat your experiment at least two times.

4. Record your data on a chart like the one below.

Do you notice anything you would like to check about these results? Do you see why scientists repeat an experiment many times?

Data Table to Record Observations

Length of String	Trial 1 Depth of Crater	Trial 1 Width of Crater	Trial 2 Depth of Crater	Trial 2 Width of Crater
10 cm	1 cm	4 cm	2 cm	3 cm
20 cm	2.5 cm	5 cm	2 cm	4 cm
30 cm	3 cm	7 cm	4 cm	6 cm

5 IE 6.c. Plan and conduct a simple investigation based on a student-developed question and write instructions others can follow to carry out the procedure.

Collecting and Analyzing Data

How do you know if your results are good? One way is to repeat your experiment several times. See if you get similar results. Another way is to have others conduct the same experiment. Compare their results to yours. Many tests should show that your findings are accurate.

To compare observations and results, scientists must present their data in a way that is clear to others. They use graphs, charts, diagrams, and other visual tools.

The students decided to make a line graph of their results. They put their independent variable on the x axis, and the dependent variable on the y axis as shown.

The students concluded that the distance an object is dropped will affect the size of the crater it makes.

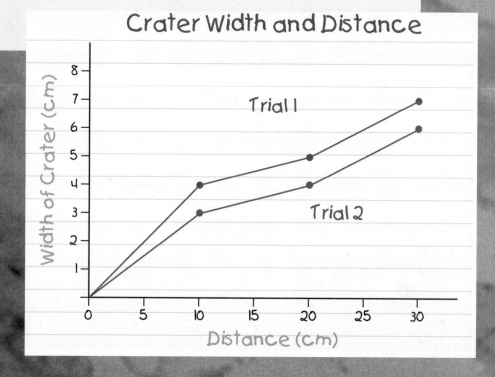

Crater Width and Distance

 5 IE 6.g. Record data by using appropriate graphic representations (including charts, graphs, and labeled diagrams) and make inferences based on those data. • **5 IE 6.h.** Draw conclusions from scientific evidence and indicate whether further information is needed to support a specific conclusion. • **5 IE 6.i.** Write a report of an investigation that includes conducting tests, collecting data or examining evidence, and drawing conclusions.

Forming New Questions

Scientists can use the information from experiments like this one to make new discoveries. Some of these discoveries may be about the surface of Mars, or the Moon, or Earth. What discoveries have you learned about?

One of the most exciting things about science experiments happens after the experiment itself. That is when new ideas, questions, and solutions to problems arise.

What do you think caused this crater? What have scientists learned about it? What tools would they have used to find out about it?

Meteor Crater in Arizona is more than one kilometer wide!

5 IE 6.b. Develop a testable question.

Life Science

Redwoods are the tallest trees in the world.

Structure of Living Things

 What are living things made of?

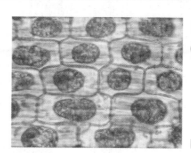
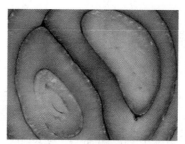

5 LS 2. Plants and animals have structures for respiration, digestion, waste disposal, and transport of materials.

Literature

MAGAZINE ARTICLE

ELA R 5.2.3. Discern main ideas and concepts presented in texts, identifying and assessing evidence that supports those ideas.

ELA W 5.2.4. Write persuasive letters or compositions: **b.** Support a position with relevant evidence.

from **SCHOLASTIC SUPERSCIENCE**

Cancer-Sniffing Canines

People already use the super-sniffing nose power of dogs for many important jobs, like finding people trapped in avalanches. Now scientists have discovered that man's best friend can also use its nose to detect cancer.

Cancer is a disease in which cells (the body's most basic unit of life) multiply without stopping. For a long time scientists suspected that these cells give off a unique smell. To find out for sure, they put six dogs to the test.

The dogs were trained to sniff samples and lie down next to the one that came from a patient suffering from cancer. The dogs picked the correct sample almost half the time.

Scientists hope to use this information to create tests that will check a cell's odor to determine whether a person has cancer. Who says you can't teach an old dog new life-saving tricks?

▲ This dog was trained to find the sample with cancer cells.

▲ A cancer cell. Cancer cells divide much more rapidly than normal cells.

Write About It

Response to Literature
In this article you learned that dogs are being used to detect cancer. Write a letter to the editor of your local newspaper. State your position about using dogs for research. Include convincing evidence that backs up your position.

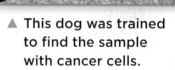

Cells

Look and Wonder

All living things are made of very similar tiny structures. The ones you see here are part of a plant. What is it about these structures that allows us to be alive?

 Building block lesson for 5 LS 2.a. Students know many multicellular organisms have specialized structures to support the transport of materials.

What are plants and animals made of?

Make a Prediction

Animals and plants are living things. Think about the differences between plants and animals. Do you think these differences mean that the parts that they are made of are similar or different?

Test Your Prediction

1 Observe Look at the prepared slide of a leaf under the microscope. For help using the microscope, ask your teacher and look at page 469.

2 Record Data Draw what you see.

3 Observe Look at the prepared slide of blood under the microscope.

4 Record Data Draw what you see.

Draw Conclusions

5 Compare How were the plant leaf slide and animal blood slide alike? How were they different?

6 Communicate Write a report explaining whether or not your observations supported your prediction.

Explore More

Examine the drawings you made and think about the living things they came from. Do you think that a leaf from another plant would look the same? Make a prediction and plan an experiment to test it.

Materials

- microscope
- prepared slides of leaf cells
- prepared slides of blood cells

Step 1

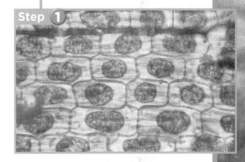

Step 2

Step 3

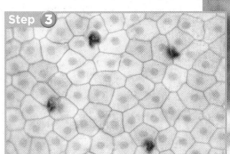

 5 IE 6.i. Write a report of an investigation that includes conducting tests, collecting data or examining evidence, and drawing conclusions.

Main Idea

Plants and animals are made of cells. Cells are the smallest units that can carry out life processes.

Vocabulary

cell, p.26

organelle, p.27

cell membrane, p.29

cytoplasm, p.29

nucleus, p.29

mitochondria, p.29

vacuole, p.29

cell wall, p.31

chloroplast, p.31

microscope, p.32

LOG ON e-Glossary
@ www.macmillanmh.com

Reading Skill

Summarize

Summary

What are plants and animals made of?

Plants, animals, and all living things are made of cells. A **cell** (SEL) is the smallest unit of a living thing that can carry out the basic processes of life. Grass and mountain lions are made of cells. Your own body is made up of trillions of these tiny building blocks.

▼ **This mountain lion and the grass are made of many cells.**

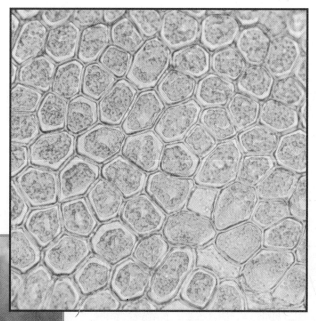

▲ plant cells

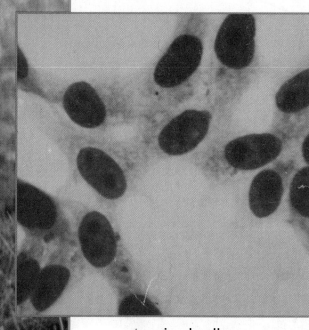

▲ animal cells

The cells of different living things are similar in many ways. All cells need energy to carry out life processes. All cells have structures, called **organelles** (awr•guh•NELZ) that work together to help them perform life processes. These organelles have jobs that must be done to keep the cell alive.

The cells of living things also have some important differences. For example, many plants need to grow tall to reach the sunlight. This means they need something in their cells to provide extra support. Plants can't move to find water when it doesn't rain. So plant cells need to be able to store a lot of water. Plants usually don't eat other living things, so their cells need special organelles to produce their own food.

Unlike plants, animals move around from place to place. They need cells that are more flexible and allow more movement. Since animals can move to find water, their cells do not need to store as much water as plant cells. Animals do not have cells that produce their food. They must get their energy from eating other living things.

 Quick Check

Summarize Describe the relationship between a cell and a living thing.

Critical Thinking What is the difference between a living thing and a nonliving thing?

What are the organelles in animal cells?

If you look at cells through a microscope, you can see that cells have several organelles in them. These organelles work together to keep the cell alive. Look at the diagram of the animal cell to learn about its different parts.

Animal Cell

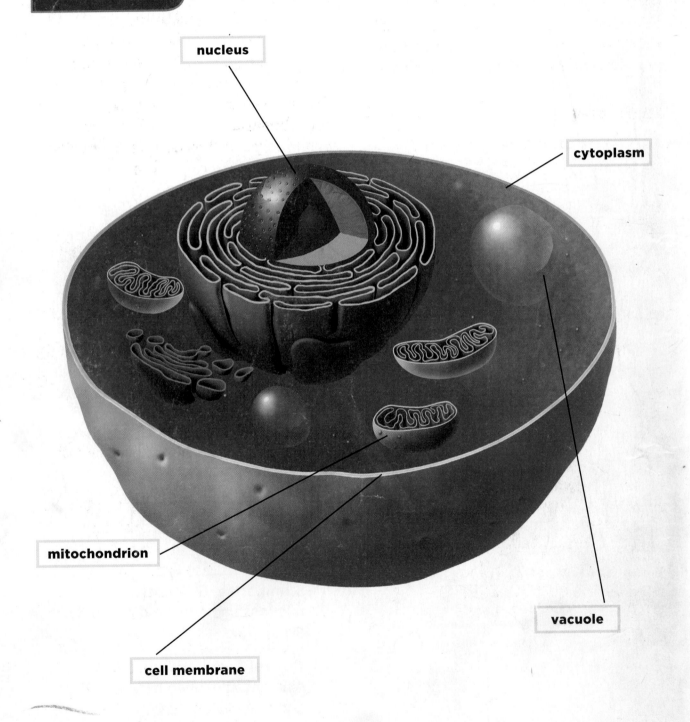

nucleus

cytoplasm

mitochondrion

vacuole

cell membrane

Cell Membrane

All animal cells have a **cell membrane** (MEM•brayn). The cell membrane is a layer around the outside of the cell. It gives the cell shape and controls what moves in and out of the cell.

The cell membrane only allows certain materials to enter and exit the cell. It is very selective. It wraps around the outside of the cell in somewhat the same way your skin wraps around you.

Cytoplasm

Inside the cell membrane is the **cytoplasm** (SIGH•tuh•PLAZ•uhm). The cytoplasm is a gel-like substance that supports all of the organelles that carry out the different jobs in the cell. Cytoplasm is constantly moving through the cell in a stream-like motion.

Nucleus

The **nucleus** (NEW•klee•uhs) is a large spherical structure found in the center of the cell. It has a double membrane with pores, or openings, to allow certain materials to pass in and out.

The nucleus controls all of the activity in the cell. It sends signals to the other parts of the cell. The nucleus tells the cell when it is time to break down food, to grow, to move, and even when it's time for the cell to die.

Mitochondria

Cells have many oval sacs called **mitochondria** (migh•tuh•KON•dree•uh). These sacs have a folded inner membrane. The folds give the mitochondria more surface area. The increased surface area allows the mitochondria to do more work for the cell. A *mitochondrion* (migh•tuh•KON•dree•uhn), a single mitochondria, breaks down food and turns it into energy for the cell to use. The more energy a cell needs, the more mitochondria that cell will have. Very active cells, such as human liver cells, need a lot of mitochondria.

Vacuoles

Cells also contain organelles called **vacuoles** (VAK•yew•ohls) that store water, food, and wastes. The nucleus can signal a vacuole to release whatever it is holding. Animal cells may have many small vacuoles and some may not have any vacuoles.

 Quick Check

Summarize Describe the parts of animal cells.

Critical Thinking Do you think a cell would function without a nucleus? Explain.

What are the organelles in plant cells?

Plant cells have the same organelles as animal cells. They also have some structures that animal cells do not have. Look at the diagram of the plant cell to learn about its parts.

Plant Cell

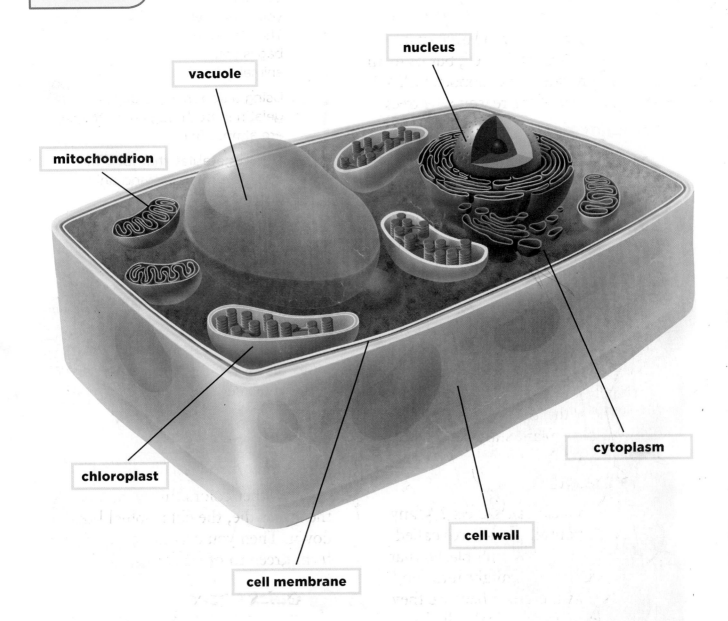

Reading Diagrams

Which structures in plant and animal cells are the same?
Draw a Venn diagram to answer the question.

Clue: Look at the labels in this plant cell diagram and the animal cell diagram on page 28.

Cell Wall

Plant cells have an additional layer around the outside of the cell. This layer is called the **cell wall**. Cell walls are made from a hard, specialized sugar called cellulose. Cellulose protects plant cells and gives them their shape.

The cell wall lets food and wastes move in and out of the cell, but its main job is to provide extra support. Cell walls are part of the reason why trees can grow as tall as they do.

Vacuole

Unlike animal cells, plant cells have one large central vacuole that stores water and also provides support. Have you seen what happens to a plant when it doesn't get enough water? The vacuoles release the water they were storing into the cells. This causes the vacuoles to shrink, which makes the cells become smaller. This makes the plant wilt, or bend over. Once you water the plant, the vacuoles have water again and the plant stands back up.

Chloroplasts

What makes plants green? Many plant cells contain structures called **chloroplasts** (KLAWR•uh•plasts) that turn energy from sunlight into food. Chloroplasts are green because they contain a green chemical called *chlorophyll* (KLAWR•uh•fil). Some plants have chemicals that make other colors. However, there is usually so much more chlorophyll that you don't

see the other colors. In the fall, as the leaves die, the chlorophyll breaks down. Then you can see leaves change from green to other colors.

 Quick Check

Summarize What do vacuoles do in plant cells?

Critical Thinking Do you think desert plants have vacuoles?

How can cells be seen?

For thousands of years people didn't realize that living things as tiny as cells existed. This is because cells are so small they cannot be seen with our eyes only. A **microscope** (MIGH•kruh•skohp) is an instrument that magnifies objects, or makes them look bigger. It took almost 200 years after the first cells were seen under a microscope before scientists realized that all living things are made of cells.

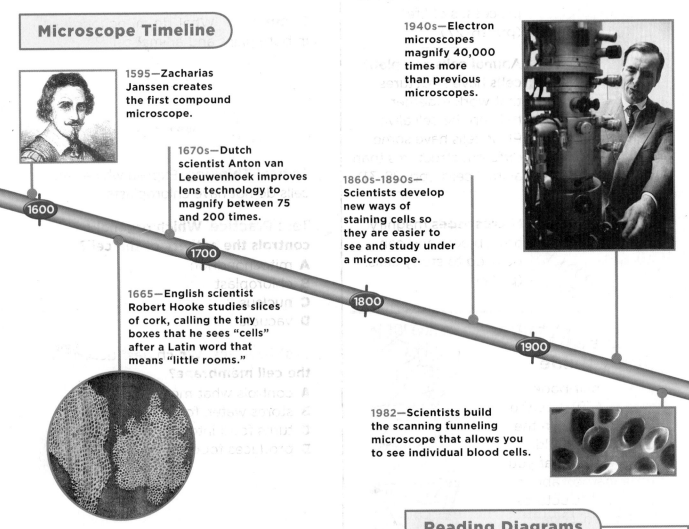

Microscope Timeline

1595—Zacharias Janssen creates the first compound microscope.

1670s—Dutch scientist Anton van Leeuwenhoek improves lens technology to magnify between 75 and 200 times.

1600

1700

1665—English scientist Robert Hooke studies slices of cork, calling the tiny boxes that he sees "cells" after a Latin word that means "little rooms."

1860s–1890s— Scientists develop new ways of staining cells so they are easier to see and study under a microscope.

1800

1900

1940s—Electron microscopes magnify 40,000 times more than previous microscopes.

1982—Scientists build the scanning tunneling microscope that allows you to see individual blood cells.

✔ Quick Check

Summarize What prevented people from realizing that cells and other tiny living things existed?

Critical Thinking What are some reasons that it is important for scientists to be able to see cells clearly?

Reading Diagrams

In what year did Robert Hooke first see cork cells?

Clue: Look at the diagram for the picture of cork cells. Read the caption and look for the year.

Lesson Review

Summarize the Main Idea

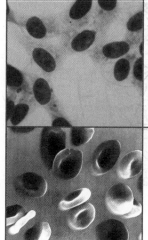

All living things are made of **cells**, which are the smallest units of a living thing that can carry out the basic processes of life. (pp. 26–27)

Animal cells and **plant cells** have structures that work together to keep the cell alive. Plant cells have some different structures than animal cells. (pp. 28–31)

Microscopes magnify tiny objects and can be used to study cells. (p. 32)

Make a FOLDABLES™ Study Guide

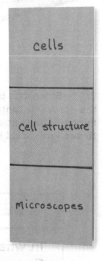

cells

cell structure

microscopes

Make a half-book (see p. 479). Use the titles shown. On the inside of the fold, summarize what you have learned about cells, cell structures and microscopes.

Think, Talk, and Write

1. **Main Idea** What are cells? *are the smallest of living things that can carry out the basic process of life*

2. **Vocabulary** A structure that stores food, water, and wastes in plant and animal cells is a _vacuole_

3. **Summarize** What do mitochondria do in both plant and animal cells?

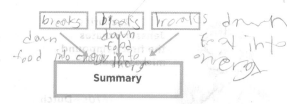

breaks down food into energy *breaks down food into energy* *breaks down food into energy*

Summary

4. **Critical Thinking** Explain why animal cells do not have chloroplasts. *animals don't have leaves*

5. **Test Practice** Which organelle controls the activity of the cell?
   - **A** mitochondrion
   - **B** chloroplast
   - **C** nucleus
   - **D** vacuole

6. **Test Practice** Which *best* describes the cell membrane?
   - **A** controls what moves in and out
   - **B** stores water, food, and wastes
   - **C** turns food into energy
   - **D** produces food for the cell

 **Writing Link**

Expository Writing

Select an organelle and research what it does in the cell. Explain its function in the cell.

 Math Link

How small are cells?

Animal cells can be as small as 1/1000 of a millimeter. Write this number as a decimal and as a percent.

Experiment

All living things are made up of cells. Every cell has a cell membrane, or a layer around the outside of the cell. A cell membrane acts like the door to the cell. It lets things in and out of the cell. One way to learn more about how cell membranes work is by doing an **experiment**.

❶ Learn It

An **experiment** is a test that supports or disproves a hypothesis. To carry out a successful **experiment** you need to perform a test that examines the effects of one variable on another using controlled conditions. You can then use your data to draw a conclusion about whether or not the hypothesis has been supported.

In the following **experiment**, you will test the effects of variables on a cell membrane. Using vinegar, you will dissolve the shells of two eggs to expose the egg membranes. Then you will gather and analyze data to support or disprove the following hypothesis: *If the liquid outside a membrane is thicker than the liquid inside the membrane, then the liquid inside the membrane will move out to balance the concentration.*

❷ Try It

▶ Pour 200 mL of vinegar into two jars with lids and carefully lower two eggs into the jars of vinegar. Tighten the lids and leave the eggs inside for one day.

▶ Use a spoon to carefully remove the eggs and rinse them under water.

▶ Measure each egg using either a measuring tape, metric measuring cup, or balance. Record the measurements in your chart.

▶ Pour 200 mL of water into a beaker and 200 mL of corn syrup into another beaker. Carefully lower an egg into each beaker. Leave the eggs inside for one day.

5 IE 6.f. Select appropriate tools (e.g., thermometers, meter sticks, balances, and graduated cylinders) and make quantitative observations. • 5 IE 6.c. Plan and conduct a simple investigation based on a student-developed question and write instructions others can follow to carry out the procedure.

▶ Use the spoon to carefully remove the eggs and rinse them under water.

▶ Measure the eggs again using the same measuring tool you used earlier. Record the measurements in your chart.

	Measurement Tool Used	Initial Measurement	Final Measurement
Egg in Vinegar			
Egg in Water			
Egg in Corn Syrup			

❸ Apply It

Now it is time to analyze your data and observations. Use your chart to compare your initial and final measurements of the eggs.

▶ Did both eggs change in size? Did one change more than the other?

▶ Why do you think this happened? Does this support or disprove the hypothesis?

From Cells to Organisms

Look and Wonder

You could say that the levels of organization of a school are bricks, walls, rooms, and finally the school building. Living things also have levels of organization. How are organisms, like an onion plant, organized?

Building block lesson for 5 LS 2.a. Students know many multicellular organisms have specialized structures to support the transport of materials.

What are the levels of organization of living things?

Purpose

To research the levels of organization of an onion plant.

Procedure

1. Peel the skin of an onion.

2. Make a wet-mount slide by placing a small piece of the onion skin in the center of the slide, then put a drop of water on the onion skin. Carefully put a cover slip on top.

3. **Observe** View the onion skin under low power. What do the cells looks like? Draw what you see.

4. **Observe** Use the hand lens to observe another piece of onion skin. Draw what you see.

5. Take the remaining onion and remove all of its parts. Make a diagram of the structure of the onion.

- gloves
- goggles
- onion
- slides
- water
- microscope
- hand lens

Draw Conclusions

6. **Compare** Are the various onion cells you observed in the onion layer similar or different?

7. **Infer** How do these cells work together?

Step 1

Explore More

Research the levels of organization of the onion plant. Answer these questions with a labeled diagram. What is an onion? Is it part of the root or the stem?

Step 2

 5 IE 6.g. Record data by using appropriate graphic representations (including charts, graphs, and labeled diagrams) and make inferences based on those data.

How are living things organized?

Main Idea

Cells make up tissues, which make up organs, which make up organ systems.

Vocabulary

unicellular, p.38

organism, p.38

multicellular, p.39

tissue, p.40

organ, p.40

organ system, p.41

 LOG ON e-Glossary
@ www.macmillanmh.com

Reading Skill

Compare and Contrast

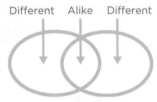
Different   Alike   Different

SCIENCE QUEST Explore the levels of organization from cells to organs with Team Earth.

As you have learned, cells are the smallest units of living things that can carry out the basic processes of life. **Unicellular** (YEW•nuh•SEL•yuh•luhr), or one-celled, organisms (AWR•guh•niz•uhm) can carry out all of the processes of life within a single cell. An **organism** is an individual living thing. Diatoms are examples of unicellular organisms. Diatoms live in fresh water and salt water. They float on the water's surface and are eaten by many other organisms. They have glass-like cell walls.

▼ Diatoms are unicellular living things found in fresh water and salt water.

Organisms that are made of many different kinds of cells are **multicellular** (mul•tee•SEL•yuh•luhr). Animals and plants are examples of multicellular organisms.

In multicellular organisms, every cell carries out its own life processes. The cells also work together to take care of different functions for the organism. For example, all of your heart muscle cells carry out their own life processes and they work together to keep your heart beating.

▼ This mountain lion cub is a multicellular organism.

Life Processes in Living Things	
Growth	The ability to increase in size
Response	The ability to react to changes in surroundings
Reproduction	The ability to produce offspring
Nutrition	The ability to take in food or raw materials to support other life processes
Respiration	The ability to break down food into energy
Excretion	The removal of waste

 Quick Check

Compare and Contrast What activities are common to all living things?

Critical Thinking Are multicellular organisms made of unicellular organisms? Explain your answer.

Reading Charts

What is respiration?
Clue: Look at the rows in the chart. Find the row that gives information about respiration.

How do cells work together?

A group of similar cells that do the same job in an organism is called a **tissue** (TISH•ew). Both plants and animals have tissues. Muscle cells in your legs make up muscle tissue, which allows you to move your legs. Other kinds of tissues in an animal's body include blood, nerves, bone, and skin.

One kind of plant tissue carries water and minerals from a plant's roots through the stems to the leaves. Another example of a plant tissue is the flesh of fruits. The function of this tissue is to protect the plant's seeds.

In plants and animals, tissues of different kinds come together to make up an **organ** (AWR•guhn). Stems and fruits

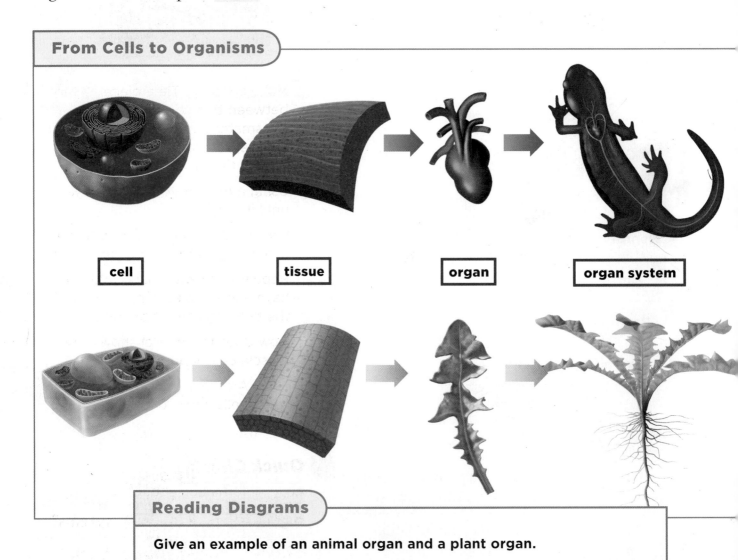

From Cells to Organisms

cell   tissue   organ   organ system

Reading Diagrams

Give an example of an animal organ and a plant organ.

Clue: Use the labels in the diagram to find the answer.

LOG ON   *Science in Motion*   Watch how multicellular living things are organized to form organisms @ **www.macmillanmh.com**

are examples of a plant's organs. The onion is an example of an organ that stores food. The brain, lungs, heart, and stomach are examples of animal organs.

A group of organs that work together to do a certain job is an **organ system**. Organ systems, like the different transport systems in animals and plants, help carry out an organism's life processes.

organism

Muscle Tissues

1. **Make a Model** Tie a piece of yarn between two chairs. Have two classmates sit on each chair. This yarn represents one cell in your muscle tissue.

2. Using a metal ruler, twist the yarn until it snaps.

3. Now tie two pieces of yarn to the chairs. Try to break the yarn again.

4. Repeat this experiment until you have enough pieces of yarn that the twisting cannot break it.

5. How does this model show how muscle cells work in your body?

6. **Infer.** Are your muscles stronger when cells work together?

✓ Quick Check

Compare and Contrast How do organs compare to organ systems?

Critical Thinking Do you think cells from different organs, like the heart and lungs, can be switched? Explain.

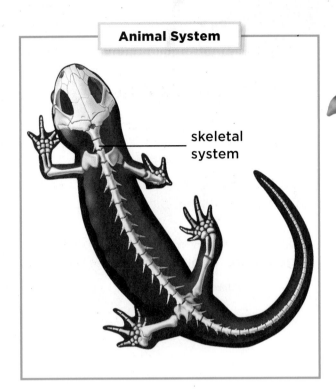

Animal System

skeletal
system

▲ The skeletal system is a
support system in animals.

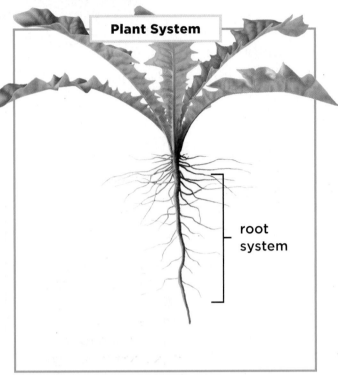

Plant System

root
system

▲ The root system is a
transport system in plants.

What are some plant and animal organ systems?

Multicellular organisms, like a dandelion plant or a salamander, have several organ systems. Plants and animals use different organ systems to carry out their life processes.

The roots of a dandelion, and other plants, are the main organ in the root system. Stems and leaves are organs of the shoot system. Plants also have other systems for transporting materials and for reproduction.

The salamander, like other animals, has an organ system that breaks down food for energy. The stomach is part of this system. The bones, muscles,

and brain are part of systems that control the salamander's movements and responses. The salamander has an organ system for respiration. Its skin and lungs are organs in this system. The skin is also part of the organ system that protects the salamander. The salamander's heart is part of the organ system that transports its blood and other materials.

✓ Quick Check

Compare and Contrast Which organ systems of plants and animals carry out similar functions?

Critical Thinking Can an organ be part of two organ systems?

Lesson Review

Summarize the Main Idea

A **unicellular** organism carries out life processes within one cell. A **multicellular** organism has specialized cells to carry out life processes. (pp. 38–39)

A **tissue** is a group of cells that work at the same job. Tissues form **organs**, which work together and form **organ systems**. Organ systems make up the organism. (pp. 40–41)

Plants and animals have many different **organ systems** to carry out life processes. (p. 42)

Make a FOLDABLES™ Study Guide

Make a half-book (see p. 479). Use the titles shown. On the inside of the fold, compare and contrast each of the topics.

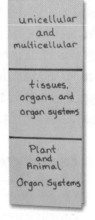

unicellular and multicellular

tissues, organs, and organ systems

Plant and Animal Organ Systems

Think, Talk, and Write

1. **Main Idea** What are multicellular organisms made up of?

   many cells

2. **Vocabulary** A group of similar cells that work together is a(n) _____ *tissue*.

3. **Compare and Contrast** Compare the organization in plants and animals.

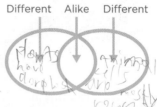

Different   Alike   Different

Plants have chloplasts *animals kills are mostly round*

4. **Critical Thinking** Could an organism survive without one of its organs?

   NO

5. **Test Practice** Which of the following life processes removes wastes?
   A response
   B reproduction
   C excretion
   D nutrition

6. **Test Practice** Which of the following is a unicellular organism?
   A a human
   B a plant
   C a diatom
   D an animal

Writing Link

Explanatory Writing
Research one of your organs, such as your heart. Write about the functions of this organ and its organ system.

Math Link

Your skin is the largest organ in your body. You lose about 30,000 dead skin cells every minute. How many skin cells does your body lose in a day?

 **e-Review** Summaries and quizzes online @ **www.macmillanmh.com**

43
EVALUATE

Materials

microscope

muscle slide

skin slide

nerve slide

colored pencils

Inquiry Structured

How do cells from different tissues in the human body compare?

Form a Hypothesis

A cell can be an organism that carries out its own life processes. Bacteria and protists are unicellular organisms. A cell can also be a part of a multicellular organism. Cells in multicellular organisms might have a single, very specific, function. For example, a cell in the stomach might only be responsible for producing one digestive chemical.

Do you think cells from different tissues in the human body have different forms? Are all cells from the human body alike or different? Write your answer as a hypothesis in the form *"If cells belong to different tissues in the human body, then ..."*

Test Your Hypothesis

1. **Experiment** Place the muscle slide on the microscope stage. Follow your teacher's instructions to focus the microscope.
⚠ **Be careful.** Tell your teacher immediately if a slide breaks.

2. **Observe** Use colored pencils and draw the image you see in your journal. Label your drawing.

3. **Experiment** Repeat steps 1 and 2 with the skin and nerve slides.

Step 1

Step 2

 5 IE 6.b. Develop a testable question. • **5 IE 6.c.** Plan and conduct a simple investigation based on a student-developed question and write instructions others can follow to carry out the procedure.

Draw Conclusions

1. **Communicate** Describe the cell size and shape for each cell type.

2. **Compare** What similarities and differences did you see?

3. Did the experiment support or disprove your hypothesis? Explain your answer.

Inquiry Guided

How do cells from different plant tissues compare?

Form a Hypothesis

You have already learned about the differences between animal and plant cells. You also know that, like animals, plants are made up of cells that form tissues. Do you think cells from different tissues in a plant have different forms? Write your answer as a hypothesis in the form *"If cells belong to different tissues in a plant, then ..."*

Test Your Hypothesis

Design a plan to test your hypothesis. Then write out the materials, resources, and steps you need. Record your results and observations as you follow your plan and conduct your experiment.

Draw Conclusions

Did your experiment support your hypothesis? Why or why not? Present your results to your classmates.

Remember to follow the steps of the scientific process.

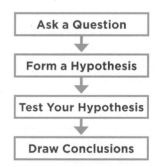

Inquiry Open

What else can you learn about cells and tissues in plants and animals? For example, how many types of tissues do we have? Determine the steps you would follow to answer your question. Record and document the resources you would use during your investigation.

Diversity of Organisms

Look and Wonder

Scientists estimate that there are more than 10 million organisms that have yet to be discovered. What do scientists do when they find an organism they've never seen before? How do they classify it?

Building block lesson for 5 LS 2.a. Students know many multicellular organisms have specialized structures to support the transport of materials.

How would you classify a new plant?

Purpose

You are part of an expedition that is studying plants in the jungle. You find a plant you've never seen before. How do you classify it? You could use a classification key. A classification key lists traits of organisms. It gives directions that lead you to the organisms' identities. Use this classification key to classify plants.

Procedure

① **Observe** Choose a plant and examine its structures with the hand lens.

② Use the classification key to identify your plant. Start with the first pair of traits and choose the trait that applies to your plant.

③ Repeat steps 1 and 2 for the other four plants.

Draw Conclusions

④ Why do you think classifying organisms helps scientists? Explain.

⑤ **Infer** Which of the plants you classified are more similar, or more closely related, to each other? Explain.

Explore More

What traits could you use to identify other organisms, such as birds? Research another group of organisms and create a classification key for them. Your key should begin with general traits and end with traits that are more specific.

 5 IE 6.a. Classify objects (e.g. rocks, plants, leaves) in accordance with appropriate criteria.

Materials

- water plant, such as an elodea
- flowering plant, such as a geranium
- small pine or other conifer
- moss plant
- fern plant
- hand lens

Step ①

Step ②

Classification Key for Plants

1. Stem.....................Go to 2
   No stem...................Moss

2. Produces flowers ...... Geranium
   No flowers ....Go to 3

3. Waxy leaves............Conifer
   Non-waxy leaves .... Go to 4

4. Grows in soil .... Fern
   Grows in water ....Elodea

Main Idea

Living things are classified in kingdoms so they can be studied.

Vocabulary

kingdom, p.48

vertebrate, p.50

invertebrate, p.50

vascular, p.52

nonvascular, p.53

fungus, p.54

bacteria, p.55

protist, p.56

LOG ON ℮-Glossary
@ www.macmillanmh.com

Reading Skill

Main Idea

Main Idea	Details

How are living things grouped together?

With millions of organisms on Earth, scientists need a way to organize the information they discover about them. Classifying organisms, or putting them into groups, helps scientists study, identify, and name organisms. It shows which organisms are most similar to one another. It can also show the order in which they appeared on Earth.

One widely used classification system divides living things into six kingdoms. A **kingdom** is the broadest group into which organisms are classified. Kingdoms are then divided into smaller and smaller groups. As the groups become smaller, the organisms in each group are more alike.

How can you tell which organisms should be grouped together? You would never think that a horse had anything in common with a spider, but they are actually in the same kingdom! Scientists classify organisms into kingdoms by carefully comparing their cells, tissues, organs, and organ systems.

After being classified into a kingdom, organisms with more similarities are grouped into a *phylum* (FIGH•luhm). *Phyla*, the plural of phylum, are separated into *classes*, classes into *orders*, orders into *families*, families into *genera*, and genera into *species*. A horse and a zebra share many traits but they are not similar enough to be the same species. A species is the narrowest group in the classification system, so it only contains organisms that are very closely related.

◄ The scientific name for this horse is *Equus caballus.* The first part of the name is the genus. The second part is the species.

Classification of Horses

Kingdom

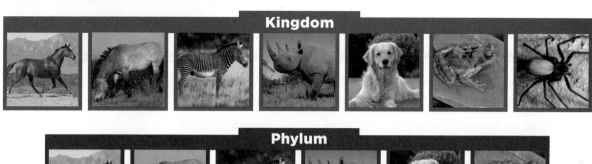

Phylum

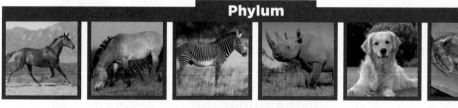

Class

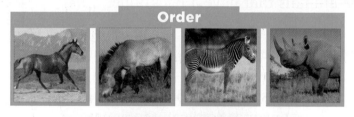

Order

Family

Genus

Species

✓ Quick Check

Main Idea How do classification systems organize organisms?

Critical Thinking Do you think cats belong in a group with horses? Explain.

What do animals have in common?

Animals are multicellular organisms that get energy from eating other living things.

All animals belong to the Animal Kingdom. The Animal Kingdom is divided into many phyla. Some phyla are made up of animals that are invertebrates. **Invertebrates** (in•VUR•tuh•brayts) are animals without a backbone.

Most of the animals you are familiar with—such as dogs, cats, and horses—belong to one phylum, called *Chordata* (KAWR•day•ta). Members of this phylum have a supporting rod that runs the length of the body for at least part of their life.

The phylum Chordata also includes some unusual animals such as sea squirts. Sea squirts are invertebrates. Most chordates, however, are vertebrates. **Vertebrates** (VUR•tuh•brayts) are animals that have a backbone.

There are five basic kinds of vertebrates. These are fish, amphibians (am•FIB•ee•uhns), reptiles, birds, and mammals. *Fish* are vertebrates that live in water. Their bodies are covered by scales. *Amphibians* spend part of their lives in water and part of their lives on land. Some amphibians

◀ giraffe eating from a tree

▲ monarch butterfly on daisy flower

Reading Photos

What do these two organisms have in common?

Clue: Observe the organisms in the photos. Think about what both organisms are doing in the photos.

Animal Phyla without Backbones		Phylum Chordata: Classes with Backbones	
Phylum	**Example**	**Class**	**Example**
Sponges	glass sponges	Jawless fish	lampreys
Cnidarians	jellyfish, corals	Cartilaginous fish	sharks, skates, rays
Flatworms	planarians, tapeworms	Bony fish	most saltwater and freshwater fish
Roundworms	hook worm, vinegar eel	Amphibians	frogs, salamanders, toads
Mollusks	clams, oysters, squid, snails	Reptiles	snakes
Segmented worms	earthworms	Birds	ducks, chickens, robins, ostriches, penguins
Arthropods	insects, spiders, lobsters, crayfish, millipedes, centipedes	Mammals	dogs, cats, squirrels, cows, tigers, lions, humans
Echinoderms	sea stars, sand dollars, sea cucumbers, sea urchins		

include frogs, salamanders, and toads. *Reptiles* are land vertebrates with thick, dry, scaly skin. Snakes, lizards, turtles, and alligators are all reptiles. *Birds* have wings and feathers. Ducks, chickens, and robins are all birds. *Mammals* have hair and are fed from their mothers' bodies when they are young.

Some invertebrate phyla are sponges, *mollusks* (MOL•uhsks), and *arthropods* (AHR•thruh•pods). Sponges are simple animals that live in water. Their bodies are hollow tubes with small holes in them. Sponges eat by using their cells to trap food that is carried into their bodies by water. Mollusks are invertebrates with an internal or an external shell. Snails and clams are mollusks with external shells. Octopuses are mollusks with internal shells. Arthropods have a hard outer skeleton, jointed legs, and bodies that are broken up into sections.

✓ Quick Check

Main Idea What are the main characteristics of organisms in the animal kingdom?

Critical Thinking What is the first thing scientists would want to know about a new animal in order to classify it?

What do plants have in common?

All of the organisms in the plant kingdom produce their own food. Like the animal kingdom, the plant kingdom is separated into two major groups. The difference between these divisions is based on how plants transport water, nutrients, and waste.

If you were to look inside a plant's stem, you would see long tubes that run up and down. Water taken in by the plant's roots moves up one set of tubes toward the leaves and flowers. At the same time, food made in the leaves move down through another set of tubes that lead to all parts of the plant.

The tubes are vascular tissue. **Vascular** (VAS•kyuh•luhr) means "composed of or containing vessels." Scientists call plants that have these tissues vascular plants. Vascular plants can grow tall because these tubes let the plants move food and water around to where it is needed. Trees, bushes, grasses, and cacti are all vascular plants.

The trees that grow by this waterfall are examples of vascular plants. The moss that grows on the rocks is nonvascular.

Plant Kingdom

nonvascular

liverwort

moss

hornwort

vascular

gerber flower

pumpkin

pine tree

Reading Diagrams

How are plants divided?

Clue: Look at the chart and observe how it is divided. Use the headings to answer the question.

If you were to look at a piece of moss under a microscope, you would notice that all of its cells look very much alike. Mosses transport water and other substances directly from the ground into their cells. Mosses are called **nonvascular** (non•VAS•kyuh•luhr) plants because they do not have vascular tissue. This makes it impossible for these plants to grow tall.

✓ Quick Check

Main Idea What is the major difference between plants?

Critical Thinking Could you tell whether a plant is vascular or nonvascular by looking at it? Why?

What are fungi?

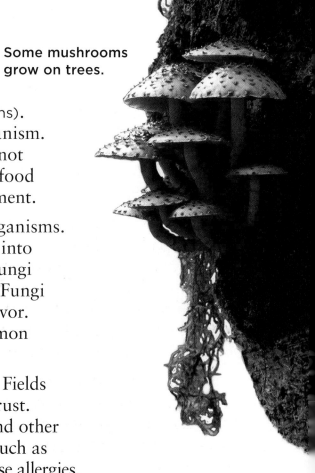

▶ Some mushrooms grow on trees.

If you have had sourdough bread or mushrooms, you have eaten a fungus (FUNG•guhs). A **fungus** can be a unicellular or multicellular organism. *Fungi* (FUN•jigh) is the plural of fungus. Fungi cannot make their own food. Instead they usually absorb food from decaying or dead organisms in their environment.

The fungus kingdom includes many types of organisms. Fungi in soil break down dead plants and animals into nutrients that can be reused by other organisms. Fungi called yeast can be added to bread to make it rise. Fungi are added to some cheeses to give them a tangy flavor. They are also used in medicines. Penicillin, a common medicine, was first produced by a bread mold.

Some fungi can be harmful for other organisms. Fields of wheat can be attacked by a fungus called wheat rust. Many wild mushrooms are poisonous to humans and other animals. Fungi can cause diseases on human skin, such as athlete's foot. Mold and mildew are fungi that can cause allergies.

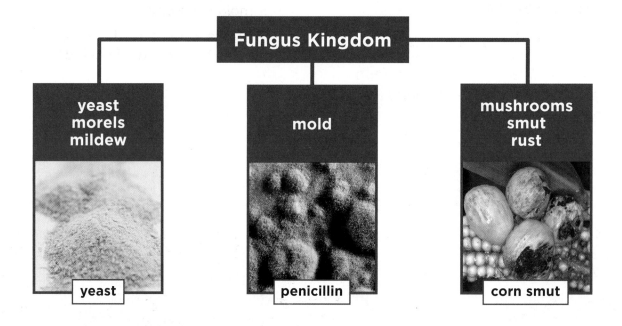

Fungus Kingdom

yeast morels mildew	mold	mushrooms smut rust
yeast	penicillin	corn smut

 Quick Check

Main Idea What is a fungus?

Critical Thinking How are mushrooms similar to molds?

What are bacteria?

Bacteria (bak•TEER•ee•uh) are tiny unicellular organisms with a cell membrane and a cytoplasm. Most bacteria also have cell walls. However, they do not have a distinct nucleus like plant and animal cells.

Bacteria are classified into two kingdoms called "ancient" bacteria and "true" bacteria. Ancient bacteria are the oldest living organisms on Earth. Many of them are found in harsh environments, such as hot springs, salt water, and acidic environments.

True bacteria usually live in or on other organisms. Some true bacteria cause diseases in plants and animals, such as "strep" throat, pneumonia, and Lyme disease.

 Quick Check

Main Idea What is bacteria?

Critical Thinking Create a Venn diagram that compares bacteria cells to plant cells.

Quick Lab

Bread Mold Activity

1. Trace the outline of a slice of bread on graph paper.

2. Put a drop of water on one corner of the bread and put it in a bag. Place the bag in a warm, dark corner.

3. **Observe** On the first day you see mold, sketch the shape of the moldy area on your graph paper.

4. For the next three days, use a different color to sketch the new growth.

5. **Record Data** Count the number of squares that were covered with mold each day.

6. Create a graph to show the growth of the mold each day.

Two Bacteria Kingdoms

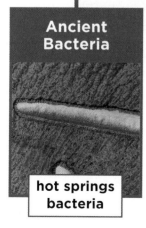

Ancient Bacteria

hot springs bacteria

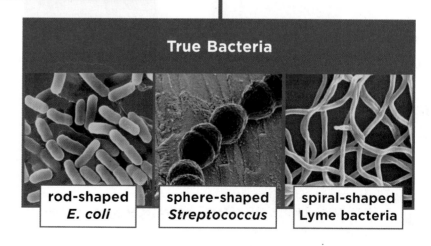

True Bacteria

rod-shaped *E. coli*

sphere-shaped *Streptococcus*

spiral-shaped Lyme bacteria

What are protists?

Protists (PROH•tists) are unicellular or multicellular organisms that either make their own food or eat other living things. These organisms don't fit into the other kingdoms, so scientists classify them together. Unlike bacteria all organisms in the protist kingdom have a distinct nucleus in their cells. Unlike animals, plants, and fungi, protists have simple body structures and they lack specialized tissues. Most protists live in water.

Plant-like Protists

These protists can produce their own food like plants. Some are green because they have chlorophyll. Others produce food using different chemicals that make them look red or brown. Red, brown, and green *algae* (AL•gee) are all plant-like protists.

Animal-like Protists

These protists cannot produce their own food. They use their cell membranes to absorb other organisms. Like animals, these protists eat and move. Some move using hairlike structures that stick out of their cell membranes. Others move by shifting cytoplasm in their cells. Two common protists in this group are *amoeba* (uh•MEE•buh) and *paramecium* (par•uh•MEE•shee•uhm).

Fungi-like Protists

Like fungi, these protists break down dead organisms for food. The slime mold is an example of this group of protists. Many of these protists behave like molds, but they have different cell structures.

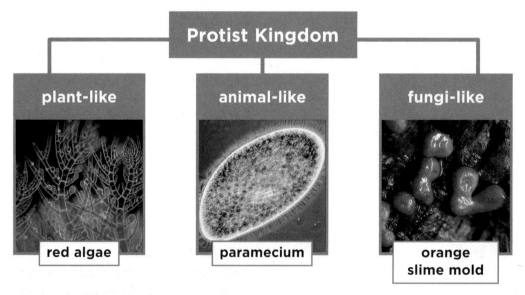

Protist Kingdom

plant-like | animal-like | fungi-like

red algae | paramecium | orange slime mold

**Quick Check**

Main Idea What are the three main groups of protists?

Critical Thinking What stops scientists from classifying plant-like protists as plants?

Lesson Review

Summarize the Main Idea

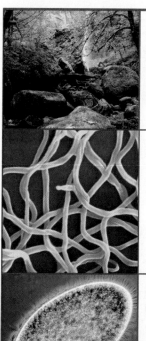

Animals can be vertebrate or invertebrate. **Plants** can be vascular or nonvascular. (pp. 48-53)

Fungi absorb food from decaying organisms. **Bacteria** are unicellular organisms. There are two groups, ancient and true. (pp. 54-55)

Protists can be unicellular or multicellular. The cells of protists all have a distinct nucleus. (p. 56)

Make a FOLDABLES™ Study Guide

Make a layered-look book (see p. 481). Use the titles shown. List the main ideas for each type of organism.

Diversity of Organisms
Animals
Plants
Fungi
Bacteria
Protists

Think, Talk, and Write

1. **Main Idea** What are the main characteristics of the six kingdoms?

2. **Vocabulary** Animals without a backbone are called _____ .

3. **Main Idea** How are organisms in the plant kingdom divided?

Main Idea	Details

4. **Critical Thinking** Why can fungi be called recyclers?

5. **Test Practice** In which of the following kingdoms should mold be classified?
   A fungus
   B plant
   C protist
   D animal

6. **Test Practice** A rabbit is a(n)
   A invertebrate.
   B protist.
   C vertebrate.
   D plant.

Writing Link

Expository Writing

Research an organism and classify it. Tell about its traits and explain why you classified it into each group.

Health Link

Helpful Bacteria

Washing your hands destroys many bacteria that could make you sick. However, most bacteria are not harmful and some are even helpful. Research bacteria and tell how they can be helpful.

Meet Angelique Corthals

reptile cells

fish cells

▲ Angelique is an archaeologist. That's a scientist who studies how people lived in the past. She specializes in the preservation of the information in cells, such as the ones shown.

How can you fit thousands of organisms into one small room? Angelique Corthals knows. She's a scientist at the American Museum of Natural History and she's been busy preserving tissue samples of many different organisms from around the globe, including samples from species that have already become extinct. A species is extinct when it has died out completely.

Angelique works in the museum's frozen tissues lab. She collects, preserves, and organizes the cells of all sorts of living things from bacteria to insects to mammals. Angelique stores the organisms' cells in small plastic tubes the size of your finger and freezes them. Just like food stays fresh in the freezer, freezing the cells prevents them from spoiling or decomposing. The tubes are stored in large tanks containing liquid nitrogen. At $-150°C$ $(-238°F)$, this liquid is so cold that all of the cells' biological processes stop.

ELA R 5.2.3. Discern main ideas and concepts presented in texts, identifying and assessing evidence that supports those ideas.

▶ Angelique can learn about organisms, such as the humpback whale and the fruit fly, by studying their cells.

By using this freezing process, the cells can be preserved for many years. When a scientist needs to study an organism, she can request a cell sample from the lab. Whether it's from a small fly or a large humpback whale, each of their cells contains information about the whole organism. Scientists can use this information to learn how different organisms are related. They can also use this information to learn about living things that have already become extinct and to understand why they died out.

Soon, the collection will be home to one million frozen tissue samples. One day, the museum expects to have a record of most of the organisms on the planet.

Write About It

Summarize

Make a chart that tells the steps for preserving cells. Use your chart to write a summary of the process Angelique uses to freeze cells from organisms.

LOG ON e-Journal Write about it online @ www.macmillanmh.com

Summarize

▶ To summarize the passage, briefly retell it in your own words.

▶ Focus on the most important events or pieces of information.

AMERICAN MUSEUM OF NATURAL HISTORY

Writing in Science

Two Desert Creatures

A good fictional story

▶ has an interesting beginning, middle, and end.

▶ describes a setting that tells when and where the story takes place.

▶ has a plot that centers around a problem or conflict.

▶ has characters that move the action along.

It was a cool night in the California desert. The kangaroo rat crawled out of his underground burrow. He hopped on his long back legs to some nearby bushes. There he found some seeds on the ground. He was so busy stuffing seeds into his cheek pockets that he did not hear the soft rattling noise coming from behind him.

"Hello, furry friend," said the rattler. The moonlight shone on the brown diamond shapes along his back. "I'm very hungry. Are those seeds-s-s-s any good?"

"Stay back!" screeched the kangaroo rat when he saw the snake slithering closer.

"Don't be silly. I won't eat you, I just want some of your seeds-s-s-s," hissed the snake. But he quickly moved to within striking distance. The kangaroo rat tried to hop away, but it was too late.

Write About It

Fictional Writing

Choose two other organisms that are very different from each other. Write a fictional narrative in which these two organisms are in a conflict.

LOG ON **e-Journal** Write about it online @ www.macmillanmh.com

ELA W 5.2.1. Write narratives: a. Establish a plot, point of view, setting, and conflict.

Math in Science

It Is All Part of Growing

Some organisms, like bacteria, grow in number very quickly. One bacterium can generate more than one billion offspring in one day! This chart represents the reproduction rate of one type of bacteria in minutes. Using the data in the chart you can create a graph. Each point on the graph represents an ordered pair. An ordered pair gives the location of a point on a graph.

Making a line graph

▶ decide on a scale for the bottom and side of the graph.

▶ use the numbers from your chart to plot the ordered pairs.

▶ connect the points with a line.

Bacteria Growth

Time in Minutes	0	20	40	60	80	100
Number of Bacteria	20	40	80	160	320	640

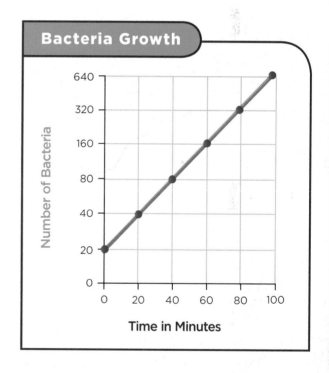

Bacteria Growth

Solve It

1. California redwood trees are the tallest trees in the world. Assume a redwood is now 25 years old and it has grown 3 feet per year. Fill in the chart and graph the growth data. How tall is the redwood after 25 years?

California Redwood Tree Growth

Age in years	1	3	5	7	9	11	13	15	17	19	21	23	25
Height in feet	3	9	15	21	27	33	39	45	51				

 MA AF 5.1.5. Solve problems involving linear functions with integer values; write the equation; and graph the resulting ordered pairs of integers on a grid.

CHAPTER 1 Review

Vocabulary

Summarize the Main Ideas

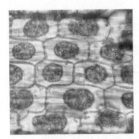

Plants and animals are made of cells. Cells are the smallest units that can carry out life processes.
(pp. 24–33)

Cells make up tissues, which make up organs, which make up organ systems.
(pp. 36–43)

Living things are classified in kingdoms so they can be studied.
(pp. 46–57)

Make a FOLDABLES™ Study Guide

Take a sheet of paper and tape your lesson study guides as shown.

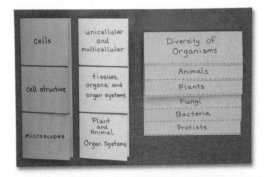

Fill each blank with the best word from the list.

cell membrane, p. 29   **organ**, p. 40

nucleus, p. 29   **organ system**, p. 41

chloroplast, p. 31   **tissue**, p. 40

invertebrate, p. 50   **vertebrate**, p. 50

1. A group of cells that works together forms a(n) _____. 5 LS 2.a

2. Organs in plants and animals are part of a(n) _____. 5 LS 2.a

3. A bird is a(n) _____ because it has a backbone. 5 LS 2.a

4. Plant cells, but not animal cells, contain an organelle called a(n) _____. 5 LS 2.f

5. The _____ controls the flow of materials in and out of a cell. 5 LS 2.f

6. The structure of an insect allows it to be classified as a(n) _____.
5 LS 2.a

7. The heart is an example of a(n) _____. 5 LS 2.a

8. All of the activities of a cell are controlled by its _____. 5 LS 2.f

Answer each of the following in complete sentences.

9. Summarize Explain how the parts of an organism are organized from most simple to most complex. 5 LS 2.a

10. Compare and Contrast How do plants and animals obtain energy differently? 5 LS 2.a

11. Experiment You discover a new organism. Describe an experiment to test whether it is a plant or animal. 5 LS 2.a

12. Critical Thinking Humans, cats, dogs, and cows are all classified as mammals because they share certain characteristics. A platypus lives most of its life in water, lays eggs, has hair, and provides its young with milk. What characteristics of this animal allow it to be classified as a mammal? 5 LS 2.a

13. Fictional Narrative Different parts of a cell do different jobs to keep the cell alive. Suppose you are a cell part. Write a story telling what you do in the cell. 5 LS 2.f

 What are living things made of?

CHAPTER 1

Classifying Organisms

Your goal is to classify an organism found in California, such as the sea otter.

What to do

1. Use the Internet, a textbook, or other sources to make a classification chart for an organism. Classify the organism into a kingdom, phylum, class, order, family, genus, and species.

2. After you have classified the organism into these groups, describe what characteristics allow it to be classified into these groups.

Analyze your results

▶ Identify two other organisms that could be classified in the same kingdom as your organism.

▶ Why is classifying a useful tool in science?

 5 IE 6.a. Classify objects (e. g., rocks, plants, leaves) in accordance with appropriate criteria.

1 Which of the following *best* describes cells?

A membranes that control the movement of materials

B tube-like structures that go up and down in plants

C smallest units of living things that can carry out the basic processes of life

D large specialized structures that work together to do a job

2 Which of the following organisms is most likely a protist?

A multicellular organism with vascular tissues

B unicellular organism without a distinct nucleus

C unicellular organism that can produce its own food

D multicellular organism with a backbone

3 Which part of a plant cell breaks down food into energy?

A cytoplasm

B mitochondrion

C cell wall

D vacuole

4 A student classified some organisms in the chart below.

Plants	
Group A	Group B
cacti	moss
tree	liverworts
grass	hornworts

Which of the following traits did the student most likely use to classify the organisms? 5 IE 6.a

A cell walls or no cell walls

B vascular or nonvascular

C vertebrate or invertebrate

D protists or fungi

5 A scientist finds a unicellular organism that consumes decaying materials. In which of the following kingdoms should the organism be classified?

A plant

B bacteria

C animal

D fungi

6 Which list gives the correct order of the largest classification group to the smallest?

A phylum, kingdom, class, order, family, genus, species

B species, genus, family, order, class, kingdom, phylum

C kingdom, phylum, class, order, family, genus, species

D kingdom, phylum, class, family, order, species, genus

7 Which of the following structures allow plants to make their own food?

A mitochondria
B chloroplasts
C vacuoles
D cell walls

8 Which of the following *best* describes a tissue?

A group of similar organs that do the same job in an organism
B system that breaks down food in an organism
C group of similar cells that do the same job in an organism
D system that transports blood in an organism

9 Which of the following animals are classified as amphibians?

A chicken, duck, goose
B frog, salamander, toad
C alligator, turtle, lizard
D whale, dog, horse

10 Which list gives the correct order of the smallest level of organization of an organism to the largest?

A organ system, organs, cells, tissues
B organs, organ system, tissues, cells
C cells, organs, tissues, organ system
D cells, tissues, organs, organ system

11 Why do plant cells have one large, central vacuole?

A The vacuole gives extra support and stores water.
B Plant cells need a large vacuole for food storage.
C Plant cells would wilt if they had more than one.
D The vacuole controls the activity of the plant cell.

12 The diagram below shows a cell.

The cell in the diagram is a(n)

A plant cell.
B fungus cell.
C animal cell.
D bacteria cell.

 Building Block questions for 5 LS 2.a. Students know many multicellular organisms have specialized structures to support the transport of materials.

CHAPTER 2

Plant Structures and Functions

 How do plants produce, transport, and use food?

 5 LS 2. Plants and animals have structures for respiration, digestion, waste disposal, and transport of materials.

Literature

POETRY

ELA R 5.3.5. Describe the function and effect of common literary devices (e.g., imagery, metaphor, symbolism).

ELA W 5.2.3. Write research reports about important ideas, issues, or events by using the following guidelines:

a. Frame questions that direct the investigation

b. Establish a controlling idea or topic.

c. Develop the topic with simple facts, details, examples, and explanations.

BRANCHES

Against the blowing sky
the stiff
fabric of branches and twigs
grows up and
up into the light

Spreading
unseen beneath the tree
a tangle of roots —
secret fingers
that feel their way
through the unmapped
country
underground

Veins
thread their thin pattern
through every leaf Look
how they hold each green
hand
open to the sun
collecting light and the green
diamond-drops of water!

 Write About It

Response to Literature

The poet creates a vivid impression of a leaf collecting light and water. Do print and online research to find out what happens as a plant grows new leaves. Then, write an explanation of this sequence of events.

LOG ON **e-Journal** Write about it online @ **www.macmillanmh.com**

Vascular Plants

Look and Wonder

Cactus plants need to store and retain water. Their spines protect the stored water from thirsty animals. What do cactus plants have in common with other vascular plants?

Building block lesson for 5 LS 2.a. Students know many multicellular organisms have specialized structures to support the transport of materials.

What are the parts of vascular plants?

Purpose

You have learned that all vascular plants have vessels in their stems. What else do vascular plants have in common? You will examine several vascular plants to find out.

Procedure

1. Examine each plant. Look at the roots, stems, and leaves.

2. **Record Data** Make a chart for each plant. Draw what the plant's root, stem, and leaves look like. Record the color, size, and shape of each plant part.

3. **Compare** Which of the plant parts look similar? Which parts look different?

Draw Conclusions

4. How do the stems of the water plant and the cactus compare? Why do they have these differences?

5. **Infer** Would the flowering plant be able to survive in a hot, dry area? Why or why not?

6. **Infer** Would the water plant be able to survive out of the water? Why or why not?

Explore More

Look at the plants where you live. Observe three plants and compare them to these three plants. Based on your observations, decide if each of the plants you observed are also vascular plants.

 5 IE 6.g. Record data by using appropriate graphic representations (including charts, graphs, and labeled diagrams) and make inferences based on those data.

Materials

- cactus plant
- water plant
- flowering plant
- disposable plates
- gloves

Step 1

Step 2

Flowering Plants				
What the Plant Part Looks Like	Color	Size	Shape	Other Observations

Read and Learn

Main Idea

Vascular plants are classified as seedless and seed plants. Most seed plants have flowers.

Vocabulary

spore, p.73

seed, p.73

angiosperm, p.74

gymnosperm, p.75

pollination, p.76

LOG ON e-Glossary
@ www.macmillanmh.com

Reading Skill

Sequence

First
↓
Next
↓
Last

What are vascular plants?

Think about the plants you see every day. If you go to the park you might see lots of grass, trees, and shrubs. Your family might grow roses or have a vegetable garden in your backyard. You might find ferns and other potted plants in your house or classroom. What do all of these plants have in common? They are all vascular plants.

Vascular plants have specialized cells and tissues that form vessels. These vessels work together to transport water, food, and waste to and from all parts of the plant. The main parts of vascular plants are roots, stems, and leaves.

The roots of the vascular plant form the root system. The root system is usually the portion of the plant found below the ground. The main functions of this system are anchorage and absorption. This means the roots hold the plant in place and take in nutrients and water from the soil. Roots can also store food for the plant.

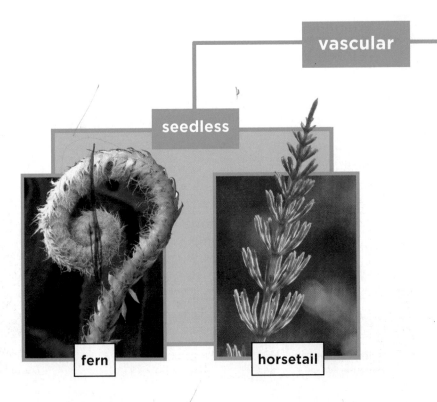

vascular

seedless

fern

horsetail

▲ The morning glory is a vascular plant with seeds and flowers.

The stem and the leaves of the plant are part of the shoot system. The shoot system is usually the above-ground portion of the plant. The main functions of the shoot system are to support the plant, to transport materials, and to produce food.

If you were to study the life cycles of vascular plants, you would probably notice that some vascular plants have seeds and others don't. Because of this, scientists have classified vascular plants into seedless plants and plants with seeds. Seedless plants develop from spores and seed plants develop from seeds. A **spore** (spawr) is a single cell that can develop into a new plant that is exactly like the plant that produced it. A **seed** contains an undeveloped plant, stored food, and a protective covering.

Plants with seeds are further divided into plants that produce flowers and plants that do not produce flowers.

✔ Quick Check

Sequence What steps would you take to classify a plant?

Critical Thinking What kind of vascular plant is an apple tree?

seed

no flower

flowers

evergreen

cycad

flowering plant

gerbera daisy

How are seedless and seed plants different?

Most of the plants that you see every day produce seeds. Grasses, flowering plants, and trees are all seed plants. Seed plants have male and female structures that produce male and female cells. Seeds are formed when a male cell and a female cell join.

The undeveloped plant in the seed uses the stored food to develop and grow into a new plant. This new plant shares the characteristics of the two plants that produced the seed.

Seedless vascular plants, such as horsetails, club mosses, spike mosses, and ferns, do not produce or grow from seeds. Instead, these plants use spores to reproduce.

Plants that grow from spores, such as ferns, first grow a stalk with leaves, or fronds. The underside of the fronds have capsules, or spore cases. Each capsule is filled with thousands of tiny spores. When the capsule opens, some spores drop to the ground near the parent plant. Other spores are blown away by the wind. Spores have a tough outer covering. It protects them from drying out until they find the right conditions to grow. Spores will not grow and produce new plants unless they land near water.

Seed plants

A seed plant that produces flowers is called an **angiosperm** (AN•jēē•uh•spurm). Fruits, vegetables, grains, and almost all nuts come from angiosperms. Angiosperms are the most abundant plants. There are more than 235,000 different kinds of angiosperms.

Spores and Seeds

▲ These spore cases, or capsules, are arranged at the bottom of a fern frond, or leaf. They contain many tiny spores.

▼ fern fronds

A seed plant that does not produce flowers is called a **gymnosperm** (JIM•nuh•spurm). Gymnosperms produce seeds inside a cone. When the cone falls, it breaks and releases seeds. The seeds are blown by the wind, washed away by water, or moved by animals until they reach a place where a new plant can grow.

Most gymnosperms are evergreens. *Evergreens* are trees that lose only a few leaves at one time and constantly replace the leaves they have lost. So, they look green all the time.

✓ Quick Check

Sequence How do seed and seedless plants develop? List the steps for each.

Critical Thinking How are spores and gymnosperm seeds similar?

Quick Lab

Fern Spores

1. **Observe** Carefully examine a fern leaf. Draw what you see and write down any observations.

2. Place a drop of water on a slide.

3. Use a toothpick to scrape one of the spore cases into the drop of water.

4. **Observe** Examine the spore case under the microscope on low power. What does the spore case contain?

5. Draw what you see and write down any observations.

6. **Infer** How does the size of the fern spores relate to their function?

▼ Apples are fruits that contain seeds. The seeds can be planted to grow new apple trees.

◄ apple tree branch

Reading Photos

How are spores and seeds different?

Clue: Look at the size and covering of spores and the seeds.

What do flowers do?

Flowers are the reproductive organs of angiosperms. Flowers usually have both male and female structures. The male part of the flower, the *stamen* (STAY•muhn), produces *pollen grains* which contain male cells. Pollen grains are transferred from the top of a stamen to the female part of the flower, the *pistil* (PIS•tuhl), or to another flower's pistil. This transfer is called **pollination** (pol•uh•NAY•shuhn).

Flowers have bright colors, scents, and nectar to attract animals such as insects, birds, and small mammals. These animals become pollinators when they accidentally transfer pollen from one flower to another.

Once the flower is pollinated, the pollen travels down the pistil until it reaches the female cell, the egg cell. When the pollen and egg cell join, they form a seed. This is called *fertilization*

(fur•tuh•luh•ZAY•shuhn). As the seed develops, the ovary enlarges until it becomes a fruit. The fruit protects the seeds inside it.

Seeds are *dispersed* (di•SPURSD), or scattered, in many ways. Some seeds have structures, like wings, that enable them to be carried by the wind. Other seeds are moved by animals. Some have hooks that get stuck to an animal's fur or feathers. Animals that eat fruit cannot digest the seeds. They help with dispersal by depositing the seeds in their waste. If a seed reaches a place where conditions are right for a new plant to grow, it will sprout.

✔ Quick Check

Sequence What are the steps of pollination?

Critical Thinking What flowering plants do we eat?

Structure of Flowers

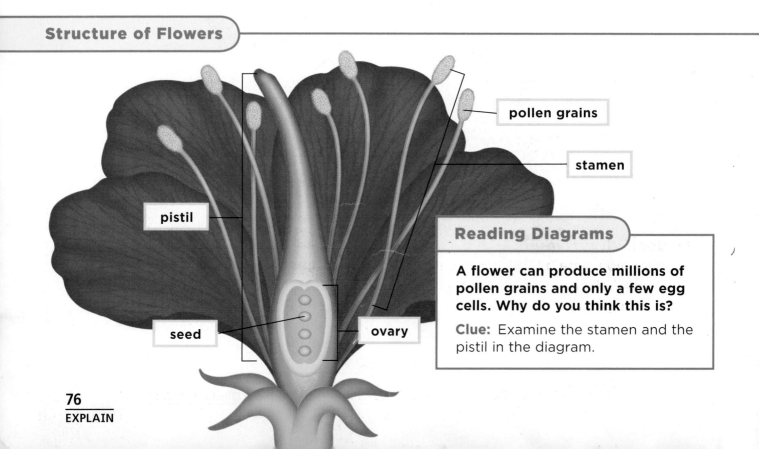

pollen grains

stamen

pistil

seed

ovary

Reading Diagrams

A flower can produce millions of pollen grains and only a few egg cells. Why do you think this is?

Clue: Examine the stamen and the pistil in the diagram.

Lesson Review

Summarize the Main Idea

Scientists classify **vascular plants** by whether they produce spores or seeds, and flowers or no flowers. (pp. 72–73)

Some plants grow from **spores**. Others grow from **seeds**. (pp. 74–75)

Flowers are reproductive organs that produce seeds. (p. 76)

Make a FOLDABLES™ Study Guide

Make a tri-fold book (see p. 480) Use the titles shown. Summarize each item.

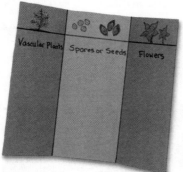

Think, Talk, and Write

1. **Main Idea** How are vascular plants classified?

2. **Vocabulary** Plants that have seeds but do not have flowers are called _____.

3. **Sequence** How are plant seeds dispersed?

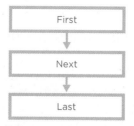

| First |
| Next |
| Last |

4. **Critical Thinking** Why do many seedless plants, such as mosses, grow near water?

5. **Test Practice** **Which of the following plants produce spores?**
   A angiosperms
   B gymnosperms
   C seedless vascular plants
   D vascular plants with flowers

6. **Test Practice** **All of the following are part of a flower EXCEPT**
   A the stamen.
   B the ovary.
   C the petal.
   D the spore.

 Writing Link

Fictional Narratives

Suppose you were a tiny pollen grain or a seed. Tell about the things that happen as you are dispersed.

 Math Link

Calculate Seeds

Apples have about 12 seeds. Suppose only 1/4 of the seeds will grow into new trees. If a tree grows 150 apples, how many seeds will become new trees?

Focus on Inquiry Skills

Classify

When scientists **classify**, they place things that share traits or characteristics into groups. In order to do that, scientists need to compare and contrast. Remember, to compare you look for how things are alike. To contrast you look for how they are different.

➊ Learn It

Classifying is a useful tool for organizing and analyzing things. When you **classify**, you can learn the characteristics of millions of things, without actually having to learn about each one. For example, you may not know all the different kinds of bicycles there are in the world, but you know something about all bicycles: Bicycles have two wheels.

It is a good idea to keep notes of the criteria, or rules, you use to **classify** things. An example of a criterion is the number of wheels something has. If you decide to **classify** things by the number of wheels they have, cars, pickup trucks, and carts would be in the same group because they all have four wheels. Motorcycles and bicycles would be in the same group because they have two wheels.

One way to **classify** things is by their shape. You can **classify** leaves by the shape of their edges. Here are some examples of the different types of leaf edges.

palmate leaf

smooth leaf

toothed leaf   **pinnate leaf**   **lobed leaf**

 5 IE 6.a. Classify objects (e.g., rocks, plants, leaves) in accordance with appropriate criteria.

❷ Try It

▶ Find ten leaves of different kinds, shapes, and sizes.

▶ Examine each of your ten leaves one at a time.

▶ Draw your leaves on a chart similar to the one shown.

▶ Write a description of each leaf next to the picture.

▶ **Classify** your leaves according to the type of edge each has. Use the leaves on the previous page as a guideline. Record the type of edge on your chart.

❸ Apply It

▶ Look around you for more things to **classify**. Choose something you are interested in or enjoy. Think of things you see every day, such as plants, rocks, or animals.

▶ **Classify** them by size, shape, color, or any other characteristic that they have in common. Share your findings with the class.

Leaf Classification

Leaf	What It Looks Like	Description	Classification
1.		veins smooth edges	smooth
2.			

Plant Transport Systems

Look and Wonder

Mangrove trees are very important to shoreline environments. Their large, entangled roots provide protection for smaller organisms. How do their large roots help the mangroves get water?

 5 LS 2.a. Students know many multicellular organisms have specialized structures to support the transport of materials. • **5 LS 2.e.** Students know how sugar, water, and minerals are transported in a vascular plant.

How does water move in a plant?

Make a Prediction

What will happen if you leave a celery stalk in colored water? Make a prediction.

Test you Prediction

1 **Observe** Use a hand lens to look at the celery stalk.

2 Place the celery stalk in a container with water.

3 Put three drops of food coloring into the container. Stir the water until the food coloring is thoroughly mixed.

4 **Record Data** Use colored pencils to draw a picture of the celery stalk. Record the date and time.

5 **Observe** On the following day, use the hand lens to look at the celery stalk. Note any changes.

6 **Record Data** Use colored pencils to draw a picture of the celery stalk. Record the date and time.

- hand lens
- celery stalk
- colored pencils
- food coloring
- water
- container
- spoon

Step 3

Draw Conclusions

7 What can you conclude about how water moves in a plant?

8 **Communicate** Write a report of your investigation. Describe any differences between your results and those of your classmates.

Step 4

Explore More

You used a celery stalk in this experiment. What do you think would have happened if you used a plant that had a white flower? Answer this question by making a prediction and a plan to test it. Then follow your plan and write a report of your results.

5 IE 6.i. Write a report of an investigation that includes conducting tests, collecting data or examining evidence, and drawing conclusions.

Read and Learn

Main Idea 5 LS 2.a

Vascular plants have special structures for the transport of materials such as sugar, water, and minerals.

Vocabulary

xylem, p.84
phloem, p.84
cambium, p.84

LOG ON **e-Glossary**
@ www.macmillanmh.com

Reading Skill

Cause and Effect

Cause → Effect
→
→
→
→

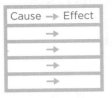

petiole

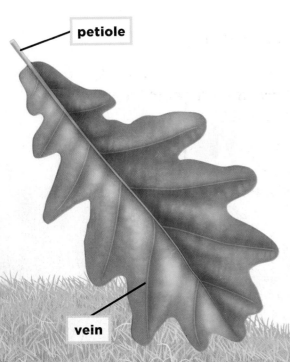

vein

How do different materials move in plants?

Vascular plants are constantly moving materials through the specialized cells in their transport system. The transport system includes the roots, the stem, and the leaves. Water and minerals are moved up from the roots to the leaves. Sugar is transported from the leaves to all other parts of the plant.

Root

A *root* is the part of a plant that absorbs water and minerals, stores food, and anchors the plant. The roots of a plant usually spread out and down into the soil. Each root contains thousands of tiny root hairs. The cells of the root system carry the water and minerals up the stem and to the leaves.

Stem

A *stem* is the main stalk of a plant. The stem develops buds and shoots and usually grows above the ground. Inside the stem, materials move up and down through the tissues of the transport system. A trunk is the main stem of a tree.

Leaf

A *leaf* usually grows from the stem of a plant. The *petiole* (PET•ee•ohl) connects the leaf to the stem or branch. Water and minerals are transported from the roots to the leaves. Veins carry these materials throughout the leaf. Leaves take in and release gases into the air. They use water and carbon dioxide to produce sugar. Once the sugar is made, the transport system moves it throughout the plant so other plant cells can use the sugar as food.

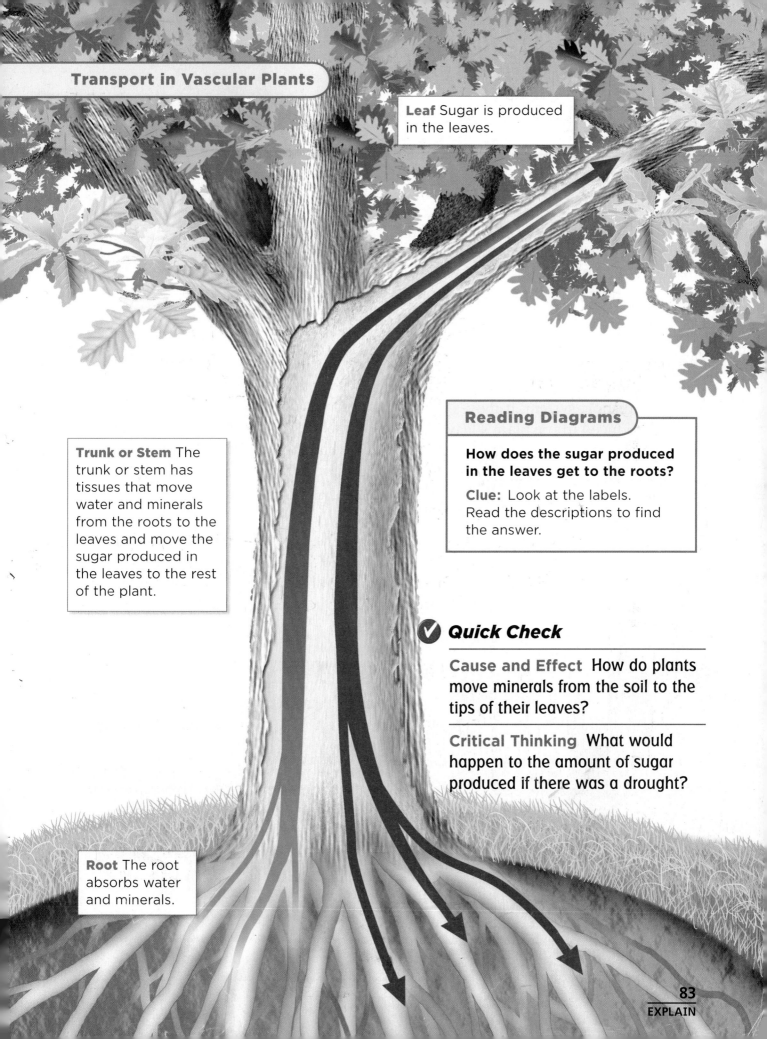

Transport in Vascular Plants

Leaf Sugar is produced in the leaves.

Trunk or Stem The trunk or stem has tissues that move water and minerals from the roots to the leaves and move the sugar produced in the leaves to the rest of the plant.

Root The root absorbs water and minerals.

Reading Diagrams

How does the sugar produced in the leaves get to the roots?

Clue: Look at the labels. Read the descriptions to find the answer.

✓ Quick Check

Cause and Effect How do plants move minerals from the soil to the tips of their leaves?

Critical Thinking What would happen to the amount of sugar produced if there was a drought?

What is the transport system made of?

When you cut a thin slice of a plant stem or root and look at it under a microscope, you can see the tissues that form the transport system.

One of these tissues is xylem (ZIGH•luhm). **Xylem** moves water and minerals up from the roots. As water moves up the plant, some of it is stored in the vacuoles of the xylem tissue cells. Most of the layers of a tree trunk are made of xylem.

Phloem (FLO•em) is the other tissue in the transport system. It moves the sugar produced in the plant's leaves to its other parts.

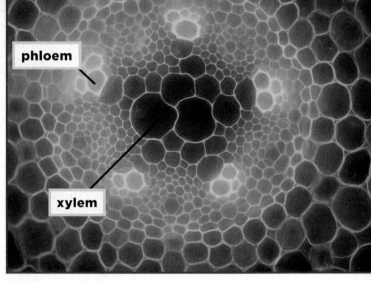

▲ This is a magnified cross section of a buttercup root.

Many stems have a layer of cells that separate the xylem from the phloem. This layer is called the cambium (KAM•be•uhm). The **cambium** is where new xylem and phloem cells are produced.

Woody and Soft Stems

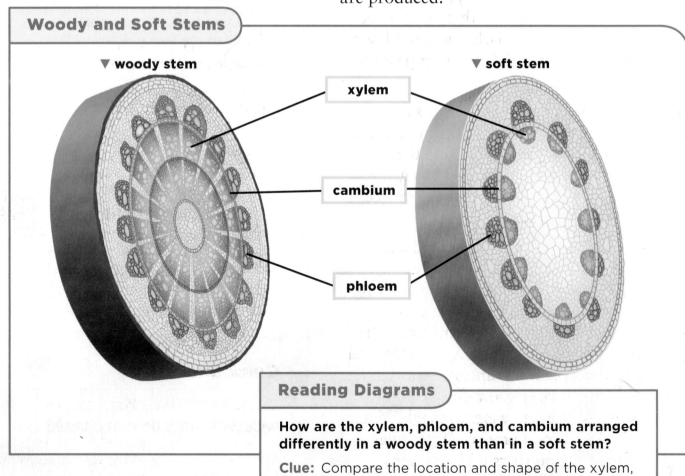

▼ woody stem

▼ soft stem

xylem

cambium

phloem

Reading Diagrams

How are the xylem, phloem, and cambium arranged differently in a woody stem than in a soft stem?

Clue: Compare the location and shape of the xylem, phloem, and cambium in each stem.

▲ Tree rings can be used to determine a tree's age. The oldest living tree, a bristlecone pine, is in California. It is 4,767 years old.

The outer layer of a woody stem, such as a tree trunk, is called bark. *Bark* is a tough outer covering that serves as a protective layer for the tree. It can be thin or very thick with deep ridges. Inside the bark, there is a layer of phloem. Inside the layer of phloem is more xylem.

Each year, a new layer of xylem forms an annual ring. You can estimate the age of a tree by counting the number of annual rings. Trees grow out in a circle, so the center of a tree is the oldest part.

You can also use the annual tree rings to tell what the weather was as the tree was growing. Each annual ring is made up of a lighter and a darker part. The lighter rings form during the spring when there is plenty of water and growing conditions are good for the tree. The darker rings grow during autumn when there is less water available. Years with lots of rain produce larger rings of growth and years with less rain produce much smaller rings.

Quick Lab

Root Cross Section

1 **Observe** Examine a cross section of a root with a hand lens. Draw what you see.

2 Place the cross section and a few drops of water on a slide. Cover it with a cover slip. Look at it under a microscope at low power.

3 Draw what you see. Label the parts that you can identify.

4 **Draw Conclusions** Which parts of the root carry water? How can you tell?

5 **Communicate** Other groups in your class have looked at different kinds of roots. Discuss whether their cross sections were similar or different from yours.

✔ Quick Check

Cause and Effect What causes wide, light rings on a tree trunk?

Critical Thinking Why are trees important to historians?

Dandelions have taproots.

Grass has fibrous roots.

Corn plants have prop roots.

How are roots different?

There are several different kinds of roots. *Taproots* have one large root with a few branching, hairy roots. Dandelion, carrot, and beet plants have taproots. Taproots tend to grow deep into the soil and can often reach underground sources of water.

Fibrous roots are made up of thin, branching roots. Grasses have this type of root. Fibrous roots can have huge networks of roots underground.

Prop roots grow like fingers out of the bottom of the stem. These roots help support, or prop up, the plant. Corn plants and mangrove trees have prop roots.

Some plants have *aerial roots*, or roots that never touch the ground. Plants with these roots include some types of ivy and orchids. Some orchids live high in the branches of rain forest trees. Since their roots cannot reach the ground, the roots of these plants take in water from moisture in the air.

 Quick Check

Cause and Effect What causes taproots to grow deep into the soil?

Critical Thinking How could aerial roots help a plant stay in place?

Lesson Review

Summarize the Main Idea

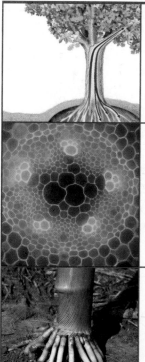

Vascular plants have a **transport system** made up of roots, stems, and leaves. (pp. 82–83)

Xylem carries water and minerals from the roots to the leaves. **Phloem** carries food from the leaves to the rest of the plant. (pp. 84–85)

Different plants have different kinds of roots. **Roots** absorb water and minerals into the plant. (p. 86)

Make a FOLDABLES™ Study Guide

Make a three-tab book (see p. 481). Use the titles shown. On the inside of each fold, summarize the functions of that plant structure.

Transport System

Xylem and Phloem

Roots

Think, Talk, and Write

1. **Main Idea** What tissues are a part of the plant transport system?

2. **Vocabulary** Water is transported to the leaves by the _____.

3. **Cause and Effect** What would happen to a plant without functional phloem cells?

Cause	→	Effect
	→	
	→	
	→	
	→	

4. **Critical Thinking** Why are weeds, like dandelions, hard to pull out?

5. **Test Practice** **Which of the following is found in the stem of a plant?**
   A xylem
   B leaves
   C root hairs
   D aerial roots

6. **Test Practice** **Which types of roots help support plants?**
   A fibrous roots
   B taproots
   C prop roots
   D aerial roots

 Writing Link

Persuasive Writing

Write a letter persuading your teacher to take your class to a botanical garden. Tell about the things you can learn there.

 Math Link

Measuring Tree Age

You count the annual rings on five of the largest trees in a forest. You find that the trees are 24, 27, 22, 26, and 28 years old. What is their average age?

Be a Scientist

Materials

4 annual bedding plants in pots

water

4 plastic bags

string

spray bottle

light source

metric balance

Inquiry **Structured**

How does water move in and out of plants?

Form a Hypothesis

Plants need water to survive. If a plant loses too much water it will wilt and eventually die. How do plants lose water? Plants lose water through transpiration, the evaporation of water from the leaves. As the water evaporates, it pulls water from the roots up through the xylem tissue. The rate of transpiration changes depending on a number of variables. How does the amount of light a plant receives affect its transpiration rate? Write your answer as a hypothesis in the form *"If the amount of light a plant receives is increased, then the rate of transpiration…"*

Test Your Hypothesis

1. Use the spray bottle to water the 4 plants. Be sure to give all of the plants the same amount of water.

2. Place each of the plants' pots in a plastic bag and use the string to tie the bag around the stem of each plant.

3. **Record Data** Weigh all 4 plants using the metric balance. Record their masses.

4. **Use Variables** Place 2 of the plants under the light source. Place the other two plants away from the light source.

5. **Record Data** After 10 minutes weigh all 4 plants again. Record their masses.

6. Return the plants to their original locations.

7. Repeat step 5 every 10 minutes for 30 minutes.

Step 1

Step 2

Step 3

 5 IE 6.b. Develop a testable question. • **5 IE 6.c.** Plan and conduct a simple investigation based on a student-developed question and write instructions others can follow to carry out the procedure. • **5 IE 6.e.** Identify a single independent variable in a scientific investigation and explain how this variable can be used to collect information to answer a question about the results of the experiment.

Draw Conclusions

1 What is the independent variable in the investigation?

2 **Analyze Data** Did the mass of any of the plants change? Did your data show a correlation between the transpiration rates and the amount of light?

3 Did your results support your hypothesis? Why or why not?

Inquiry Guided

How is water loss in plants affected by changes in the environment?

Form a Hypothesis

You have seen how light affects the rate of transpiration. What other variables affect the rate of transpiration? How about wind? Write your answer as a hypothesis in the form "*If wind increases, then the rate of transpiration…*"

Test Your Hypothesis

Design a plan to test your hypothesis. Then write out the materials, resources, and steps you need. Record your results and observations as you follow your plan.

Draw Conclusions

Did your results support your hypothesis? Why or why not? Present your results to your classmates.

Remember to follow the steps of the scientific process.

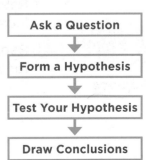

Inquiry Open

What other conditions in the environment can affect the rate of transpiration? Come up with a question to investigate. For example, how does humidity affect the rate of transpiration? Design an experiment to answer your question. Your experiment must be organized to test only one variable, or item being changed.

Photosynthesis and Respiration

Look and Wonder

Leaf cells contain the most abundant type of factories in the world. Do you know what these factories manufacture?

 5 LS 2.f. Students know plants use carbon dioxide (CO_2) and energy from sunlight to build molecules of sugar and release oxygen. • **5 LS 2.g.** Students know plant and animal cells break down sugar to obtain energy, a process resulting in carbon dioxide (CO_2) and water (respiration).

What do plants produce?

Materials

Purpose

You will observe elodea, a water plant, to find out what it produces.

Procedure

1. Mix 200 mL of water and 10 g of baking soda in the beaker. Baking soda is a source of carbon dioxide.

2. Pour water from the beaker into the large plastic cup until the cup is half full.

3. Place the elodea into the test tube with the cut end facing up. Fill the test tube with water from the beaker.

4. Place your thumb over the end of the test tube. Turn the tube upside down and lower it to the bottom of the plastic cup.

5. Place the plastic cup near a lamp or sunny window. Draw a diagram of the plant and water level.

6. **Observe** On the next day, look closely at the elodea and at the water level in the test tube. Draw a diagram of the plant and water level.

- water
- baking soda
- glass beaker
- spoon
- large plastic cup
- water plant, such as elodea
- large test tube
- light source

Step **3**

Conclusion

7. **Compare** Look at your two diagrams. What did you observe? Why do you think this happened?

Explore More

What are the variables in this experiment? Did light have something to do with your results? Would you get the same results without the baking soda? Form a hypothesis and design an experiment to test it.

 5 IE 6.e. Identify a single independent variable in a scientific investigation and explain how this variable can be used to collect information to answer a question about the results of the experiment.

Step **4**

Main Idea 5 LS 2.f. • 5 LS 2.g

Plants use carbon dioxide and sunlight to build sugar and release oxygen. Plants and animals break sugar down to release energy, carbon dioxide, and water.

Vocabulary

photosynthesis, p.92
stomata, p.92
carbohydrate, p.94
cellular respiration, p.95

LOG ON e-Glossary
@ www.macmillanmh.com

Reading Skill

Draw Conclusions

Text Clues	Conclusions

SCIENCE QUEST Explore photosynthesis and respiration with Team Earth.

What do leaves do?

You have learned that roots absorb water. You have also learned that the water is carried to the leaves by the xylem tissue in the veins. Now you will see how the leaves use water.

Leaves capture and use energy from the sun, water absorbed by the roots, and carbon dioxide from air to make food for the plant. This food-making process is called **photosynthesis** (foh•tuh•SIN•thuh•sis). The carbon dioxide that plants need to carry out photosynthesis is taken in from the air. It enters the plant through tiny pores called **stomata** (STO•muh•tuh). A single pore is called stoma. These are usually found at the bottom of leaves, but are also found on stems. Stomata open and close to let in and give off the gases carbon dioxide and oxygen. They also open to give off excess water vapor.

The job of opening and closing a stoma belongs to two guard cells that surround it. The guard cells open and close stomata in response to the amount of water and light the plant receives. When a plant has too little water, the guard cells will close the stomata to preserve water.

Parts of a Leaf

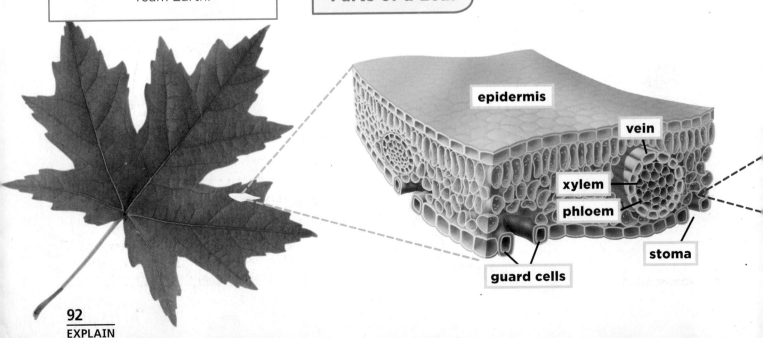

epidermis

vein

xylem

phloem

stoma

guard cells

Photosynthesis takes place in the chloroplasts of cells. This is why chloroplasts are also known as food factories. In most plants, photosynthesis occurs in the chloroplasts of the cells that are underneath the *epidermis* (ep•i•DUR•mis). The epidermis is the outermost layer of a leaf. In some plants, like cactus plants, photosynthesis occurs in the chloroplasts of the cells that are on the stem. As you have learned, chloroplasts contain chlorophyll, a chemical that absorbs and traps the energy of the sunlight.

Carbon dioxide and water enter the chloroplasts and combine in the presence of light energy. This combination results in sugars and oxygen. The plant uses the sugars it produces as food. The sugars are transported to all of the plant's cells by the phloem tissue. Most of the oxygen leaves the plant through the stomata as a waste product.

Scientists express what happens during photosynthesis using a chemical equation. The equation shows how the materials of photosynthesis react together and what they produce.

✔ Quick Check

Draw Conclusions How are the chloroplasts like tiny factories?

Critical Thinking How would a drought affect a plant's ability to produce food?

$$6CO_2 \ + \ 6H_2O \ + \ energy \ \longrightarrow \ C_6H_{12}O_6 \ + \ 6O_2$$

carbon dioxide   water   sugar   oxygen

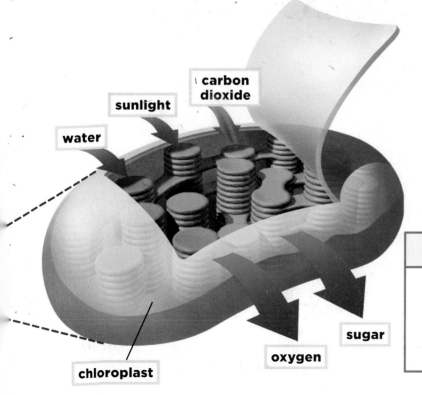

carbon dioxide

sunlight

water

sugar

oxygen

chloroplast

Reading Diagrams

What part of the leaf is made up of xylem and phloem tissue?

Clue: Look at the labels on the diagram. Use them to help you answer the question.

What is the photosynthesis and respiration cycle?

All living things need energy to carry out their life processes. The photosynthesis and respiration cycle provides energy to plants and animals.

The sugar that plants produce during photosynthesis is a carbohydrate (kahr•boh•HIGH•drayt). **Carbohydrate** is the name given to a group of substances made from carbon, hydrogen, and oxygen. Simple carbohydrates can be stored as food or

Photosynthesis and Respiration Cycle

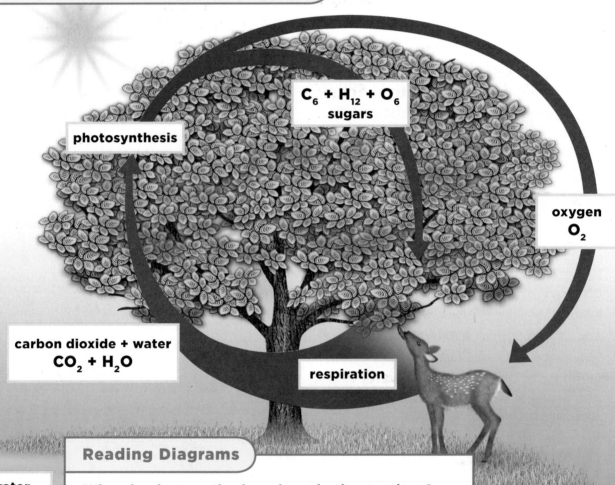

$C_6 + H_{12} + O_6$
sugars

photosynthesis

oxygen
O_2

carbon dioxide + water
$CO_2 + H_2O$

respiration

water

Reading Diagrams

What do photosynthesis and respiration produce?

Clue: Observe the direction of the arrows. Compare what they are pointing to and where they are pointing from to answer the question.

LOG ON ⊖-**Science in Motion** Watch the photosynthesis and respiration cycle @ **www.macmillanmh.com**

modified to make structural materials. When plants store sugar, they usually store it as starch. The cell walls of plant cells are made of *cellulose*. Starch and cellulose are complex carbohydrates made of thousands of simple sugar units.

Animals also depend on photosynthesis as their source of energy. When an animal eats part of a plant, it takes in the carbohydrates stored in the plant. Even when animals are carnivores and eat other animals, they are taking in the carbohydrates that these animals took from eating a plant in the first place.

The oxygen that plants produce during photosynthesis is breathed in by animals during respiration. Some of the oxygen is also used by plants. When plant or animal cells need energy, they use oxygen to break down stored carbohydrates. This is a process known as **cellular respiration** (SEL•yuh•luhr res•puh•RAY•shuhn).

You can think of respiration and photosynthesis as the opposite of each other. During cellular respiration, plant and animal cells produce carbon dioxide and water, which are then released back into the air. Plants use the released carbon dioxide along with water to produce sugars during photosynthesis. And the cycle begins again.

✔ Quick Check

Draw Conclusions In what ways do animals depend on plants?

Critical Thinking Is there more energy in the plant before or after photosynthesis?

Quick Lab

The Food in Leaves

1. Place a leaf in a jar. Fill the jar 3/4 full with rubbing alcohol. Replace the lid on the jar. Alcohol breaks down some of the structures in the leaf.

2. Draw a picture of the jar. Record the date and time.

3. Leave the leaf in the jar for 24 hours.

4. Remove the leaf from the jar and blot it dry with a paper towel.

5. Place the leaf in a petri dish. Add enough iodine to cover the leaf.

6. **Observe** Look at the leaf and draw a picture of it. Record the date and time.

7. **Draw Conclusions** What food do you think is in the leaf? Hint: In the presence of starch, iodine turns black.

8. **Communicate** Discuss your results with other groups of students. Were your results the same or different? If they were different, suggest a reason for the variation.

Where does respiration happen?

Cellular respiration occurs in mitochondria. Mitochondria provide the energy that plant and animal cells need to grow and to repair themselves. This is why they are known as the power houses of the cell.

A typical cell holds about 1,000 mitochondria. Oxygen and sugar produced during photosynthesis enter the cell and go into the mitochondria. The mitochondria use oxygen to break down the stored carbohydrates to release energy. Carbon dioxide and water are also released as products of this reaction.

In the mitochondria, the released energy is changed into a substance called ATP. The ATP is like a battery that goes where the cell needs energy. These batteries are constantly being used. The energy that it takes for you to read this page is coming from ATP.

The chemical equation for cellular respiration is:

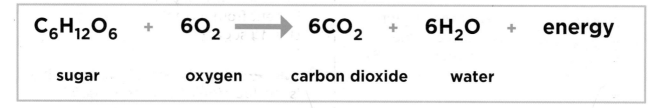

$$C_6H_{12}O_6 \; + \; 6O_2 \longrightarrow 6CO_2 \; + \; 6H_2O \; + \; \text{energy}$$

sugar   oxygen   carbon dioxide   water

Cellular Respiration

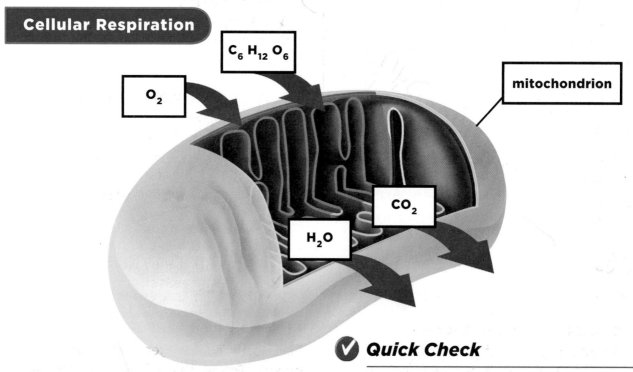

$C_6 H_{12} O_6$

O_2

mitochondrion

CO_2

H_2O

✔ Quick Check

Draw Conclusions Why are the mitochondria in plant cells important?

Critical Thinking Why does a cell need energy?

Lesson Review

Summarize the Main Idea

Leaves capture and use the energy of the sun to make food through photosynthesis. (pp. 92–93)

Photosynthesis uses light energy, carbon dioxide, and water to produce oxygen and sugar. Sugar is used for food in plants. (pp. 94–95)

Cellular respiration takes place in the mitochondria. (p. 96)

Make a FOLDABLES Study Guide

Make a layered look book (see p. 481). Use the titles shown. On the inside of each fold, summarize what you learned about each title.

Think, Talk, and Write

1. **Main Idea** How do plants produce their own food?

2. **Vocabulary** In the process of photosynthesis, _____ is captured.

3. **Draw Conclusions** What happens when a plant needs energy?

Text Clues	Conclusions

4. **Critical Thinking** How do animals benefit from a plant's method of storing sugar?

5. **Test Practice** Which of the following is the location of photosynthesis?
   A mitochondria
   B chloroplasts
   C stomata
   D cuticle

6. **Test Practice** What are the products of photosynthesis?
   A sugar and carbon dioxide
   B carbon dioxide and water
   C sugar and oxygen
   D carbon dioxide and oxygen

Math Link

Calculate Grams of Sugar
An apple has about 13.8 g of carbohydrates. Sugars make up 75% of the carbohydrates in an apple. How many grams of sugar does it have?

Health Link

House Plants
Plants produce oxygen and carbon dioxide. Research the health benefits of having plants in your house. Is it healthy to keep plants in your bedroom?

A Year in the Life of a Forest

Did you know that forests breathe? Scientists can measure the gases in the forest air to gather data about the photosynthesis and respiration of the trees, animals, and other organisms that live there.

Take a look at the carbon dioxide data that scientists measured in the air from Howland Forest, a deciduous forest in Maine. Howland Forest has cold and snowy winters and hot and humid summers. How do these changes in seasons affect the amount of carbon dioxide in the air?

Spring

As the days become longer and warmer, activity in the forest grows. This increased activity results in higher levels of respiration, so the amount of carbon dioxide measured in the air starts to rise. The trees sprout new leaves and begin to photosynthesize.

Summer

Summer days are the longest and warmest of the year. Because the forest is so active, a lot of photosynthesis and respiration occurs. During the day, the amount of carbon dioxide is low. That's because the trees are transforming the carbon dioxide into food to store in their roots. During the night, the amount of carbon dioxide is high. That's because all of the life forms in the forest are respiring, and the trees are not photosynthesizing. These two processes together result in the different day and night carbon dioxide levels you see in the chart.

Fall

Shorter days mean fewer hours of sunlight. Trees begin to lose their leaves and the forest becomes less active. The forest is photosynthesizing and respiring less. Day and night carbon dioxide levels are similar.

Winter

Winter days are the shortest and coldest of the year. The forest is much less active. Most of the trees have lost their leaves, and there is no photosynthesis. These two processes together result in different day and night carbon dioxide levels.

ELA R 5.2.1. Understand how text features (e.g. format, graphics, sequence, diagrams, illustrations, charts, maps) make information accessible and usable. •
ELA R 5.2.2. Analyze text that is organized in sequential or chronological order.

Spring | Summer

Winter | Fall

Sequence

▶ The sequence of events is the order in which events happen in time.

▶ Look for the event that happens first, then fill in what happens next and last.

▲ These photos show Howland Forest at all four seasons.

Write About It

Sequence

Create a sequence of events timeline based on the information in the article. Tell what happens first, next, and last as the seasons change in Howland Forest. Then use your timeline and the chart from the article to summarize the data collected from Howland Forest.

LOG ON **e-Journal** Write about it online @ **www.macmillanmh.com**

AMERICAN
MUSEUM of
NATURAL
HISTORY

CO₂ Concentration (parts/million)		
Month	Minimum CO₂	Maximum CO₂
Jan	378	388
Feb	377	385
March	377	384
April	376	388
May	371	393
June	362	413
July	356	427
Aug	355	424
Sep	362	418
Oct	358	386
Nov	366	379
Dec	368	377

Saving Water the Yucca Plant Way

Yucca plants grow in the deserts of California and the southwest parts of North America. They have long, narrow leaves they use to save water. Yuccas use a special kind of photosynthesis called CAM photosynthesis.

Most plants open their stomata during the day. They need carbon dioxide for photosynthesis. Yucca plants only open their stomata at night. This keeps the yucca from losing water through evaporation in the hot desert sun. During the day, the yucca plant uses its stored carbon dioxide for photosynthesis. Desert plants that use CAM photosynthesis, like the yucca, lose much less water than other plants.

Good expository writing

▶ develops the main idea with facts and supporting details.

▶ gives information about a topic.

▶ uses transition words to connect ideas.

▶ draws a conclusion.

The yucca plant has long, thin leaves. ▼

 ### Write About It

Explanatory Writing Write an article for young gardeners. Explain the process of CAM photosynthesis. Add a diagram to help explain. Research facts and details for your article.

 e-Journal Write about it online @ www.macmillanmh.com

 ELA W 5.2.3.c. Write research reports about important ideas, issues, or events by using the following guidelines: Develop the topic with simple facts, details, examples, and explanations.

Leave It Be!

Some leaves, like the tiny pine needle, barely have any surface area. Others, like the very large banana plant leaf, have a very large surface area.

The surface area of leaves is directly connected to the amount of sugar and oxygen they produce. One could assume that a single pine needle does not produce as much sugar and oxygen as a banana leaf.

How can you find the surface area of a leaf?

Calculating Area

To find the area of an irregular figure,

▶ trace the figure on graph paper.

▶ count the number of whole square units.

▶ count the number of partial square units and divide this number by 2.

▶ add the two numbers.

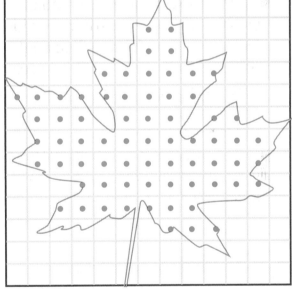

 ### Solve It

1. Find a leaf. Calculate the area of your leaf.

2. Compare the area of your leaf to the area of the maple leaf above.

3. Which produces more sugar and oxygen?

whole squares	+	partial squares / 2	= area
43	+	$\frac{24}{2}$	= area
43	+	12	= 55

 MA MG 5.1.4. Differentiate between, and use appropriate units of measures for, two-and three-dimensional objects (i.e. find the perimeter, area, volume)

Summarize the Main Ideas

Vascular plants are classified as seedless and seed plants. Most seed plants have flowers. (pp. 70-77)

Vascular plants have special structures for the transport of materials such as sugar, water, and minerals. (pp. 80-87)

Plants use carbon dioxide and sunlight to build sugar and release oxygen. Plants and animals break sugar down to release energy, carbon dioxide, and water. (pp. 90-97)

Make a **FOLDABLES**™ Study Guide

Take a sheet of paper and tape your lesson study guides as shown.

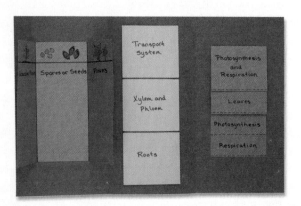

Fill each blank with the best word from the list.

angiosperm, p. 74

cellular respiration, p. 95

gymnosperm, p. 75

phloem, p. 84

photosynthesis, p. 92

seed, p. 73

spore, p. 73

xylem, p. 84

1. Sugar combines with oxygen to produce carbon dioxide, water, and energy during _____. 5 LS 2.f

2. Water and minerals move through _____ from roots to leaves. 5 LS 2.a

3. Plants use _____ to make their own food. 5 LS 2.f

4. A single cell that develops into a plant identical to its parent is a(n) _____. 5 LS 2.a

5. A plant that produces flowers is a(n) _____. 5 LS 2.a

6. A plant that produces cones is a(n) _____. 5 LS 2.a

7. When a male cell and a female cell join, a(n) _____ forms, which will develop into a plant that shares the characteristics of its two parent plants. 5 LS 2.a

8. Sugars move through _____ from leaves to other parts of a plant. 5 LS 2.a

Answer each of the following in complete sentences.

9. Sequence What are the main steps of photosynthesis? 5 LS 2.f

10. Draw Conclusions What part of a plant would you assume had been damaged if its leaves began to wilt? Explain. 5 LS 2.a

11. Classify Upon seeing a tree, how would you determine whether it should be classified as a gymnosperm or an angiosperm? 5 LS 2.a

12. Critical Thinking Some scientists believe that increased levels of carbon dioxide in the air are causing changes in our climate. How might the cutting down of forests make this problem worse? 5 LS 2.f • 5 LS 2.g

13. Expository Writing Write a paragraph that describes how energy moves between plants and animals. 5 LS 2.f • 5 LS 2.g

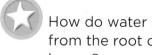

How do water and nutrients travel from the root of a plant to its leaves?

Light Up a Problem!

You have learned that plants need light to carry out photosynthesis. Your task is to find out whether different kinds of plants need different amounts of light to produce the food they need to stay healthy.

What to do

1. Gather data on the amount of light plants need to produce the food they need to stay healthy. Use the Internet, books, or visit a plant nursery or florist shop to find information.

2. Design a chart that shows the amount of light needed for different plants. Include illustrations of the plants in your chart.

Analyze your results

▶ Based on the information you have collected, explain whether different plants need similar or different amounts of light to stay healthy.

▶ Suggest places where each kind of plant might grow best.

 5 LS 2.f. Students know plants use carbon dioxide (CO_2) and energy from sunlight to build molecules of sugar and release oxygen.

1 **All of the following are vascular plants EXCEPT** 5 LS 2.a

A trees.

B mosses.

C ferns.

D grasses.

2 **Why do plants *most* likely have fruit?**

5 LS 2.a

A Pollen is produced by fruit.

B Fruit protects spores.

C Fruit protects seeds.

D Pollen is transferred by fruit.

3 **The picture below shows the roots of a corn plant.**

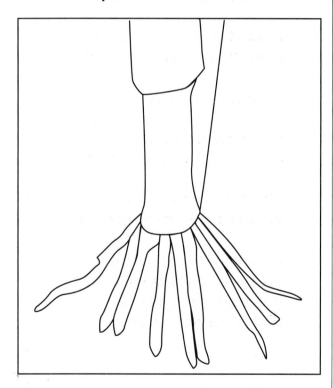

Which type of root is illustrated in the picture? 5 LS 2.a

A prop root

B taproot

C fibrous root

D aerial root

4 **Why are *most* living things on Earth dependent on photosynthesis?**

5 LS 2.f

A It produces food energy and carbon dioxide.

B It produces water and light.

C It produces food energy and oxygen.

D It produces carbon dioxide and oxygen.

5 **Which of the following *best* describes the function of stomata?**

5 LS 2.e

A convert carbon dioxide, oxygen, and water into food energy

B allow gases and water to enter and exit a plant

C circulate minerals through the xylem and phloem of the plant

D transport carbon dioxide and oxygen through the plant

6 **Which of these supports a plant and usually grows above ground?** 5 LS 2.a

A flower

B leaf

C root

D stem

7 The following diagram illustrates some of the parts of a leaf.

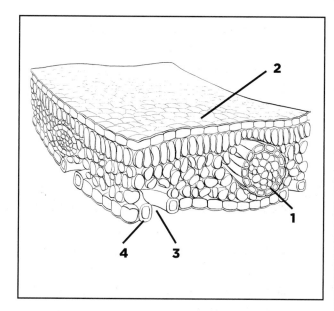

Which location on the diagram represents a stoma? 5 LS 2.a

A 1
B 2
C 3
D 4

8 The food produced during photosynthesis is transported by

5 LS 2.e

A roots.
B xylem.
C phloem.
D leaves.

9 Light Energy + Carbon Dioxide + Water → _____ + Oxygen
Which of the following is missing from the chemical equation above? 5 LS 2.f

A chloroplast
B energy
C sugar
D chlorophyll

10 Which of the following are seed plants that produce flowers? 5 LS 2.a

A mosses
B hornworts
C gymnosperms
D angiosperms

11 Which of the following are the products of cellular respiration?

5 LS 2.g

A oxygen and sugar
B carbon dioxide and oxygen
C water and sugar
D carbon dioxide and water

12 Which list gives the correct order of pollen traveling through a flower?

5 LS 2.a

A stamen, egg cell, pistil
B egg cell, pistil, stamen
C stamen, pistil, egg cell
D pistil, stamen, egg cell

CHAPTER 3

Human Body Systems

 How does your body work?

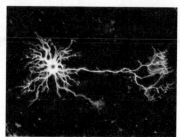

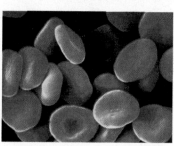
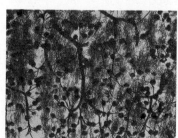
 5 LS 2. Plants and animals have structures for respiration, digestion, waste disposal, and transport of materials.

107

Literature

MAGAZINE ARTICLE

ELA R 5.2.3. Discern main ideas and concepts presented in texts, identifying and assessing evidence that supports those ideas.

ELA W 5.1.2. Create multiple-paragraph expository compositions: c. Offer a concluding paragraph that summarizes important ideas and details.

from *CURRENT HEALTH*

Bigger MUSCLES or A Stronger Heart?

Different kinds of activities have different effects on the body. If you dance, jump rope, ride your bike, or do anything else that makes you breathe hard and increases your heartbeat for an extended period of time, you're doing aerobic exercise. (Aerobic means "with oxygen.") Aerobic exercise is very good for the health of the heart and lungs, although it's usually not good to exercise so hard that it hurts or is difficult to breathe.

Another kind of exercise, called anaerobic, involves short bursts of intense activity, such as sprinting over a short distance or lifting weights. Anaerobic exercise is an excellent way to help build muscle.

For kids, aerobic exercise is considered the most healthful kind. However, any exercise, whether it's walking, hiking, skating, or practicing karate, is better than none.

Write About It

Response to Literature In this article, you learned about the difference between aerobic and anaerobic exercise. Write a summary. Start by telling the main idea of the article. Then include important facts and details. Reach a conclusion at the end.

 e-Journal Write about it online @ **www.macmillanmh.com**

The Human Body

Look and Wonder

Cells like this one carry the brain's messages to all parts of your body. What activities do you use your brain for?

5 LS 2.a. Students know many multicellular organisms have specialized structures to support the transport of materials.

What parts of your body are you using?

Make a Prediction

Pick one of the following activities:

▶ Write your name.

▶ Pick a pencil up from the floor.

▶ Whistle or hum a tune.

Predict the body parts that you will use as you do this activity.

- craft paper
- markers
- colored pencils

Test Your Prediction

1 Trace an outline of your partner's body on craft paper.

2 Start from a sitting position at your desk. Do the activity you chose.

3 On your body outline, color or circle all of the parts of the body that you used during your activity. How much of your body did you use?

Draw Conclusions

4 **Compare** What differences do you see between your original list and the body parts you circled on your outline?

5 What part of your body controlled the activity you did?

6 How did your body get the energy it needed to do the activity? What body parts turn food into the energy that you used when you moved?

Step 1

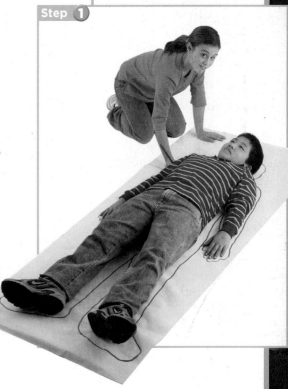

Explore More

Think about all the activities you do in one day. Keep track of all of the things you do. What part of your body do you use to complete every activity? Write a report that explains your observations.

5 IE 6.i. Write a report of an investigation that includes conducting tests, collecting data or examining evidence, and drawing conclusions.

Read and Learn

Main Idea 5 LS 2.a

Your body has many organ systems that transport materials and information so you can do your life processes.

Vocabulary

skeletal system, p.115

muscular system, p.115

respiratory system, p.115

circulatory system, p.115

excretory system, p.115

nervous system, p.115

digestive system, p.115

integumentary system, p.115

immune system, p.115

endocrine system, p.115

reproductive system, p.115

LOG ON e-Glossary
@ www.macmillanmh.com

Reading Skill

Main Idea

Main Idea	Details

What are the organ systems in your body?

The human body is a complex machine that carries out multiple jobs at the same time. As you learned in Chapter 1, the smallest unit of life in the human body is a cell. A group of similar cells that work together to carry out a function make up a tissue. In turn, different tissues are organized into various organs. The organs then work together as part of an organ system to perform specific activities or functions.

Suppose you are riding a bicycle. Your skeletal system (SKEL•i•tuhl SIS•tuhm) supports your body as you move your legs to pedal. Your muscular (MUS•kyuh•luhr) system lets you tighten your hand around the handlebars to steer the bicycle.

As you pedal faster, the speed of your breathing increases. This means that your

Human Body Systems

System	Function
skeletal system	support
muscular system	movement
respiratory system	oxygen/carbon dioxide exchange
circulatory sytem	transport
excretory system	waste removal
nervous system	control
digestive system	food absorption
immune system	protection
integumentary system	protection
endocrine system	regulation and control
reproductive system	reproduction

Reading Tables

What organ systems help protect your body?

Clue: Look at the function column of the chart.

respiratory (RES•puhr•uh•tawr•ee) system is breathing in more oxygen for your cells to use. Your circulatory (SUR•kyuh•luh•tawr•ee) system carries this oxygen throughout your body to all of your cells.

As you ride farther, you may sweat, meaning your excretory (EK•skri•tawr•ee) system is removing waste materials that your body does not need. This system also keeps your body from overheating. When you are done riding, your nervous (NUR•vuhs) system may send signals that you are hungry. If you then eat an apple, your digestive (di•JES•tiv) system breaks it down to provide energy for your body.

Your integumentary (in•TE•gyuh•men•tuh•ree) system, or your skin and hair, covers your body

and acts as a barrier to protect it from damage, much the way your helmet protects you from injuries. If you fall while riding your bicycle and cut your knee, your immune (i•MYEWN) system helps you heal.

Your endocrine (EN•duh•krin) system controls your body's growth and responses. Your endocrine system would be activated if you are nervous about falling off of your bicycle or excited about competing in a race.

 Quick Check

Main Idea What are your organ systems?

Critical Thinking What system would be activated if you were surprised?

▼ As this boy rides his bicycle, he uses all of his body's organ systems.

What do your organ systems do?

Your organ systems work together to carry out your life processes. Each system works like parts of a machine.

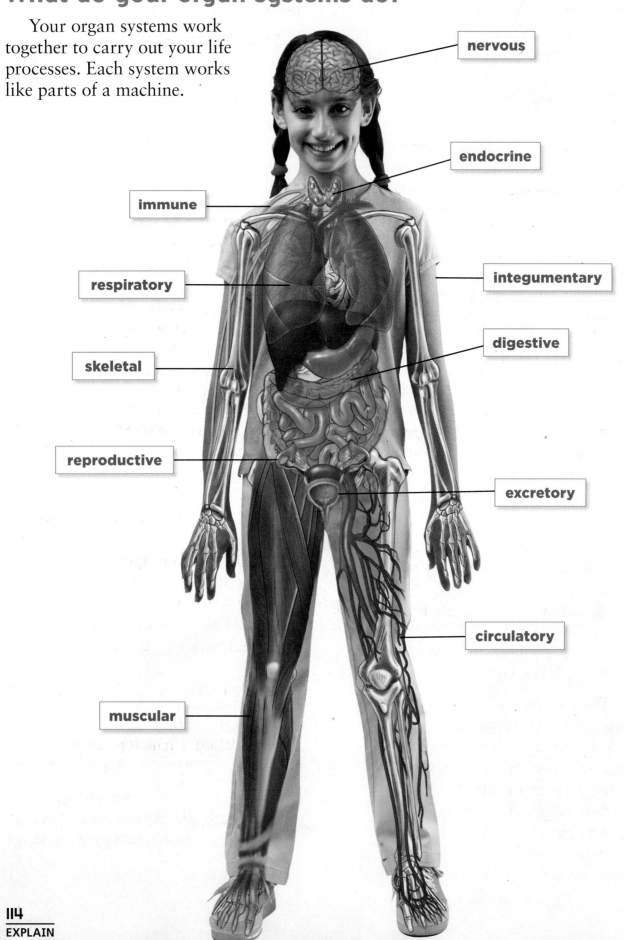

nervous

endocrine

immune

respiratory

integumentary

digestive

skeletal

reproductive

excretory

circulatory

muscular

The **nervous system** includes the brain, spinal cord, and nerves. It carries messages in your body and controls your senses. Without your nervous system, you wouldn't be able to taste, smell, hear, think, write, or move.

The skeletal and muscular systems work together to help you move. The 206 bones of the **skeletal system** give the body its shape and protect the organs. The **muscular system** is made up of muscles that are attached to and move bones. Some organs are also made up of muscle tissue.

The integumentary and the immune systems protect the body. The **integumentary system** includes skin, hair, and nails. It protects the body from injury and infection and removes waste. The **immune system** protects and fights against disease and illness and helps heal injuries. The immune system has cells that attack and kill disease organisms in your tissues.

The **endocrine system** produces chemicals that regulate and control body functions. The chemicals of the endocrine system also help to control the reproductive (ree•pruh•DUK•tiv) system. The **reproductive system** produces offspring.

The digestive, respiratory, circulatory, and excretory systems transport materials in the body. The **digestive system** turns food into nutrients that are suitable for use by the body cells. The **respiratory system** carries oxygen into the lungs, where it is transferred to the blood. It removes carbon dioxide from the

Quick Lab

The Skeletal System

1. Take two chenille sticks. Bend a loop in one end of each.

2. **Make a Model** Alternatively string pasta wheels and hard candy circles on one chenille stick.

3. Alternatively string pasta wheels and soft candy circles on the other chenille stick.

4. Fold the ends of the chenille sticks so the pasta and candy do not fall off.

5. **Compare** Slowly bend each model. How far can you bend each model?

6. **Infer** Which model better represents the structure of your backbone? Explain your answer.

blood and releases it from the body. The **circulatory system** uses blood and blood vessels to move oxygen and nutrients to the cells. It also removes carbon dioxide and other waste from the cells. The **excretory system** moves waste materials out of the body.

✔ Quick Check

Main Idea What do the digestive, respiratory, circulatory, and excretory systems have in common?

Critical Thinking What would happen to the human body if one of the organ systems stopped working?

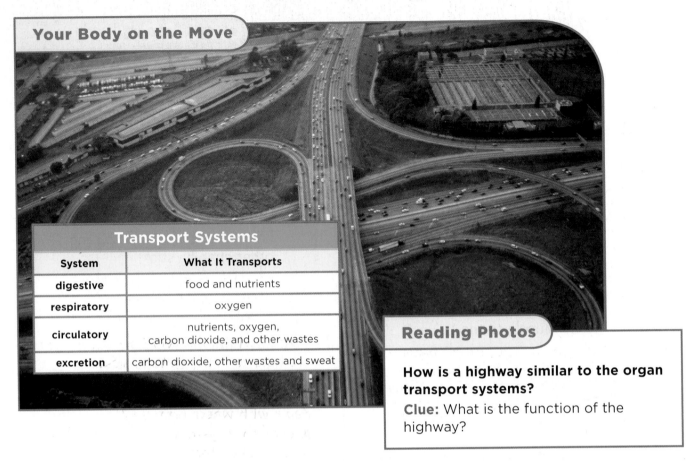

Your Body on the Move

Transport Systems	
System	**What It Transports**
digestive	food and nutrients
respiratory	oxygen
circulatory	nutrients, oxygen, carbon dioxide, and other wastes
excretion	carbon dioxide, other wastes and sweat

Reading Photos

How is a highway similar to the organ transport systems?
Clue: What is the function of the highway?

How are body materials transported?

Your body needs to move materials, such as nutrients, gases, and waste, from one place to another. How does your body transport these materials?

Your digestive system breaks the food that you eat into nutrients that are suitable for use by your cells. The breakdown of food starts in your mouth and continues in your stomach. Food is broken down into nutrients which move into your circulatory system.

When you breathe, your respiratory system moves oxygen into your body through your nose and your mouth. The oxygen travels into your lungs, where it passes into your circulatory system.

Your circulatory system carries oxygen and nutrients around your body to your cells. As oxygen moves into your cells, carbon dioxide moves out into your blood. As nutrients move into your cells, waste moves out into your blood.

Your excretory system removes waste from your body. The carbon dioxide in your blood is carried back to your lungs, where it is breathed out. Waste in your blood is filtered out of your body.

 Quick Check

Main Idea What does your circulatory system transport?

Critical Thinking Why do you need an excretory system?

Lesson Review

Summarize the Main Idea

Your body's **organ systems** enable it to carry out life processes. (pp. 112–113).

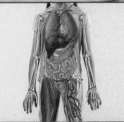

Each organ system has a specific **structure** and **function**. (pp. 114–115)

Your **organ transport systems** move materials throughout your body. (p. 116)

Make a FOLDABLES™ Study Guide

Make a three-tab-book (see p. 481). Use the titles shown. On the inside of each tab, tell the main idea of each title.

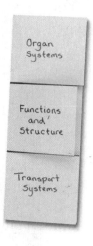

Organ Systems

Functions and Structure

Transport Systems

Think, Talk, and Write

1. **Main Idea** What do organ systems do?

2. **Vocabulary** The system that functions as a framework for the body and as a place for muscles to attach is the _____.

3. **Main Idea** List five organ systems and their functions.

Main Idea	Details

4. **Critical Thinking** Which organ system protects you from getting sick?

5. **Test Practice** **Which organ system deals with waste removal?**
   A excretory system
   B skeletal system
   C nervous system
   D reproductive system

6. **Test Practice** **Which of the following is a function of the integumentary system?**
   A transports gases
   B protects the body
   C breaks down food
   D produces offspring

Writing Link

Personal Narrative

Write about a time you performed an activity, such as competing in a sport or acting in a play. Tell about at least two organ systems you think you used to perform your activity.

Health Link

Healthful Diet

Research the effects of a healthful diet on your organ systems. Tell how the organ systems benefit from a diet low in fat and high in fruits and vegetables.

 **e-Review** Summaries and quizzes online @ www.macmillanmh.com

Form a Hypothesis

The nervous system allows the brain to communicate with every part of the body. It controls your senses and your body movements. Your ability to react to stimuli, such as catching a ball, depends on how fast messages get transmitted, or sent to or from your brain.

The time between when you sense something and when you act is called reaction time. Scientists study people's reactions to various situations to learn more about how the nervous system works. Scientists use what they learn to **form a hypothesis**. When you **form a hypothesis**, you make a testable statement about what you think is logically true.

❶ Learn It

A **hypothesis** is a statement about the effect of one variable on another. It should be based on observations or collected data. For example, when you play baseball, you might notice that you catch the ball more times when you keep your eyes on the ball. Based on this observation, you might form the **hypothesis**: *"If I keep my eyes on the ball, then I'll hit the ball more often."*

A **hypothesis** is tested using an experiment. You might test this **hypothesis** by trying to hit a ball several times with your eyes on the ball and elsewhere. The results of the experiment will either support or disprove the **hypothesis**.

❷ Try It

▶ Test your reaction time by trying to catch a falling object. Think about any observations you've made in the past about reaction times. What variables might affect your reaction time? Will you react faster to a sound or a sight? Write your answer as a **hypothesis** in the form *"If my eyes are shut then ... "*

5 IE 6.b. Develop a testable question. • **5 IE 6.e.** Identify a single independent variable in a scientific investigation and explain how this variable can be used to collect information to answer a question about the results of the experiment.

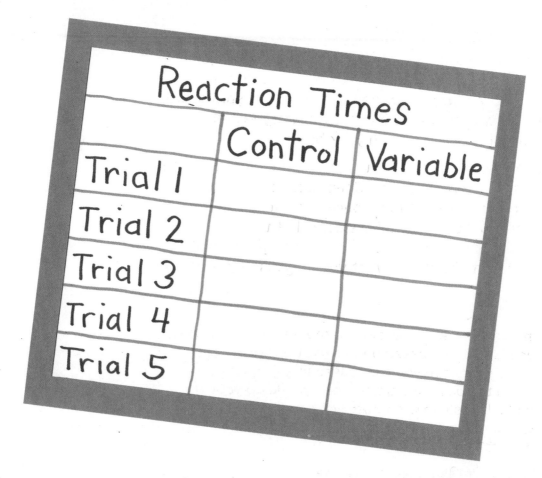

Reaction Times

	Control	Variable
Trial 1		
Trial 2		
Trial 3		
Trial 4		
Trial 5		

▶ Create a chart like the one shown to record the results.

▶ Hold a ruler at the highest number. Have your partner put one hand at the bottom of the ruler without touching it.

▶ Drop the ruler and observe the spot where your partner caught the ruler. This is the control. The closer to the bottom numbers, the quicker the reaction. Repeat the test 5 times.

▶ Repeat this activity, but this time have your partner cover their eyes and make a noise as you drop the ruler. This is the variable. Repeat the test 5 times and record your results.

▶ Now have your partner drop the ruler for you, and record your results.

❸ Apply It

▶ Now it's time to analyze your data. Compare your reaction times. Do you notice any patterns? Does your data support or disprove your **hypothesis**?

▶ What will happen to your reaction time if you try the same experiment with your other hand? Write your answer as a hypothesis in the form *"If I use my other hand then…"*

▶ Test your **hypothesis** and record the results during five attempts. Analyze the results to find out if they support or disprove your **hypothesis** and share them with the class.

The Digestive System

Look and Wonder

Your small intestine is full of folds. Stretched out it is about as long as a school bus! How does this structure help you absorb nutrients?

5 LS 2.c. Students know the sequential steps of digestion and the roles of teeth and the mouth, esophagus, stomach, small intestine, large intestine, and colon in the function of the digestive system.

Why is the small intestine full of folds?

Make a Prediction

Compare the structure of the construction paper, the computer paper, and the paper towels. Make a prediction about the type of paper that will absorb the most water.

Test Your Prediction

1. Pour the same amount of water into each graduated cylinder. Observe and record the water levels of the graduated cylinders.

2. Fold the construction paper twice lengthwise.

3. Dip the construction paper into a graduated cylinder until half is covered in water.

4. After 30 seconds remove the paper. Observe and record the water level in the graduated cylinder.

5. Repeat steps 2–4 for the other paper types.

Draw Conclusions

6. Which type of paper absorbed the most water? Do these results support your prediction?

7. **Compare** How does the structure of the paper that absorbed the most water compare to the small intestine?

8. **Infer** What is the function of the small intestine?

Step 2

Step 3

Explore More

What do you think would happen if you repeat the experiment using a bath towel? Form a hypothesis and test it. Analyze your results and write a report explaining them.

5 IE 6.i. Write a report of an investigation that includes conducting tests, collecting data or examining evidence, and drawing conclusions.

Main Idea 5 LS 2.c

The digestive system includes the mouth, esophagus, stomach, small intestine, large intestine, and colon.

Vocabulary

digestion, p.122

saliva, p.124

pharynx, p.125

esophagus, p.125

stomach, p. 126

small intestine, p.127

large intestine, p.128

colon, p.128

LOG ON e-Glossary
@ www.macmillanmh.com

Reading Skill

Sequence

First
Next
Last

SCIENCE QUEST Explore the body systems with Team Earth.

What is digestion?

Your cells need energy to perform life processes and do work for your body. They get this energy from the food you eat. Eating is like putting gas in a car. But the food you eat is too big and complex for your tiny cells. **Digestion** (die•JES•chuhn) breaks down food into smaller and simpler substances that your body can absorb.

Your body breaks down food physically and chemically. When you take a bite of food, your teeth and tongue break down food physically by chewing it into smaller pieces. Chemicals produced by *glands* further break down the bits of food into nutrients. A *nutrient* is any substance found in food that is useful for your body.

Nutrients pass from your digestive system into tiny blood vessels in your circulatory system. They are then carried by your blood to all the cells of your body. Your cells draw energy from nutrients. This energy helps you grow, develop, and perform daily activities, like reading this textbook or riding a bicycle.

▶ The digestive system breaks down the food we eat into substances the body can absorb.

Mouth The mouth is where digestion begins.

Esophagus The esophagus is a tube that connects your mouth to your stomach.

Liver The liver adds digestive juices to food.

Stomach The stomach is a hollow bag with muscular walls.

Pancreas The pancreas is an organ about 6 inches long that produces several digestive juices.

Small Intestine The small intestine connects the stomach and the large intestine. It absorbs digested food.

Gall Bladder The gall bladder is a pear-shaped organ that stores digestive juices produced by the liver.

Large Intestine The large intestine eliminates undigested waste.

 Quick Check

Sequence What is the first step in digestion?

Critical Thinking Are solids or liquids easier to digest?

Where does digestion begin?

Suppose that you just bit into a nice, juicy apple. Your front teeth, the *incisors* and *canines*, tear through the tough apple skin. Your back teeth, the *molars*, grind the apple into a ball of food called a *bolus* (BOH•luhs).

What does the apple taste like? As the apple touches your tongue, your 10,000 taste buds tell you it is sweet. The *salivary glands* in your mouth and throat produce a watery fluid called saliva (seh•LIE•vuh). **Saliva** helps to moisten and soften the bolus and to break it down chemically.

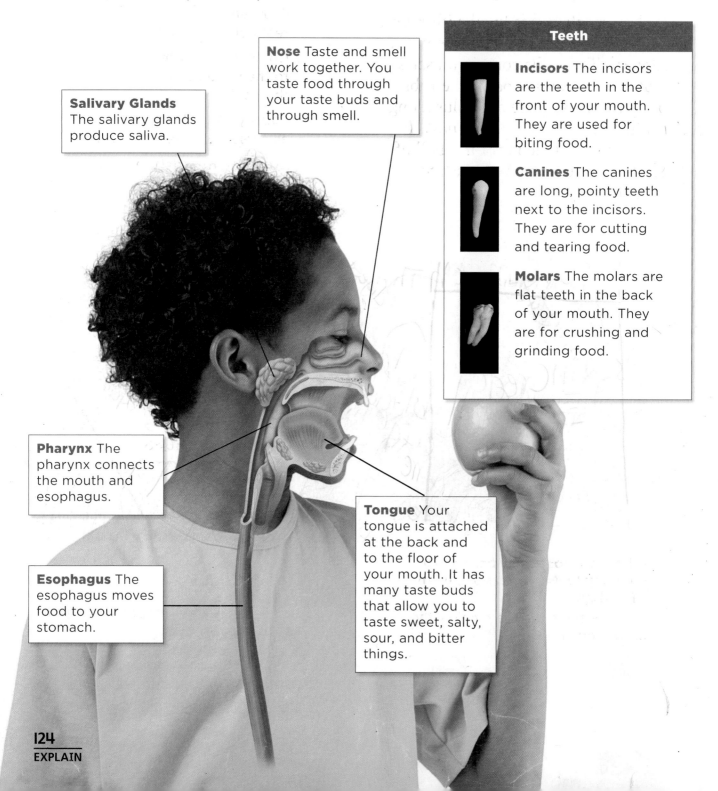

Nose Taste and smell work together. You taste food through your taste buds and through smell.

Salivary Glands The salivary glands produce saliva.

Pharynx The pharynx connects the mouth and esophagus.

Esophagus The esophagus moves food to your stomach.

Tongue Your tongue is attached at the back and to the floor of your mouth. It has many taste buds that allow you to taste sweet, salty, sour, and bitter things.

Teeth

Incisors The incisors are the teeth in the front of your mouth. They are used for biting food.

Canines The canines are long, pointy teeth next to the incisors. They are for cutting and tearing food.

Molars The molars are flat teeth in the back of your mouth. They are for crushing and grinding food.

Next, your tongue moves the chewed up apple to the back of your mouth. The bolus moves to the **pharynx** (FAR•ingks), another name for the portion of the throat that connects the mouth to the digestive tube. Now you swallow, and the bolus passes into a long, muscular tube called the **esophagus** (i•SOF•uh•guhs).

The esophagus is lined with *mucus*, (MYOO•kuhs) which makes the inside slippery. The walls contain muscles that contract and expand like rubber bands. They squeeze the bolus along toward the stomach (STUM•uhk). It takes about 10 seconds for a ball of food to move from the mouth to the stomach.

Quick Lab

Your Teeth

1. Use a mirror to observe your teeth.
2. Count your teeth and record the number in a chart.
3. Draw each of your teeth on your chart.
4. Compare your chart to the pictures of the teeth in the book.
5. Classify each of the teeth you drew as incisors, canines, or molars.
6. **Compare** How do the shapes of your teeth compare to each other?

Human Mouth X ray

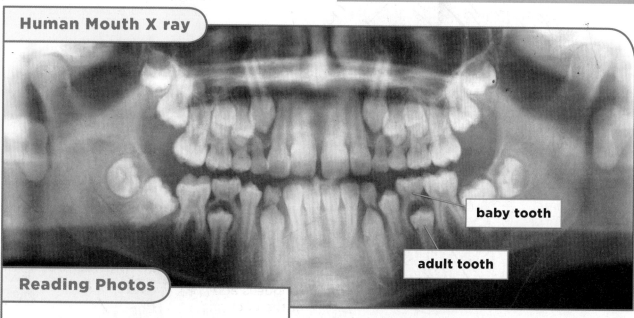

baby tooth

adult tooth

Reading Photos

What will most likely happen to the baby teeth that are shown in this X ray?

Clue: Observe the teeth below the baby teeth in the photo.

✓ **Quick Check**

Sequence What happens after you swallow food?

Critical Thinking What would happen if your salivary glands did not secrete saliva?

How is food broken down further?

Now the ball of chewed apple has reached the stomach. The **stomach** is a digestive organ with thick muscular walls. When the stomach is empty it has folds that resemble wrinkles. When the stomach fills up with food, the folds expand and smooth out. The stomach can hold more than a liter when it is full.

The wall of the stomach has glands that produce chemicals, such as acids, that break down food. It also contains mucus that keeps food moist and slippery.

Three layers of muscles in the stomach squeeze the food with wave-like motions. The muscles of the stomach contract and relax to create the movement. While the stomach is moving, it adds mucus and digestive acids to the food. The muscles squeeze and mix the bolus until it is changed into a thick, soupy liquid. After about 4 to 6 hours of mixing and squeezing, the liquid food is released into the small intestine (in•TES•tin).

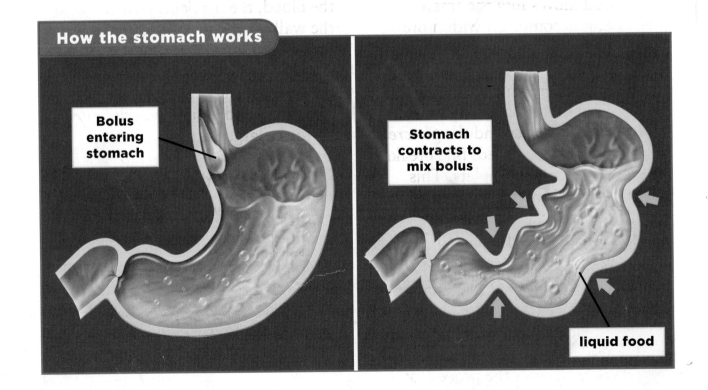

How the stomach works

Bolus entering stomach

Stomach contracts to mix bolus

liquid food

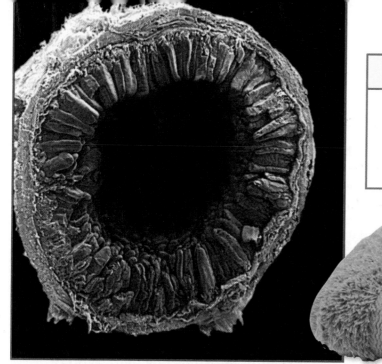

▲ The fingerlike bumps and hairs in the small intestine absorb nutrients.

Reading Photos

How are the inside of the small intestine and towel similar?

Clue: Compare the photos and read the captions to answer the question.

▲ The folds of fabric in a towel increase absorption.

The **small intestine** is a coiled, tubular organ that is connected to the stomach. As the partially digested liquid food moves into the small intestine, it is combined with more digestive juices. The digestive juices break down the nutrients from the food into smaller, simpler forms. *Bile* (BIGHL) and other digestive juices produced by the liver and the *pancreas* (PAN•kree•uhs) are added. Bile breaks down fat into small droplets. This digestive juice is produced by the liver and is stored in the *gall bladder* (GAWL BLAD•uhr) until needed. The pancreas produces digestive juices that help digest carbohydrates, fats, and proteins.

The nutrients are absorbed by the small intestine. *Absorption* (ab• SAWRP•shuhn) is the process in which tissues take in nutrients. The inside of the small intestine has many bumps called *villi* (VIL•igh) that look like hairy fingers. They increase absorption like a fuzzy towel. To reach the blood, the nutrients pass through the walls of the small intestine and into tiny blood vessels. Blood carries the nutrients to the rest of the body by way of the circulatory system. The remaining undigested material moves on to the large intestine.

 Quick Check

Sequence What happens to the nutrients right before they leave the small intestine?

Critical Thinking Explain the steps of digestion with a diagram. Start with the stomach and end with the small intestine.

What are the parts of the large intestine?

Much of the apple that you chewed has already been digested and sent to the circulatory system. The parts of the apple that you could not digest moves on to the large intestine. The **large intestine** is a thick, tubular organ that removes undigested waste. It is shorter and thicker than the small intestine.

The *cecum* (SEE•kuh) is the first and shortest part of the large intestine. It connects directly with the small intestine. The **colon** (KOH•luhn) is the widest part of the large intestine. Some water and some minerals are absorbed in the colon and are carried to your body tissue by the blood.

The last part of the large intestine is the *rectum* (REK•tuhm). Solid waste called *feces* (FEE•seez) is stored in the rectum until strong muscles push it out of the body through the *anus* (AY•nuhs). This process is called *elimination* (i•limuh•NAY•shuhn).

✔ Quick Check

Sequence What happens to undigested waste in the large intestine?

Critical Thinking Do you think the large intestine has villi? Why or why not?

Large Intestine

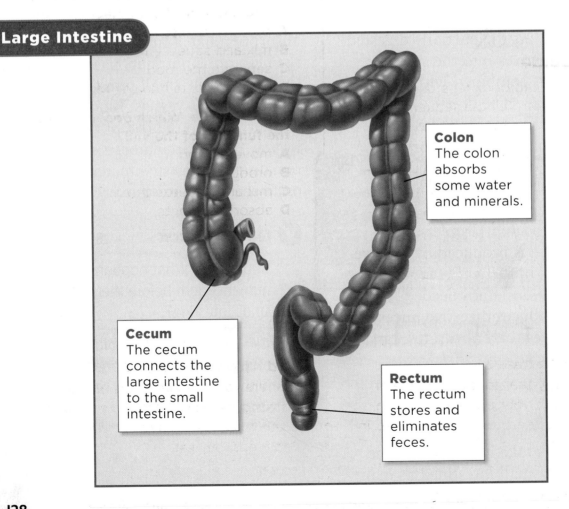

Colon
The colon absorbs some water and minerals.

Cecum
The cecum connects the large intestine to the small intestine.

Rectum
The rectum stores and eliminates feces.

Lesson Review

Summarize the Main Idea

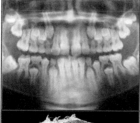
Digestion breaks down food into smaller pieces your body can use. It begins in the **mouth.** (pp. 122–125)

Chemical breakdown of food occurs mostly in the **small intestine.** Absorption takes place in the small intestine. (pp. 126–127)

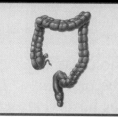
Water and minerals are removed from undigested food in the **large intestine.** (p. 128)

Make a FOLDABLES™ Study Guide

Make a three-tab book (see p. 481). Use the titles shown. Tell the sequence of events that occur for each title.

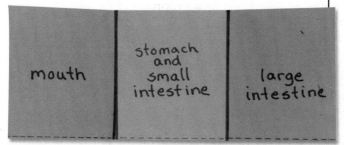

mouth | stomach and small intestine | large intestine

Think, Talk, and Write

1. **Main Idea** What happens to food before it can be used by the body?

2. **Vocabulary** The tube that connects the mouth and the stomach is the _____.

3. **Sequence** What happens to food in the small intestine?

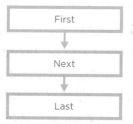

First

↓

Next

↓

Last

4. **Critical Thinking** Why might babies need to eat soft food?

5. **Test Practice** **Which of the following is a function of the stomach muscles?**
   A produce digestive juices
   B mix and squeeze food to liquid
   C separate the food
   D pass nutrients into the blood

6. **Test Practice** **Which *best* describes the function of the villi?**
   A move the food
   B produce bile
   C mix and squeeze the food
   D absorb nutrients

 Writing Link

Fictional Narrative
Write a story that follows a piece of food through your digestive system. Tell what happens to it at each step in the digestion process.

 Social Studies Link

Food Around the World
What are your favorite foods? People all around the world eat different foods. Research another culture and find out what foods they eat.

Meet George Barrowclough

When most people think of predators, they picture long, sharp teeth that can rip into flesh. But did you know that some predators, like owls, have no teeth at all? Owls are predators, animals that hunt other animals, that eat and digest their food in an interesting way.

George Barrowclough is an ornithologist at the American Museum of Natural History. An ornithologist is a scientist who studies birds. He investigates a bird called the northern spotted owl, found only in California, Oregon, Washington, and parts of Canada. Northern spotted owls are excellent hunters. They mostly catch rodents, including flying squirrels, woodrats, and mice.

▲ northern spotted owl

▼ **George is a scientist that studies birds.**

AMERICAN MUSEUM OF NATURAL HISTORY

 ELA R 5.2.3. Discern main ideas and concepts presented in texts, identifying and assessing evidence that supports those ideas.

When you eat, you chew first to break the food apart before swallowing it down to your stomach. Most of the time, when an owl eats a mouse it swallows it whole. Then it relies on a part of its stomach called the gizzard to break the food down. The gizzard has digestive fluids that dissolve the soft tissues of the mouse.

The skeleton, teeth, fur, and claws don't have a lot of nutrients and are very hard for the owls to digest. Instead they are squeezed into a tight ball in the gizzard. Several hours later, the owl closes its eyes, coughs it up, and spits it out. This mass of mixed-up fur and bones is called a pellet.

Owl pellets may look gross to some people, but scientists like George find them fascinating. That's because scientists get a lot of information from owl pellets. They can find out what kinds of animals the owls prey on and how they hunt. This information is especially important because the northern spotted owl is an endangered species of bird. The more we learn about these owls and what they need to survive, the better we are able to protect them.

▲ George working in the field holding a northern spotted owl chick.

▶ owl pellets

Write About It

Main Idea

Think about the article you just read. Look for the main topic or central idea of the article. Write the main idea of the article and give one detail from the article that supports the main idea.

LOG ON e-Journal Write about it online @ www.macmillanmh.com

Main Idea

▶ Look for the central point of a selection to find the main idea.

▶ Details are important parts of the selection that support the main idea.

The Respiratory System

Look and Wonder

Your lungs have more than a million of these tiny air sacs. How much air can they hold?

5 LS 2.b. Students know how blood circulates through the heart chambers, lungs, and body and how carbon dioxide (CO_2) and oxygen (O_2) are exchanged in the lungs and tissues. • 5 LS 2.g. Students know plant and animal cells break down sugar to obtain energy, a process resulting in carbon dioxide (CO_2) and water (respiration).

How much air do you breathe?

Materials

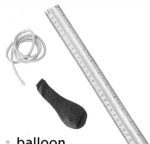

- **balloon**
- **string**
- **ruler**

Purpose

The purpose of this activity is to see how much air you can hold in one breath.

Procedure

1. Breathe in as much air as you can.

2. Breathe out into the balloon and quickly tie the balloon shut.

3. Holding one end of a piece of string, wrap the string around the balloon at its widest point.

4. Mark the other end of the string with a pen.

5. Use a ruler to measure the length of the string. The string represents the amount of air you breathe out.

6. **Record Data** Keep track of the number of times you breathe in for one minute.

Draw Conclusions

7. **Communicate** Compare the length of your string and the number of times you breathed in to those of your classmates. Were they the same or different? Why do you think this is?

8. **Analyze Data** What relationship, if any, can you see between the breathing rate and how much air can be held in one breath?

Step 2

Step 4

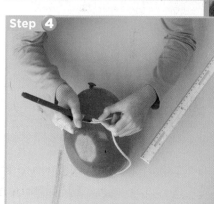

Explore More

How would your breathing rate and the amount of air you breathe out change if you tried the activity after exercising? Form a hypothesis and test it. Then analyze your results and write a report explaining them.

 5 IE 6.i. Write a report of an investigation that includes conducting tests, collecting data or examining evidence, and drawing conclusions.

What does the respiratory system do?

Your respiratory system is made up of a series of tubes and passages that transport the air you breathe. It allows an exchange of gases between the air, your blood, and your tissues.

When you **inhale** (in•HAYL), or breathe in, air enters your body through your mouth and nose. Your **lungs** are organs that fill with air when you inhale. They expand like balloons. Then they empty of air when you **exhale** (eks•HAYL), or breathe out. This movement is controlled by the contractions of a large, flat sheet of muscle called the **diaphragm** (DIGH•uh•fram). Air is drawn down into your lungs through a series of narrowing, branched tubes. The tubes are surrounded by capillaries (KAP•uh•ler•ees). A **capillary** is a tiny blood vessel. Oxygen from the air in the tubes enters the blood cells in the capillaries. They take the oxygen to the rest of your cells.

As blood passes through the lungs, it takes in oxygen and releases carbon dioxide. As you know, carbon dioxide is a waste product of cellular respiration. Along with water vapor, carbon dioxide, is exhaled out of the body through the respiratory system.

▶ Some people, like this girl, need medicine to help them breathe.

The Respiratory System

Nose You inhale and exhale air through your nose. The passages in the nose heat and moisten the air.

Mouth The air from your nose enters your mouth. You also inhale and exhale through your mouth.

Epiglottis This flap of tissue protects you from choking. It closes when you swallow to prevent food from entering the airway.

Throat Air from the mouth flows down into your pharynx and passes over your voice box, called the larynx.

Trachea The trachea is a strong tube that is divided into two branches that connect to the lungs.

Lungs You have a right and left lung. The lungs fill with air when you inhale.

Diaphragm Air is pulled into and pushed out of the lungs by the muscular diaphragm.

Bronchi These are the branches of the trachea inside the lungs. Each branch, which divides into smaller and smaller branches, is called a bronchus.

Alveoli The alveoli are small, thin sacs at the end of each bronchus. Gas exchange takes place here.

✓ Quick Check

Main Idea What is the main function of the respiratory system?

Critical Thinking Explain how the diaphragm and lungs work together.

Where does gas exchange take place?

As you inhale, air travels from your nose and mouth to your lungs through a series of tubes in your respiratory system. The journey begins at the *trachea* (TRAY•kee•uh). The trachea divides into two tubes leading into the lungs. Once inside the lungs, the tubes branch out into smaller tubes. The tiniest of these tubes, the *bronchi* (BRONG•kigh), have branches like a tree. These branches empty the air into very thin-walled air sacs, called **alveoli** (al•VEE•uh•ligh).

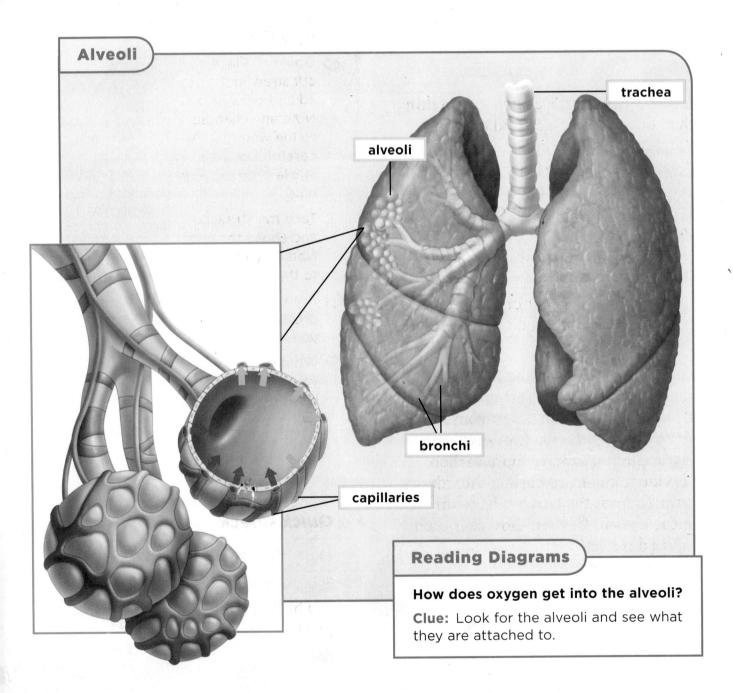

Alveoli

trachea

alveoli

bronchi

capillaries

Reading Diagrams

How does oxygen get into the alveoli?

Clue: Look for the alveoli and see what they are attached to.

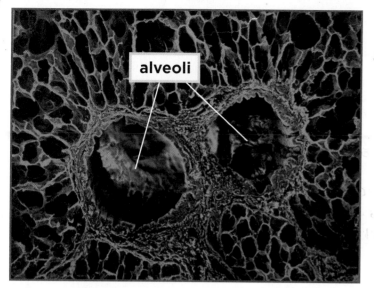

▲ These two alveoli are surrounded by a network of capillaries.

The walls of the alveoli are so thin that gases like oxygen and carbon dioxide can pass through them by diffusion (di•FYEW•zhuhn). **Diffusion** is the movement of particles from areas of high concentration to low concentration.

The alveoli are surrounded by capillaries. The walls of these tiny vessels are also very thin. The blood cells trade the carbon dioxide for the oxygen.

The blood cells in the capillaries have less oxygen than air in the alveoli, so oxygen diffuses from the air to the blood cells. Likewise, cells in the capillaries have more carbon dioxide than air, so carbon dioxide diffuses from the blood cells to air in the alveoli. Carbon dioxide is then exhaled out through the organs of your respiratory system.

Quick Lab

The Gas You Exhale

Bromothymol blue (BTB) can be used to indicate the presence of carbon dioxide. If CO_2 is present, BTB in water changes from blue to yellow.

1. Pour 1 cup of water into a plastic cup with a lid.

2. Using an eye dropper, add drops of BTB slowly until the water turns blue.

3. **Observe** Place a cut straw in the cup lid and blow into it. Note any changes to the water. △ **Be careful.** Do not inhale bromothymol blue.

4. Take the straw out and shake the cup. Note any changes to the water.

5. **Draw Conclusions** What gas is present when you exhale? How do you know?

6. What do you think will happen if you run in place and then blow into the BTB solution?

✔ Quick Check

Main Idea What is gas exchange?

Critical Thinking Carbon dioxide is a human waste. Is this true for plants, too?

How does cellular respiration happen in animal cells?

You may recall that animal cells, much like plants cells, need oxygen to carry out cellular respiration.

Blood cells in the capillaries collect oxygen from the air in the alveoli, and nutrients from the small intestine. As capillaries throughout the body come in contact with other body cells, the oxygen and the nutrients diffuse out of the blood cells and into other body cells.

Oxygen and sugar enter the cell and once in the cell enter the mitochondria. The mitochondria break down the sugar with oxygen, releasing the energy stored in the sugar. This energy is saved in ATP. Like plant cells, animal cells use ATP to carry out cellular processes.

The reaction between sugar and oxygen also produces carbon dioxide and water. Carbon dioxide and water diffuse from the cells, back into the blood cells in the capillaries. The capillaries take carbon dioxide-rich cells back to the lungs so they can be oxygenated.

✔ Quick Check

Main Idea What is the main function of the mitochondria?

Critical Thinking Why is water considered a waste product in cellular respiration?

Cellular Respiration

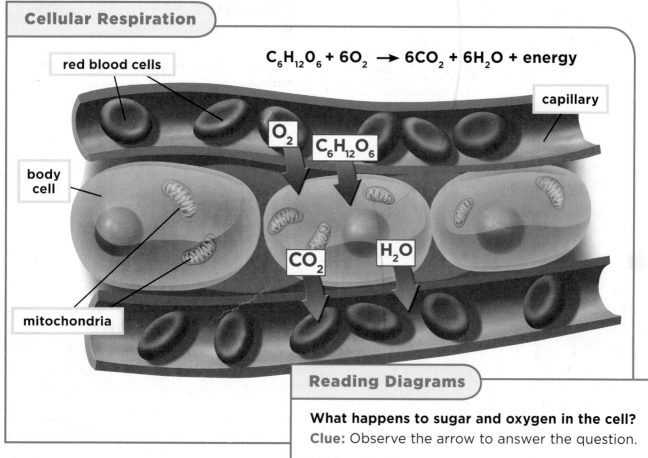

$$C_6H_{12}O_6 + 6O_2 \rightarrow 6CO_2 + 6H_2O + energy$$

red blood cells

capillary

O$_2$

C$_6$H$_{12}$O$_6$

body cell

CO$_2$

H$_2$O

mitochondria

Reading Diagrams

What happens to sugar and oxygen in the cell?
Clue: Observe the arrow to answer the question.

Summarize the Main Idea

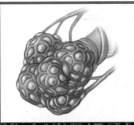

The **respiratory system** passes the air you breathe into the lungs for gas exchange. (pp. 134–135)

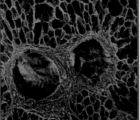

Oxygen and carbon dioxide are transferred between the **alveoli** and red blood cells during **gas exchange**. (pp. 136–137)

Cells get their energy from glucose through the process of **cellular respiration**. (p. 138)

Make a FOLDABLES™ Study Guide

Make a three-tab book (see p. 481). Use the titles shown. List the main idea and details for each title.

Think, Talk, and Write

1. **Main Idea** What would happen if your cells did not get oxygen?

2. **Vocabulary** The tubed branches in the lungs are called _____ .

3. **Main Idea** Describe the process of gas exchange.

Main Idea	Details

4. **Critical Thinking** What would happen if you did not have an epiglottis?

5. **Test Practice** Which organ is a flat muscle?
   A lung
   B bronchus
   C diaphragm
   D windpipe

6. **Test Practice** Which *best* describes cellular respiration?
   A Oxygen combines with water.
   B Air moves into cells.
   C Air moves in and out of the lungs.
   D Oxygen breaks down sugar.

 Writing Link

Persuasive
Research the damaging effects of smoking on your respiratory system. Write a persuasive editorial to your school newspaper convincing your friends not to smoke.

 Math Link

Measuring the Air You Breathe
Every minute you breathe in about 13 pints of air. How many pints of air will you breathe in after 2 hours? How many gallons of air does that equal?

Be a Scientist

Materials

2 600 mL beakers

2 test tubes

3 droppers

bromothymol blue

sugar, yeast

goggles, gloves

warm water

Inquiry Structured

What are the products of respiration?

Form a Hypothesis

During cellular respiration, living cells use oxygen to break down sugar and release energy. This process also produces carbon dioxide. Yeast cells will be placed in water and in a sugar solution. What will happen to the level of carbon dioxide when sugar is present? Write your answer as a hypothesis in the form "*If sugar is present, then…*"

⚠ **Be careful.** Wear goggles and gloves. If bromothymol blue comes in contact with skin, wash that area immediately. Do not inhale bromothymol blue.

Test Your Hypothesis

1. Make 2 solutions. In Solution A, mix 2 teaspoons of yeast, 3 tablespoons of sugar, and 1.5 cups of warm water. In Solution B, mix 2 teaspoons of yeast and 1.5 cups of warm water.

2. Fill one dropper with Solution A. Fill the other dropper with the Solution B.

Step 2

3. Pour water into 2 test tubes until they are 3/4 full. Put three drops of bromothymol blue in each test tube. Observe and record the color of the water.

Step 3

4. Place each (solution-filled) dropper into a test tube with the opening of the dropper pointed up. Add water if the opening of the dropper is not covered.

5. Place each test tube in a beaker of warm water.

6. Observe the droppers and water color every 15 minutes for 45 minutes. Record what you see.

Step 4

5 IE 6.b. Develop a testable question. • **5 IE 6.e.** Identify a single independent variable in a scientific investigation and explain how this variable can be used to collect information to answer a question about the results of the experiment.

Draw Conclusions

1 As you know, bromothymol blue changes from blue to yellow in the presence of carbon dioxide. Based on this information, what do your observations of the color of the water in the test tubes indicate?

2 Do your results support your hypothesis? Explain why or why not.

Inquiry Guided

How does temperature affect the respiration rate of cells?

Form a Hypothesis

Sometimes a cell's temperature will increase due to an increase in activity. How do yeast cells react to an increase in temperature? Write your answer as a hypothesis in the form *"If the temperature increases, then…"*

Test Your Hypothesis

Design a plan to test your hypothesis. Then write out the materials, resources, and steps you need. Record your results and observations as you follow your plan.

Draw Conclusions

Did your experiment support your hypothesis? Why or why not?

Inquiry Open

What else would you like to learn about respiration or the respiratory system? Come up with a question to investigate. For example, how does your respiration rate change when you exercise? Design and carry out an experiment to answer your question. Your experiment must be organized to test only one variable, or one item being changed.

Remember to follow the steps of the scientific process.

Ask a Question
↓
Form a Hypothesis
↓
Test Your Hypothesis
↓
Draw Conclusions

The Circulatory System

Look and Wonder

Driven by the heart, your blood cells travel around your body carrying chemicals and oxygen to your cells. What does your heart do when your body needs more oxygen?

 5 LS 2.b. Students know how blood circulates through the heart chambers, lungs, and body and how carbon dioxide (CO_2) and oxygen (O_2) are exchanged in the lungs and tissues.

When does your heart work the hardest?

Form a Hypothesis

When you exercise, your body requires more oxygen. What happens to your heart when you exercise? Write your answer as a hypothesis in the form *"If the body requires more oxygen, then …"*

Test your Hypothesis

1. Take your pulse when you are resting. Press lightly on the skin on the inside of your wrist until you feel a beat. Then count how many beats you feel in 15 seconds. Record this number in a chart.

2. Walk in place for one minute. When you are done, take your pulse. Record your data.

3. Run in place for one minute. When you are done take your pulse. Record your data.

4. **Record Data** Make a bar graph of your heartbeats when resting, walking, and running.

Draw Conclusions

5. Did your results support your hypothesis?

Explore More

Repeat the above experiment, but this time measure your pulse for 1 minute after every step. Now multiply your results in the first experiment to convert the unit into minutes. How do the two sets of experiment results compare? Which set of results is more accurate?

 5 IE 6.g. Record data by using appropriate graphic representations (including charts, graphs, and labeled diagrams) and make inferences based on those data.

- **stopwatch**
- **graph paper**

Step 1

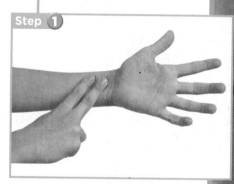

Step 2

How are materials transported through your body?

If it were possible to journey around the human body, a red blood cell would be your best guide. Red blood cells travel through the entire circulatory system. The circulatory system is the transport system made up of the heart, blood vessels, and blood. This system is also known as the *cardiovascular* (kahr•dee•oh•VAS•kyuh•luhr) *system*.

Your circulatory system is like a postal system for your body, with the blood cells bringing things to and from your body cells. Your **heart** is a muscular organ that is constantly pumping blood through your body.

First, blood from your heart is pumped into your arteries (AHR•teer•ees). An **artery** carries blood mixed with oxygen away from your heart. Your organs, tissues, and cells take the oxygen, food, and nutrients they need from your blood. They also release waste into your blood. Oxygen and waste, like carbon dioxide, move in and out of your blood through the walls of your capillaries. From the capillaries, the blood carrying carbon dioxide moves into your veins (VAYNS). A **vein** takes the blood cells carrying carbon dioxide back to your heart.

▶ Local blood drives collect blood for patients who need it.

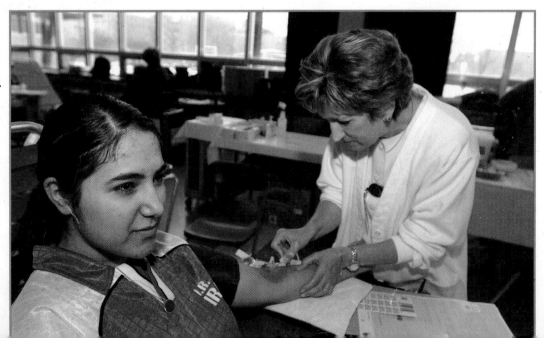

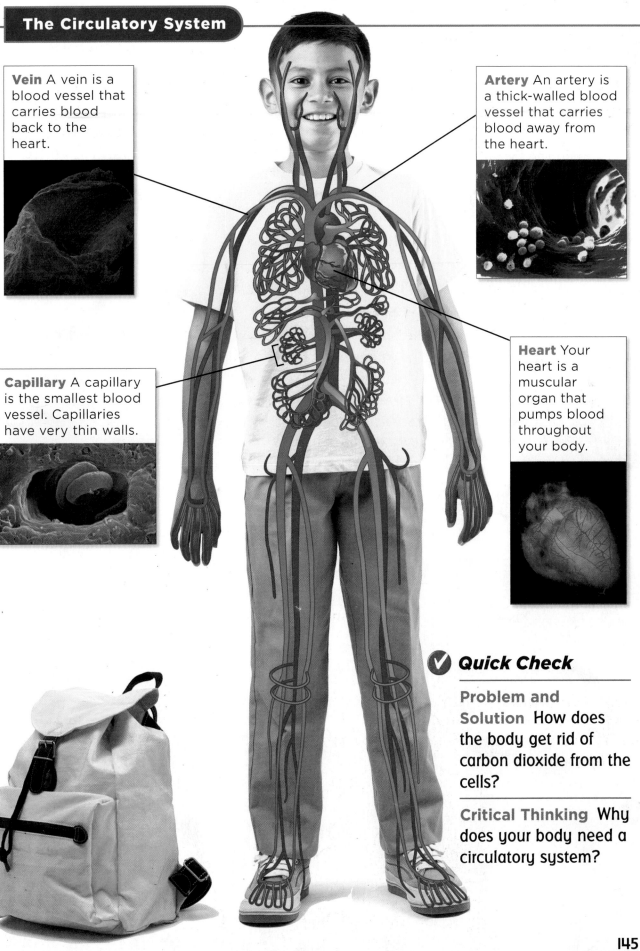

Vein A vein is a blood vessel that carries blood back to the heart.

Artery An artery is a thick-walled blood vessel that carries blood away from the heart.

Capillary A capillary is the smallest blood vessel. Capillaries have very thin walls.

Heart Your heart is a muscular organ that pumps blood throughout your body.

✔ Quick Check

Problem and Solution How does the body get rid of carbon dioxide from the cells?

Critical Thinking Why does your body need a circulatory system?

What are the parts of the heart?

Your heart is a very strong muscle about the size of your fist. It is located in the center of your chest behind a bone called the *sternum* (STUR•nuhm). A protective sac of tissue called the *pericardium* (per•i•KAHR•dee•uhm) surrounds the heart. The heart is always pumping blood through your body. In one year, a person's heart pumps enough blood to fill 4 large swimming pools!

The heart has two sides, the right side and the left side, that are separated by a muscular wall. Each side of the heart has two chambers, or hollow sacs. The upper chamber is called an *atrium* (AY•tree•uhm). The lower chamber is called a *ventricle* (VEN•tri•kuhl). There are *valves* (VALVS) connecting the upper chamber and lower chamber. Valves are like automatic doors that close to prevent blood from flowing in the wrong direction.

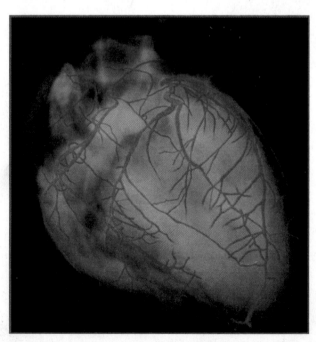

▲ The human heart beats about 70 to 90 times a minute.

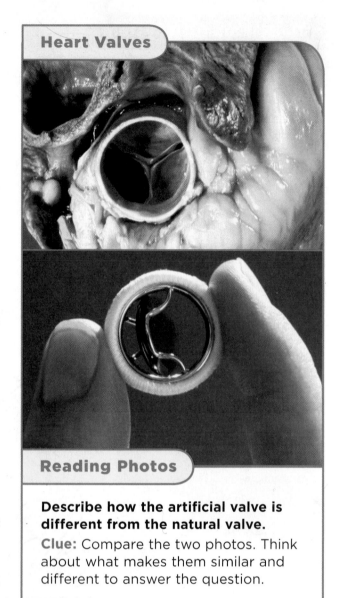

Heart Valves

Reading Photos

Describe how the artificial valve is different from the natural valve.

Clue: Compare the two photos. Think about what makes them similar and different to answer the question.

The right atrium receives blood from two large veins, the superior *vena cava* (VEE•nuh KAY•vuh) and the inferior vena cava. The superior vena cava brings blood from the upper part of the body and the head. The inferior vena cava brings blood from the lower part of the body. This blood flows into the right ventricle. It is then pumped out of the heart through the *pulmonary* (POOL•muh•nuh•ee) artery which leads to the lungs.

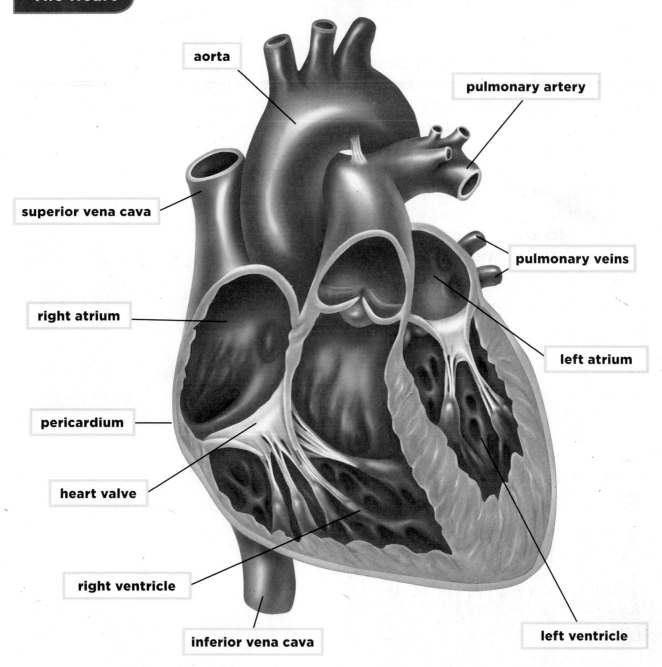

aorta

pulmonary artery

superior vena cava

pulmonary veins

right atrium

left atrium

pericardium

heart valve

right ventricle

inferior vena cava

left ventricle

The left atrium receives blood from the pulmonary veins which come from the lungs. This blood flows into the left ventricle. It is then pumped out of the heart through a large artery called the *aorta* (ay•AWR•tuh). The aorta brings blood to the rest of the body.

 Quick Check

Problem and Solution How does the heart prevent blood from flowing in the wrong direction?

Critical Thinking What do you think happens to a person when the heart valves are not working?

147
EXPLAIN

How do blood and blood vessels work?

Blood is a liquid tissue that contains *plasma* (PLAZ•muh), red blood cells, white blood cells, and *platelets* (PLAYT•lits). Plasma is a clear liquid that makes up about 56% of blood. The red blood cells, the white blood cells, and the platelets are suspended in the plasma. Plasma is made up of water and proteins. Plasma transports the nutrients and vitamins obtained from the digested food you eat.

Red blood cells make up about 40% of your blood. The oxygen your body needs is transported by red blood cells to your body cells. Red blood cells also transport carbon dioxide.

White blood cells and platelets make up about 4% of your blood. White blood cells fight off any germs that enter the body. They are like soldiers that protect your body from any invaders. They also break down dead cells. White blood cells are larger than red blood cells.

▼ This vial contains blood that has been separated.

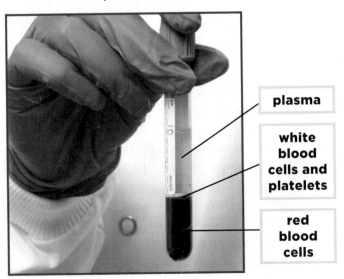

plasma

white blood cells and platelets

red blood cells

Platelets are small cell fragments. They help your body fix itself after you get hurt. If you cut your finger, the platelets clump or stick together. They form a clot or a scab to make your finger stop bleeding. Platelets also prevent your blood from leaking through broken blood vessels. They repair the blood vessels by sticking to the broken spots.

▲ White blood cells attack any germs or invaders in your body.

How Platelets Heal

Platelets help heal cuts by clotting or sticking together.

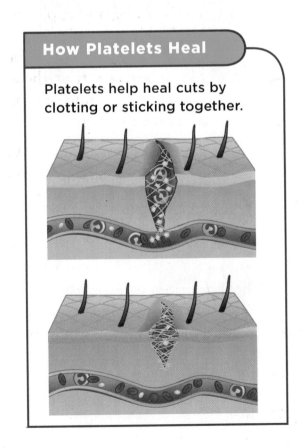

Structure of Vein Valves

vein valve

Blood is transported through the body in arteries, veins, and capillaries. The muscular walls of arteries and veins have three layers. The walls of the veins are thinner and narrower than those of arteries. They prevent nutrients and gases from passing through.

Like the heart, some veins in your arms and legs have valves that prevent the blood from flowing in the wrong direction. The valves close to stop blood from backing up.

Capillaries are tiny blood vessels that connect veins and arteries. Gas exchange of carbon dioxide and oxygen takes place through the thin walls of capillaries. Oxygen and carbon dioxide pass through the walls of the capillaries, where they are picked up by red blood cells.

Quick Lab

Vein Valves

1. ⚠ **Be Careful!** Cut a slit in the center of a cardboard tube.

2. Insert a small piece of cardboard through the tube sideways, so that it touches the other side of the tube.

3. Stand the tube up vertically so the piece of cardboard is pointing down.

4. Pour some kidney beans through the top of the tube.

5. **Observe** Look inside the tube. Describe what happened to the beans.

6. Now turn the tube over so the piece of cardboard is pointing up. Repeat Step 4.

7. **Infer** How is this model similar to your veins?

✔ Quick Check

Problem and Solution How does your body fight infection?

Critical Thinking Why are there more red blood cells than white blood cells?

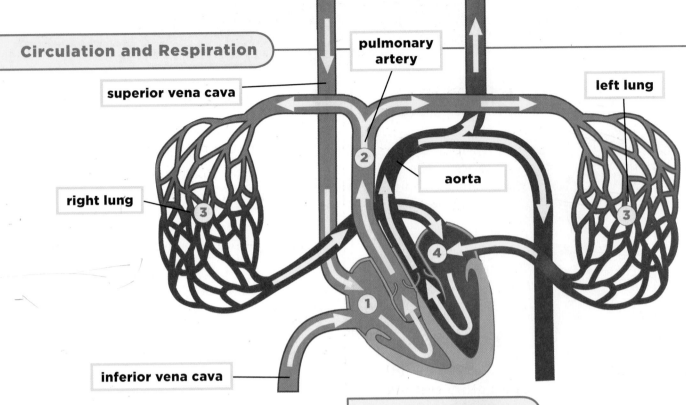

pulmonary artery

superior vena cava

left lung

right lung

aorta

inferior vena cava

Reading Diagrams

What are the main steps in circulation and respiration?

Clue: Follow the arrows. Red represents oxygen-rich blood. Blue shows oxygen-poor blood.

LOG ON *Science in Motion* Watch how the circulatory and respiratory systems work together@ **www.macmillanmh.com**

How do the circulatory and the respiratory systems work together?

Your circulatory and respiratory systems work together to transport oxygen and carbon dioxide through your body.

① Carbon dioxide-rich blood from the superior vena cava and inferior vena cava enters the right atrium. Then it flows into the right ventricle and is pumped out through the pulmonary artery.

② The carbon dioxide-rich blood flows through the pulmonary artery into the lungs.

③ In the lungs, the blood drops off carbon dioxide and picks up oxygen.

④ Oxygen-rich blood from the lungs flows into the left atrium through the pulmonary veins. Then it goes into the left ventricle where it is pumped out to the body through the aorta.

✔ Quick Check

Problem and Solution How does the heart get rid of the carbon dioxide in the blood?

Critical Thinking What might happen if someone's lungs were not working properly?

Summarize the Main Idea

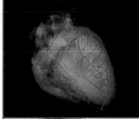

The **circulatory system** is a transport system. It consists of the heart, blood vessels, and blood. (pp. 144–47)

Blood is made up of red blood cells, plasma, white blood cells, and platelets. (pp. 148–149)

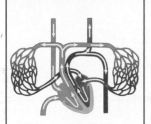

The **circulatory** and the **respiratory systems** work together to transport oxygen to your cells and carbon dioxide out of your cells. (p. 150)

Make a FOLDABLES™ Study Guide

Make a three-tab book (see p. 481). Use the titles shown. Write a summary for each title.

Think, Talk, and Write

1. **Main Idea** What keeps the blood moving through the circulatory system?

2. **Vocabulary** Blood with carbon dioxide is carried back to the heart in _____ .

3. **Problem and Solution** How does blood get to the heart from the lungs?

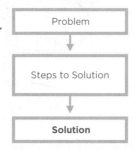

4. **Critical Thinking** Why is the heart made up of two separate pumps?

5. **Test Practice** **Which carries blood away from the heart?**
   A capillaries
   B veins
   C artery
   D vena cava

6. **Test Practice** **What do white blood cells do?**
   A carry oxygen to the heart
   B fight off germs
   C form blood clots
   D transport carbon dioxide

Writing Link

Fictional Narrative
Pretend that you are a red blood cell. Tell a story about your travels through the body. What things do you see? What do you transport?

Art Link

Drawing
Draw a picture of your heart. Label each of the important parts and tell what they do for your body.

Reading in Science

Meet Adriana Aquino

Water covers about three-quarters of Earth's surface, and fish live in almost every corner of it. In tropical seas where coral reefs are found, the water is warm. In oceans near the poles, the water is below freezing. How do fish survive in these different conditions?

Adriana Aquino is a scientist at the American Museum of Natural History. She studies several fish species from around the world. The fish she studies are from many different environments. Adriana specializes in their body structure and form. Some of the fish she is interested in have developed amazing adaptations to their circulatory systems that allow them to live in these different environments.

One of these adaptations allows fish to live in some of the coldest places on Earth, like the icy cold waters of the Arctic and Antarctic oceans. You might think that the fish swimming in water below 0°C would freeze solid, but they do not. What stops them from freezing?

▲ Adriana is an ichthyologist. That's a scientist who studies fish.

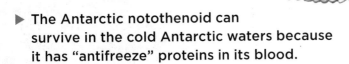

▶ The Antarctic notothenoid can survive in the cold Antarctic waters because it has "antifreeze" proteins in its blood.

ELA R 5.2.3. Discern main ideas and concepts presented in texts, identifying and assessing evidence that supports those ideas.

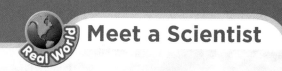

▲ The Arctic cod lives in cold Arctic waters. "Antifreeze" proteins in its blood prevent it from freezing.

These fish have a special protein in their blood. This "antifreeze" protein in the circulatory systems of these fish stops the blood from freezing. Even a single ice crystal can be deadly to a fish. Once one crystal grows, others can cluster around it, eventually freezing the blood. If the blood freezes, the circulatory system fails. The frozen blood stops circulating and no longer carries oxygen and nutrients to cells. The antifreeze proteins stop this from happening by surrounding any ice crystals and binding to their sides. This stops the crystals from clustering. And that's how these fish can survive in the coldest waters of the world.

Main Idea

▶ Look for the central point of a selection to find the main idea.

▶ Details are important parts of the selection that support the main idea.

 Write About It

Main Idea

Tell how the fish that live in Arctic and Antarctic oceans are able to keep from freezing. Explain what would happen if a fish did not have this adaptation to the cold water. Research and explain other adaptations fish in cold environments use to survive.

 e-Journal Write about it online @ **www.macmillanmh.com**

AMERICAN
MUSEUM ᵒᶠ
NATURAL
HISTORY

The Excretory System

Look and Wonder

Your kidneys have millions of these tiny bumps. How does the structure of the kidneys help them filter the blood?

5 LS 2.d. Students know the role of the kidney in removing cellular waste from blood and converting it into urine, which is stored in the bladder.

How do your kidneys filter out waste?

- cornstarch
- measuring spoon
- water
- eye dropper
- 2 beakers
- spoon
- iodine
- cellophane bag
- twist ties

Purpose

Your kidneys filter waste out of your blood using a special kind of membrane. The membrane has very small openings that allow some molecules to pass through and not others. Waste particles are kept inside the kidneys and useful substances are sent back into the body. Make a model of a kidney's membrane.

Procedure

1. **Experiment** Mix 1 teaspoon of cornstarch and 200 mL of hot water in a beaker.

2. Mix 150 mL of water and 5 mL of iodine in the other beaker.

3. Pour 50 mL of the cornstarch water into the bag and close it with a twist tie.

4. Gently place the bag in the iodine solution without letting the twisted top get wet.

5. **Observe** Check the beaker every 3 minutes for 15 minutes. Write down your observations.

Draw Conclusions

6. What happened to the cornstarch in the bag? Why do you think this happened?

7. How is the bag similar to the membrane of the kidneys?

Step 3

Explore More

Would you expect salt or pepper to filter through the bag? Make a prediction. Plan and conduct a test to test you prediction. Then write a report of your results.

Step 4

5 IE 6.i. Write a report of an investigation that includes conducting tests, collecting data or examining evidence, and drawing conclusions.

Read and Learn

Main Idea 5 LS 2.d

The kidneys remove waste from the blood and produce urine, which is stored in the bladder.

Vocabulary

urinary system, p.156
kidneys, p.156
urine, p.156
nephron, p.158
bladder, p.160
urethra, p.160

LOG ON e-Glossary
@ www.macmillanmh.com

Reading Skill

Summarize

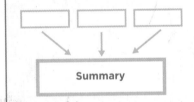

What does the excretory system do?

The cells in your body produce waste that cannot be used by your body. The excretory system removes these waste products from your body.

Waste leaves your body as:

- solid waste through the digestive system.

- carbon dioxide through the respiratory system.

- liquid waste through the urinary (YUR•uh•ner•ee) system.

- sweat through the integumentary system.

You have learned how your body produces and releases waste through the digestive system and the respiratory system. The **urinary system** includes your kidneys (KID•nees), bladder, and urinary tract. Waste products are carried in the blood from the liver to the kidneys. **Kidneys** are bean-shaped organs that filter waste out of the blood. The kidneys send useful particles back into the blood and produce **urine** (YUR•in), which consists of waste and excess water.

Your integumentary system is also part of your excretory system. Your body gets rid of waste through sweat glands in your skin. In these glands, excess water, salts, and a small amount of a waste build up. These substances then leave your body through the skin as sweat.

▶ Your body gets rid of waste through your skin as sweat.

Liver The liver breaks down toxins in the blood.

Kidney The kidneys filter waste out of the blood and produce urine.

Ureters The ureters are tubes that carry urine from the kidneys to the bladder.

Bladder The bladder stores urine until it can be released.

Urethra The urethra is a tube that carries urine from the bladder to the outside of the body.

 **Quick Check**

Summarize What systems are part of the excretory system?

Critical Thinking What makes something a waste?

How does your body filter blood?

As you have learned, the liver is part of the digestive system. It also plays an important role in your excretory system. Your liver breaks down *toxins* in the blood. A toxin is a poisonous substance. The toxins are later filtered out of the blood by the kidneys.

All of your blood passes through your kidneys about 60 times a day. The kidneys remove substances from the blood that your body no longer needs. At the same time, they return substances to the blood that your body does need. Your kidneys control the amount of chemicals in your blood.

Blood enters the kidneys through the renal artery and flows into smaller capillaries. The capillaries then carry the blood to tiny filters called nephrons (NEF•rons). A **nephron** is the structure in the kidneys that separates waste from the useful materials in the blood.

The Kidney

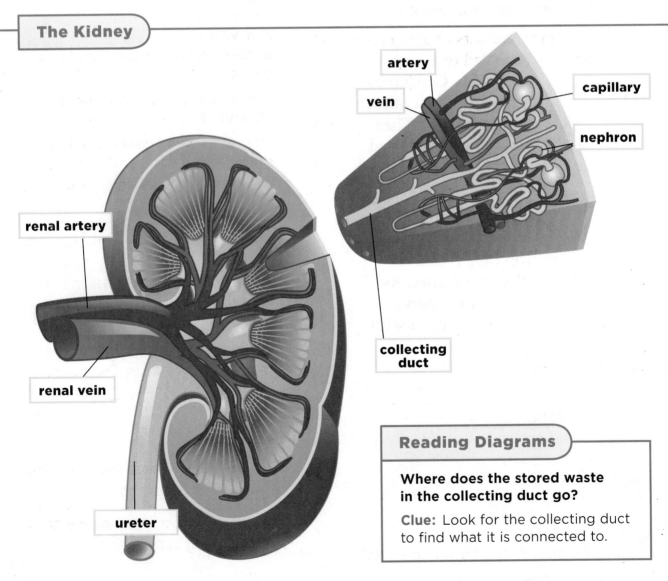

artery

vein

capillary

nephron

renal artery

renal vein

collecting duct

ureter

Reading Diagrams

Where does the stored waste in the collecting duct go?

Clue: Look for the collecting duct to find what it is connected to.

▲ **Each kidney has more than 1 million nephrons.**

This is how a nephron works:

- A nephron consists of a cup-like capsule connected to a long, slightly coiled tube. Capillaries form a tightly coiled ball near the capsule of the nephron. When blood flows through the coiled ball of capillaries, waste and blood plasma are forced through the walls of the capillaries and into the nephrons.

- The nephron tube is also surrounded by capillaries. As the waste and plasma move down the nephron tube, useful substances, such as nutrients, pass out of the tube and back into the capillaries.

- Capillaries surrounding the nephron capsule and tube lead to a renal vein, which carries the cleansed blood out of the kidneys.

- The nephron tube feeds into a collecting duct that is connected

to many nephrons. At this point, the liquid in the collecting duct contains only excess water and waste. The water and waste are processed into urine.

Every day your kidneys produce about 2.5 pints of urine from the 45 gallons of blood they filter.

✔ Quick Check

Summarize What are the functions of the liver and kidneys?

Critical Thinking Why are nephrons surrounded by capillaries?

How does your body eliminate waste?

The **bladder** (BLAD•der) is an organ that temporarily stores urine. Humans can comfortably store urine for several hours. The bladder can hold up to one and a half pints of urine. When the bladder is empty, it is about the size of a plum. When it is full, it is about the size of a large grapefruit. The muscle in the bladder wall is capable of great shrinking and stretching.

Urine flows from your kidneys to your bladder through tubes called *ureters* (yu•REE tuhrs). When the bladder is holding a lot of urine, a signal is sent to your brain through your nervous system telling you it is time to empty your bladder. *Urination* (yur•in•NAY•shuhn) occurs when urine is released from the bladder and flows into the urethra (yu•REE thruh). The **urethra** is the tube that carries urine from your bladder to the outside of your body.

Comparison of an Empty and Full Bladder

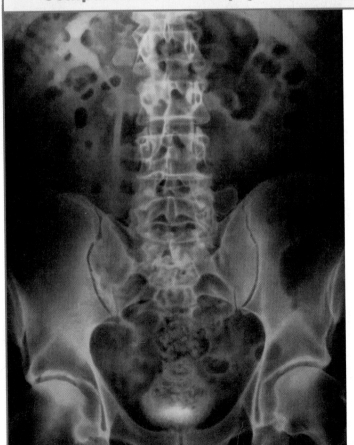 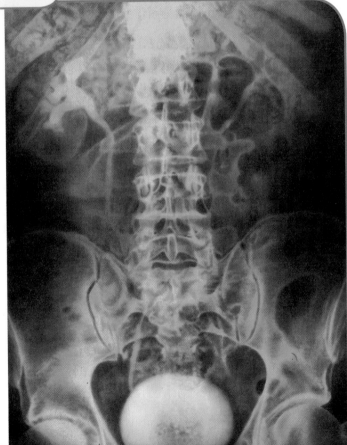

Reading Photos

Describe how the empty bladder and the full bladder are different.

Clue: Look at the highlighted part of the photos.

Structure of Skin

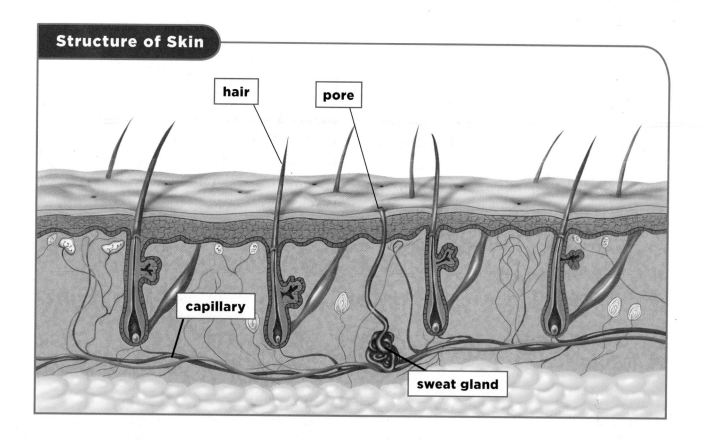

hair

pore

capillary

sweat gland

Your body also eliminates waste through the skin. Sweat is made of water, excess salts, and other waste products. Apart from getting rid of waste, sweat is like an air conditioner for your body. It helps your body get rid of excess heat and keeps your body at a constant temperature.

Your skin has tiny openings called *pores* (PAWRS). Pores are connected to sweat glands. You have about 2.6 million sweat glands in your skin. These glands produce sweat when your body needs to cool down.

When enough sweat collects in the gland, it is pushed up to the surface of the skin as droplets. Once sweat reaches the surface of the skin, the air and your body heat causes the water in the sweat to evaporate. The evaporating water removes the excess heat and cools your body down.

 Quick Check

Summarize What is sweat?

Critical Thinking How do urine and sweat leave your body?

What happens if the kidneys stop working?

More than 13 million people in the United States suffer from some form of kidney disease. The function of the kidneys can weaken for many reasons such as cancer, other diseases, or injury. When the kidneys stop working properly, they can no longer filter the blood. Without the kidneys, waste products and other chemicals build up in the blood. The raised levels of these chemicals in the blood can cause a person to become sick.

Dialysis (digh•AL•uh•sis) is a treatment that carries out the functions of healthy kidneys. It does not cure kidney disease, but it helps people who have kidney disease stay healthy. It removes the waste and extra water from the blood and prevents them from building up. It keeps the levels of chemicals in your blood safe.

When a patient undergoes dialysis, their blood is redirected through a tube to an artificial kidney machine. The kidney machine filters the blood and then flows the blood back to the patient's circulatory system. The kidney machine filters all of the patient's blood in about four hours.

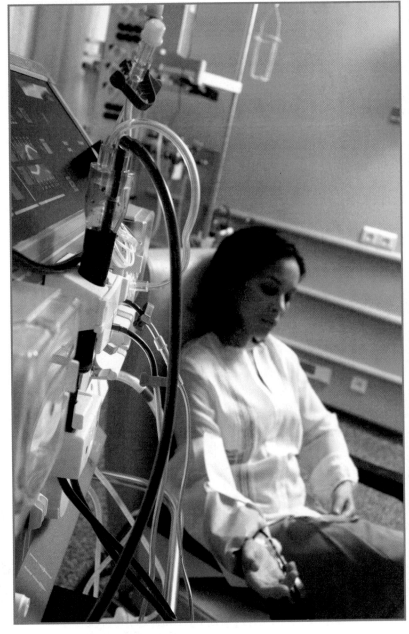

▲ This patient is having a dialysis treatment to filter her blood.

 Quick Check

Summarize What is dialysis?

Critical Thinking Why do people need dialysis?

Lesson Review

Summarize the Main Idea

The **liver** and the **kidneys** filter waste from the blood. (pp. 156–159)

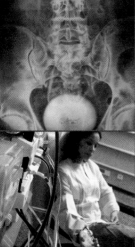
Urine is stored in the **bladder** and leaves the body through the urethra. **Sweat** is waste that is removed through the skin. (pp. 160–161)

Dialysis is a treatment to help people with kidney disease. It filters the blood. (p. 162)

Make a FOLDABLES™ Study Guide

Make a folded book (see p. 479). Use the title shown. On the inside, summarize how the liver, kidneys, and bladder work together.

Excretory System

Think, Talk, and Write

1. **Main Idea** What is the function of the excretory system?

2. **Vocabulary** The organ that stores urine is the _____ .

3. **Summarize** How does waste leave the body?

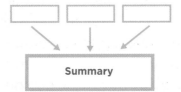

4. **Critical Thinking** How does the liver help the body stay healthy?

5. **Test Practice** Which step happens last in the kidneys?
   A Blood flows in through an artery.
   B Urine is formed.
   C Waste collects in tubes.
   D Nephrons filter waste.

6. **Test Practice** Which part of the excretory system helps to cool the body?
   A bladder
   B liver
   C kidneys
   D sweat glands

Writing Link

Expository Writing
Compare the functions of your liver and your kidneys. Write about how these two organs are similar and how they are different.

Art Link

Make a Poster
Make a poster that illustrates how the nephron filters waste from the blood.

 e-Review Summaries and quizzes online @ **www.macmillanmh.com**

DR. KOLFF
GREAT INVENTOR

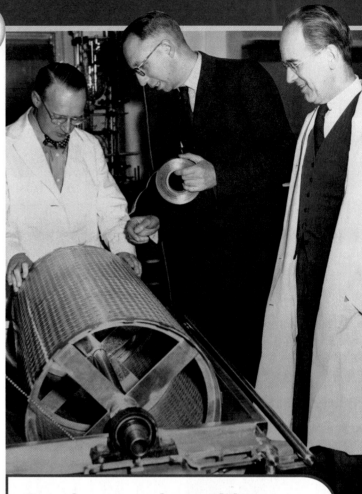

The first artificial kidney machine was invented in 1945 by Dr. Willem Kolff. (center) ▶

In my opinion, Dr. Willem Kolff should be considered one of the great inventors of the twentieth century. This doctor's amazing inventions have saved millions of lives.

In 1940, many doctors thought it was impossible for a machine to replace a kidney. Kidneys filter waste from the blood. Patients died when their kidneys no longer worked.

Dr. Kolff decided to build an artificial kidney. At this time, his country, Holland, was in the middle of a war. Dr. Kolff had few supplies, but he never stopped working. Finally in 1945, this remarkable man proved that his machine could save lives.

Dr. Kolff went on to design many more helpful inventions. He worked on artificial eyes, ears, and arms. He even helped develop the first artificial heart. Dr. Kolff's inventions continue to improve and save lives. This incredible man is truly a great inventor.

Good persuasive writing

▶ clearly states the opinion of the writer.

▶ uses convincing reasons to influence an audience.

▶ organizes reasons in a logical order.

 ## Write About It

Persuasive Writing Suppose your school wants to give someone an award. Write a letter that persuades your principal to give the award to Dr. Kolff. Use convincing facts and details to back up your arguments.

e-Journal Write about it online @ **www.macmillanmh.com**

 ELA W 5.2.4. Write persuasive letters or compositions. • 5.2.4.a. State a clear position in support of a proposal. • 5.2.4.b. Support a position with relevant evidence. • 5.2.4.c. Follow a simple organizational pattern.

Moo!

California has the largest dairy farms in the United States. Each dairy farm has an average of 659 cows. Each cow produces 7.5 gallons of milk every day.

You can use this information and math notation to calculate that the average dairy farm produces 1,804,012.5 gallons of milk in one year. This is how:

1 cow = 7.5 gallons (gal)/day(d)

Multiply by number of days in 1 year (yr):
7.5 gal/d x 365d = 2737.5 gal/yr

Then multiply by number of cows:
2,737.5 gal/yr x 659 cows = 1,804,012.5 gal/yr

Cows also produce solid waste, or manure, from their excretory system. Cow manure is used as fertilizer in gardens and for many crops. One dairy cow produces 106.5 pounds of manure every day.

Multiplying by decimals

To multiply by decimals:

▶ multiply as with whole numbers,

▶ count the number of decimal places in each factor,

▶ add the total number of decimal places,

▶ move the decimal point that many places to the left in the product.

 ## Solve It

1. Determine how many pounds of manure the average California dairy farm produces per year. Show your work and explain your answer.

 MA NS 5.2.1. Add, subtract, multiply, and divide with decimals; add with negative integers; subtract positive integers from negative integers; and verify the reasonableness of the results. • MA MR 5.2.4. Express the solution clearly and logically by using the appropriate mathematical notation and terms and clear language; support solutions with evidence in both verbal and symbolic work.

Summarize the Main Ideas

Your body has many organ systems to transport materials and information so you can do your life processes. (pp. 110–117)

The digestive system includes the mouth, esophagus, stomach, small intestine, large intestine, and colon. (pp. 120–129)

Carbon dioxide and oxygen are exchanged in the lungs and in body cells. (pp. 132–139)

Materials needed by the cells are carried in the blood, which is pumped through the body by the heart. (pp. 142–151)

The kidneys remove waste from the blood and produce urine, which is stored in the bladder. (pp. 154–163)

Make a FOLDABLES™ Study Guide

Take a sheet of paper and tape your lesson study guides as shown.

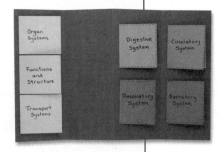

Fill each blank with the best word from the list.

diaphragm, p. 134   **skeletal system**, p. 115

esophagus, p. 125   **circulatory system**, p. 115

urethra, p. 160   **kidneys**, p. 156

vein, p. 144   **small intestine**, p. 127

1. The heart, veins, and arteries are parts of the _____. 5 LS 2.a

2. The tube that connects the mouth to the stomach is the _____. 5 LS 2.c

3. The organs are protected by the _____. 5 LS 2.a

4. Blood is cleansed of waste by the _____. 5 LS 2.d

5. During digestion, the absorption of nutrients occurs in the _____. 5 LS 2.c

6. Blood moving inside a(n) _____ is on its way to the heart. 5 LS 2.b

7. Urine passes from the bladder, through the _____, then out of the body. 5 LS 2.d

8. A muscle called the _____ allows a person to inhale or exhale. 5 LS 2.b

Answer each of the following in complete sentences.

9. **Main Idea** What is the main function of the respiratory system? 5 LS 2.b

10. **Sequence** List the organs of the digestive system in order from the first part that receives the food to the last. 5 LS 2.c

11. **Form a Hypothesis** As you climb up a mountain, the oxygen level in the air drops. How do you think this affects the number of breaths mountain climbers take in one minute? Form a hypothesis to answer the question. How could you test it? 5 LS 2.b

12. **Critical Thinking** If the number of white blood cells in a person's body fell below normal, what might happen to the person? Why? 5 LS 2.b

13. **Persuasive Writing** Pretend you are a medical student researching dialysis. Write a letter to persuade your school to give you money toward your research. 5 LS 2.d

How does your body work?

CHAPTER 3

Health Kick!

Your goal is to investigate the health benefits of the foods you eat and explain why certain foods are better for your body than others.

What to do

1. Think about the foods you usually eat. Design a chart to keep track of all the food you eat for one week.

2. Foods that are low in fat and calories and high in vitamins and fiber are good for your body. Research to find out why these foods are good for you.

3. Use the Internet, books, magazines, and food labels to research the amount of calories, fats, fiber, and vitamins in the food you ate. Record your results in your chart.

Analyze your results

▶ Did you eat foods that were good for you? Which types of foods that you ate were healthy for your body?

▶ Explain why foods that are high in fat and calories are unhealthy.

1 Which of the following human body systems is a transport system?

5 LS 2.a

A muscular system

B reproductive system

C respiratory system

D immune system

2 Which of the following *best* describes veins? 5 LS 2.b

A blood vessels that carry blood back to the heart

B blood vessels that carry blood to the body

C blood vessels that carry blood to the lungs

D blood vessels that carry blood away from the heart

3 Which of the following equations represents cellular respiration?

5 LS 2.g

A sugar + water → oxygen + energy + carbon dioxide

B oxygen + carbon dioxide → energy + sugar + water

C sugar + oxygen → carbon dioxide + water + energy

D sugar + carbon dioxide → water + energy + oxygen

4 Which of the following organs absorbs nutrients during digestion?

5 LS 2.c

A kidney

B small intestine

C large intestine

D liver

5 The following diagram illustrates some of the organs involved in digestion.

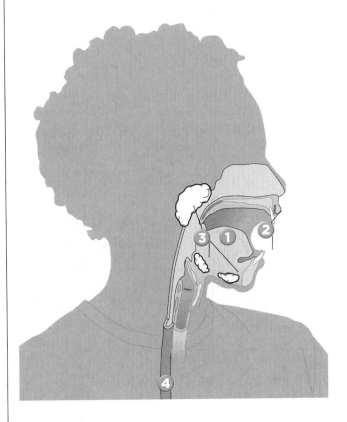

Which location on the diagram represents the esophagus? 5 LS 2.c

A 1

B 2

C 3

D 4

6 Where does gas exchange take place? 5 LS 2.b

A heart

B alveoli

C stomach

D nephrons

7 Which of the following pairs of organs are part of the excretory system? 5 LS 2.d

A tongue, stomach
B heart, arteries
C trachea, lungs
D kidneys, bladder

8 The diagram below shows how the circulatory system and the respiratory system work together.

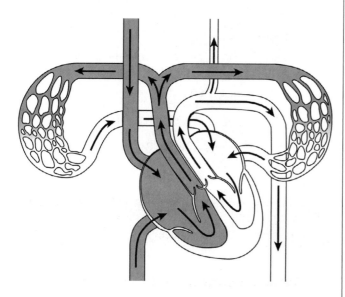

In which direction will oxygenated blood move? 5 LS 2.b

A from the lungs to the heart
B from the lungs to the body
C from the body to the heart
D from the heart to the lungs

9 Which part of blood fights off germs that enter the body? 5 LS 2.b

A red blood cells
B white blood cells
C platelets
D plasma

10 Which of the following parts of the body take in oxygen and release carbon dioxide? 5 LS 2.b

A mouth, stomach, small intestine
B nose, mouth, lungs
C heart, arteries, veins
D bones, muscles, nerves

11 Which *best* describes the circulatory system? 5 LS 2.b

A breaks down food to release as energy for the body
B contracts and expands muscles to move the body
C filters the blood and removes waste from the body
D pumps blood, which transports materials through the body

12 Which list gives the correct order of the air traveling through the respiratory system after it is inhaled? 5 LS 2.b

A pharynx, trachea, bronchi, alveoli
B pharynx, trachea, alveoli, bronchi
C bronchi, pharynx, trachea, alveoli
D trachea, pharynx, alveoli, bronchi

Adventures in
EATING

You just take a bite, chew, swallow, and that's that. Right? Well, dinner isn't always as cooperative as that. For some animals, eating is quite an adventure!

Thorny

How about dinner with a view? A giraffe uses its extra-long neck to stretch to the treetops. There, it munches on leaves—up to 34 kg (75 pounds) of them each day! Giraffes even eat the leaves of thorny acacia trees.

The giraffe's long flexible tongue weaves past the thorns, curls around a leaf, and tugs it free. If it grabs a thorn by mistake, thick, gooey saliva inside the giraffe's mouth and throat protects it from the sharp spines.

▽ giraffe eating acacia tree leaves

① ② ③

▲ African egg-eater swallowing an egg

Bigger than Bite-Size

The African egg-eater is a snake made for snagging egg snacks. It can eat eggs four times the size of its head! (That would be like you swallowing a whole watermelon.) How is that possible? ① First, the snake opens its mouth and unhinges its jaw. ② The skin on its neck stretches as it slowly begins to swallow the egg. ③ The egg stops partway down the snake's throat. Sharp points on the snake's backbone puncture the eggshell. As muscles in the snake's body crush the egg, the snake swallows the food inside. Then it spits out the shell.

Creepy-Crawly

▽ giant anteater

This giant anteater has all the right tools to keep it in business. What business is that? Eating ants, of course! Nose to the ground, the anteater sniffs out an ant nest. It breaks a hole with a sharp claw, pokes in its long snout, and sticks out its tongue. This is no ordinary tongue. It is two feet long and covered with tiny spines and sticky saliva. It flicks in and out more than 150 times a minute, slithering through the tunnels where ants live and slurping as many as 30,000 of them a day.

All animals have to eat, of course. Yet as you can see, giraffes, anteaters, and egg-eating snakes have some special adaptations that help them succeed in their eating adventures!

 5 LS 2.c. Students know the sequential steps of digestion and the roles of the teeth and the mouth, esophagus, stomach, small intestine, large intestine, and colon in the function of the digestive system. • **ELA R 5.2.3.** Discern main ideas and concepts presented in texts, identifying and assessing evidence that supports those ideas.

Gardener

Think about a garden or park that you enjoy visiting. What comes to mind? Chances are you will think about plants, such as trees, shrubs, grass, and flowers. The beauty of gardens and parks depends on the work of gardeners. These are people who plant seeds and graft, or join, two plants together, and then take care of the plants that grow. Do you like to work outdoors? Do you have a "green thumb?" If both your answers are "yes," then you might like a career as a gardener. As a high school graduate, you can get a job as a gardener. Among the rewards of being a gardener is the enjoyment of the beauty you help to create.

▼ **a gardener working with tomato plants**

▼ **a plant ecologist observing pitcher plants**

Plant Ecologist

Do you have a strong love of nature, especially plants? If so, then you might want to become a plant ecologist. Ecology is the study of the relationships between living things and their environments, and plant ecologists study the ecology of plants. Their concerns include natural resources, the protection of endangered species, and conservation issues. In California's Central Valley, for example, plant ecologists are concerned with a type of wetland ecosystem known as vernal pools, in which many animals and plants are endangered. A bachelor of science degree is needed for a beginner in this field, after which you might do graduate work.

Chapter 4

Chapter 5

Chapter 6

Earth Science

About three-quarters of Earth's surface is covered with water.

Earth's Water

⭐ **Where does the water you use come from?**

 5 ES 3. Water on Earth moves between the oceans and land through the processes of evaporation and condensation.

Literature

ESSAY

ELA R 5.2.4.
Draw inferences, conclusions, or generalizations about text and support them with textual evidence and prior knowledge.

ELA W 5.2.1.
Write narratives:

a. Establish a plot, point of view, setting, and conflict.

b. Show, rather than tell, the events of the story.

Mono Lake

Saltwater shrimp

from **CALIFORNIA, THE BEAUTIFUL**
a selection from the Federal Writers Project, 1939

MONO LAKE

Though it appears fresh and inviting, is actually a briny deep, in which nothing but one small species of saltwater shrimp and the larvae of one tiny black fly can live. ... But the water that feeds Mono Lake will not go to waste much longer, for, soon purified, it will go into the new Mono Basin Aqueduct and help to slake the thirst of metropolitan Los Angeles.

Write About It

Response to Literature This essay supports the construction of the Mono Basin Aqueduct to solve the water crisis in Los Angeles in 1939. Pretend it is 1939. Write an essay that either supports or opposes the construction of the Aqueduct.

LOG ON e-Journal Write about it online @ **www.macmillanmh.com**

Los Angeles in 1939

Earth: The Blue Planet

Look and Wonder

If you have ever seen ocean waves like this one, you already know oceans are really big. How much of the water on Earth do you think is in the oceans?

 5 ES 3.a. Students know most of Earth's water is present as salt water in the oceans, which cover most of Earth's surface.

How much of Earth's water is salty and how much is fresh?

Purpose

To make a model that shows how much of Earth's water is salty and how much is fresh.

Procedure

1. Fill the 1-liter bottle with water. The water in this bottle represents all of the water on Earth. Remember, 1 liter (L) holds 1,000 milliliters (mL).

2. Label the cups frozen water, liquid water, and water vapor.

3. **Measure** Using the water in the 1-liter bottle, measure 28 mL of water in the metric measuring cup. This cup represents all of Earth's fresh water.

4. **Measure** From the metric measuring cup, pour the following:

Frozen water cup	22 mL
Liquid water cup	6 mL
Water vapor cup	1 drop

Draw Conclusions

5. **Infer** What kind of water is represented by the remaining water in the 1-liter bottle?

6. **Use Numbers** About how many times more salt water than fresh water does Earth hold?

7. **Interpret Data** People can only easily use fresh liquid water. What percentage of Earth's water is available for people to use?

Explore More

Describe how you would make a model to show the proportions of the different types of fresh water on Earth.

 5 ES 3.a. Students know most of Earth's water is present as salt water in the oceans, which cover most of Earth's surface.

Materials

- 1-liter bottle
- metric measuring cup
- metric measuring spoons
- eye dropper
- 3 small clear plastic cups
- marker
- water

Step 3

Step 4

Read and Learn

▶ Main Idea 5 ES 3.a

Oceans cover most of Earth's surface.

▶ Vocabulary

ocean, p.180
fresh water, p.182
evaporation, p.183
water vapor, p.183
ice sheet, p.184
glacier, p.184

e-Glossary
@ www.macmillanmh.com

▶ Reading Skill

Summarize

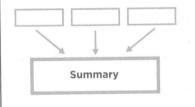

Summary

▼ Dungeness crabs are a natural resource found along the coasts of the Pacific Ocean. They are a popular food in California.

How much of Earth's surface is covered by water?

If you stand on a sandy beach on California's coast, the ocean stretches as far as you can see. The world's oceans do not really have an end. They flow uninterrupted around all of the continents and islands on our planet.

An **ocean** is a large body of salt water. The oceans cover about 70% of Earth's surface. The remaining 30% of Earth's surface is mostly land. Other bodies of water cover a small fraction of the surface.

People use different kinds of natural resources from the oceans. The organisms that live in the ocean are one valuable resource. Many people eat fish, shrimp, crabs, lobsters, squid, and seaweed.

Resources such as oil and natural gas are extracted from beneath the ocean floor. The oceans have other resources that we may be able to get from ocean water in the future, such as gold.

People also use the oceans for recreation and for transport of goods. People swim, surf, scuba dive, and sail in ocean water. For much of history, sailing across the oceans was the only way to move goods and people.

The World's Oceans

Although ocean water flows uninterrupted around Earth, *oceanographers*, or scientists who study oceans, have divided the water into several distinct oceans. They make the divisions based on many different factors. One factor includes physical separation caused by continents. Other factors that make the oceans different include the temperatures and saltiness of the oceans.

The Pacific Ocean is the largest ocean on Earth. It is bordered on the east by North America and South America, and in the west by Asia and

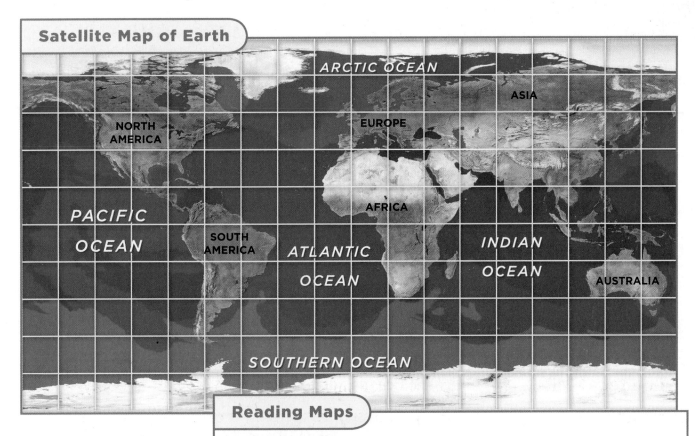

ARCTIC OCEAN

ASIA

EUROPE

NORTH AMERICA

PACIFIC OCEAN

AFRICA

SOUTH AMERICA

ATLANTIC OCEAN

INDIAN OCEAN

AUSTRALIA

SOUTHERN OCEAN

Reading Maps

Estimate the percentage of Earth's surface that is covered by ocean water.

Clue: Count the number of squares that are more than half blue. Divide by the total number of squares. Then multiply by 100.

Australia. It spreads over 156 million square kilometers (60 million square miles). The Pacific Ocean covers about 28% of the surface of the world.

The Pacific Ocean is also the deepest ocean on Earth. At one spot near the Philippine Islands, the bottom of this ocean is 11,033 meters (36,198 feet, or over 6 miles) below the surface.

The Atlantic Ocean is about half the size of the Pacific Ocean. The Atlantic Ocean separates the continents of North and South America from Europe and Africa. The next largest ocean, the Indian Ocean, lies between Australia on the east and Africa on the west.

The Arctic Ocean surrounds Earth's North Pole above North America, Europe, and Asia. Some oceanographers think that the Arctic Ocean is part of the Atlantic Ocean. Others think that the ocean waters around Antarctica are so different from the other oceans that they should be considered a separate ocean, called the Southern Ocean.

 **Quick Check**

Summarize Describe Earth's oceans.

Critical Thinking How have you used the ocean's natural resources?

What makes the oceans salty?

Have you ever tasted ocean water? It is much too salty to drink. However, the water in the rivers that run into the ocean does not taste salty. Where does all the salt in the ocean come from?

Water that falls as rain is fresh water. **Fresh water** is water that contains little or no dissolved salts. As rain runs downhill, it picks up salt in the dirt and rocks.

The flowing water forms tributaries. A *tributary* is a small river or stream that flows into a larger river. River water does not taste salty because it has only very small amounts of salts. However, rivers carry small amounts of salt into the ocean all the time.

Waves pounding on shores pick up salt from rocks and sand, adding more salts to the oceans. Volcanoes erupting under the oceans add even more salts.

rain

tributaries

river

Reading Diagrams

What path does water take as it collects salt while flowing to the ocean?

Clue: Follow the water starting from the top of the mountain.

LOG ON *Science in Motion* Watch water flow to the ocean @ www.macmillanmh.com

When sunlight shines on the ocean, it heats the water, causing it to change from a liquid to a gas. **Evaporation** (i•vap•uh•RAY•shuhn) is the process of a liquid turning into a gas. When water turns into a gas, it is called water vapor. Water vapor is an invisible, colorless, odorless, and tasteless gas.

Evaporation happens at the surface of a body of water constantly when heat is present. Sunlight provides the heat to make water evaporate. When more heat is present, such as when sunlight shines on a cloudless day, evaporation happens faster. Evaporation also happens faster when the surface of the body of water is larger.

Salt Does Not Evaporate

When water evaporates from the ocean, the salts remain behind. As water evaporates, there is less water in the ocean but the amount of salt stays the same. This means the remaining water becomes saltier.

The concentration of salt in the ocean has increased over millions of years. Today, every 100 grams (3.5 ounces) of ocean water holds about 3.5 grams (0.12 ounces) of salts. That means that the concentration of salt in ocean water is about 3.5 percent.

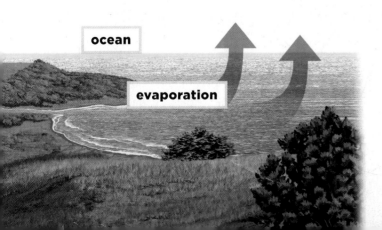

ocean

evaporation

Quick Lab

How the Ocean Becomes Salty

1. In a container, mix 2 tablespoons of salt and a few drops of food coloring. Then mix in 2 cups of dirt or sand.

2. Put the salt and dirt mixture into a pan so it is on one side.

3. Tip the pan so the side with the mixture in it is slightly off the table. Try not to knock any of the mixture to the other side.

4. As you hold the pan slightly off the table, slowly pour some water onto the mixture.

5. **Observe** Note what color the water is when it reaches the other side. How does the color of the water compare to the color of the dyed salt?

6. **Infer** How does this model resemble what happens as fresh water flows down to the ocean?

✔ Quick Check

Summarize What are three ways that salts enter the oceans?

Critical Thinking What are some reasons why the ocean might be more salty in some areas than others?

Where is fresh water found in Earth's surface?

Only about 1% of Earth's surface is covered by fresh water. Where is fresh water found?

 If all the water on Earth's surface were the size of this page, fresh water would be about the size of this square.

Frozen Water

Of all the fresh water on Earth's surface, 78% is frozen. Most of this water is in ice sheets. An **ice sheet** is a huge slab of ice and snow that covers a very large area of land for thousands of years. Currently, Antarctica and Greenland have the only ice sheets in the world. On average, the Antarctica ice sheet is 1.6 kilometers (1 mile) thick. In the thickest places, the ice sheet is up to 4 kilometers (2.5 miles) deep. Some fresh water is also frozen in glaciers. A **glacier** (GLAY•shuhr) is a large body of ice that moves slowly over land.

Liquid Water

Twenty-one percent of the fresh water on Earth's surface is liquid. Most of this water is in rivers and lakes. Thousands

▲ Liquid water flows down to the ocean.

of freshwater rivers cross Earth's surface. The water in a river starts out as a trickle of water high in the mountains. As other trickles join it, the water becomes a river that flows into an ocean.

Most lakes hold fresh water. A lake is a small to medium-sized body of water surrounded by land. Some lakes, such as Mono Lake in California, contain salt water. Saltwater lakes lose water rapidly through evaporation.

✔ Quick Check

Summarize In what form is most of Earth's fresh water found?

Critical Thinking Why might a lake in a hot, dry region contain salt water?

▼ Most of Earth's fresh water is frozen in Antarctica's huge ice sheet.

Lesson Review

Summarize the Main Idea

Almost three-fourths of Earth's surface is covered by water. Most of the water on Earth is **salt water**. (pp. 180–181)

Flowing water, waves pounding on shores, and volcanos under the ocean add salt to the ocean. (pp. 182–183)

Most of the **fresh water** on Earth is **frozen** in ice sheets. (p. 184)

Make a FOLDABLES™ Study Guide

Make a three-tab book (see p. 481). Use the titles shown. On the inside of each tab, summarize what you know about that topic.

Think, Talk, and Write

1 **Main Idea** What is Earth's surface covered by?

2 **Vocabulary** A large body of ice that moves slowly over land is a _____ .

3 **Summarize** Discuss the path a drop of rain takes as it travels to the ocean.

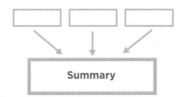

4 **Critical Thinking** When have you observed that salts are left behind when water evaporates?

5 **Test Practice** **Where is the largest amount of fresh water found?**
 A in oceans
 B in ice sheets
 C in rivers
 D in lakes

6 **Test Practice** **How much of Earth's surface is covered by salt water?**
 A 70%
 B 30%
 C 97.2%
 D 2.8%

Writing Link

Descriptive Writing
Write about what would happen to the oceans if an ice sheet rapidly melted. Discuss the effect a sudden change in the concentration of salt might have.

Math Link

Salt Concentration
You take a 100-gram sample of water from a nearby river. After letting the water evaporate, you find 2 grams of salt. What percentage represents the amount of salt in the river water?

Focus on Inquiry Skills

Observe and Measure

The amount of salt in the ocean has increased over millions of years. Oceans are salty because the salt is left behind when fresh water evaporates. Does all of the salt stay in the ocean? Scientists often think of questions that have not been answered yet. To find the answers, they measure and observe things around them.

① Learn It

When you observe, you use one or more of your senses to identify or learn about an object. When you measure, you find the size, distance, time, volume, area, mass, weight, or temperature.

It is important to record measurements and observations you make during your experiment. You can organize this kind of data on a chart or graph so you can compare information at a glance. Once you have enough information, you can make predictions about what might happen if you changed a variable in the experiment.

② Try It

What Happens to the Salt in the Ocean When Water Evaporates?

▶ **Measure** Add 225 milliliters of water to each of two large clear plastic cups. Mark the level of the water in each cup on the outside.

▶ Dissolve a teaspoon of salt in each cup. Stir each cup to mix the salt and water as much as possible.

▶ **Use variables** Place one cup in a warm location, such as in sunlight or under a lamp. Place the second cup in a cooler location, such as in a refrigerator or a shady spot.

5 IE 6.f. Select appropriate tools (e.g., thermometers, meter sticks, balances, and graduated cylinders) and make quantitative observations.

▶ **Record data** Mark the level of the water on each cup every other day until all of the water has evaporated. Using a chart, record the temperature in each spot each time you measure the level of the water. Also record any other observations you made.

▶ **Measure** Once the water has evaporated, measure the amount of salt left in each cup. Record the measurements.

③ Apply It

Use the information from your measuring and observing to answer these questions.

▶ **Analyze data** How does temperature affect the rate of evaporation?

▶ How much of the original teaspoon of salt was left in each cup after the water evaporated?

▶ Can you predict what would happen if you used more salt than water? What if you used equal parts of salt and water?

Observations and Measurements	Shady Cup	Sunny Cup
Day 0		
Day 2		
Day 4		

The Water Cycle

Look and Wonder

Although it did not rain, water droplets appeared on this spider web and on the grass overnight. What caused these water droplets to form?

5 ES 3.b. Students know when liquid water evaporates, it turns into water vapor in the air and can reappear as a liquid when cooled or as a solid if cooled below the freezing point of water. • **5 ES 3.c.** Students know water vapor in the air moves from one place to another and can form fog or clouds, which are tiny droplets of water or ice, and can fall to Earth as rain, hail, sleet, or snow.

How do water droplets form?

Form a Hypothesis

One of the variables that can affect water droplet formation is temperature. You will use a glass filled with room temperature water and a glass filled with ice water to see if water droplets form on the sides of the glasses. Before you begin, write a hypothesis in the form *"If the glass is . . . then water will . . ."*

Test Your Hypothesis

1. Fill one glass completely with ice. In a separate glass, add a few drops of food coloring to some cold water and stir. Then pour the water into the glass that is full of ice.

2. Fill the empty glass with room temperature water. Add a few drops of food coloring to the water and stir.

3. Sprinkle salt onto each saucer. Then put one glass on each saucer. Let the glasses sit for half an hour.

4. **Observe** What do you see on the sides of either glass?

Step 1

Draw Conclusions

5. **Draw Conclusions** Are the water droplets dyed? What does this indicate about where the water droplets came from?

6. **Use Variables** The independent variable in this experiment was temperature. What was the dependent variable in this experiment?

7. **Infer** Why do you think water droplets formed where they did?

Step 3

Explore More

What happened to the salt under the glass with water droplets? Plan and carry out an experiment that shows where the salt is.

 5 IE 6.d. Identify the dependent and controlled variables in an investigation.

Read and Learn

▶ **Main Idea** 5 ES 3.b • 5 ES 3.c
Liquid water can evaporate and turn into water vapor. Water vapor in the air can form clouds, fog, rain, hail, sleet, or snow.

▶ **Vocabulary**

condensation, p.190
sea breeze, p.192
land breeze, p.192
fog, p.194
precipitation, p.196
water cycle, p.198

LOG ON ℮-Glossary
@ www.macmillanmh.com

▶ **Reading Skill**

Sequence

First
↓
Next
↓
Last

What makes water change form?

You have seen water in three different forms, or states. When you drink a glass of water, you are using water in the liquid state. When you put ice cubes in your glass, you are using water in the frozen state. The water you breathe out with each breath is in the gaseous state.

Where can you see water changing states? Look at what happens to the water in a pond as a year goes by. In the spring and fall, the pond has water in it. In the winter, the water turns into a solid and forms ice. During the summer, the level of water in the pond may drop as more water evaporates.

What caused the water to change from one state to another? In order to answer this question, you need to look at the variable that changed during the year.

As fall turns to winter, the cooling temperature removes heat from liquid water, causing it to freeze into solid water. As winter turns to spring, the warming temperature adds heat to the frozen water, causing ice to melt.

As spring turns to summer, hotter temperatures cause liquid water to evaporate, lowering the level of water in the pond. As summer turns to fall, cooler temperatures cause water vapor to condense into liquid water. The process of water vapor changing to liquid water is called **condensation** (kon•den•SAY•shuhn). When water vapor in the air condenses in the fall, it rains. The rain replaces the water that was lost due to evaporation over the summer.

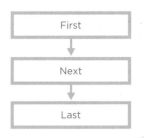

◀ The water in the lemonade is liquid, the ice is solid. Water vapor turns to water droplets on the side of the glass.

Changes in State of Water in a Pond

Heat Removed

Heat Added

solid water

freezing

melting

liquid water

condensation

evaporation

water vapor

Reading Diagrams

What is the process called when you are removing heat and going from a gas to a liquid?

Clue: Look on the diagram for an arrow where heat is being removed and where water vapor is changing to a liquid.

Water changes state from gas to liquid and from liquid to solid when heat is taken away from water. When heat is added to water, the reverse happens, and water changes state from solid to liquid and from liquid to gas.

✓ Quick Check

Sequence What happens to water in a pond during the year?

Critical Thinking Why is the water in the pond at the same level in the spring and in the fall?

What happens to water after it evaporates?

When water evaporates and becomes water vapor in the air, it is carried around with the air. Moving air is called a wind or a breeze. Winds can carry water vapor from one place to another. What causes the air to move?

Air is made up of tiny particles of gases, including nitrogen and oxygen. As the particles are heated, they move faster and farther apart. Thus, as the air warms, it expands to take up more space.

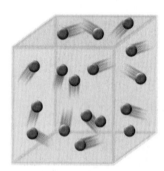

warm

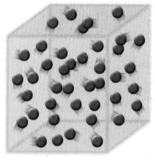

cold

▲ Cold air is more dense than warm air.

If you measure the number of particles in a specific volume of cold air and compare it to the number of particles in a specific volume of hot air, the cold air will have more particles. Thus, the cold air is more *dense*, or more packed with particles, than the warm air is. Because it has more particles in it, cold air is heavier than the same amount of warm air. Cold air sinks while warm air rises. This is why hot air balloons, which are full of warm air, rise in the sky.

Sea Breezes and Land Breezes

If you visit a beach during the day, you feel the wind blowing from the ocean onto the land. If you are at the beach in the evening, you feel the wind blowing from the land onto the ocean. Why does the wind change direction?

During the day, the sun shines on the water and the land and warms them both. Land warms faster than water. As the land warms up, it heats the air above it. The warm air over the land rises, and the cooler air over the water moves in to replace it. The movement of air from the water to the land is called a **sea breeze**.

As night falls, the land and water both begin to cool. Land also cools faster than water. Now the air over the water is warmer than the air over the land. The air over the water rises. Cooler air from the surface of the land moves toward the water. The movement of air from the land to the water is called a **land breeze**.

 Quick Check

Sequence How does a breeze form during the day?

Critical Thinking What makes air move?

Air Movement in Sea and Land Breezes

Sea Breezes

cold air

warm air

Land Breezes

warm air

cold air

Reading Diagrams

In which direction does air move in sea breezes and in land breezes?

Clue: Look at the direction of the arrows to see which way the air is moving.

How do clouds form?

Clouds are made up of tiny water droplets or ice crystals. What has to happen for a cloud to form?

Air is filled with water vapor. As warm air rises and cools, the water vapor condenses. The water vapor condenses around tiny dust particles in the air, forming water droplets.

Clouds look different depending on how high they are and what they are made of. Cirrus clouds form high in the sky. They are usually made of ice crystals. Clouds made of ice crystals have fuzzy edges.

Cumulus clouds and stratus clouds form lower in the sky. They are made of water droplets. Clouds made of water droplets have sharp, well-defined edges. They are darker than cirrus clouds because sunlight is unable to pass through.

Clouds that form closest to the ground are better known as fog (FAWG). **Fog** is a cloud that forms near the ground.

① Air rises and cools when it is pushed upward over mountains, ② when air near the ground is warmed by the Sun, or ③ when warm air is pushed upward by cool air.

Cirrus Clouds

▲ Cirrus clouds form at high altitudes and are wispy and featherlike with fuzzy edges.

Cumulus Clouds

▲ Cumulus clouds are puffy clouds that appear to rise up from a flat bottom.

Stratus Clouds

▲ Stratus clouds form in blanket-like layers at low altitudes.

≡Quick Lab

Types of Clouds

1. **Predict** Which type of clouds do you see most frequently?

2. Look for clouds in the sky. How many types of clouds do you see?

3. **Record Data** Make a chart to record what you see.

4. **Classify** Do the clouds that you see look like cirrus, cumulus, or stratus clouds?

Cloud Observation

	Cirrus	Cumulus	Stratus
Day 1			
Day 2			
Day 3			

5. Continue your data collection for one week.

6. **Analyze Data** Which type of cloud did you see most frequently?

7. **Communicate** Write a report about the types of clouds that you saw. Do you think you would get different results at a different time of year?

✓ Quick Check

Sequence How do clouds form?

Critical Thinking Why is it likely to rain when clouds are gray?

Will it rain?

When clouds are made of liquid water, the water is in the form of very small, light drops. The drops are pulled down by their weight, but winds keep blowing them up away from the ground. As time passes, these drops collide with one another and combine to form larger, heavier drops.

Soon the drops become too large and too heavy for the winds to keep them in the air. They will then fall to the ground as precipitation.

Precipitation (pri•sip•i•TAY•shuhn) is water that falls from the air to the ground as rain, sleet, hail, or snow.

Rain, Sleet, Hail, and Snow

If the temperature of the air is cool enough, water vapor will condense to form liquid precipitation, or raindrops. When the temperature is below the freezing point of water, water vapor and raindrops can form other kinds of precipitation. Sleet, hail, and snow are forms of solid precipitation.

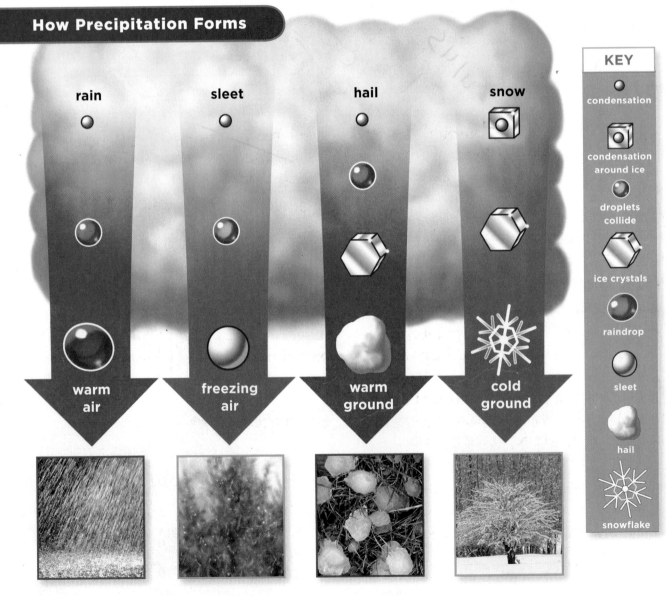

How Precipitation Forms

rain   sleet   hail   snow

warm air   freezing air   warm ground   cold ground

KEY

condensation

condensation around ice

droplets collide

ice crystals

raindrop

sleet

hail

snowflake

How Hailstones Form

1. Strong winds move drops of water and ice around in a cloud.

2. The water and ice collide and form a hailstone.

3. Upward moving winds, called updrafts, push the falling hailstones back into the cloud.

4. Hailstones grow larger as more drops of water collide with them.

5. Hailstones fall to the ground.

When raindrops fall through a layer of very cold air, they freeze, changing into tiny bits of ice. These bits of ice are called sleet. Sleet only reaches the ground when air temperatures are cold near the ground. If the air above the ground is warm, sleet will melt and turn back into raindrops.

Hail (HAYL) forms when drops of water in a cloud collide with bits of ice. The drops freeze to the ice, forming a hailstone. Upward moving winds push the falling hailstones back into the cloud. The hailstones keep growing larger as they are repeatedly pushed back up into the cloud.

Most hailstones are between 5 millimeters (0.2 inches) and 75 millimeters (3 inches) in diameter.

The largest hailstones that have been found have been about as big as a softball.

Snowflakes are formed when the temperature is so cold that water vapor turns directly into a solid. The water vapor in the clouds turns into crystals. A *crystal* (KRIS•tuhl) is a solid that has a repeating pattern in its shape. If you look carefully at snowflakes landing on a window or windshield, you may see the crystals before they melt.

✔ Quick Check

Sequence What similar steps occur in all forms of precipitation?

Critical Thinking Why do some types of precipitation occur only when the temperature near the ground is cold?

How is water recycled?

Water on Earth is never lost. It changes form and moves from place to place in a process called the water cycle. The **water cycle** is the continuous movement of water between Earth's surface and the air as it changes from liquid to gas to solid to liquid.

As you learned, water vapor evaporates from the ocean and condenses into clouds. Water falls as precipitation and runs down to the ocean. From the ocean, it evaporates again.

 Quick Check

Sequence How does the water cycle work?

Critical Thinking As time passes, what happens to the amount of water on Earth?

The Water Cycle

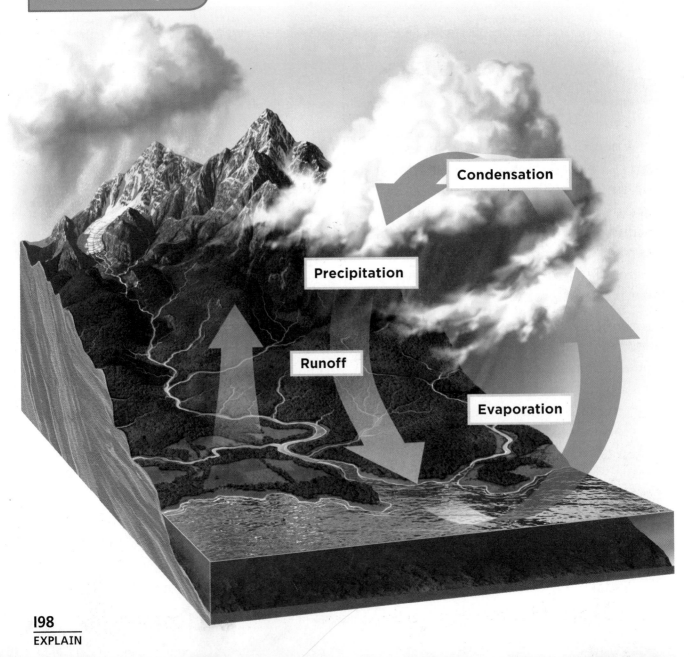

Condensation

Precipitation

Runoff

Evaporation

Lesson Review

Summarize the Main Idea

Condensation occurs when a gas changes into a liquid. **Evaporation** occurs when water changes from a liquid to a gas. (pp. 190–195)

Precipitation falls as rain, sleet, hail, or snow. (pp. 196–197)

Water changes form and moves from place to place in the **water cycle**. (p. 198)

Make a FOLDABLES™ Study Guide

Make a Four-Door Book (see p. 482). Use the titles for the tabs as shown. On the inside of each tab, write the sequence that occurs for each topic.

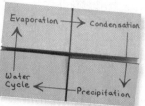

Think, Talk, and Write

1 **Main Idea** Where does water vapor form in the water cycle?

2 **Vocabulary** Water that falls from the air to the ground as rain, sleet, hail, or snow is called _____ .

3 **Sequence** How are large hailstones formed?

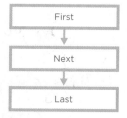

4 **Critical Thinking** Changes in what type of energy cause the water cycle to work?

5 **Test Practice** What happens when water vapor condenses?
   A Air blows from the ocean toward land.
   B Particles of water speed up and are blown up.
   C Particles of water vapor come together to form liquid drops.
   D Air blows from land toward the ocean.

6 **Test Practice** What is liquid precipitation?
   A rain
   B snow
   C hail
   D sleet

Writing Link

Descriptive Writing
Write about a time in your life when you were affected by precipitation. Include details about what you did and why.

Math Link

Average Hailstone Size
You find five hailstones that are 7, 8.5, 10, 25, and 45 mm in diameter. What is the average diameter of these hailstones?

Be a Scientist

How can you tell that water vapor is in the air?

Form a Hypothesis

Water is constantly evaporating. You will cover a cup of water and use cobalt chloride to find out if this is true. Cobalt chloride paper is blue. It turns pink in air that has water vapor in it. Write a hypothesis in the form *"If water is constantly evaporating, then the amount of water vapor in the air…"*

Test Your Hypothesis

1. ⚠ **Be Careful!** Cut the tops off of the two clear plastic bottles.

2. Tape one strip of cobalt chloride paper in the bottom of each plastic bottle.

3. Place one bottle upside down over an empty plastic cup. Place the second bottle upside down over a cup half-full of water.

4. Tape a third strip of cobalt chloride paper to a sheet of paper. Leave it in open air.

5. **Observe** Examine the color of the cobalt chloride paper.

6. **Record Data** Write down your observations of any changes in color of the cobalt chloride paper. Also record any changes in the level of water in the cup.

Materials

2 clear plastic bottles

2 clear plastic cups

cobalt chloride paper

scissors

tape

sheet of paper

Step 1

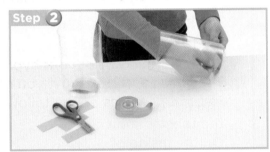
Step 2

Step 3

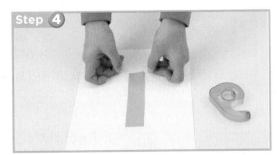
Step 4

5 IE 6.c. Plan and conduct a simple investigation based on a student-developed question and write instructions others can follow to carry out the procedure. • **5 IE 6.d.** Identify the dependent and controlled variables in an investigation.

Draw Conclusions

1. **Use Variables** Identify the variables in this experiment. What purpose does the cobalt chloride paper that is taped to the piece of paper serve?

2. **Draw Conclusions** Does the evidence from your observations support your hypothesis?

Inquiry Guided

How does surface area affect how fast water evaporates?

Form a Hypothesis

You have already learned that water evaporates and can be detected as water vapor in the air. Does water evaporate faster from a body of water with a bigger surface area? Write your answer as a hypothesis in the form *"If you increase the surface area of water, then the evaporation of the water will…"*

Test Your Hypothesis

Design a plan to test your hypothesis. Write out the materials, resources, and steps that you need to take. Record your results and observations as you follow your plan.

Draw Conclusions

Did your test support your hypothesis? Why or why not? Present your results to your classmates.

Inquiry Open

How would being near a larger body of water affect the rate of precipitation in an area? What effect does wind have on the evaporation rate of water? Come up with a question to investigate. Design an experiment to answer your question. Your experiment must be organized to test only one variable, or one item being changed. Your experiment must be written so that another group can complete the experiment by following your instructions.

Remember to follow the steps of the scientific process.

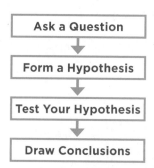

Ask a Question
↓
Form a Hypothesis
↓
Test Your Hypothesis
↓
Draw Conclusions

Freshwater Resources

Look and Wonder

Every day, 100 million gallons of fresh water flow through Burney Falls in Northern California. Does this sound like a lot of water? How much fresh water do you use?

5 ES 3.d. Students know that the amount of fresh water located in rivers, lakes, underground sources, and glaciers is limited and that its availability can be extended by recycling and decreasing the use of water. • **5 ES 3.e.** Students know the origin of the water used by their local communities.

How much fresh water do you use?

Make a Prediction

How much water do you use in a day for a particular activity such as brushing your teeth or washing your hands?

Test Your Prediction

1 Put the container in the sink.

2 Turn the water on and pretend to brush your teeth or wash your hands. Run the water as long as you would if you were really doing that activity. Once you are done, turn the water off.

3 **Measure** Using the measuring cup, scoop water out of the container into the sink. Keep track of each cup that you pour so you can estimate the total amount of fresh water you used in that activity.

Draw Conclusions

4 **Communicate** Discuss how much water you used with your classmates. Exchange data for the amount of water you used for your chosen activity. Whose use of water was closest to their prediction?

5 **Use Numbers** Figure out how many gallons of fresh water you use for the activity in a week, a month, and a year. Remember to include how many times each day you do that task.

6 **Analyze Data** Design and complete a table or graph to display your results.

Materials

- container
- sink
- measuring cup

Step 2

Step 6

Activity: _____

Cups	
I week	
I month	
I year	

Explore More

Think of a way you can reduce the amount of water that you use. Predict how much water you can save. Redo the activity you chose using your new idea. Were you able to save water? Discuss your idea and its result with your classmates.

 5 IE 6.g. Record data by using appropriate graphic representations (including charts, graphs, and labeled diagrams) and make inferences based on those data.

Read and Learn

Frankey

Where is Earth's usable fresh water found?

As you have learned, much of Earth's fresh water is frozen in ice sheets and glaciers. Ice sheets and glaciers are usually far from cities and towns, so the fresh water in them is not available to most people. Most of the fresh water that people use for drinking, washing, and cooking is obtained from running water, standing water, and groundwater.

Running Water

If you look at a map, you may notice that many cities and towns are built next to streams, rivers, or some other source of running water. People build near fresh water because they need a steady source of fresh water for their homes, farms, and businesses.

Usable Fresh Water Sources

snow

streams

reservoir

aquifer

watershed

well

water table

Standing Water

Lakes, ponds, and reservoirs (REZ•uhr•vwahrs) are examples of standing fresh water. These bodies of water fill holes in the ground.

Lakes usually fill deep holes. Ponds are much smaller and shallower than lakes. Their smaller size means they are often not reliable sources of fresh water for people to use.

A **reservoir** is an artificial lake that is used to store water. Reservoirs are usually made by building a **dam** across a stream or river. Water builds up behind the dam and is stored there until it is needed. At many reservoirs, activities such as swimming and boating are restricted so the water supply remains clean.

The water stored behind reservoirs is measured in acre-feet. One acre-foot is a unit of volume that is defined as the volume of water necessary to cover one acre of surface area to a depth of one foot. It is equal to about the amount of water used annually by a family of four.

Reading Diagrams

What are two ways that people obtain water using artificial construction?

Clue: Look for artificial construction.

Groundwater

Communities, homes, farms, and factories that are far from running or standing freshwater sources can get fresh water from groundwater. **Groundwater** is water beneath Earth's surface. Groundwater seeps into the ground through aquifers (AK•wuh•fuhrs). An **aquifer** is an underground layer of rock or soil which is capable of absorbing water. As it seeps down through the ground, the water eventually runs into a layer of rock that does not absorb water. Then the fresh water collects and builds up, forming a water table.

The level of the water table changes as water seeps down from the surface and is removed. Aquifers fill over a period of years. When water is removed from the aquifer, the aquifer requires time to refill. Groundwater is most useful to people when it is close enough to the surface that it is easy to reach by drilling or digging wells into the ground.

✔ Quick Check

Problem and Solution How is the water supply in reservoirs protected?

Critical Thinking What are some other bodies of water that people can use as a source of water?

dam

river

What is a watershed?

Each day, about 16 trillion liters (4.2 trillion gallons) of rainwater fall on the United States. About two-thirds of this rainwater evaporates back into the air. A very small amount seeps into the ground. The rest of the rainwater runs into rivers and then into the ocean. A **watershed** is the name for an area of land in which water drains into a specific river.

California has ten major watersheds. In Northern California, there are three watersheds: North Coast, Sacramento River, and North Lahontan. In central California, there are five watersheds: San Francisco Bay, Central Coast, San Joaquin River, Tulare Lake, and South Lahontan. In Southern California, there are two watersheds: South Coast and Colorado River.

As water flows through a watershed, it replaces the water that rivers, lakes, and oceans lose through evaporation. It also adds to supplies of groundwater. Watersheds refill many sources of water that people use, so it is important not to disturb the flow of water through watersheds.

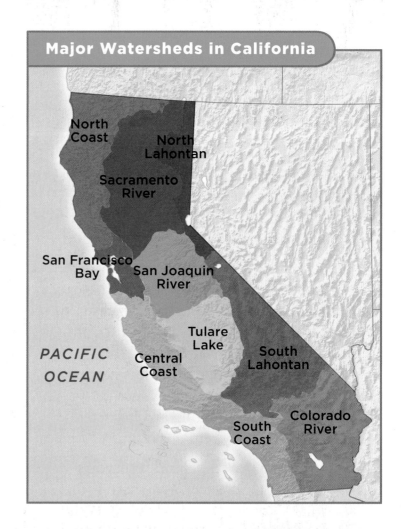

Major Watersheds in California

Water runs through the San Joaquin River and Sacramento River watersheds into the Pacific Ocean. ▶

Reading Photos

Which photo shows damage to a watershed?
Clue: Compare the edges of the river.

Plants help control the flow of water in a watershed. The roots grow down into the soil and hold it in place. The soil can then soak up water that runs down mountain slopes and hills. If many roads are built in a watershed, or if many trees are cut down, there will be fewer plants to help hold back the flow of water. You may have noticed that water runs over paved roads much more quickly than over grass.

Sometimes, fast-flowing water enters rivers more rapidly than the rivers can carry it away. A **flood** occurs when water pours over the banks of a body of water and spreads over the land. Floods can damage property by submerging streets and homes. During a flood, water can carry away things as heavy as cars!

Changes in a watershed can also cause water to flow in a different direction. If that water flowed into a stream, the stream may now get smaller or dry up completely. People who rely on these streams and rivers for fresh water could face a water shortage.

Quick Check

Problem and Solution How can flood damage to a watershed be prevented?

Critical Thinking How could changes made to land far away from a river affect its flow?

What causes polluted water?

Although water that falls from the sky is not salty, it sometimes has other substances in it that cause it not to be clean enough for you to drink. Water that runs across the land may also pick up substances that contaminate (kuhn•TAM•uh•nayt) the water. To **contaminate** means to dirty, or **pollute**, a material such as fresh water. Contaminated water cannot be used by people for drinking, washing, cooking, or swimming.

What are some signs that water is polluted? It might smell. It might be cloudy, a strange color, or have dead fish in it. However, you can't always tell that water is contaminated by looking at it. It might look clear and still contain chemicals or harmful organisms that could make you sick.

Contamination of Fresh Water

Farmers and homeowners use different kinds of chemicals to help their crops and lawns grow. People also use chemicals to kill organisms that are harmful to plants. Some factories and farms produce polluting waste products.

Water flowing over polluted ground becomes contaminated. It spreads chemicals and harmful organisms throughout the watershed. It contaminates sources of fresh water like streams and rivers. Water seeping through the ground can carry the chemicals into groundwater.

When a community is built in a watershed, water flows through the community on the way to streams and rivers. As it rushes over streets, it can pick up contaminants such as salt used to melt ice and snow, spilled motor oil, and trash.

▼ Chemicals used to protect crops against insects, such as the cucumber beetle, can pollute freshwater supplies.

▲ Pollution can make water so dirty that almost nothing can live in it.

Laws That Protect Freshwater Resources

Local and state governments, as well as the United States government, have passed laws to control water pollution. The U.S. government has passed two important laws to keep freshwater supplies clean.

In 1974 Congress passed the Safe Drinking Water Act. This law sets rules that communities all over the United States must follow to keep drinking water clean and safe.

Three years later, Congress passed the Clean Water Act of 1977. This law made it illegal to throw pollutants into surface waters, such as streams, rivers, lakes, and oceans. People or businesses that break this law can be fined.

✔ Quick Check

Problem and Solution Why do farmers and homeowners use products that can contaminate fresh water?

Critical Thinking What are some ways that people could prevent contamination of fresh water?

≡ Quick Lab

Cleaning Polluted Water

1. Make a model of polluted water by mixing 3 liters of fresh water with soil, rocks, and leaves of different sizes.

2. Cut the tops off of three clear 2-liter plastic bottles.

3. Fill the first bottle with 3 inches of sand. Fill the second bottle with 3 inches of sand and then a layer of 3 inches of pebbles. Fill the third bottle with 3 inches of sand, 3 inches of pebbles, and a top layer of 3 inches of rocks.

4. Carefully make a hole in the side of each container near the bottom.

5. **Experiment** Hold a clear plastic cup up to the hole in the first bottle. Then pour about 1/3 of the polluted water into the bottle. Collect the water coming from the hole. Repeat these steps for the second and third bottles using different cups.

6. **Observe** Compare the water in each cup.

7. **Communicate** Explain the differences you observe. Which cup had the clearest water? Why?

How are fresh water resources cleaned?

The water that flows to houses and businesss in your community is *treated* or cleaned in a water treatment plant. There, fresh water from a lake or reservoir runs through several tanks. In each tank, a different step takes place. The steps may vary depending on the quality of the source of water.

First, sticky particles are added to the water to attract any dirt in it. This step is called *coagulation*. In the next tank, *sedimentation* takes place. This is when the heavy clumps of dirt and sticky particles fall to the bottom of the tank. Then, the water passes through a series of filters, which are layers of sand, gravel, and charcoal. These filters remove any remaining bits of soil or other particles. After water leaves this tank, chemicals such as chlorine are added to the water to kill harmful bacteria. This step is called *disinfection*. Finally, the clean water is stored in a tank or storage area before it flows to the community.

 Quick Check

Problem and Solution How do water treatment plants prevent harmful bacteria from traveling in the water?

Critical Thinking How would you change the steps in a treatment plant if water was heavily polluted?

Water Treatment Plant

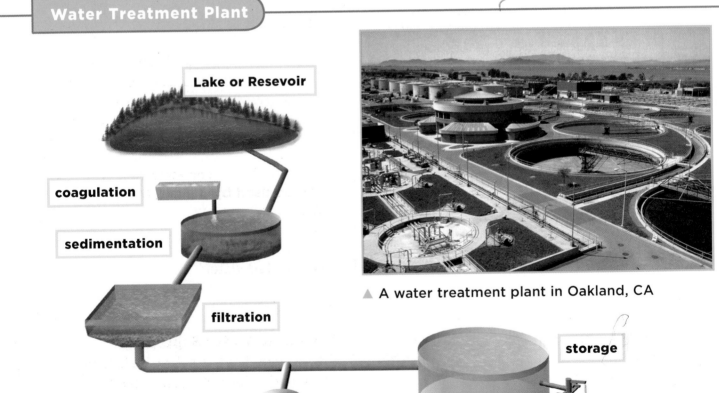

Lake or Reservoir

coagulation

sedimentation

filtration

disinfection

storage

▲ A water treatment plant in Oakland, CA

Summarize the Main Idea

Usable fresh water **comes from** running water, standing water, and groundwater. (pp. 204–205)

Fresh water from rain **runs through watersheds**. Plants, buildings, and roads all affect this flow. (pp. 206–207)

Fresh water **can be polluted** by human activities. It is protected by government laws and cleaned in water treatment plants. (pp. 208–210)

Make a FOLDABLES™ Study Guide

Make a three-tab book (see p. 481). Use the titles shown. On the inside of each tab, discuss a problem and solution related to that topic.

Think, Talk, and Write

1. **Main Idea** Where can people find useable sources of fresh water?

2. **Vocabulary** Water pours over the banks of a body of water when there is a _____ .

3. **Problem and Solution** How do governments protect fresh water?

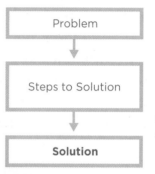

4. **Critical Thinking** Why is groundwater usually less polluted than surface water?

5. **Test Practice** **What is an aquifer?**
   A a man-made lake used to store water
   B water beneath Earth's surface
   C a layer of rock that absorbs water
   D water that pours over the banks of a river

6. **Test Practice** **The following sources can be used by people, EXCEPT**
   A running water
   B standing water
   C groundwater
   D polluted water

🎨 Art Link

Research ways you can protect the watersheds in California. Draw a poster demonstrating one of these ways.

➕ Math Link

Measuring Water Supply

If a reservoir holds 3 million gallons of water and a California town uses 10,000 gallons a day, for how many days can the reservoir supply the town with water?

Writing in Science

KEEP OUR WATER CLEAN!

Laura needed people in her town to help clean up trash that had been dumped in the local stream. She wrote an e-mail to the mayor and asked him to put her message on the town Web site.

Laura_Email.com   Send   Cancel

Our supply of fresh water is limited to what we can get from streams, rivers, lakes, and under the ground. If we pollute these sources of water, we will run out of fresh water to use! I believe that adopting a local stream, creek, or watershed is one way you can protect your water.

Come this weekend and help clean up our stream. We will pick up the trash and plant trees and grasses that will keep the dirt near the creek from washing away. We will also put up signs to remind people not to dump trash in our stream.

Don't take the water near you for granted. Take care of it!

Write About It

Persuasive Write a letter to the mayor of your town. Explain a need that the students in your community have and why people should help. State your position clearly and support it with relevant facts and evidence organized in a logical way.

LOG ON e-Journal Write about it online @ **www.macmillanmh.com**

What is Above Average Rainfall?

Geographic areas such as towns, cities, states, countries, deserts, and mountain ranges get different amounts of rain. Rain forests can have up to 30 inches of rain in one month, while deserts may have less than 3 inches in one year! Scientists measure and record the amount of rain that falls so they can keep track of how much rain an area gets. One reason to keep these records is to notify people living in the area if the amount of rainfall is above average. When more rain falls, it increases the risk of floods and mud slides.

Finding averages:

The mean is the average value of a group of numbers. To find the mean of a group of numbers, find the total sum of the numbers and divide that total by the number of numbers in the group.

Example:
0 + 5 + 7 + 6 + 2 + 10 = 30

30 / 6 = 5

The mean of these numbers is 5.

Monthly Rainfall (in inches)

	Jan	Feb	Mar	Apr	May	Jun	Jul	Aug	Sep	Oct	Nov	Dec
San Francisco	4.4	3.1	3.1	1.3	0.4	0.2	0.0	0.1	0.3	1.1	2.9	3.6
San Diego	2.2	1.6	2.0	0.8	0.2	0.1	0.0	0.1	0.2	0.2	1.2	1.4

Source: National Oceanic and Atmospheric Administration

 Solve It

1. Use the chart to find the mean rainfall for San Francisco.

2. Use the chart to find the mean rainfall for San Diego.

3. Using the Internet or another reference source, find the rainfall data for your hometown or city for one year. Use that data to calculate the mean rainfall.

 MA NS 5.2.1. Add, subtract, multiply, and divide with decimals; add with negative integers; subtract positive integers from negative integers; and verify the reasonableness of the results. • MA SDAP 5.1.1. Know the concepts of mean, median, and mode; compute and compare simple examples to show that they may differ.

California's Water Supply

Look and Wonder

In 2000, 9.5 million people lived in Los Angeles County, and 1.3 million more people are expected to live there by 2020. However, the supply of fresh water will have hardly changed during that time. How will Californians get the water they need?

5 ES 3.d. Students know that the amount of fresh water located in rivers, lakes, underground sources, and glaciers is limited and that its availability can be extended by recycling and decreasing the use of water. • **5 ES 3.e.** Students know the origin of the water used by their local communities.

How much precipitation falls in your community?

Purpose

To measure the amount of precipitation in your area and see if your community gets enough water from precipitation to supply what your families use every day.

Procedure

1. △ **Be careful.** Use the scissors to cut the top off of the carton.

2. Tape your carton into the baking pan and put the pan on the ground outside in an open area.

3. **Measure** At the same time every day, check the carton to see if there is any water inside. If there is water, measure the height in inches of water in the container.

4. **Record Data** Write down the daily results on a table. Then empty the carton and put it back in the same spot outside.

Draw Conclusions

5. **Analyze Data** Design and complete a graph to display your results.

6. **Use Numbers** How can you convert your daily measurement of inches of precipitation into gallons? HINT: The conversion rate is 1 cubic inch = 0.004 gallons.

7. **Draw Conclusions** An average family in California uses 224 gallons of water every day. Did you get that much water in precipitation?

Step 2

Step 3

Explore More

How close were your results to an official rain measurement for your area? Were there any problems that you ran into with the experiment? How could you improve the data collection?

5 IE 6.g. Record data by using appropriate graphic representations (including charts, graphs, and labeled diagrams) and make inferences based on those data.

Reading Maps

How much precipitation falls on Crescent City?

Clue: Look at the color near Crescent City, then use the map key to figure out how many inches of rain that color represents.

Where does California's fresh water come from?

Most of California's people live in the southern part of the state. However, most of California's precipitation falls on the watersheds in the northern part of the state. That means that people need more fresh water where the least amount of fresh water is available from precipitation.

Californians get water from running water, standing water, and groundwater. However, many of these sources of water in California supply less water when there is a drought (DROUT). A **drought** is a long period of dry weather.

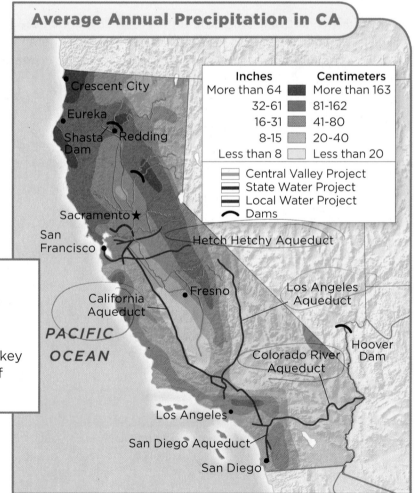

Average Annual Precipitation in CA

Inches		Centimeters
More than 64		More than 163
32-61		81-162
16-31		41-80
8-15		20-40
Less than 8		Less than 20

Central Valley Project
State Water Project
Local Water Project
Dams

▲ The Saugus Water Reclamation Plant in Santa Clarita, California, cleans 7 million gallons of water per day.

Aquifers usually supply about 30% of California's fresh water. However, when a drought occurs, that figure can increase to more than 60%. Taking this much groundwater out decreases the amount of water in an aquifer. Less water reaches the aquifer and more water is taken out. When the water table drops too low, the ground above the aquifer may collapse.

Reclaiming Used Water

Because of the problems associated with water shortages during droughts, people in California run used fresh water through reclamation plants.

Reclamation means to recycle or to make usable again. To reclaim used water, it must be cleaned and purified. Water reclamation plants use a variety of systems to filter and clean water. California's state government set strict standards for the quality of the reclaimed water. One use of reclaimed water is to refill aquifers. By refilling aquifers with this clean water, the level of the water table is raised, and wells can more easily reach groundwater.

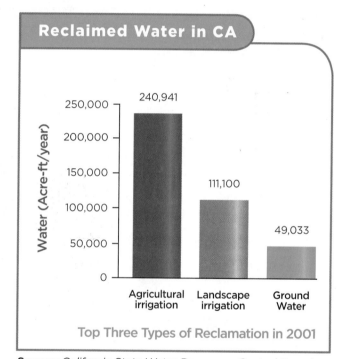

Reclaimed Water in CA

Water (Acre-ft/year)

240,941 — Agricultural irrigation
111,100 — Landscape irrigation
49,033 — Ground Water

Top Three Types of Reclamation in 2001

Source: *California State Water Resources Control Board, Office of Water Recycling*

Quick Check

Main Idea What are the sources of fresh water in California?

Critical Thinking What is the relationship between the location of precipitation and the location of water users in California?

▲ The Hoover Dam blocks the Colorado River, forming a reservoir called Lake Mead.

▼ Water runs from Lake Mead through the Los Angeles Aqueduct.

How is fresh water supplied to Californians?

For more than 100 years, local communities and state and federal governments have built different ways to store and transport fresh water in California. California's government manages the State Water Project, which supplies water to 23 million Californians, or more than 65% of the state's population.

The U.S. government built the Central Valley Project. This project includes dams such as the Shasta Dam on the Trinity River. Dams hold river water in reservoirs. Water is moved from north to south and from east to west through aqueducts (AK•kwee•dukts). An **aqueduct** is a channel built by people to move water long distances through mountains and across rivers.

Los Angeles receives water from several aqueducts. When the first aqueduct was designed in the early 1900s, there was controversy over the plan because it would change the route of the Owens River and dry up the water supply of farmers in the Owens Valley.

In the 1930s the aqueduct was extended to draw water from the rivers that run into Mono Lake. Mono Lake's saltwater environment provides a home for brine shrimp, which many different species of birds eat. As less water ran into the lake, the number of shrimp decreased, which meant less food for the birds. People realized that the decrease in water was harming the Mono Lake environment. Now the amount of water drawn from Mono Lake is limited to keep the water in the lake at a certain height.

The Colorado River is another important source of water for Los Angeles. The Colorado River watershed runs through several states. Since many communities share this source of water, water shortages during severe droughts can cause conflicts between the states.

The water supply in California is limited, and people have different needs and opinions about its uses. This is why Californians have to make agreements about the best uses of their water.

▼ **Water from Lake Mead is used in Los Angeles, CA.**

Quick Lab

Your Water Sources

1. Look at the map on page 216. Use modeling clay to make a map of California. Make sure to include the mountain ranges.

2. Use a different color of modeling clay to show the routes of the major aqueducts in California.

3. Does your community get its water from an aqueduct? Use a piece of string to trace the route that your community's water travels to get to you.

✓ Quick Check

Main Idea How is water stored and moved in California?

Critical Thinking How could the loss of water to agricultural water users affect urban water users?

Supply and Uses	Wet year (1998)	Normal year (2000)	Dry year (2001)
Total water supply	336.9	194.7	145.5
Urban uses	7.8	8.9	8.6
Agricultural uses	27.3	34.2	33.7
Environmental uses	59.4	39.4	22.5

Source: *California Water Plan Update* Units: million acre-feet

Reading Charts

Which of the uses of water has the largest difference between a wet year and a dry year?

Clue: Subtract the water used in wet years from the water used in dry years for urban, agricultural, and environmental uses.

How can California save water?

In a year with an average water supply, California receives about 200 million acre-feet of water. Of the total amount of water received, 50% to 60% soaks into the ground, evaporates, or is absorbed by plants. The remaining 40% to 50%, which is called the dedicated water supply, is divided into urban, agricultural, and environmental uses. Environmental uses include allowing water to run through rivers and lakes.

Californians have focused their efforts on conservation of their water supply. **Conservation** means to save. You can also think of water conservation as preventing water from being wasted.

In order to conserve water, you need to know how an average California family uses it. Watering lawns uses 50% to 70% of a household's water. One way to save water is to water your lawn less often or grow plants that do not need as much water. You can also buy appliances that use less water, turn the water off when you are not using it, and fix leaks.

Source: *American Water Works Association*

✅ Quick Check

Main Idea What happens to about half of the precipitation that falls in California?

Critical Thinking Why do you think urban water use decreases in a wet year?

Summarize the Main Idea

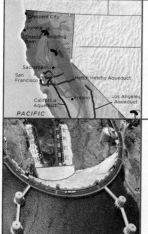

Most of California's **precipitation falls in the north**. (pp. 216–217)

A system of **aqueducts, reservoirs**, and **dams** helps to supply dry areas of California with water. (pp. 218–219)

Water conservation can help Californians meet their needs for fresh water. (p. 220)

Make a FOLDABLES™ Study Guide

Make a three-tab book (see p. 481). Use the titles shown. On the inside of each tab, write down a main idea and details related to that topic.

Think, Talk, and Write

1. **Main Idea** Where does the fresh water that you use come from?

2. **Vocabulary** A long period of dry water is a _____.

3. **Main Idea** When making agreements about water use, what do Californians need to consider?

Main Idea	Details

4. **Critical Thinking** How does conserving water help the environment?

5. **Test Practice** **How is water moved long distances in California?**
   A using reclamation
   B using aqueducts
   C using reservoirs
   D using rivers

6. **Test Practice** **Where does most of California's precipitation fall?**
   A in Northern California
   B in Oregon
   C in the Colorado River
   D in the Central Valley

Math Link

Calculating Annual Water Use
If a family of four people uses 224 gallons of water every day, how many gallons of water does the family use every year?

Social Studies Link

History of Aqueducts
Write about the history of aqueducts. Research the aqueducts built by the ancient Romans and the history of aqueducts in the United States.

Getting the Salt Out

ELA R 5.2.4. Draw inferences, conclusions, or generalizations about text and support them with textual evidence and prior knowledge.

Why does California have water shortages when it is next to the Pacific Ocean? People cannot drink ocean water because of the salts in it.

The island of Santa Catalina lies off the coast of Southern California. It is completely surrounded by the Pacific Ocean. However, people on the island use water from the ocean all the time—to water crops, to take showers, and even to drink. How can they drink and use the salty ocean water? The water is transformed from salty to fresh at the Santa Catalina desalination plant. Desalination means to remove salts.

At the desalination plant, ocean water is taken from an ocean water well. Once it is moved into the plant, salt and other impurities are removed from the water. The fresh water that is produced can now be used by people.

The Santa Catalina plant is one of the few desalination plants in the United States that produces water for public use. Desalination is an expensive process that uses a lot of energy. Despite its costs there are desalination plant projects all over the world, including places like Saudi Arabia and Japan. Desalination is generally used when a community has so little access to fresh water that they are willing to pay a high price to get it. Scientists continue to research cheaper and more efficient ways to produce fresh water from ocean water.

 Write About It

Problem and Solution

1. Why can't the people of Santa Catalina island drink and use water directly from the ocean?
2. How do the people of Santa Catalina get fresh water?

LOG ON **e-Journal** Write about it online @ **www.macmillanmh.com**

Problem and Solution

▶ Identify the problem by looking for a conflict or an issue that needs to be resolved.

▶ Think about how the conflict or issue is resolved.

 AMERICAN MUSEUM OF NATURAL HISTORY

Summarize the Main Ideas

Oceans cover most of Earth's surface. (pp. 178–185)

Liquid water can evaporate and turn into water vapor. Water vapor in the air can condense and form clouds, fog, rain, hail, sleet, and snow. (pp. 188–199)

There is only so much fresh water on Earth. To keep the supply of fresh water available to people, fresh water must be stored and recycled. (pp. 202–211)

The fresh water you use comes either from running water, standing water, or groundwater. (pp. 214–221)

Make a FOLDABLES™ Study Guide

Take a sheet of paper and tape your lesson study guides as shown.

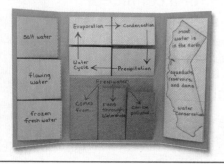

Fill each blank with the best word from the list.

aqueduct, p. 218   **glacier**, p. 184

condensation, p. 190   **precipitation**, p. 196

drought, p. 216   **reservoir**, p. 205

evaporation, p. 183   **watershed**, p. 206

1. The process of water vapor coming together to form liquid water droplets is called _____. 5 ES 3.b

2. A long period of dry weather is a(n) __drought__ 5 ES 3.d

3. An artificial lake that is used to store water is a(n) _____. 5 ES 3.d

4. Water drains from a(n) _____ into a river. 5 ES 3.e

5. A sheet of ice that moves slowly over land is a(n) _____. 5 ES 3.d

6. The part of the water cycle during which liquid water turns into water vapor is called _____. 5 ES 3.b

7. Water falling from clouds, or _____, may be rain, sleet, hail, or snow. 5 ES 3.c

8. In California, a(n) _____ is used to channel fresh water over long distances. 5 ES 3.e

Skills and Concepts

Answer each of the following in complete sentences.

9. **Sequence** Starting at any point in the water cycle, describe its stages in order. 5 ES 3.b

10. **Draw Conclusions** Why is most of Earth's fresh water not available for use by people? 5 ES 3.d

11. **Critical Thinking** How do the Pacific and Atlantic oceans compare in size and depth? 5 ES 3.a

12. **Problem and Solution** Some people have suggested that large icebergs be towed from their source to areas where fresh water is scarce. Explain why you think this is a good or bad idea. 5 ES 3.d

13. **Persuasive Writing** Assume you are a politician from Southern California. Write a speech to convince Californians to pay for a system of aqueducts. 5 ES 3.e

 Where does the water you use come from?

CHAPTER 4

Performance Assessment

Driving the Water Cycle!

Your goal is to demonstrate the role that heat plays in the water cycle.

What to do

1. Design and describe an experiment to show how the addition or removal of heat from water affects the water cycle.

2. Predict the outcome of your experiment.

Analyze your results

▶ What will the results of your experiment tell you about the relationship between heat and the water cycle?

▶ How is your experimental setup like and unlike what happens on Earth?

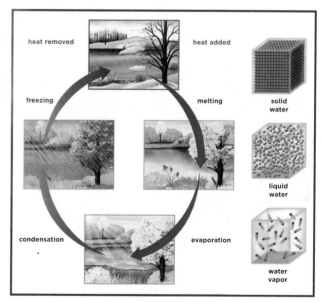

▲ changes of state for water

 5 ES 3.b. Students know when liquid water evaporates, it turns into water vapor in the air and can reappear as a liquid when cooled or as a solid if cooled below the freezing point of water.

225

1 In which three ways are dissolved salts deposited into the ocean?

5 ES 3.a

A rivers, waves, underwater volcanoes

B rain, sandy soil, streams

C rivers, rain, waves

D rivers, rain, underwater volcanoes

2 A student dissolved different amounts of salt into three cups, each containing 50 mL of water. The student placed all three cups in a sunny location. After five days, all of the water had evaporated.

Results			
	Cup A	Cup B	Cup C
Amount of salt dissolved into the water	5 g	10 g	2 g
Amount of salt after 5 days	5 g	10 g	2 g

Which conclusion could the student draw from this experiment? 5 IE 6.h

A The Sun heats the water to the same temperature.

B The salt in Cup A evaporated first.

C The amount of salt in each cup remains the same.

D The sunlight strikes the cups at the same angle.

3 Which of the following describes what happens to water vapor when it is cooled? 5 ES 3.b

A It turns into a gas.

B It turns into a liquid.

C It stays the same.

D It turns into matter.

4 What is the cycle called when fresh water evaporates, condenses, and then precipitates? 5 ES 3.b

A the rain cycle

B the condensation cycle

C the water cycle

D the precipitation cycle

5 Which of the following describes what happens when water vapor forms larger and heavier liquid drops? 5 ES 3.c

A precipitation

B the water cycle

C evaporation

D runoff

6 Which of these is a type of standing fresh water? 5 ES 3.d

A reservoir

B ocean

C river

D stream

7 What are two ways to extend the limited supplies of fresh water?

5 ES 3.d

A driving trains and riding bicycles

B planting grass and watering trees

C cleaning oceans and saving fish

D preventing pollution and cleaning water

8 **Where does most of California's precipitation fall?** 5 ES 3.e

A reservoirs throughout California
B aqueducts in the north and east
C watersheds in the north
D deserts in the south

9 **How do water projects supply water to dry areas of California?** 5 ES 3.e

A through aqueducts, dams, and reservoirs
B through aqueducts, lakes, and rivers
C through aquifers, lakes, and reservoirs
D through lakes, river, and dams

10 **This circle graph shows the average home water usage in California.**

Average home water usage in California

showers 18%

washing dishes, laundry, and cooking 12%

flushing toilets 20%

landscaping 50%

Based on the circle graph, where do Californians use the most water?

5 IE 6.g

A taking showers
B flushing toilets
C landscaping
D washing dishes

11 **Where is most of Earth's fresh water found?** 5 ES 3.a

A glaciers
B ice sheets
C lakes
D rain clouds

12 **What is it called when we use water wisely and limit our overall use of water?** 5 ES 3.e

A conservation
B reclamation
C sedimentation
D evaporation

CHAPTER 5

Earth's Weather

 How can we tell what the weather will be?

 5 ES 4. Energy from the Sun heats Earth unevenly, causing air movements that result in changing weather patterns.

Literature

MAGAZINE ARTICLE

ELA R 5.2.3. Discern main ideas and concepts presented in texts, identifying and assessing evidence that supports those ideas.

ELA W 5.2.3. Write research reports about important ideas, issues, or events by using the following guidelines:
a. Frame questions that direct the investigation.
b. Establish a controlling idea or topic.
c. Develop the topic with simple facts, details, examples, and explanations.

STRONG STORMS

LOS ANGELES, JANUARY 21, 2005
Severe weather pounded the western region of the United States last week. Part of a coastal town in California was buried in sliding soil, rocks, and mud. Thirteen homes were crushed. Rainstorms caused flooding in many areas. According to the National Weather Service, these were the wettest days in a row on record for downtown Los Angeles, California.

La Conchita, CA

▲ **A storm washed this Southern California home into a river.**

Write About It

Response to Literature This article describes the damage caused by severe rainstorms in Los Angeles. Research additional information about damage caused by severe rainstorms. Write a report about the effects of severe rainstorms. Include facts and details from this article and from your research.

 -Journal Write about it online @ **www.macmillanmh.com**

Earth's Atmosphere

Look and Wonder

As you climb a high mountain, the air becomes less dense. This can cause breathing problems and dizziness. To keep from getting sick, some mountain climbers breathe from oxygen tanks as they climb. What other variables affect the density of air?

5 ES 4.e. Students know that the Earth's atmosphere exerts a pressure that decreases with distance above Earth's surface and that at any point it exerts this pressure equally in all directions.

Explore

How does air density change if the volume is changed?

Make a Prediction

If you have a plastic bag attached to the top of a container and the container is full of air, will it be hard to push the bag into the container?

Test Your Prediction

1. **Make a Model** Set up the bag and container as shown. Make sure your set up is sealed.

2. **Observe** Have a partner place both hands on the container and hold it firmly. Slowly push the bag into the container.

3. Pull the bag back out of the container. Using a pencil, carefully poke a hole in the plastic bag.

4. **Observe** Push the bag into the container again while holding your hand near the hole in the bag.

Draw Conclusions

5. Did the volume or the amount of air change as you pushed down in Step 2?

6. **Infer** How did it feel when you pushed the bag into the container in Step 2? Why?

7. Did the volume or the amount of air change as you pushed down in Step 4? How could you tell if it was changing?

8. **Infer** How did it feel when you pushed into the container in Step 4? Why?

Explore More

Predict what will happen if you repeat the set up so the bag is tucked into the container and you pull it out of the container. Test your prediction.

 5 IE 6.b. Develop a testable question.

Materials

- plastic container
- plastic sandwich bag
- rubber band
- masking tape

Step 1

Step 2

Main Idea 5 ES 4.e

The air in Earth's atmosphere has weight and presses on all the objects it surrounds.

Vocabulary

atmosphere, p.234
troposphere, p.234
air pressure, p.235
altitude, p.236
humidity, p.237
barometer, p.238

LOG ON ℮-Glossary
@ www.macmillanmh.com

Reading Skill

Make Inferences

Clues	What You Know	Inferences

What is air pressure?

Even though air looks empty, it contains a mixture of gases such as nitrogen and oxygen. You can feel air particles when you wave your hand next to your face. You can tell that air takes up space because it fills up blimps, balloons, and car or bike tires.

The air that surrounds Earth is called **atmosphere** (AT•muhs•feer). The atmosphere forms five layers of gases around Earth. The layer of gases closest to Earth's surface is called the **troposphere** (TROP•uh•sfeer). The troposphere is between 8 and 18 kilometers (5 to 11 miles) thick. The troposphere contains 99% of the air in the atmosphere. The air is densest in this layer.

As the height above Earth increases, the number of particles of gas in the layers of the atmosphere decreases. The air gradually thins off into space. The highest layer, which is called the exosphere, ends at about 700 kilometers (435 miles) above Earth's surface. By this point, there are so few particles of gas that the average distance a particle travels without running into another particle is equal to the radius of Earth.

All of the organisms on Earth exist in the troposphere. In this layer, water vapor is found and weather occurs. Cirrus clouds, the clouds that form at the highest altitudes, form between 6 and 13 kilometers (4 to 8 miles) high. Mount Everest, the highest mountain on Earth, is 8,850 meters (29,035 feet) high.

▼ Earth's atmosphere reaches from Earth's surface about 700 kilometers into space.

▲ Air pressure pushes equally on all parts of an object such as a blimp.

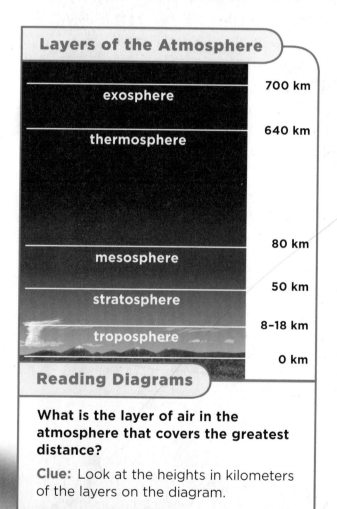

Layers of the Atmosphere

exosphere	700 km
thermosphere	640 km
	80 km
mesosphere	
	50 km
stratosphere	8-18 km
troposphere	
	0 km

Reading Diagrams

What is the layer of air in the atmosphere that covers the greatest distance?

Clue: Look at the heights in kilometers of the layers on the diagram.

The particles of gas press on Earth's surface and on everything they surround. The force put on a given area by the weight of the air above it is called **air pressure** or atmospheric pressure.

At sea level on Earth's surface, air pressure equals 1.04 kilograms per square centimeter (1.04 kg/cm^2), or 14.7 pounds per square inch (14.7 lb/in.^2). You can think of this as the weight of a column of air pressing on a patch of Earth's surface about the size of your thumbnail. You do not feel this weight because atmospheric pressure pushes in all directions and these pushes balance each other.

✔ Quick Check

Make Inferences What causes air pressure inside the blimp?

Critical Thinking Are there particles of gas in space?

What variables can change air pressure?

Many factors affect air pressure. These include height above Earth's surface, volume, temperature, and amount of water vapor.

Height Above Earth's Surface

The column of air above a mountain is shorter than the column of air above sea level. The column above the mountain weighs less and pushes with a lower pressure.

Atmospheric pressure decreases with higher **altitude** (al•ti•TEWD). Altitude is the height above Earth's surface. It is measured from sea level, which is set to be zero.

Volume

Another variable that can change atmospheric pressure is volume. Volume is a measure of how much space an object takes up. When you push down on a closed system, such as a bag sealed over a container, you are decreasing the volume. Since the amount of air cannot change because the system is closed, less space is now available for the same amount of air. The air pressure inside the system increases. The air inside the system pushes out harder than the air outside the system pushes in. That extra force pushing out is what you push against as you push the bag into the container.

▲ As the volume of the container increases, the air pressure decreases.

lower air pressure at top of mountain

higher air pressure at sea level

Temperature

Air pressure also depends on temperature. When air is heated, the gases speed up and spread out into a larger space. There are now fewer particles of gas in the original volume of air. The air pressure decreases, the density decreases and, as a result, the air weighs less.

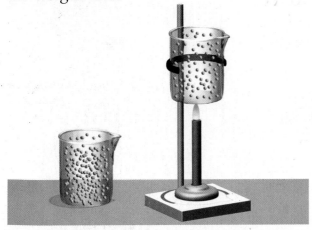

▲ As the temperature increases, the air pressure decreases.

Amount of Water Vapor

Air is a mixture of gases. Water vapor weighs less than most of the gases in air. When water vapor is added to air, the mixture of gases becomes lighter, and so exerts less pressure than dry air. The amount of water vapor in the air is called **humidity** (hew•MID•i•tee).

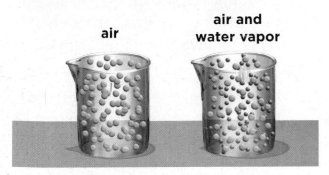

air   air and water vapor

▲ As the humidity increases, the air pressure decreases.

Quick Lab

Air Pressure and Weight

1. Tie a length of string around the middle of a meterstick so the stick is balanced. Tape the string in place. Hang the meterstick from a shelf or other object so the stick can swing freely.

2. Blow up a balloon and knot it shut. Attach it with a piece of string to one end of the meterstick. Tape the string in place.

3. Add paper clips or binder clips to the other side of the meterstick until the stick is balanced.

4. Carefully use a pin to poke a small hole in the neck of the balloon under the knot so the air will run out slowly. ⚠ **Be careful.** Do not puncture the balloon below this point.

5. **Observe** What happens to the meterstick?

6. **Infer** How do the results show that air has weight?

✔ Quick Check

Make Inferences What happens to air pressure when air is cooled?

Critical Thinking Would you expect higher atmospheric pressure on a dry day or a rainy day?

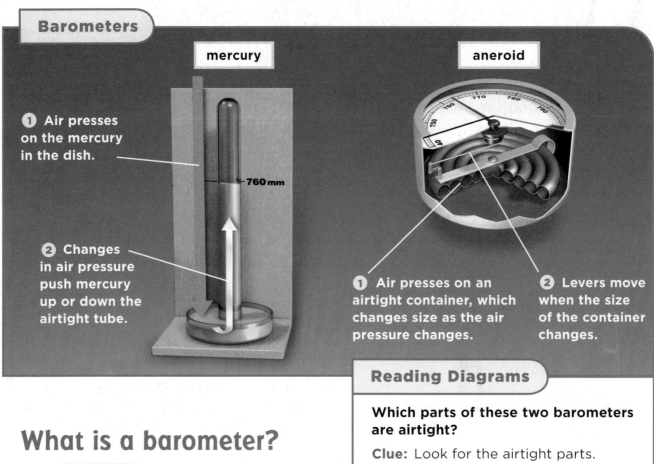

Barometers

mercury

① Air presses on the mercury in the dish.

←760 mm

② Changes in air pressure push mercury up or down the airtight tube.

aneroid

① Air presses on an airtight container, which changes size as the air pressure changes.

② Levers move when the size of the container changes.

Reading Diagrams

Which parts of these two barometers are airtight?

Clue: Look for the airtight parts.

What is a barometer?

A **barometer** (buh•ROM•i•tuhr) is an instrument that is used to measure atmospheric pressure. There are two different kinds of barometers.

A mercury barometer works by measuring the pressure of air on an airtight tube of mercury. The height to which the mercury rises in the tube is the atmospheric pressure. At sea level, the atmospheric pressure is about 760 millimeters, or 760 mm (29.9 inches).

An aneroid barometer measures changes in the size of an airtight container. As air pressure increases, the container gets smaller. As air pressure decreases, the container gets larger.

Barometers can be used to tell altitude. A measurement of 210 mm of

mercury tells pilots that their plane is about 10 kilometers above sea level. In order to get the most accurate altitude reading using a barometer, pilots adjust their barometers to account for changes caused by current temperature and humidity.

Quick Check

Make Inferences Why do pilots get more accurate readings when they adjust a barometer for the current temperature and humidity?

Critical Thinking Why do parts of both barometers need to be airtight?

Lesson Review

Summarize the Main Idea

The **properties of air** are that it has weight, takes up space, and exerts pressure. (pp. 234–235)

Changes in volume, temperature, humidity, or altitude can change **air pressure**. (pp. 236–237)

Two types of barometers are used to measure atmospheric pressure. (p. 238)

Make a **FOLDABLES**™ Study Guide

Make a three-tab book (see p. 481). Label it as shown. On the inside of each tab, compare and contrast the properties of air, factors that affect air pressure, and barometers.

Properties of Air

Air Pressure

Barometers

Think, Talk, and Write

1. **Main Idea** What properties does air have?

2. **Vocabulary** The height above Earth's surface is _____ .

3. **Make Inferences** Would you expect higher atmospheric pressure on a cold day or on a hot day?

Clues	What You Know	Inferences

4. **Critical Thinking** The barometer on a plane measured 210 mm. If the next reading showed a measurement of 400 mm, has the plane increased or decreased its altitude?

5. **Test Practice** **Which of the following is a tool used to measure air pressure?**
   A atmosphere
   B humidity
   C volume
   D barometer

6. **Test Practice** **A change in which of the following would cause a change in air pressure:**
   A mountains
   B barometer
   C altitude
   D mixtures

Writing Link

Persuasive Writing
Suppose you are an engineer working on the design of an early airplane. Write a letter to persuade the company financing the project to invest in a barometer for the planes.

Math Link

Percent of Air Pressure
Mt. Everest is the highest mountain on Earth. The air pressure is 50% less at the peak than at sea level. What air pressure does a mountain climber feel at the top of Mt. Everest?

Focus on Inquiry Skills

Communicate

When scientists complete an experiment, they **communicate** their results by writing books and articles, doing newspaper and TV interviews, and making presentations. When you **communicate**, you share information with others. You may do this by speaking, writing, drawing, using sign language, pantomiming, singing, or dancing.

❶ Learn It

In the following activity, you will do an experiment to test whether air can lift a notebook off the table. Keep notes as you do your experiment. Your notes should include a list of your materials, your observations at each step of the experiment, and whether or not you were able to prove your hypothesis.

Scientists often try new experiments based on work that other scientists have done. If you accurately **communicate** everything that you do, other people will be able to do new experiments based on what you did. If you get an unexpected result or disprove your hypothesis, you should communicate that information as well. Writing down exactly what you did also lets you plan new experiments with different materials and different variables.

❷ Try It

You know that air has weight and takes up space. Do you think air will be able to lift a notebook off a table?

▶ Place a notebook on a table. Tape two balloons to the notebook, leaving enough of the ends of the balloons sticking out for you to blow them up. Flip the notebook over.

▶ Blow into the balloons to fill them with air. When you need to take a breath, pinch the tips of the balloons to keep air from leaking out. What happens to the notebook?

▶ **Measure** Using a ruler, measure the distance between the table and the bottom of the book at the highest point.

▶ **Communicate** Exchange data with your classmates about the distance you were able to raise the notebook.

▶ **Analyze data** Using the data from your classmates. figure out the average height that your class was able to lift the notebooks. Make a bar graph to compare your results. Who was able to raise their notebook the highest? Was anyone unable to lift it?

❸ Apply It

How could you use air to lift the book even higher? Think about what you can change in the experiment you just did. What would happen if you used bigger balloons? If you placed little balloons under each corner of the notebook? Could you use the same materials to lift a heavier book?

Plan a new experiment using different materials. Test your idea and draw conclusions about using the power of air to lift objects. Finally, communicate to the class about the results of your experiment by writing a report, drawing a cartoon strip, or composing and singing a song!

 5 IE 6. i. Write a report of an investigation that includes conducting tests, collecting data or examining evidence, and drawing conclusions.

Air Currents And Wind

Look and Wonder

You know that local breezes occur because of differences in land and water temperature. Larger wind patterns occur because land and water have different temperatures in different parts of Earth. What causes the temperature difference?

 5 ES 4.a. Students know uneven heating of Earth causes air movements (convection currents).

How does the angle of sunlight affect temperature?

⚠ **Be careful.** Do not look directly at the Sun.

Materials

- **three sheets of black construction paper**
- **scissors**
- **three pieces of cardboard**
- **masking tape**
- **three thermometers**
- **protractor**

Form a Hypothesis

What happens to the temperature of Earth as the angle of sunlight increases? Write your answer as a hypothesis in the form *"If the angle of the sunlight increases, then . . ."*

Test Your Hypothesis

1. Cut a hole for your thermometer in the middle of each piece of construction paper.

2. Tape one sheet of construction paper to each of the pieces of cardboard.

3. Place a thermometer into each hole so the bulb is between the cardboard and the paper and the scale can be read.

4. Tape the thermometers in place. Leave the thermometers in the shade until they read the same temperature. Record this temperature.

5. Put the thermometers out in the sunlight.

6. **Record Data** Every two minutes, record the temperature shown on each thermometer.

Step 3

Draw Conclusions

7. What are the independent and dependent variables in this experiment?

8. **Analyze Data** Graph the change in temperature over time for each thermometer. Which thermometer's temperature rose faster?

Step 5

Explore More

How does the angle of sunlight change during different seasons? Plan an experiment to find out.

 5 IE 6.d. Identify the dependent and controlled variables in an investigation. • **5 IE 6.g.** Record data by using appropriate graphic representations (including charts, graphs, and labeled diagrams) and make inferences based on those data.

Read and Learn

▶ **Main Idea** 5 ES 4.a

When air is heated unevenly it moves around, causing winds and air currents.

▶ **Vocabulary**

convection, p. 247

global wind, p. 248

 e-Glossary
@ www.macmillanmh.com

▶ **Reading Skill**

Compare and Contrast

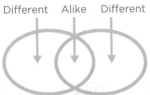

Different Alike Different

▶ **Technology**

SCIENCE QUEST Explore air currents and winds with Team Earth.

Why are temperatures different around the world?

It is the first day of spring. You live in Seattle, Washington. The sky is cloudy, and the temperature outside of your bedroom window reads 10°C (50°F). You have a friend who lives in San Diego, California, about 1,709 kilometers (1,062 miles) to the south. She says that the sky is bright and sunny and the temperature is 25°C (77°F). What causes the weather to be warmer in San Diego than in Seattle?

One reason for the difference in temperature has to do with Earth's shape. Earth is shaped like a sphere, or a ball. An imaginary line called the *equator* (i·KWAY·tuhr) runs around Earth's middle.

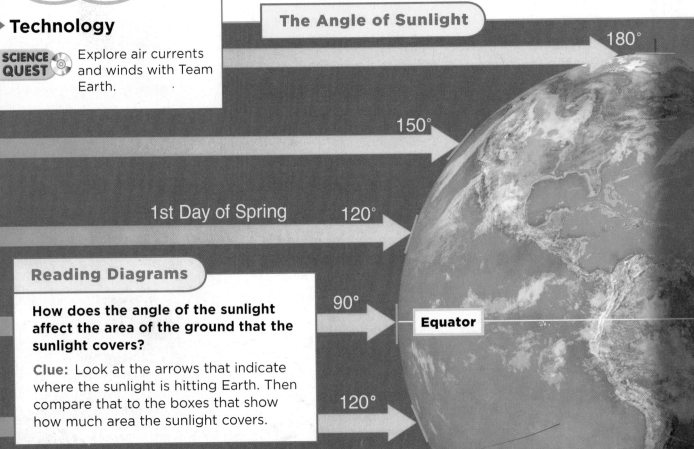

The Angle of Sunlight

180°

150°

1st Day of Spring   120°

90°   **Equator**

120°

Reading Diagrams

How does the angle of the sunlight affect the area of the ground that the sunlight covers?

Clue: Look at the arrows that indicate where the sunlight is hitting Earth. Then compare that to the boxes that show how much area the sunlight covers.

150°

When sunlight shines on Earth, heat energy from the Sun warms Earth's surface. However, it does not warm all places equally. Sunlight strikes Earth most directly at the equator. If you think of sunlight as a beam of light, the beam shines on the Earth in a circle at the equator. Since Earth's surface is curved, the same beam will strike Earth at an wider angle above or below the equator.

The beam of light always has the same amount of heat energy. However, a beam that warms the Earth in an oval covers a greater area of the Earth's surface than a beam that warms the Earth in a circle. The heat energy of the light is spread over a larger area.

Because the area is larger but the heat energy in the sunlight is the same, each part of that area receives less energy.

This is why areas that are farther north or south of the equator receive less heat energy from sunlight. Areas that are closer to the equator, such as San Diego, generally receive more heat energy and are warmer than areas farther from the equator, such as Seattle.

✅ Quick Check

Compare and Contrast Why does San Diego have warmer weather than Seattle?

Critical Thinking On what part of Earth is sunlight the least concentrated?

90° sunlight

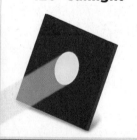
120° sunlight

150° sunlight

180° sunlight

Seattle

San Diego

▲ Seattle (top) is generally cooler than San Diego (bottom). Part of the reason for this is that the Sun's rays strike San Diego at a narrower angle than they do Seattle.

How do land and water temperatures affect air pressure?

As you learned when you studied the water cycle, if you face the ocean early in the morning, you feel a breeze on your back. In the same position later in the day you feel the breeze on your face. How do these breezes form in terms of air pressure?

Air Pressure in a Sea Breeze

During the day, land heats up faster than water. Air over the land becomes warmer than air over the sea. As it warms, the air over the land becomes less dense and the atmospheric pressure decreases. The column of air over the ocean now has a higher pressure than the column of air over the land. The air over the ocean moves toward the land.

Air Pressure in a Sea Breeze

Air Pressure in a Land Breeze

Overnight, the land cools off faster than the water. This means that the air over the ocean is warmer and has a lower pressure than the column of air over the land. The column of air over the land has a higher pressure than the column of air over the ocean.

Air moves from where the pressure is higher to where the pressure is lower. When you stand on the beach in the morning, cool air moves from the land behind you toward the ocean in front of you.

Convection

As land and water temperatures change throughout the day, the changing temperatures cause differences in air pressure. Air flows from areas of high pressure to areas of low pressure. As the air flows, it moves heat from one place to another. **Convection** (con•VEK•shuhn) is the transfer of heat through the movement of a gas or a liquid. When convection happens in air, it forms winds. These winds can be local breezes or winds that blow around the world.

✔ Quick Check

Compare and Contrast Describe the movement of air pressure during a sea breeze and compare it to the movement of air pressure during a land breeze.

Critical Thinking Why does convection happen in liquids and gases but not in solids?

≡ *Quick Lab*

Land and Water Temperatures

1. **Predict** Write down your prediction about whether water or land holds heat longer.

2. **Make a Model** Fill one container with room-temperature water. Then fill another container to the same height with sand.

3. **Record Data** Measure the initial temperature of each material by placing a thermometer about halfway down into the middle of the container. Record it on a table.

4. **Experiment** Place both containers in a tub of ice water.

5. **Record Data** Record the temperature in each container every 2 minutes.

6. **Analyze Data** Graph the change in temperature over time for both containers. Which one had a faster drop in temperature?

7. **Communicate** Write a report. Include details of the experiment and tell whether or not the evidence supports your prediction.

What are global winds?

Hundreds of years ago ships sailed around the world carrying items for trade. The captains of these ships planned their journeys so their ships could take advantage of winds that blew across the world's oceans.

When sailing from Europe to the Americas, the captains wanted to travel from northeast to southwest. They found winds that blew in these directions in bands between the equator and 30°N latitude (LAT•i•tewd). *Latitude* is a measure of how far north or south a place is from the equator. Winds that blew between 30°N latitude and 30°S latitude became known as *trade winds*.

Trade winds are part of a system of winds called global winds. A **global wind** blows steadily in predictable directions and over long distances.

Global winds blow because sunlight heats areas near Earth's equator more than it heats areas near Earth's poles. That means the air near the poles is cooler, denser, and has higher pressure than air near the equator. These differences cause warm air with low pressure near the equator to rise. Cooler polar air with high pressure moves in to take its place.

✔ Quick Check

Compare and Contrast Why is the air pressure at the poles higher than the air pressure at the equator?

Critical Thinking Why did captains need to know where global winds were found?

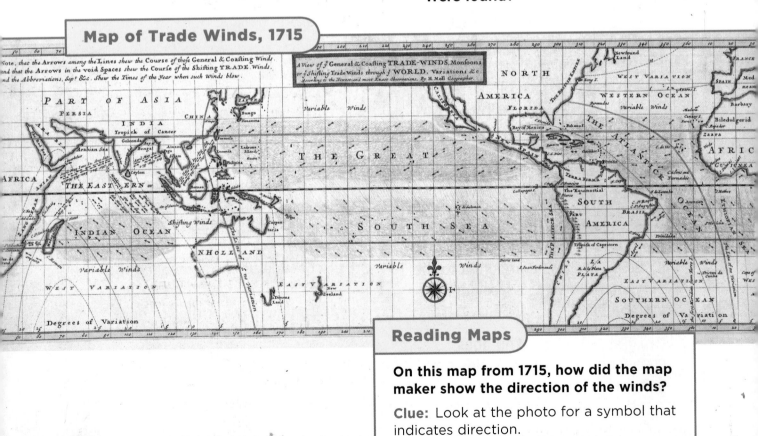

Map of Trade Winds, 1715

Reading Maps

On this map from 1715, how did the map maker show the direction of the winds?

Clue: Look at the photo for a symbol that indicates direction.

Lesson Review

Summarize the Main Idea

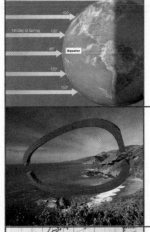

The Sun heats Earth's atmosphere unequally. (pp. 244–245)

Air moves from an area of **high pressure** to an area of **low pressure**. (pp. 246–247)

Global winds are predictable, blow steadily, and blow over long distances. (p. 248)

Make a FOLDABLES™ Study Guide

Make a three-tab book (see p. 481). Use the titles shown. On the inside of each tab, summarize what you learned about how the Sun heats Earth, how air moves, and why global winds were important to captains.

The sun heats Earth's atmosphere unequally.

Air Moves

Global Winds

Think, Talk, and Write

1. **Main Idea** What happens when air is heated unevenly?

2. **Vocabulary** Winds that blow steadily in predictable directions over very long distances are _____.

3. **Compare and Contrast** How is the heat energy per area received from sunlight different at the equator than at the poles?

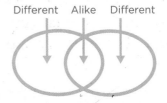

Different   Alike   Different

4. **Critical Thinking** How is a global wind different from a local wind, such as a sea breeze?

5. **Test Practice** Captains used global winds because the winds
   A blew steadily over long distances.
   B had atmospheric pressure.
   C heated Earth unequally.
   D moved air in a loop.

6. **Test Practice** What is convection?
   A air blowing toward land
   B transfer of heat through motion
   C winds that blow around the world
   D a change in air pressure

Writing Link

Fictional Narrative
Write about what you would do if you are a sailing captain on your way from Europe to the Americas and you lost your map of the trade winds.

Math Link

Calculating Global Wind Speed
The distance across the Atlantic Ocean from New York to London is roughly 3,500 miles. If it took ships using the global winds six months to cross the ocean, how far, on average, did they travel each month?

Be a Scientist

paper

scissors

string

heat source

Inquiry Structured

How does warmed air affect weather?

Form a Hypothesis

When air is warmed, it becomes less dense and has a higher pressure. How does warm air move? In this experiment, you will hold a spiral of paper over a heat source. What do you think will happen to the paper? Write your hypothesis in the form "*If the air warms, then the paper spiral will…*"

Test Your Hypothesis

1. Cut a circle of paper to form a spiral.

2. Tie a piece of string to one end of the paper.

3. Have your teacher turn on a heat source. Carefully hold or hang the spiral about 6 inches above the heat source.

4. **Observe** Describe what the spiral does.

5. While holding the spiral above the heat source, turn the heat source off. Describe what happens to the spiral.

Step **1**

Step **2**

Step **3**

5 IE 6.c. Plan and conduct a simple investigation based on a student-developed question and write instructions others can follow to carry out the procedure.

Draw Conclusions

1 Why did the spiral of paper move when the heat source was on?

2 Why did the spiral stop moving when the heat source was not on?

3 **Infer** What happens to air over ground that is warmed throughout the day?

Inquiry Guided

Which type of land changes temperature fastest?

Form a Hypothesis

You have already figured out what air does when it is warmed. Air is warmed by heat released from the land or from water. Of soil, sand, or rock, which type of land holds heat longer? Write your answer as a hypothesis in the form *"If soil, sand, or rock are heated, then…"*

Test Your Hypothesis

Design an experiment to determine which type of land holds heat longer. Write out the materials you will need and the steps you will follow. Record your results and observations as you follow your plan.

Draw Conclusions

Did your experiment support your hypothesis? Why or why not? Present your results to your classmates.

Inquiry Open

What else can you learn about air and temperature? For example, what do you think about how much heat fresh water can hold compared to ocean water? How does the size of a body of water affect how much heat it can hold? Design an experiment to answer your question. Your experiment must be organized to test only one variable, or one item being changed. Your experiment must be written so that another group can repeat the experiment by following your instructions.

Remember to follow the steps of the scientific process.

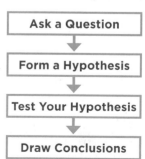

Ask a Question

↓

Form a Hypothesis

↓

Test Your Hypothesis

↓

Draw Conclusions

Oceans and Air Temperature

San Francisco ○ ○ Stockton

Look and Wonder

Stockton and San Francisco have very different temperatures during the year. Why are their temperatures so different?

5 ES 4.b. Students know the influence that the ocean has on the weather and the role that the water cycle plays in weather patterns.

What can cause two places to have different temperatures?

Make a Prediction

How does being close to an ocean affect the temperature of a city? Make a prediction.

Test Your Prediction

1. Find Stockton and San Francisco on the map of California on p. 252. Where are they located compared to the Pacific Ocean?

2. **Compare** Use the temperature data in the charts to compare the monthly high and low temperatures of the two cities.

Draw Conclusions

3. **Analyze Data** Examine the data to determine whether the temperature changes less throughout the year in one city than the other.

4. **Infer** How might the ocean affect the temperature changes in these cities?

5. **Communicate** Write a report explaining how the data for these two cities either support or do not support your prediction. Would examining data for more cities improve the accuracy of your prediction?

Explore More

Write a prediction explaining how being near an ocean will affect another weather variable. Collect and compare weather data for both cities. Write a report explaining how the data support or do not support your prediction.

 5 IE 6.h. Draw conclusions from scientific evidence and indicate whether further information is needed to support a specific conclusion.

Average High Temperature (°F)		
	San Francisco	Stockton
Jan.	55.7	53.4
Feb.	59.1	60.5
Mar.	61.3	65.9
Apr.	63.9	72.9
May	66.8	81.0
Jun.	70.0	88.4
Jul.	71.4	94.1
Aug.	72.1	92.5
Sep.	73.5	88.2
Oct.	70.2	78.4
Nov.	62.9	64.2
Dec.	56.4	53.7

Average Low Temperature (°F)		
	San Francisco	Stockton
Jan.	42.4	37.7
Feb.	44.9	40.5
Mar.	46.1	42.6
Apr.	47.6	46.1
May	50.1	51.6
Jun.	52.6	57.0
Jul.	53.9	60.4
Aug.	54.9	59.8
Sep.	54.7	57.2
Oct.	51.8	50.2
Nov.	47.3	42.2
Dec.	43.1	37.5

Read and **Learn**

▶ Main Idea 5 ES 4.b

Ocean water helps determine the weather and climate of nearby land.

▶ Vocabulary

climate, p.255

current, p.256

LOG ON ⊝-Glossary
@ www.macmillanmh.com

▶ Reading Skill

Compare and Contrast

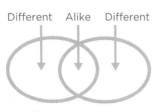

Different   Alike   Different

▲ This thermometer relies on density to measure temperature.

How do oceans affect temperature on land?

In December you hear the weather reporter say, "Temperatures inland will be in the low 40s, but they will be higher along the coast." In June you hear, "Temperatures inland will be in the 80s, but they will be lower along the coast." What causes temperatures along the coast to be lower in the summer and higher in the winter?

If you place your hand over a sink filled with warm water, you will feel warmth. That is because heat from the water is warming the air between your hand and the water. Water and land heat the air above them. Air that is in contact with water is *tempered*, or warmed in the winter and cooled in the summer.

On a summer day the ocean water may have a temperature of 20°C (68°F). The air above the water will be near 20°C. The air temperature will not increase much during the day because the water temperature under it will not increase much.

However, on that same summer day, sunlight warms the land very rapidly. Air above the land will get hotter. Air temperatures may jump 10°F or more in just a few hours. On a very hot day the temperature of the air above the land may soar to 30°C (86°F). You would feel cooler near the ocean than even a few kilometers inland.

Over the summer, the temperature of the water increases slightly as it is warmed by heat energy from sunlight. The temperature of the oceans does not change much from day to night or from season to season.

In winter, the reverse happens. During the fall and winter, the ocean slowly gives up the heat it gained during the summer. By February it may have cooled to 10°C (50°F). However, the land has cooled faster. Its temperature may now be

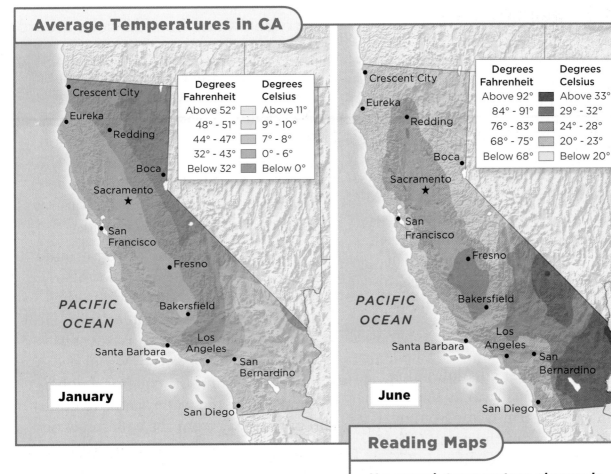

Average Temperatures in CA

Degrees Fahrenheit	Degrees Celsius
Above 52°	Above 11°
48° - 51°	9° - 10°
44° - 47°	7° - 8°
32° - 43°	0° - 6°
Below 32°	Below 0°

Crescent City
Eureka
Redding
Boca
Sacramento ★
San Francisco
Fresno
PACIFIC OCEAN
Bakersfield
Santa Barbara
Los Angeles
San Bernardino
San Diego

January

Degrees Fahrenheit	Degrees Celsius
Above 92°	Above 33°
84° - 91°	29° - 32°
76° - 83°	24° - 28°
68° - 75°	20° - 23°
Below 68°	Below 20°

Crescent City
Eureka
Redding
Boca
Sacramento ★
San Francisco
Fresno
PACIFIC OCEAN
Bakersfield
Santa Barbara
Los Angeles
San Bernardino
San Diego

June

0°C (32°F). In winter, the air over the water usually stays warmer than the air over the land.

Oceans moderate temperatures throughout the year both locally and over the entire planet. The climate of a place near the ocean is more mild than a place inland. **Climate** (KLIGH•mit) is the average weather conditions of a place or region. Climate includes average temperature, average rainfall, humidity, and wind conditions.

Differences between the temperatures near the equator and those near the poles would be much greater if Earth had no oceans. The slow warming and cooling of the oceans around the world keeps air in a narrow range of temperatures.

Reading Maps

How much temperature change is there in Santa Barbara versus San Bernardino?

Clue: Look at the key to see what the colors mean. Then figure out which city has a bigger difference in color.

✔ Quick Check

Compare and Contrast What effect do oceans have on the temperatures of places near the ocean and places further inland?

Critical Thinking What is the climate like where you live?

What are ocean currents?

A message in a bottle thrown into the Atlantic Ocean near Florida might wash up on a beach in Ireland months later. What moved the bottle thousands of kilometers from Florida to Ireland?

The Gulf Stream is a current (KUR•unht) of warm water that would have carried the bottle from the southern tip of Florida along the east coast of the United States and then across the northern Atlantic Ocean. A **current** is an ongoing movement of ocean water.

The Gulf Stream is one of many ocean currents that circulate water on Earth. Currents such as the Gulf Stream carry warm water from near the equator toward the poles. Other currents such as the California Current carry cold water from the poles toward the equator.

Since the water in a current can be warm or cold, currents also transfer heat from one place to another. The heat that they transfer through convection affects the weather and climate of the nearby land. The warm water in the Gulf Stream causes mild temperatures in the British Isles and Scotland.

Ocean currents move heat around the world in the oceans. They also move heat around the world in the atmosphere through water vapor. Heat energy from sunlight causes water vapor to evaporate from warm ocean currents around the equator. Global winds carry the water vapor to cooler regions away from the equator. As it is moved to cooler regions, the water vapor condenses.

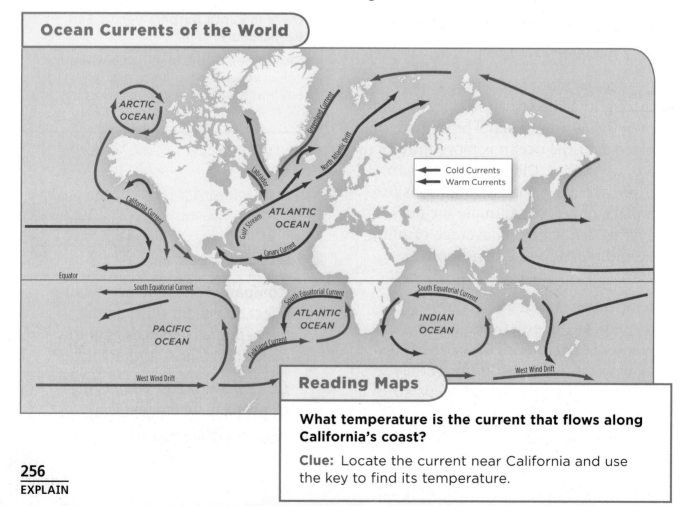

Ocean Currents of the World

ARCTIC OCEAN

Greenland Current

North Atlantic Drift

Labrador

California Current

Gulf Stream

ATLANTIC OCEAN

Canary Current

Cold Currents
Warm Currents

Equator

South Equatorial Current

South Equatorial Current

South Equatorial Current

PACIFIC OCEAN

ATLANTIC OCEAN

Falkland Current

INDIAN OCEAN

West Wind Drift

West Wind Drift

Reading Maps

What temperature is the current that flows along California's coast?

Clue: Locate the current near California and use the key to find its temperature.

Condensation is the opposite of evaporation. What do you think this means about what happens to heat when water vapor condenses into water? Heat is released into the atmosphere as water vapor condenses. The transfer of heat around the world through the atmosphere and through the water is an important way that oceans keep temperatures on Earth in a narrow range.

How do we know where the currents go? Some scientists track ocean currents by following items that are lost from cargo ships. One cargo loss that was tracked was 29,000 bathtub toys. They were lost off the coast of Alaska. About six months later, the toys began showing up along the coast of Alaska and Washington. Scientists are following the toys to see if they will be carried by ocean currents along the coast of California and out to Hawaii.

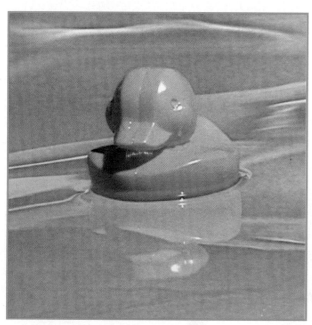

▲ This rubber duck was one of the toys used to track currents when it fell off a cargo ship in Alaska.

Quick Lab

Ocean Currents

1. Fill a white or clear wash-basin or pan with about 2 in. of water at room temperature. This represents the ocean.

2. Fill one 8-oz paper cup with ice water and several drops of blue food coloring. Fill another 8-oz paper cup with hot water and several drops of red food coloring.

3. Place the cups in the pan. Then stick a pushpin into each cup about 1 in. from the bottom.

4. **Make a Model** Gently pull out the pins to form currents.

5. **Observe** What happens to the food coloring?

6. Does the colored water float or sink?

7. How does this model resemble ocean currents?

✔ Quick Check

Compare and Contrast How do evaporation and condensation relate to heat?

Critical Thinking How much rainfall would you expect on an area near the Gulf Stream?

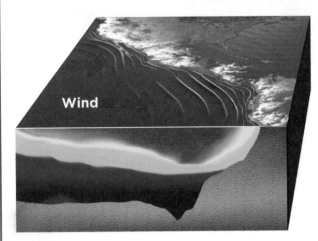

El Niño Conditions

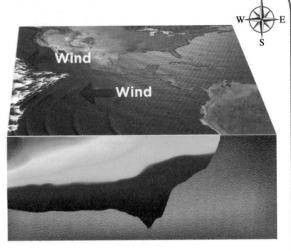

Normal Conditions

What causes El Niño?

Most of the time, a cold current along the coast of Peru keeps the temperature of the ocean water cool. This causes high air pressure along the west coast of South America. On the other side of the Pacific Ocean, the water near northern Australia is warm, which causes warm air with a low air pressure. The winds that blow across the Pacific Ocean usually blow from the high air pressure area in the east to the low air pressure area in the west.

Every two to seven years, the cold current sinks and does not push cold water up to the surface. This causes a change in weather conditions known as an *El Niño*. The warmer temperature at the surface of the water causes the air pressure over the water to fall. The air pressure changes cause the winds to blow from west to east.

The winds push ocean water in front of them and cause higher tides on the west coasts of North and South America. The winds also move moist air, causing heavy rains and storms.

The comings and goings of El Niño and the changing wind patterns are called the El Niño/Southern Oscillation, or ENSO. *Oscillation* (os•uh•LAY•shuhn) means movement back and forth. The changes that an ENSO weather pattern brings cause damage in the countries around the Pacific Ocean. Convection of heat across the Pacific Ocean changes and causes changes in weather around the world.

✔ *Quick Check*

Compare and Contrast What happens to winds before and during an El Niño?

Critical Thinking What conditions occur in Australia during an El Niño?

Lesson Review

Summarize the Main Idea

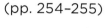

Earth's oceans keep **Earth's temperatures** moderate. (pp. 254–255)

Ocean currents move heat and water around the Earth. (pp. 256–257)

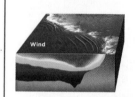

An **El Niño** can cause weather changes over a large area. (p. 258)

Make a FOLDABLES™ Study Guide

Make a three-tab book (see p. 481). Label it as shown. On the inside of each tab, summarize what you know about oceans, air temperature, currents, and El Niño.

Think, Talk, and Write

1 **Main Idea** How do oceans affect the weather and climate of nearby land?

2 **Vocabulary** The average weather conditions of a place is the _____ .

3 **Compare and Contrast** Why might two places at the same distance from the equator have different climates?

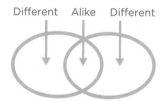

Different   Alike   Different

4 **Critical Thinking** Draw a map of the Pacific Ocean and show the changes that occur during an El Niño.

5 **Test Practice** What is an ongoing movement of water in the ocean called?
A precipitation
B El Niño
C high tide
D a current

6 **Test Practice** Oceans affect the temperature on Earth by:
A moving bottles
B washing onto beaches
C causing floods
D moving heat

 **Math Link**

Percentage of Bottles Found
50,000 bottles are lost in the ocean. Only 100 bottles are ever found. What percentage of the bottles were recovered?

 Social Studies

Protecting Ocean Currents
Write about how the United States government can pass laws to help protect ocean currents and why protecting currents is important.

LOG ON **e-Review** Summaries and quizzes online @ www.macmillanmh.com

Be a Scientist

Materials

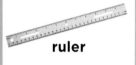

**large plastic
storage bin**

ruler

water

food coloring

**sportwater
bottle**

stopwatch

modeling clay

How does a land mass affect the speed of an ocean current?

Form a Hypothesis

If you measure the time a current takes to travel a certain distance and then measure the time the current takes to travel the same distance when it has to flow around a landmass, will the time the current takes change? Write your answer as a hypothesis in the form "*If a landmass is placed in a current, then the time the current takes will…*"

Test Your Hypothesis

1. Pour cold water in a large plastic container to a height of 4 cm.

2. Add 6 drops of food coloring to warm water and mix. Then fill a sport water bottle and put the cap on the bottle.

3. Hold the sport water bottle down at one end of the container so it touches the bottom. Have your partner get the stopwatch ready. Then squeeze the sport water bottle gently.

4. **Record Data** Record the time the current takes to reach the other side of the container.

5. Replace the cold water in the large plastic container and refill the sport water bottle with warm water and food coloring.

6. Make a landmass from modeling clay. Place the landmass in the middle of the container. Then repeat steps 3 and 4.

Step 1

Step 2

Step 3

5 IE 6.c. Plan and conduct a simple investigation based on a student-developed question and write instructions others can follow to carry out the procedure.

Draw Conclusions

① Did the test support your hypothesis? Explain why or why not.

② What is the independent variable in this experiment? What is the dependent variable?

③ **Communicate** Discuss your results with your classmates. How did your times compare with theirs?

Inquiry Guided

Will the time change if the current goes between two landmasses that are different distances apart?

Form a Hypothesis

Write your answer as a hypothesis in the form *"If the distance between two landmasses increases, then the time that the current takes to reach the other side will…"*

Test Your Hypothesis

Design an experiment to test your hypothesis. Write out the materials you will need and the steps you will follow. Carry out the procedure and record your results and observations.

Draw Conclusions

Did the data you collected support your hypothesis? Present your results to your classmates.

Inquiry Open

What else would you like to learn about ocean currents? Come up with a question and design an experiment to answer it. Your experiment must be organized to test only one variable. Write instructions that another group could follow.

Remember to follow the steps of the scientific process.

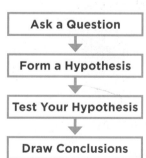

Ask a Question
↓
Form a Hypothesis
↓
Test Your Hypothesis
↓
Draw Conclusions

Severe Weather

Look and Wonder

On any given day, more than 40,000 thunderstorms are rumbling somewhere on Earth. What causes these spectacular storms?

 5 ES 4.c. Students know the causes and effects of different types of severe weather.

What happens when masses of air meet?

Materials

Form a Hypothesis

What happens to air when it meets warmer air? Write your answer as a hypothesis in the form *"If a mass of air meets warmer air, then . . ."* Like air, water flows and carries heat. Using water as a model for air can help you test your hypothesis.

- scissors
- cardboard
- aluminum foil
- cold water
- warm water
- 2 containers
- food coloring
- clear plastic box

Test Your Hypothesis

1. **Measure** Cut the cardboard so it fits tightly in the clear box. Wrap the cardboard in aluminum foil.

2. Pour 4 cups of cool water into one container, and 4 cups of warm water into the other one. Place a few drops of food coloring into the cool water container.

3. Hold the cardboard tightly against the bottom of the box. Pour the cool water on one side and the warm water on the other.

4. **Observe** Watch the box from the side as you remove the cardboard.

5. Repeat the experiment using warm water in both containers and food coloring in one.

Step 3

Step 4

Draw Conclusions

6. What are the variables in this experiment?

7. **Infer** Which experiment looked more like it would create storms? Why?

Explore More

Will a greater difference in temperature between the warm and cold water increase the observable effects? Form a hypothesis and test it.

 5 IE 6.d. Identify the dependent and controlled variables in an investigation.

Read and Learn

▶ Main Idea 5 ES 4.c

Storms are caused by the collision of air masses that have different temperatures and humidities.

▶ Vocabulary

air mass, p.265

front, p.265

thunderstorm, p.266

tornado, p.268

low pressure closure, p.268

hurricane, p.270

storm surge, p.271

cyclone, p.271

monsoon, p.272

LOG ON e-Glossary
@ www.macmillanmh.com

▶ Reading Skill

Cause and Effect

Cause → Effect
→
→
→
→

What causes severe weather?

It is a warm and sunny day. Suddenly the temperature drops. Puffy white clouds appear in the western sky. As time passes, the clouds grow taller. The drop in temperature and the change in the clouds indicate that something is happening in the atmosphere.

▼ Have you ever seen clouds like these? They could indicate that a storm is approaching.

Air Masses and Fronts

The air in the atmosphere is not the same all over the United States. Weather is affected by the air mass that is passing through your area. An **air mass** is a large region of air that has a similar temperature and humidity.

Air masses can cover thousands of square kilometers of land and water. Depending on where they form, air masses can be cold, warm, dry, or moist. An air mass that forms above a warm area of water will be warm and humid. An air mass that forms over a cold area of land will be cool and dry.

As air masses move they cause changes in the weather. These changes happen where one air mass meets a different air mass. This meeting place between air masses is called a **front**. This boundary marks the front edge of the oncoming air mass.

What happens when a cold and dry air mass runs into a warm and moist air mass? The cold air, which is dense and heavy, moves under and pushes the lighter warm air up. As the warm air rises, the moisture in the warm air condenses. Towering clouds form and storms may follow.

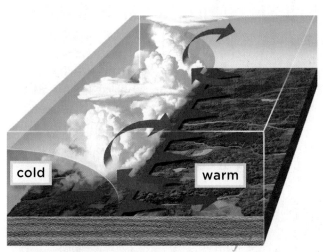

▲ warm front approaching a cold air mass

▲ cold front approaching a warm air mass

✔ Quick Check

Cause and Effect What happens when a cold air mass moves into an area where the air is warm?

Critical Thinking How can you tell that a front is passing through your area?

What causes thunderstorms?

Lightning flashed through the sky of Los Angeles, California, and thunder rumbled over the city. In some places almost 13 centimeters (about 5 inches) of rain fell in just 2 hours. Streets flooded and sheets of rain fell on stranded cars.

Thunderstorms similar to this one happen all over the world. A **thunderstorm** is a rainstorm that includes lightning and thunder.

How a Thunderstorm Forms

① cold front

② ③

① **Fronts** A cold front moves in, pushing warm, humid air upward. As the warm, humid air rises, it expands and cools.

② **Thunderheads** As the warm, humid air cools, some of the water vapor condenses. This releases energy and warms the air around it. The warm air rises further, forming a thunderhead. The cloud flattens out when winds at higher altitudes blow the condensation away.

③ **Precipitation** The water droplets combine and grow larger until they fall.

Reading Diagrams

What happens to the temperature of air in a thunderhead?
Clue: Red represents hot and blue represents cold.

LOG ON *Science in Motion* Watch how thunderstorms form
@ www.macmillanmh.com

Lightning and Thunder

Lightning is the spark caused when the electricity in a thunderhead discharges. Lightning can jump from one part of a cloud to another or between a cloud and the ground.

Scientists have not completely figured out what causes lightning. One theory is that moving air causes particles of ice and rain that are rushing upward to rub against particles rushing downward. As the particles rub, different amounts of electricity build up in different parts of the cloud.

This is similar to what happens when you shuffle your feet across a carpet and a charge of static electricity builds up in your body. When you touch your finger to a doorknob, you feel a tingle as a spark jumps between you and the door. That spark is a discharge of electricity.

Lightning raises the temperature of the air around it to more than five times the temperature of the surface of the Sun. This burst of heat makes the air expand violently. The sound of the rapidly expanding air is *thunder*.

Thunderstorms can bring severe winds that can knock over trees and heavy rains that can cause flooding. Lightning can hurt people or animals. It can also start wild fires.

✔ Quick Check

Cause and Effect What is one theory about how lightning forms?

Critical Thinking How is the production of thunder similar to the "pop" produced by a pricked balloon?

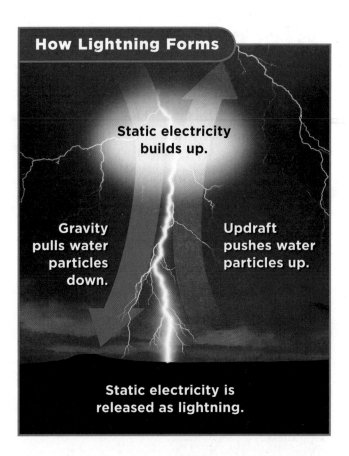

How Lightning Forms

Static electricity builds up.

Gravity pulls water particles down.

Updraft pushes water particles up.

Static electricity is released as lightning.

▼ Lightning can cause fires and damage trees.

What are tornadoes?

Under the right conditions, a thunderstorm can turn into a tornado (tawr•NAY•doh). A **tornado** is a rotating funnel-shaped cloud that contains winds that blow up to 480 kilometers per hour (299 miles per hour). People commonly call these storms "twisters."

Tornados begin to form when warm air moves upward in a thunderhead, creating an area of low pressure. The low air pressure draws air inward and upward. When an area of low pressure air is surrounded by higher pressure air, it is called a **low pressure closure**.

As air flows into the low pressure closure, it rotates around in a circle faster and faster. From the ground, the shape of the cloud looks like a funnel. Warm air rises up the center of the spinning cloud. Rain falls outside of the cloud. When the tip of the funnel cloud touches the ground, it becomes a tornado.

Because only a small section of the tornado actually touches the ground, tornadoes have been known to destroy houses on one side of a street while leaving houses on the other side untouched. The powerful winds that spin upward in a tornado can lift heavy objects, including cars. Papers and lighter objects have been found up to 201.17 kilometers (125 miles) away from the location that the tornado hit.

How a Tornado Forms

thunderhead

funnel cloud

❶ **Warm air moves upward in a thunderhead.**

❷ **A funnel is formed when the air starts rotating.**

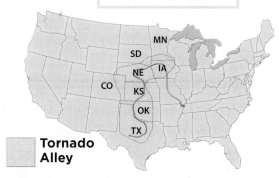

Tornado Alley

□ Tornado Alley

Tornados occur all over the United States, but they are generally worst and most frequent in an area called Tornado Alley. Tornado Alley is located where cold, dry air from Canada meets warm, moist air from the Gulf of Mexico. These weather conditions favor the formation of thunderstorms and tornadoes.

tornado

❸ The funnel cloud becomes a tornado when it touches the ground.

≡*Quick Lab*

Tornado in a Bottle

❶ Fill a 2-liter plastic bottle one-third full of water.

❷ Place an empty 2-liter plastic bottle upside down over the mouth of the first bottle. Tape them together.

❸ Holding the bottles by the necks, flip them upside down so the bottle with the water in it is now on top. Place the bottles on a desk. What do you see?

❹ **Make a Model** Swirl the water and turn the bottles over again. Then put them down and observe.

❺ How is this model similar to a tornado?

Reading Photos

Describe the appearance of the clouds as the tornado forms.

Clue: Look at the photos from left to right to see how the appearance of the cloud changes.

✔ *Quick Check*

Cause and Effect What causes winds to rotate in a tornado?

Critical Thinking Why might differences in air pressure cause buildings to explode outward when a tornado passes over them?

What are hurricanes?

A thunderstorm over the Atlantic Ocean can turn into a tropical storm. A tropical storm has rotating winds with low pressure at its center. As you know, the water near the equator is warm. Water vapor evaporates into warm air and the warm air rises. As cooler air flows toward the space where the warm air used to be, a low pressure center forms.

The low pressure causes more water to evaporate, which lowers the air pressure even more. The movement of air from the high air pressure surrounding the storm into the low air pressure center causes winds that blow in toward the center. As in a tornado, the air in a tropical storm rotates in a circle.

A tropical storm turns into a **hurricane** (HUR•i•kayn) when the wind speed reaches more than 119 kilometers (74 miles) per hour. Hurricanes are large enough to cover several states at a time!

The spinning of hurricanes is related to the rotation of Earth. If you look at Earth from space, you can see that it rotates from west to east. As it rotates, it causes air above the surface to be deflected to the right in the Northern

▼ Hurricane Katrina was the third-strongest hurricane to strike the United States.

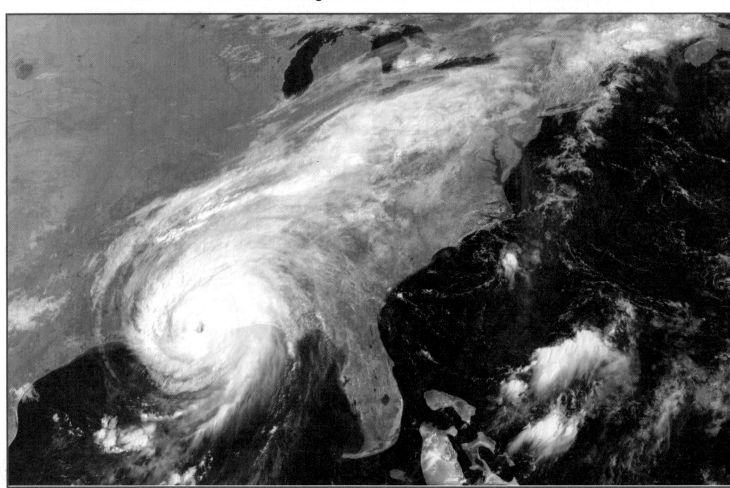

▲ Waves caused by storm surge can damage houses near the water.

hurricane

WIND

EARTH'S ROTATION

Hemisphere. This is called the *Coriolis effect*.

The Coriolis effect causes hurricanes to rotate counter-clockwise in the Northern Hemisphere. The rotating winds also help create the hurricane by pulling thunderstorm clusters together.

From space, fully developed hurricanes look like a spiral of clouds with a hole in its middle. The hole is the low pressure center, which is called the "eye" of the hurricane. Clouds form a border around the eye and

spread out beyond it. A hurricane's fastest winds and heaviest rains occur next to the eye. Winds near an eye can reach speeds of about 320 km an hour (almost 200 miles an hour) inside the most intense hurricanes. Within the eye, there is little precipitation and light winds.

Hurricane winds whip up large waves in the ocean. These waves create a bulge of water in the ocean known as a **storm surge**. As a storm moves over a coast, the storm surge can cause flooding as water levels suddenly rise, or surge, several feet.

Any storm with a low pressure center and a counter-clockwise rotation is called a **cyclone** (SIGH•klohn). Hurricanes and tornadoes both have low pressure centers and spinning winds. They are types of cyclones.

✔ Quick Check

Cause and Effect What causes the size of a hurricane to increase?

Critical Thinking Is a thunderstorm a type of cyclone?

monsoon

fog

What are other forms of severe weather?

Did you know that heavy rain is a severe form of weather? When a lot of rain falls in a short period of time, flooding often occurs because the ground cannot absorb all the water. Floods can occur rapidly, and make roads unsafe for drivers. Heavy rains can also cause mud slides and landslides.

A **monsoon** (mAHn•SOON) is a seasonal wind that brings heavy rain. Monsoon winds occur in Southeast Asia. They also occur in the southwestern United States.

Fog is considered to be a form of severe weather when it is dense enough to limit what can be seen beyond one-fourth of a mile. Dense fog can interfere with safety at airports and on highways. When it occurs, dense fog warnings are issued. Coastal California has an annual average of 60 days of dense fog warnings.

Ground fog usually forms when cool, clear nights occur after a sunny day. During the day, the ground is warmed by the Sun. After the Sun sets, a low layer of warm air begins to cool. The water vapor the air contained condenses and forms ground fog. In the Central Valley, this type of fog is often called Tule fog.

Advection fog forms when warm, humid air flows over cold ground or water. This often occurs along the California coast in the spring and early summer as warm air from the land moves toward the colder air over the ocean. When the warm air meets the cold air over the ocean, the air cools. Water vapor condenses, creating the fog. Because it is caused by warm air blown by a wind, advection fog usually continues until the wind changes direction.

Quick Check

Cause and Effect What causes ground fog to form?

Critical Thinking What types of severe weather have you seen?

Lesson Review

Summarize the Main Idea

When air masses with different temperatures and humidity meet, they cause changes in air pressure that can lead to **thunderstorms**. (pp. 264–267)

Cyclones, such as hurricanes and tornadoes, are storms with a low pressure center that cause a circular pattern of winds to form. (pp. 268–271)

Other types of severe weather include monsoons and fog. (p. 272)

Make a **FOLDABLES™** Study Guide

Make a three-tab book (see p. 481). Label as shown. On the inside of each fold, list the causes and effects of the types of severe weather.

Think, Talk, and Write

1. **Main Idea** What causes storms?

2. **Vocabulary** Tornadoes and hurricanes are examples of _____ .

3. **Cause and Effect** Why are tornadoes generally severe in Tornado Alley?

Cause → Effect	
→	
→	
→	
→	

4. **Critical Thinking** Why do you think most thunderstorms never become cyclones?

5. **Test Practice** **What is a storm surge?**
   A a circular pattern of winds
   B a bulge of water in the ocean
   C a cloud that forms near the ground
   D a large region of cold air

6. **Test Practice** **Fog that forms when warm, humid air flows over cold ground or water is:**
   A lake fog
   B ground fog
   C advection fog
   D Tule fog

Writing Link

Explanatory Writing
Write about the possible effects of fog on automobile and airport safety in California. Explain why it is important to issue dense fog warnings.

Math Link

Measuring Flood Waters
During a 5 A.M. flood watch report, water is reported to be rising at a rate of 11 inches an hour. If the water continues to rise at this rate, how many more inches will it have risen by 10 A.M.?

Writing in Science

Mudslides occur after periods of constant rainfall or rapid melting of snow. They usually start on steep hillsides, where the extra water and the dirt on the hill mix and turn into mud. As it pours down the hill, the mud may pick up rocks, trees, and cars. Read below for a story written by a California girl who experienced a mudslide.

A good personal narrative

▶ tells a story from personal experience.

▶ expresses the writer's feelings by using the first-person point of view.

▶ uses time-order words such as *first, next,* and *finally* to connect ideas and show the sequence of events.

April 15

Yesterday it rained very hard. As I was getting ready to leave for school this morning, I heard loud booming and cracking sounds. My whole family ran out of the house in our pajamas. Dad said, "It must be a mudslide. We have to get to higher ground."

First, Dad got us all in the van and drove to the top of a nearby hill. Then we turned on the car radio. We heard that about a half mile below us, the mudslide was carrying cars and trees down the road. A few people had been taken to the hospital with minor injuries, but no one was killed or badly hurt.

We could not go back home for hours. Finally, we were told that it was safe to return. We were lucky that our house was only damaged a little.

Write About It

Narrative Writing Write a personal narrative about a storm, mudslide, or other severe weather condition that you have experienced. Use a clear sequence of events to tell what happened and what you did.

 e-Journal Write about it online @ **www.macmillanmh.com**

ELA W 5.1.1. Create multiple-paragraph narrative compositions: a. Establish and develop a situation or plot. b. Describe the setting. c. Present an ending.

Math in Science

How Far Away Is Lightning?

Thunder travels at the speed of sound—about 1/5 of a mile per second. When you see a bolt of lightning, count the seconds until you hear thunder. If you know how to multiply fractions, you can use this information to find out how far away the lightning is.

Solve It

1. A rumble of thunder takes 15 seconds to reach your ears. How far away is it?

2. You see a bolt of lightning and 25 seconds later you hear thunder. How far away is it?

3. If a lightning flash is seen 12 seconds before the thunder is heard, how far away did the lightning strike?

Multiply fractions

To multiply a fraction by a whole number,

▶ write the whole number as a fraction by placing it over the denominator 1.

▶ then multiply numerators and denominators.

$$\frac{3}{4} \times 5 = \frac{3}{4} \times \frac{5}{1} = \frac{15}{4}$$

MA NS 5.2.5. Compute and perform simple multiplication and division of fractions and apply these procedures to solving problems.

Predicting the Weather

Look and Wonder

Looking at the color of the sky let sailors guess what kind of winds to expect the next day. How else could sailors know the direction that winds were blowing?

 5 ES 4.d. Students know how to use weather maps and data to predict local weather and know that weather forecasts depend on many variables.

How can you tell the direction that wind is blowing?

Purpose

To make a weather vane and record the direction of the wind.

Procedure

1. Carefully use scissors to cut an arrow shape with a tab out of a piece of cardboard or heavy construction paper.

2. Squeeze the end of one straw and insert it in the other one to make a longer tube. Put the tab of the arrow in one end of the straw. Put the other end of the straw in the bottle.

3. Put the bottle in a pan and pile rocks around it to keep it steady when the wind blows.

4. Use a compass to find north, then mark the four sides of the pan *North*, *South*, *East*, and *West* with a marker.

5. Set your weather vane in a high, open place.

6. **Record Data** For a week, record the direction of the wind every morning.

Draw Conclusions

7. **Analyze Data** Find the wind direction from a local weather station. Make a graph to compare your data with the data of the local station.

8. **Communicate** Write a report about your weather vane project. Include details about its construction and accuracy.

Explore More

How can you measure wind speed? Research the Beaufort Wind Scale. Suggest and test a scale to use for wind speed measurements in your area.

Materials

- cardboard
- scissors
- 2 straws
- 1-liter bottle
- pan
- rocks
- compass
- marker

Step 1

Step 2

 5 IE 6.g. Record data by using appropriate graphic representations (including charts, graphs, and labeled diagrams) and make inferences based on those data.

Main Idea 5 ES 4.d

Weather maps tell you what the weather is and help you predict the weather.

Vocabulary

forecast, p.278

meteorologist, p.278

weather map, p.279

LOG ON e-Glossary
@ www.macmillanmh.com

Reading Skill

Compare and Contrast

Different   Alike   Different

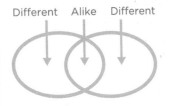

Who needs to know what the weather will be?

Think about someone who is about to push a toy car down a hill. If you are asked to guess which path the car will take as it goes down the hill, how often do you think you will be correct? What you predict is likely to be more accurate if you know some of the variables, such as how smooth the surface of the hill is or how fast the car is going when it starts.

To **forecast** (FOR•kast) is to make your best guess before something happens. Forecasting weather is more complicated than forecasting the path of the toy car because there are more variables involved. Meteorologists pay close attention to variables such as wind speed and air pressure so they can improve the accuracy of their predictions.

A **meteorologist** (mee•tee•uh•ROL•uh•jist) is a scientist who specializes in the study of Earth's atmosphere and weather. Meteorologists may

▼ Pilots and farmers need reliable weather forecasts.

farmer, Carmel, California

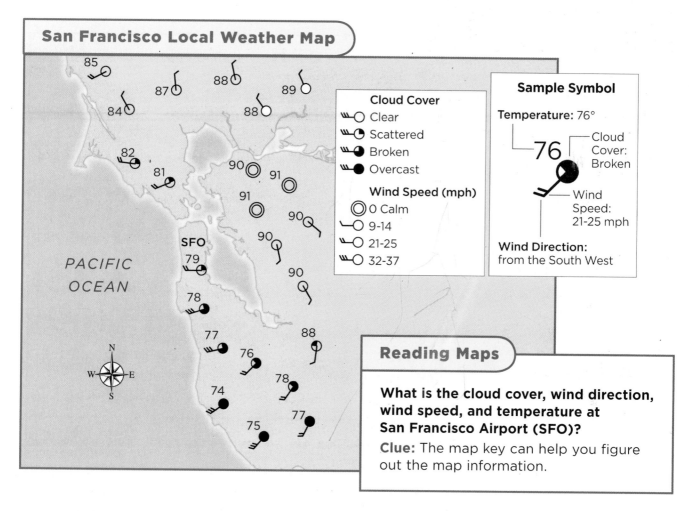

San Francisco Local Weather Map

Cloud Cover
Clear
Scattered
Broken
Overcast

Wind Speed (mph)
0 Calm
9-14
21-25
32-37

PACIFIC OCEAN

SFO

Sample Symbol

Temperature: 76°

76

Cloud Cover: Broken

Wind Speed: 21-25 mph

Wind Direction: from the South West

Reading Maps

What is the cloud cover, wind direction, wind speed, and temperature at San Francisco Airport (SFO)?

Clue: The map key can help you figure out the map information.

predict what the weather will be for the next day, for the next five days, or even for the next few months.

Who needs accurate weather forecasts? Airplane pilots need to know what the weather conditions are going to be in order to take off and land safely. Farmers need to know when rain is coming so they can make sure their crops get enough water.

Weather Maps

A **weather map** shows the weather in a specific area at a specific point in time. Many different kinds of weather maps exist. They may show only one variable, such as temperature, or they may show many different variables.

The weather map on this page uses symbols to show you the wind speed, cloud cover, air temperature, and precipitation for specific weather station locations around San Francisco. If you tracked the weather at your school every day, you could make this kind of weather map.

✔ Quick Check

Compare and Contrast Why might some weather conditions be good for a farmer but bad for a pilot?

Critical Thinking What are other symbols you could use to show on a map how cloudy the sky is?

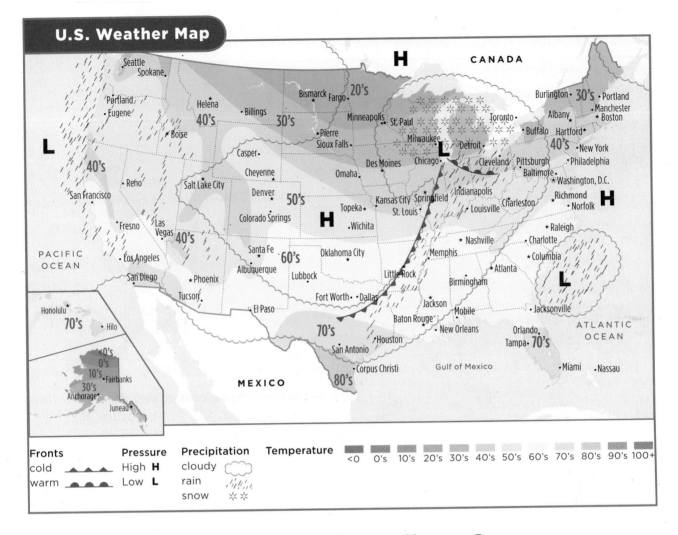

Fronts
cold ▲▲▲
warm ◠◠◠

Pressure
High **H**
Low **L**

Precipitation
cloudy ☁
rain ///
snow ✳✳

Temperature
<0 0's 10's 20's 30's 40's 50's 60's 70's 80's 90's 100+

What do weather fronts tell you?

Warm and cold fronts tell you what the weather is going to be like in the future. As you know, warm and cold fronts are the leading edges of air masses. Fronts move steadily, dragging warm and cold air along with them.

On weather maps such as the one on this page, cold fronts are marked with the symbol of a blue line of triangles. The triangles point in the direction that the cold front is moving. Warm fronts are marked with the symbol of a red line of half circles, which point in the direction that the warm front is moving.

What makes these gigantic systems move? You have learned about trade winds, one type of global wind. Another type of global wind is high altitude winds called the jet stream.

The jet stream is caused by temperature differences between air masses. The jet stream is higher than any mountains or buildings, so there is nothing to slow it down. The jet stream winds can exceed speeds of 240 kilometers per hour (150 miles per hour).

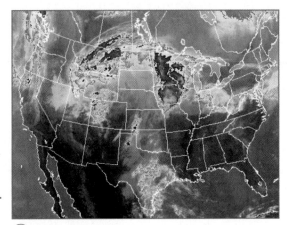

① **May 12, 2:00 P.M. Satellite image showing front over Utah, Idaho, and Montana.**

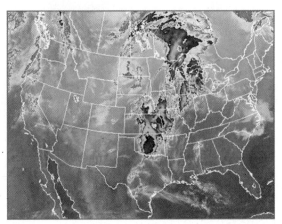

② **May 13, 2:00 P.M. Satellite image showing front over Canada.**

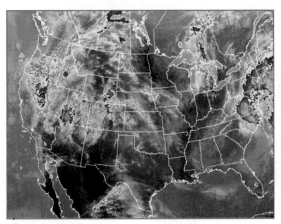

③ **May 14, 2:00 P.M. Satellite image showing front over New York, Pennsylvania, and Virginia.**

The West to East Rule

The jet stream winds blow from west to east. Since the jet stream winds push air masses, almost all weather fronts in North America move from west to east as well.

Today's weather is likely to be similar to whatever yesterday's weather was further west. As you can see in the first photo, a front is over Utah, Idaho, and Montana. As the jet stream winds blow that front to the east, the front behind it is pushed east as well. With data on wind speed, you could accurately figure out how long it would take for fronts to move across the United States.

✔ Quick Check

Compare and Contrast How does what low and high pressure systems tell you differ from what warm and cold fronts tell you?

Critical Thinking Looking at the weather map, what kind of weather is Saint Louis likely to have tomorrow?

Reading Photos

In which direction is this front moving?

Clue: Look at the satellite photos and the captions to find the direction in which the front is moving.

What do lows and highs tell you?

If you look at the map on page 280, you will see the letters L and H. These letters indicate where low pressure systems, or lows, and high pressure systems, or highs, are located. Low and high pressure systems tell you what the local weather conditions are. Here's how they work.

Low Pressure Systems

A low pressure system is a large mass of air with a low pressure center.

1. Air moves inward toward the low pressure center from all directions.

2. The air is turned to the right because of the rotation of Earth.

3. As a result, the wind in a low pressure system turns in a counterclockwise direction.

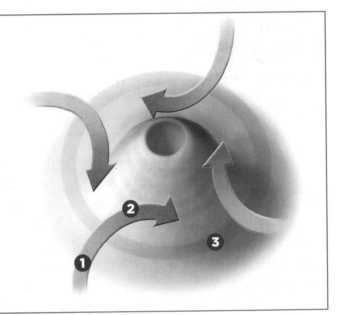

High Pressure Systems

A high pressure system is a large mass of air with the highest air pressure in the center.

1. Air moves outward from the high pressure center in all directions.

2. The air is turned to the right because of the rotation of Earth.

3. As a result, the wind in a high pressure system turns in a clockwise direction.

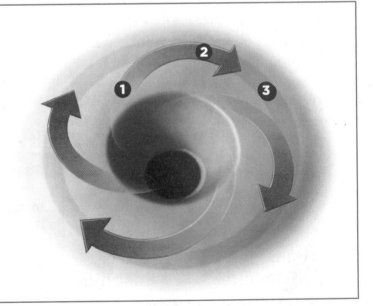

▲ A low pressure system moves across a city.

Since warm and humid air has low pressure, low pressure systems usually bring warm and stormy weather. Moisture that was held in a low pressure air mass condenses as it rises and cools, bringing clouds, rain, and other types of precipitation.

Since cool and dry air has high pressure, high pressure systems usually bring dry, clear weather. Any moisture carried in a high pressure system tends to evaporate, clearing the sky of clouds and bringing fair weather.

✓ Quick Check

Compare and Contrast Why do winds rotate in different directions in low pressure and high pressure systems?

Critical Thinking Why would knowing where the low and high pressure systems are moving help you forecast the weather?

≣ Quick Lab

Highs and Lows

How do winds in high and low pressure systems rotate?

1. **Make a Model** To model a high pressure system, stand one step away from your partner facing in the same direction. You represent the wind. Your partner represents the high pressure center.

high pressure system

2. Walk two steps away from your partner and turn to your right. Walk around your partner. In what direction is the wind moving around the high pressure center?

3. **Make a Model** To model a low pressure system, stand four steps away from your partner. You represent the wind. Your partner represents the low pressure center.

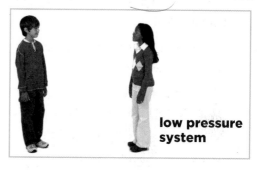

low pressure system

4. Walk two steps toward your partner and turn to your right. Walk around your partner. In what direction is the wind moving around the low pressure center?

How do weather forecasters collect data?

You may not think of yourself as a meteorologist. However, every time you have seen dark clouds in one area of the sky and guessed that rain is on the way, you have been forecasting the weather. Immediate forecasts about weather are more accurate than forecasts for the distant future.

Forecasts become less accurate as time passes because there are so many variables. A change in one variable can change the forecast from sunny to rainy. As time passes, it is increasingly likely that a variable will change. Most 12- to 24-hour forecasts are accurate, but after two or three days they are less reliable.

When you observed the color of the clouds you gathered data. Meteorologists use instruments on Earth's surface, in the sky, and in space to gather data about changes in Earth's atmosphere. They also consider what happened in the past when similar weather conditions occurred.

▲ Satellites take pictures of the movement of clouds and storms from space.

▲ Weather balloons carry instruments that measure temperature, air pressure, and humidity.

✔ Quick Check

Compare and Contrast How is the data from weather balloons and satellites different?

Critical Thinking Why does having additional data help meteorologists make forecasts more accurate?

▲ Doppler radar detects the speed and direction of clouds and rain.

Lesson Review

Summarize the Main Idea

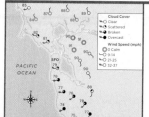

Weather maps show the weather in an area at a specific point in time. (p. 279)

Movements of masses of air with different pressures bring **changes in weather**. (pp. 280–283)

Weather data comes from observations and instruments. (p. 284)

Make a FOLDABLES™ Study Guide

Make a tri-fold book (see p. 480). Label as shown. On the inside of each fold, compare and contrast what you know about that title and forecasting the weather.

Think, Talk, and Write

1. **Main Idea** What information do weather maps tell you and help you predict?

2. **Vocabulary** The weather in a specific area at a specific point in time can be found on a(n) _____.

3. **Compare and Contrast** What type of weather do low and high pressure systems bring with them?

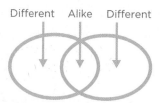

4. **Critical Thinking** What properties will a mass of air that formed over the ocean by Alaska most likely have?

5. **Test Practice** **What kind of weather data can a weather satellite gather?**
   A temperature
   B precipitation
   C air pressure
   D storm movement

6. **Test Practice** **What is a variable that meteorologists track to make weather forecasts?**
   A traffic
   B air pressure
   C barometer
   D population

Writing Link

Fictional Narrative

Write about what it would be like to work as a meteorologist or weather data observer. Include the daily tasks you would have to do.

Math Link

Measuring Wind Speed

If the wind is blowing from the northeast at 25 mph, how many hours will it take for the wind to move dense rain clouds through a 50-mile area?

Museum Mail Call

Scientists at the American Museum of Natural History study the natural world and the people who live in it. They collect stories and objects from people around the world. Read these letters to find out how weather affects children in different countries at the same time of the year.

June 13

Dear Museum Scientists,

Hola! (That's "hello" in Spanish.) It's the dry season here in Palmdale right now and it's *muy caliente*—very hot! We haven't had rain in weeks.

It's usually hot and dry here from May to November. We don't have a lot of water, so it has to be piped in from other areas. People have to watch how much water they use. Restaurants only serve water to people who ask for it.

Some people plant cacti and shrubs around their home. These plants need a lot less water than a thick, green lawn. I planted jalapeno peppers with *mi hermana*, my sister. We water the plants in the evening. That way the hot sun won't dry up all of the water.

Carlos

▲ Carlos and his sister Alicia plant jalapeño peppers.

ELA R 5.2.4. Draw inferences, conclusions, or generalizations about text and support them with textual evidence and prior knowledge.

June 23

Dear Museum Scientists,

The *gío múa*, or monsoons, have brought wet weather to our land. Everything here is soaked! Our monsoon season lasts from May to October. Many inches of rain can fall during heavy storms. But the storms only last for about an hour each day. It's very hot, so we don't mind getting wet. It's actually a lot of fun, and we dry off right away.

Our farm is near the Mekong River. Water floods our rice fields and helps the rice grow. It's hard work walking through the swampy ground. We carry the rice with *quang ganh*. These are baskets that we balance on the end of a pole.

People here are used to a lot of water. We build our homes on stilts so the water won't get in. We ride boats down the river and sell our rice on a floating market. Some years, there is more water than we expect!

Vang

▲ *Quang ganh* are used to carry rice.

Write About It
Compare and Contrast

1. How is the weather in Palmdale compared to the weather near the Mekong River?
2. What activity do both Carlos and Vang do?

LOG ON ℮-Journal Write about it online
@ www.macmillanmh.com

Compare and Contrast

▶ To compare, look for similarities, or things that are the same.

▶ To contrast, look for differences, or things that are not the same.

Summarize the Main Ideas

The air in Earth's atmosphere has weight and presses on all the objects it surrounds. (pp. 232–239)

When air is heated unevenly it moves around, causing wind and air currents. (pp. 242–249)

Ocean water helps determine the weather and climate of nearby land. (pp. 252–259)

Storms are caused by the collision of air masses that have different temperatures and humidities. (pp. 262–273)

Weather maps tell you what the weather is and help you predict the weather. (pp. 276–285)

Make a FOLDABLES™ Study Guide

Take a sheet of paper and tape your lesson study guides as shown.

Fill each blank with the best word from the list.

barometer, p. 238   **tornado**, p. 268

climate, p. 255   **global wind**, p. 248

front, p. 265   **troposphere**, p. 234

hurricane, p. 270   **weather map**, p. 279

1. There is more air in the _____ than anywhere else in Earth's atmosphere.   5 ES 4.e

2. An instrument used to measure atmospheric pressure is a(n) _____.   5 ES 4.e

3. Air that blows steadily over long distances is called a(n) _____.   5 ES 4.a

4. The average weather of an area is its _____.   5 ES 4.b

5. A meeting place between two air masses is called a(n) _____.   5 ES 4.d

6. A rotating funnel-shaped cloud with strong winds is called a(n) _____.   5 ES 4.c

7. A tropical storm turns into a(n) _____ when its wind speed reaches more than 73 miles per hour.   5 ES 4.c

8. Symbols on a(n) _____ show variables such as wind speed, cloud cover, air temperature, and precipitation.   5 ES 4.d

Answer each of the following in complete sentences.

9. **Communicate** Explain what weather you would expect behind a cold front that has run into a warm front.
5 ES 4.d

10. **Compare and Contrast** How is sunlight reaching Earth's polar regions different from sunlight reaching Earth's equatorial regions?
5 ES 4.a

11. **Compare and Contrast** Why do air temperatures tend to be more moderate near coasts than inland?
5 ES 4.b

12. **Critical Thinking** What is the relationship between heat energy and condensation and evaporation?
5 ES 4.b

13. **Personal Narrative** You are a weather forecaster. Write a script for a television show in which you discuss a hurricane.   5 ES 4.d

 How can we tell what the weather will be?

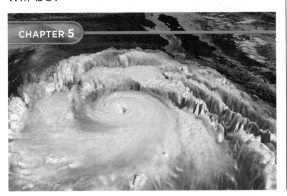
CHAPTER 5

Weather Clues!

Your goal is to infer the atmospheric conditions today in your area.

What to do

1. Observe the weather conditions.

2. Make a chart of your observations. Include a description of cloud cover, precipitation (if any), winds, and general temperature.

Analyze your results

▶ Estimate the air temperature and air pressure. You may use actual numbers or statements, such as "below normal," "about normal," or "above normal."

▶ Check your estimates against reports by television or radio weather forecasters.

▲ funnel cloud

 5 ES 4.d. Students know how to use weather maps and data to predict local weather and know that weather forecasts depend on many variables.

1 Which of the following *best* describes the force of atmospheric pressure on a blimp? 5 ES 4.e

A presses on the top

B presses on all sides

C presses on the top and bottom

D presses on the left and right

2 What happens because air has weight? 5 ES 4.e

A Air lifts objects.

B Air pushes on objects.

C Air drops objects.

D Air pulls objects.

3 In which season does California receive the *most* direct sunlight?

5 ES 4.a

A spring

B summer

C fall

D winter

4 What type of breeze is it when air moves from the land behind you toward the ocean in front of you? 5 ES 4.a

A sea breeze

B air breeze

C land breeze

D dense breeze

5 The table compares the temperatures of two cities at the same latitude.

Average Daily Tempertures		
City	January	July
San Francisco, CA	High 57° Low 46°	High 66° Low 54°
Wichita, KS	High 41° Low 21°	High 92° Low 70°

Which of the following identifies the independent variable in this investigation? 5 IE 6.d

A temperature

B month

C charts

D latitude

6 In which of the following processes does the atmosphere release heat? 5 ES 4.b

A precipitation

B evaporation

C condensation

D exploration

7 Which of the following *best* describes a cold front? 5 ES 4.c

A the cold, dry air of an air mass

B the leading edge of a warm air mass

C the leading edge of a cold air mass

D the warm, wet air of an air mass

8 **How does a hurricane form?** 5 ES 4.c

A Warm air rises over warm ocean water and becomes less dense. Surrounding air begins to spin in a counterclockwise direction.

B Cool air rises over cool ocean water and becomes more dense. Surrounding air begins to spin in a clockwise direction.

C Warm air rises over cool ocean water and becomes less dense. Surrounding air begins to spin counterclockwise direction.

D Cool air rises over warm ocean water and becomes more dense. Surrounding air begins to spin in a clockwise direction.

9 **A student collected this weather data from the local newspaper.**

Weekly Weather Data				
	Cloudiness	Temperature (°F)	Wind direction	Wind speed (mph)
Mon	Sunny	70	W	5
Tues	Cloudy	68	W	15
Wed	Partly Cloudy	64	W	15
Thu	Sunny	67	W	20
Fri	Sunny	65	W	2

What conclusion could she draw from this data? 5 IE 6.i

A This is the rainiest week in history.

B It is always sunny on Fridays.

C Mondays are warmer than Thursdays.

D The wind blew west all week.

10 **In North America, in what direction do cold and warm fronts tend to move?** 5 ES 4.d

A south to north

B north to south

C east to west

D west to east

11 **A student climbs over a mountain range. Which of the following describes the atmospheric pressure as the student climbs further up?** 5 ES 4.e

A The atmospheric pressure stays the same.

B The atmospheric pressure increases.

C The atmospheric pressure decreases.

D The atmospheric pressure changes rapidly.

12 **Which of the following describes why Earth's atmosphere is warmed unevenly by the Sun's heat?** 5 ES 4.a

A The sea heats more quickly than the atmosphere or the land.

B The land heats more quickly than the atmosphere or the sea.

C The sea cools more quickly than the atmosphere or the land.

D The atmosphere heats more quickly than the sea or the land.

CHAPTER 6

The Solar System

 What makes the planets move around the Sun?

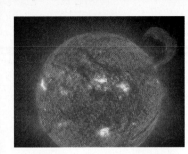

 5 ES 5. The solar system consists of planets and other bodies that orbit the Sun in predictable paths.

Literature

POEM

ELA R 5.3.7. Evaluate the author's use of various techniques (e.g., appeal of characters in a picture book, logic and credibility of plots and settings, use of figurative language) to influence readers' perspectives.

ELA W 5.2.1. Write narratives:
a. Establish a plot, point of view, setting, and conflict.
b. Show, rather than tell, the events of the story.

Stopping By A Planet on A Snowy Evening

Which world this is I do not know.
It's in our solar system though.
I'm thinking that it might be Mars,
Because it has that reddish glow.

But you know it could be Venus.
And if that's true, then just between us,
It might be wise to leave before
Any locals might have seen us.

Could be Pluto. Might be Neptune.
Don't they both have more than one moon?
I'm running out of oxygen.
I'd better figure this out soon.

Yes space is lovely, dark and deep.
For one mistake I now do weep:
In science class I was asleep.
In science class I was asleep…

Write About It

Response to Literature The space traveler in this poem cannot tell where he or she is. Write a fictional narrative as if you were the space traveler in this poem and were landing on this planet.

LOG ON **e-Journal** Write about it online @ **www.macmillanmh.com**

The Sun

Look and Wonder

On January 20, 2005, satellites that carried cell phone and cable signals suddenly shut down. They had been struck by a burst of energy. Where did this energy come from?

5 ES 5.a. Students know the Sun, an average star, is the central and largest body in the solar system and is composed primarily of hydrogen and helium.

How do the sizes of Earth and the Sun compare?

Purpose

To study the size difference between Earth and the Sun.

Procedure

1. **Use Numbers** What proportion does the size of Earth have to the size of the Sun?

2. **Use Numbers** What would the diameter of the Sun be if the diameter of Earth was 0.5 cm?

3. **Make a Model** Use appropriate tools to design a model of earth and the Sun to this scale.

4. How many Earths would it take to cover the length of the model Sun's diameter?

Draw Conclusions

5. **Communicate** Explain why this model does, or does not, show an accurate comparison between the diameters of the Sun and Earth.

Explore More

How does the Moon's diameter compare with that of Earth? Do research to answer this question and make a model to represent the difference in their sizes.

 5 IE 6.f. Select appropriate tools (e.g., thermometers, meter sticks, balances, and graduated cylinders) and make quantitative observations.

- **meter stick**
- **ruler**
- **colored pencils**
- **clear tape**

Step **2**

	Diameter
The Sun	1,390,000 kilometers
Earth	12,760 kilometers

Step **3**

Read and Learn

Main Idea 5 ES 5.a

The Sun is a star made of hydrogen and helium. The Sun is located at the center of the solar system and is also its largest object.

Vocabulary

star, p. 299

astronomical unit, p. 299

fusion, p. 302

LOG ON **e-Glossary**
@ www.macmillanmh.com

Reading Skill

Draw Conclusions

Text Clues	Conclusions

Sun

Earth

Earth and the Sun are shown here on a scale of 1 centimeter = 50,000 kilometers. At this size, Earth and the Sun are 2,992 centimeters (about 98 feet) apart.

What is the Sun?

The Sun is a star. A **star** is an object that produces its own energy, including heat and light. The planets and the other objects in the solar system are not stars because they do not produce their own light.

The stars that produce the most energy make about ten million times more energy than the Sun. The least-productive stars make only one-hundreth as much energy as the Sun.

The Sun is an average-sized star and the largest object in the solar system. The Sun's diameter is about 1,390,000 kilometers (863,706 miles). If the Sun were a hollow ball, more than a million Earths could fit inside it. The Sun looks larger than the other stars that can be seen in the night sky because it is much closer to Earth.

The mean, or average, distance between the Sun and Earth is 149,591,000 kilometers (92,960,000 miles). This number is known as one **astronomical** (as•truh•NAH•mi•kulh) **unit** (AU). The closest stars to the solar system are found in the Alpha Centauri star system. They are about 271,931 AUs away.

Finding the Sun's Mass

It is impossible to measure the weight of the Sun. After all, the Sun cannot be put on a scale.

However, you can measure the *mass* of the Sun, or the amount of matter in it. The mass of the Sun can be calculated if you know two facts. The first fact is the length of time it takes for a planet to make one trip around the Sun (for Earth, that is 365.24 days). The second is the distance between the planet and the Sun (for Earth, that is 149,591,000 kilometers).

Using this information, scientists have calculated the Sun's mass to be 2 million trillion trillion kilograms. That's 2,000,000,000,000,000,000, 000,000,000,000 kilograms! This is 745 times greater than the mass of all the other objects in the solar system put together. As a matter of fact, the mass of the Sun makes up 99.8% of all the mass in the solar system.

 Quick Check

Draw Conclusions Why are the planets not stars?

Critical Thinking Why are astronomical units used to measure distances rather than kilometers?

What are the parts of the Sun?

The Sun is a huge sphere made up mostly of two very light gases, hydrogen and helium. About 71% of the Sun's mass is made up of hydrogen. Another 27% is made up of helium. Other materials, such as oxygen and carbon, make up the remaining 2% of the Sun's mass.

Most of the energy that the Sun produces is formed in its core. At its core, the Sun has a temperature of 10 million to 20 million degrees Celsius. The pressure is more than 1 billion times greater than the air pressure at sea level on Earth.

The radiation layer, which is next to the core, moves the energy produced in the core in every direction. It can take millions of years for energy to move out of this layer.

In the convection layer, gases with different energies move in circles in a way similar to air with different densities. Energy moves out of this layer in about a week.

The photosphere is the visible surface of the Sun. It is not a solid surface, but rather a layer of gases. The photosphere is cooler than the core. Its temperature is about 5,730°C (10,346°F).

The next layer of the Sun is the chromosphere, or the inner layer of the Sun's atmosphere. When it can be seen, it looks like a red circle around the Sun.

The corona is the outermost layer of the Sun's atmosphere. The corona takes on different shapes around the Sun depending on changes in the temperature of the photosphere.

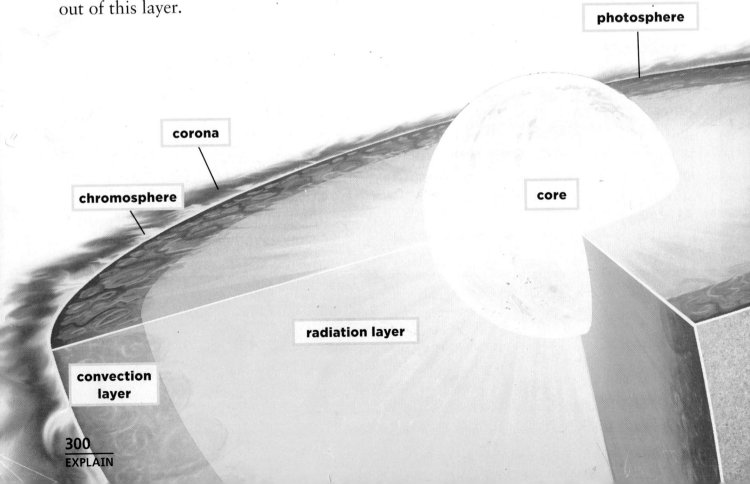

photosphere

corona

chromosphere

core

radiation layer

convection layer

Solar Flares

Solar flares are bursts of heat and energy that stretch out from the corona and chromosphere into space. Sometimes this energy disrupts satellites, interfering with TV, radio, and cell phone communication systems.

Energy from solar flares also causes displays of different-colored lights in the upper atmosphere. These lights are called the *aurora borealis* (uh•RAW•uh bawr•ee•AL•is), or northern lights. The northern lights are most often seen in Alaska, Canada, and the northern United States. They are only seen in the southern United States when the Sun releases large amounts of energy.

Solar flares are also sometimes associated with sunspots. Sunspots, or dark spots on the Sun, are regions of the photosphere that have a lower temperature than the surrounding regions.

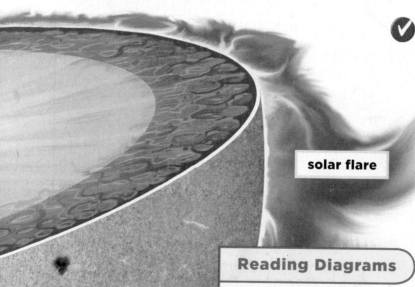

solar flare

sunspot

✔ Quick Check

Draw Conclusions Why does it take millions of years for energy that moves in every direction to leave the radiation layer?

Critical Thinking Which three layers of the Sun can be seen?

Reading Diagrams

What is the layer of the Sun between the core and the convection layer called?

Clue: Find the labels on the diagram for the core and for the convection layer, and look for the name of the layer between them.

How does the Sun produce energy?

More than 100 years ago, Albert Einstein discovered a relationship between energy and mass. He expressed the discovery in what has become one of the most famous equations in science:

$$E = mc^2$$

The E stands for energy. The m stands for mass. The c represents the speed of light. The little 2 over the c means that the speed of light is squared, or multiplied by itself. This equation tells us that a little bit of mass can be changed into a lot of energy.

As you learned earlier in this lesson, the Sun is mostly made up of hydrogen. Hydrogen has very little mass. However, inside the Sun hydrogen particles smash together to make helium. This smashing together of particles is called **fusion** (FYEW•zhuhn). A little bit of mass is lost when hydrogen particles combine to make helium. According to Einstein's equation, that little bit of mass is changed into energy. We experience this energy as light and heat, as well as other kinds of energy that cannot be seen.

✔ Quick Check

Draw Conclusions What happens when hydrogen particles collide?

Critical Thinking What would happen if all of the hydrogen in the Sun turned into helium?

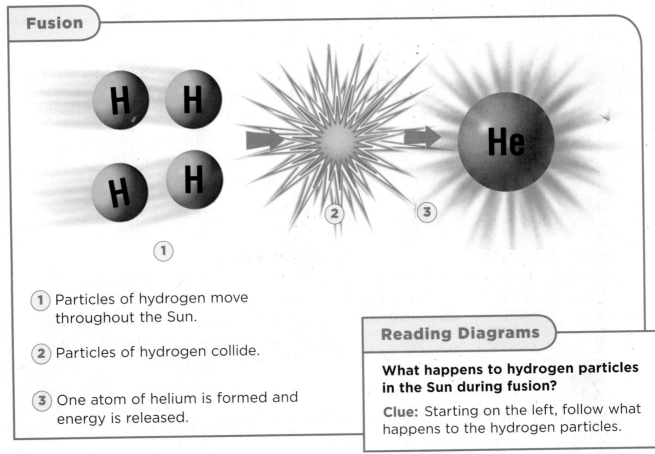

Fusion

1. Particles of hydrogen move throughout the Sun.

2. Particles of hydrogen collide.

3. One atom of helium is formed and energy is released.

Reading Diagrams

What happens to hydrogen particles in the Sun during fusion?

Clue: Starting on the left, follow what happens to the hydrogen particles.

Lesson Review

Summarize the Main Idea

The Sun is a star and the largest object in the solar system. (pp. 298–299)

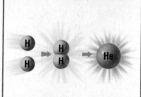

The Sun produces energy when hydrogen combines to form helium and energy. (pp. 300–302)

Make a FOLDABLES Study Guide

Make a two-tab book (see p. 481). Use the titles shown. On the inside of each tab, draw conclusions about the title.

The Sun is a star.

The Sun produces energy.

Think, Talk, and Write

1 **Main Idea** What is the largest object in the solar system?

2 **Vocabulary** An object in the solar system that produces heat and light is a _____.

3 **Draw Conclusions** What causes energy to be released inside the Sun?

Text Clues	Conclusions

4 **Critical Thinking** How would Earth be affected if the Sun stopped producing energy?

5 **Test Practice** All of the following are part of the solar system EXCEPT
A the Sun.
B Earth.
C the Moon.
D the stars.

6 **Test Practice** The Sun is made up of all of the following materials EXCEPT
A hydrogen.
B helium.
C carbon.
D steam.

Writing Link

Descriptive Writing
Using what you have learned in this lesson, write about the Sun. Discuss the layers of the Sun, fusion, and the Sun's size and mass.

Math Link

Earth's Mass
The Sun's mass is roughly 330,000 times Earth's mass. If you made a model of the Sun with a mass that was 1,000 kilograms, what would be the mass of Earth in grams?

LOG ON e-**Review** Summaries and quizzes online @ www.macmillanmh.com

Focus on Inquiry Skills

Draw Conclusions

Scientists began recording data about sunspots in 1749. After they collected years of data, scientists concluded that the number of sunspots increases and decreases during an 11-year cycle. From the beginning of the cycle, the number of sunspots tends to increase over a period of about five years to a maximum number. Over the next six years, the number of sunspots decreases to a minimum number. A new cycle begins when the number of sunspots increases.

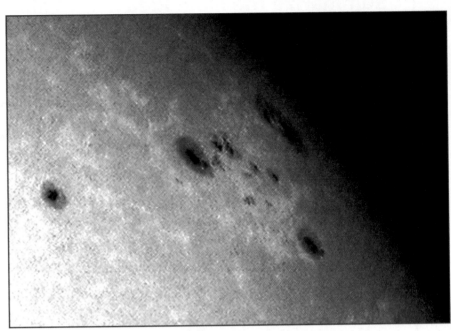

▲ Scientists collect data about the number of sunspots that occur on the Sun.

① Learn It

When you draw conclusions, you look at all the facts and decide what can be based on those facts. Be careful not to "jump to conclusions," or to draw conclusions that are not supported by the data.

Look at the chart. It lists the number of sunspots recorded each year beginning in 1750. When scientists looked at the first two years of data, they could have concluded that the number of sunspots always decreased. However, in 1752, the number of sunspots increased. This means that their conclusion was no longer supported by the data. They needed to collect more data and draw a new conclusion.

When you gather data, it is important to record it. Having a record of your data gives you the information that you need to be able to draw conclusions.

Sunspots from 1750 to 1761	
Year	Sunspots
1750	1,001
1751	572
1752	574
1753	368
1754	147
1755	115
1756	122
1757	389
1758	671
1759	648
1760	754
1761	1,030

Source: National Aeronautics and Space Administration

5 IE 6.h. Draw conclusions from scientific evidence and indicate whether further information is needed to support a specific conclusion.

❷ Try It

Use the chart of sunspots from 1750 to 1761 to draw conclusions as you answer the following questions.

▶ In which year would you conclude that this cycle began? Why?

▶ If you were a scientist studying sunspots, in which years did you observe changes in the number of sunspots that might make you question the existence of a cycle? Why?

▶ If you only had ten years of data, but you hypothesized that the sunspot cycle was longer than ten years, what would you have to do before you could draw a conclusion?

❸ Apply It

This chart shows data about sunspots and solar flares from 1993 to 2004. Use it to draw conclusions as you answer the following questions.

▶ In which year do you conclude that an 11-year cycle began? How do you know?

▶ What can you conclude about the frequency of sunspots between 1993 and 2004 compared to between 1750 and 1761?

▶ What can you conclude about the expected sunspot activity in 2005 and 2006?

▶ Scientists recently began recording data about the number of solar flares that occur every year. Their hypothesis was that solar flares increase and decrease on the same cycle as sunspots. Would you conclude that the recorded data supports this hypothesis? Why?

▶ What could you do to provide additional support for your conclusion that solar flares increase and decrease on the same cycle as sunspots?

Sunspots from 1993 to 2004		
Year	Sunspots	Solar flares
1993	657	2,541
1994	359	1,066
1995	210	639
1996	103	280
1997	258	790
1998	769	2,423
1999	1,118	3,963
2000	1,433	4,474
2001	1,331	3,597
2002	1,245	3,223
2003	763	1,552
2004	486	728

Source: National Aeronautics and Space Administration and the National Oceanic and Atmospheric Administration

The Structure of the Solar System

Look and Wonder

As the Sun sets over Paranal Observatory in Chile, you can see stars and planets in the sky. The three brighter objects are Venus (center), Mercury (below), and Saturn (left). How can you tell how far away these planets are?

5 ES 5.b. Students know the solar system includes the planet Earth, the Moon, the Sun, eight other planets and their satellites, and smaller objects, such as asteroids and comets.

How far apart are the planets?

Purpose

To learn about the distances between the planets by making a model.

Procedure

① Let the length of each paper towel equal 1 Astronomical Unit. Using the chart, lay out the number of paper towels you need to show the distance from the Sun to Pluto.

② **Make a Model** Mark the location of the Sun and each planet on the paper towels.

Draw Conclusions

③ **Analyze Data** Compare the distances between Mercury and Mars, Mars and Jupiter, and Jupiter and Neptune. Which are farthest apart?

④ **Infer** What can you conclude about the distances between the planets in the solar system?

Explore More

Your model has all of the planets in a line. Actually, the planets move in circles around the Sun. What kind of model would you make to show the positions of the planets at a specific time? Write instructions that others can follow to make the model.

 5 IE 6.c. Plan and conduct a simple investigation based on a student-developed question and write instructions others can follow to carry out the procedure.

Materials

- paper towels
- markers
- ruler

Step ①

Distances of the Planets from the Sun

Planet	Distance in A.U.
Mercury	.39
Venus	.7
Earth	1
Mars	1.5
Jupiter	5.2
Saturn	9.5
Uranus	19.2
Neptune	30

Step ②

Main Idea 5 ES 5.b

The solar system is made up of the Sun, the planets and their moons, comets, asteroids, and meteoroids.

Vocabulary

solar system, p.308
telescope, p.308
moon, p.310
satellite, p.310
asteroid, p.312
comet, p.312
meteor, p.312

LOG ON e-Glossary
@ www.macmillanmh.com

Reading Skill

Summarize

Summary

What is the solar system?

The Sun is at the center of the solar system. The word *solar* means "of the Sun." The **solar system** is a system of objects of, or around, the Sun.

Besides the Sun, the objects in the solar system include the eight planets and their moons. From nearest to farthest from the Sun, the planets are Mercury, Venus, Earth, Mars, Jupiter, Saturn, Uranus, and Neptune.

In 1610 Galileo Galilei used a telescope to observe the planets and saw moons revolving around Jupiter. A **telescope** uses lenses to see distant objects. Before Galileo's discovery, people thought that everything in the solar system revolved around Earth.

Telescopes take pictures of and collect data about objects in the solar system. Scientists have launched some telescopes into space so they can gather data without interference from Earth's atmosphere.

The solar system also contains several *dwarf planets*. These include Pluto, once considered the ninth planet, and the larger, more distant 2003 UB313 (named Eris). Ceres, the largest object in the *asteroid belt* (located between the orbits of Mars and Jupiter), is also a dwarf planet.

Space probes have examined all eight planets. Only Earth's Moon has been explored by *astronauts*—people who travel in space.

✓ **Quick Check**

Summarize How have telescopes improved our knowledge of the solar system?

Critical Thinking How did Galileo's observation provide evidence against the previous hypothesis?

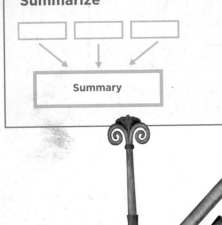

◀ Galileo discovered Jupiter's moons using this telescope.

The Solar System

Venus

Sun

Mercury

Mars

Earth

Jupiter

Uranus

Saturn

Neptune

Planetary Data from NASA

Planet Name	Radius at the Equator (km)	Mean Surface Temperature (°C)	Surface Materials	Rings
Mercury	2,440	179	Rock	No
Venus	6,052	482	Rock	No
Earth	6,378	15	Rock	No
Mars	3,397	-63	Rock	No
Jupiter	71,492	-121	Gas	Yes
Saturn	60,268	-125	Gas	Yes
Uranus	25,559	-193	Gas	Yes
Neptune	24,746	-193 to -153	Gas	Yes

Reading Charts

Which planets have gas as their only surface material?

Clue: Find Surface Materials column of the chart.

Ganymede (Jupiter)   **Moon (Earth)**

1 cm
1,000 km

Mimas (Saturn)   **Hyperion (Saturn)**

1 cm
100 km

Reading Photos

How large are these moons?

Clue: Look at the scales.

What is a moon?

A **moon** is an object that circles around a planet. Different planets have different numbers and sizes of moons. Mercury and Venus do not have moons. Earth has one moon, Mars has two, and Jupiter has at least 63 moons. Saturn has 49 moons. Astronomers have discovered at least 27 moons around Uranus and 13 moons orbiting Neptune. The dwarf planet Pluto has at least three moons.

The sizes of the moons vary. Some of the moons are very small. Seven of the moons in the solar system are actually bigger than Pluto! These include Jupiter's Ganymede, which is the largest moon, and Earth's Moon.

Moons are also called satellites (SAT•uh•lights). A **satellite** is an object in space that circles around another object. The moons of the planets are natural satellites. Man-made satellites circle around Earth. These provide weather information and are part of communication systems.

▶ Earth's Moon is the only moon that can be seen without using a telescope.

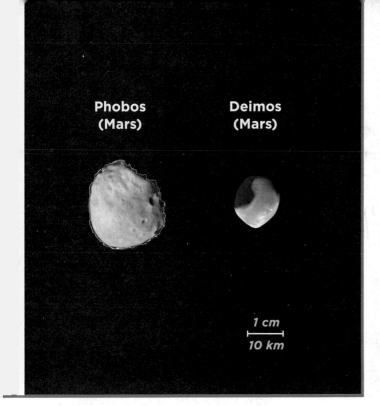

Phobos
(Mars)

Deimos
(Mars)

1 cm
10 km

Forming Craters

When objects in space collide, the impact forms a crater, or a hole. The surface of Earth's Moon has millions of these craters. The craters are easy to see because the impact knocks the surface material away so the darker rock underneath shows through.

Most objects that fall toward Earth burn up in Earth's atmosphere. Since the Moon has no atmosphere, the objects that fall toward it do not burn up. As a result, the Moon has more craters than Earth.

 **Quick Check**

Summarize Describe Earth's Moon.

Critical Thinking What is the difference between a moon and a satellite?

≡Quick Lab

Moon Craters

1 Cover the floor with newspaper and place a pan on the paper.

2 **Make a Model** Fill the pan with about 1 inch of flour. Gently tap pan until the flour layer is smooth. Then sprinkle cinnamon on top to represent topsoil.

3 Measure the diameter of three different-sized marbles.

4 Drop the largest marble from about 3 inches straight above the pan. Remove it carefully, then measure the diameter and depth of the crater.

5 Drop the other marble over different spots from the same height. Measure each crater and record the data.

6 Are the craters bigger or smaller than the diameter of the marbles?

7 What do you see at the crater sites? Why did this happen?

8 How is your model similar to what happens when an object hits the surface of the Moon?

Comets have tails of dust and gases.

What are the smaller objects in the solar system?

An **asteroid** (AS•tuh•roid) is a rock that revolves around the Sun. Most of the thousands of asteroids in the solar system are located between Mars and Jupiter in the asteroid belt. Many asteroids have irregular shapes, somewhat like a potato. Some asteroids are less than 1 mile wide, while others can be up to 500 miles wide!

A **comet** is a mixture of frozen gases, ice, dust, and rock that moves in an irregular circle around the Sun. When a comet is far from the Sun, it is usually no more than a few kilometers in diameter. However, as it gets closer, energy from the Sun warms the surface of the comet. This makes the ice melt. Then a glowing ball of gases and dust, which is called a coma, forms around the comet. Once the comet forms, the

Sun's energy shapes it into shimmering tails of dust and of gases that may stretch out millions of kilometers into space from the head of the comet.

Because the tails are produced by energy from the Sun, they always blow away from the Sun. Therefore, as a comet moves around the Sun, the comet head always stays closest to the Sun and the tails trail out behind it.

The solar system is full of other small objects. In space, these objects are called *meteoroids* (MEE•tee•uh•roids). The objects that cross paths with Earth and enter Earth's atmosphere are called **meteors** (MEE•tee•uhrs).

 Quick Check

Summarize What are asteroids, comets, and meteors?

Critical Thinking Which small objects in the solar system change names depending on where they are?

Lesson Review

Summarize the Main Idea

The Sun and eight planets and their moons make up the solar system. (pp. 308–309)

Many of the planets have **moons**. (p. 310–311)

Asteroids, **comets**, and **meteors** are smaller objects in the solar system. (p. 312)

Make a FOLDABLES™ Study Guide

Make a layered-look book (see p. 481). Use the titles shown. On the inside of each tab, summarize what you know about that topic.

Think, Talk, and Write

1. **Main Idea** What does the solar system include? *The Sun planets moons and satellites*

2. **Vocabulary** The Sun, planets, and moons are parts of the _Solar System_

3. **Summarize** Draw the orbits of the planets and describe how their temperatures relate to the distances the planets are from the Sun.

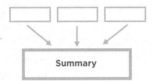

Summary

4. **Critical Thinking** Many people believed that Earth was at the center of the solar system. Explain how Galileo showed that this belief was wrong. *He saw moons orbiting around Jupiter*

5. **Test Practice** **What instrument does a scientist use to observe the solar system?**
   A microscope
   B telescope
   C magnifying glass
   D reflector

6. **Test Practice** **Mars and Mercury are alike EXCEPT**
   A they both have rocky surfaces.
   B they both are far from the Sun.
   C they both have moons.
   D they both have oxygen.

Math Link

Calculating Distance Between Planets
If Pluto is 39.4 A.U. from the Sun and Jupiter is 5.2 A.U. from the Sun, how far apart are they from each other?

Social Studies Link

Sky Observations
How long have people been watching the different objects in the sky? Use reference sources to write a report about the history of a specific object. Include current data and photographs.

Be a Scientist

Materials

spoon

frozen yogurt

seltzer water

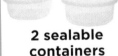
2 sealable containers

measuring cup

desk light

stopwatch

Why do comets have tails?

Form a Hypothesis

Comets are made of frozen gases, ice, dust, and rock. The orbit of a comet around the Sun is usually a long oval with the Sun closer to one end of the oval. At one end of the orbit, the gases of the comet form a tail. How does temperature affect the formation of the tail? Write your answer as a hypothesis in the form "*If temperature _____ , then gases in the comet are released to form a tail.*"

Test Your Hypothesis

1. Using a spoon, mix 2 cups of melted frozen yogurt with 1 cup of seltzer water. These ingredients represent the frozen water and frozen gases in a comet.

2. Divide the mixture into two sealable containers. Put the lids on the containers and freeze the containers overnight. Mark an oval orbit for your comet to follow.

3. **Make a Model** Take one container out of the freezer and put it 3 inches from a desk light. This container represents a comet when it is close to the Sun.

4. **Make a Model** Take the other container and put it 3 feet from the desk light. This container represents a comet when it is far away from the Sun.

5. **Observe** Watch the containers of comet material as they melt. Look for changes in the surface, such as bubbles or melting.

6. **Record Data** Note the surface changes that you see. Record the time at which you first see bubbles form and when the contents of the container look melted.

Step 1

Step 2

Step 3

Step 4

5 IE 6.c. Plan and conduct a simple investigation based on a student-developed question and write instructions others can follow to carry out the procedure.

Draw Conclusions

1️⃣ Did the test support your hypothesis? Explain why or why not.

2️⃣ **Draw Conclusions** Where on a comet's path around the Sun would you expect the most melting gas to be present?

Inquiry Guided

Does the direction of a comet's tail change as it goes around the Sun?

Form a Hypothesis

Energy from the Sun radiates out into space in all directions. What do you think this means about the direction of a comet's tail? Write your answer as a hypothesis in the form *"If energy radiates out from the Sun in all directions, then . . ."*

Test Your Hypothesis

Design a plan to test your hypothesis. Then write out the materials and resources you need and the steps you will do. Record your results and observations as you follow your plan.

Draw Conclusions

Did your test support your hypothesis? Why or why not? Present your results to your classmates.

Inquiry Open

You have studied comets that orbit in ovals around the Sun. How do you think a different-shaped orbit around the Sun would affect the tail of a comet? Come up with a question to investigate and design an experiment to answer your question. Your experiment must be organized to test only one variable, or one item being changed. Your experiment must be written so that another group can complete the experiment by following your instructions.

Remember to follow the steps of the scientific process.

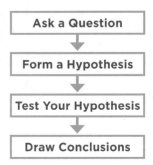

Ask a Question

↓

Form a Hypothesis

↓

Test Your Hypothesis

↓

Draw Conclusions

Gravity and Orbit

Look and Wonder

For about 4.5 billion years, the Moon has circled around Earth. What has kept the Moon in its path around Earth for so long?

5 ES 5.c. Students know the path of a planet around the Sun is due to the gravitational attraction between the Sun and the planet.

What keeps the Moon moving around Earth?

- tennis ball
- square of fabric
- 0.5-meter-long piece of string
- graph paper

Form a Hypothesis

If you let go of a ball being swung in a circle, where will the ball go? Write a hypothesis in the form *"If I let go of a ball being swung in a circle, then..."*

Test Your Hypothesis

1. Place the ball on the fabric and bring the four corners together so it covers the ball. Then tie one end of the string around the four corners, forming a pouch.

2. △ **Be Careful!** Lean forward and slowly whirl the ball in a circle near your feet.

3. **Observe** Let go of the string. Watch the path that the ball takes.

4. **Record Data** Draw and label a diagram showing the path the ball took when you let it go.

5. Repeat the experiment, letting the ball go at three different spots on the circle.

Step 1

Draw Conclusions

6. Did the experiment support your hypothesis? Why or why not?

7. If this activity models the solar system, what do you, the ball, and the string represent?

Step 2

Explore More

What results would you expect if you repeated the experiment using a lighter ball? Form a hypothesis, do the experiment, analyze your data, and write a report.

 5 IE 6.g. Record data by using appropriate graphic representations (including charts, graphs, and labeled diagrams) and make inferences based on those data.

Main Idea 5 ES 5.c

The force of gravity keeps the planets in their orbits around the Sun.

Vocabulary

gravity, p. 318

orbit, p. 320

inertia, p. 320

ellipse, p. 321

tide, p. 322

LOG ON e-Glossary
@ www.macmillanmh.com

Reading Skill

Cause and Effect

Cause → Effect
→
→
→
→

SCIENCE QUEST — Explore gravity and orbits with Team Earth.

What is gravity?

Each planet in the solar system is drawn toward the Sun by gravity. **Gravity** is a force of attraction, or pull, between any two objects. The strength of the pull of gravity is different between different pairs of objects. Gravity is affected by the mass of the two objects. It is also affected by the distances between the objects.

All objects have mass and all objects are pulled toward one another by gravity. However, the strength of the pull of gravity decreases when the mass of the two objects decreases.

As an example, look at the pull of gravity between you and Earth as compared to the pull of gravity you would feel if you were on the Moon. Your mass stays the same no matter where you are. The mass of Earth is greater than the mass of the Moon. This means that the mass of you and the Earth is greater than the mass of you and the Moon. The pull of gravity between you and the Earth is stronger than the pull between you and the Moon. In fact, the Moon's gravity is about 1/6 of Earth's gravity.

Astronaut John Young can jump higher on the Moon than on Earth because the Moon's gravity is about 1/6 of Earth's gravity.

Mass = 100
Weight = 100 lbs

Mass = 100
Weight = 236 lbs

Mass = 100
Weight = 16.5 lbs

Earth
Gravity = 1

Jupiter
Gravity = 2.36

Moon
Gravity = 0.165

Reading Diagrams

What is the relationship between weight and gravity?

Clue: Look at the weight of the person on the different planets and the gravity of each planet.

Note: Planets are not shown to scale.

Although your mass stays the same, you would weigh less on the Moon than you do on Earth. *Weight* is defined as the product of mass and gravity. This means that your weight depends on both your mass and the force of gravity wherever you are located.

Gravity is a force that acts over a distance. Two objects do not have to touch each other to produce a force of gravity between them. The strength of gravity depends on how far apart the objects are. The pull gets weaker when the objects are farther apart.

The pull of gravity between Earth and the Sun acts across about 150 million kilometers of space. Gravity also acts across roughly 6 billion kilometers of space between the Sun and Pluto. Since the distance is farther between the Sun and Pluto, the pull of gravity between the Sun and Pluto is weaker than the pull of gravity between the Sun and Earth.

Quick Check

Cause and Effect Suppose you have a dog that weighs 50 lbs. How much would it weigh on a planet that had 3.45 times Earth's gravity?

Critical Thinking Jupiter is about 320 times larger than Earth but its gravity is only 2.36 times larger than Earth's gravity. What might cause this difference?

What keeps objects in orbit?

An **orbit** is a path one object takes around another object. Planets orbit around the Sun and moons orbit around their planets. Planets are held in their orbits by the force of gravity between each planet and the Sun.

If gravity was the only force acting on a planet, the planet would be pulled into the Sun. What prevents this from happening? All objects have a property called inertia (in•UR•shuh). **Inertia** is the tendency of a moving object to keep moving in a straight line.

As a space vehicle orbits Earth, members of the crew float in the cabin. They are weightless. Why aren't the crew or other objects inside the space vehicle being pulled toward Earth by gravity?

Like all objects in an orbit, the pull of gravity on the space vehicle is balanced by its forward motion. If the space vehicle sped up, its forward motion would overcome the pull of Earth's gravity. The vehicle would pull out of that orbit and move further away from Earth.

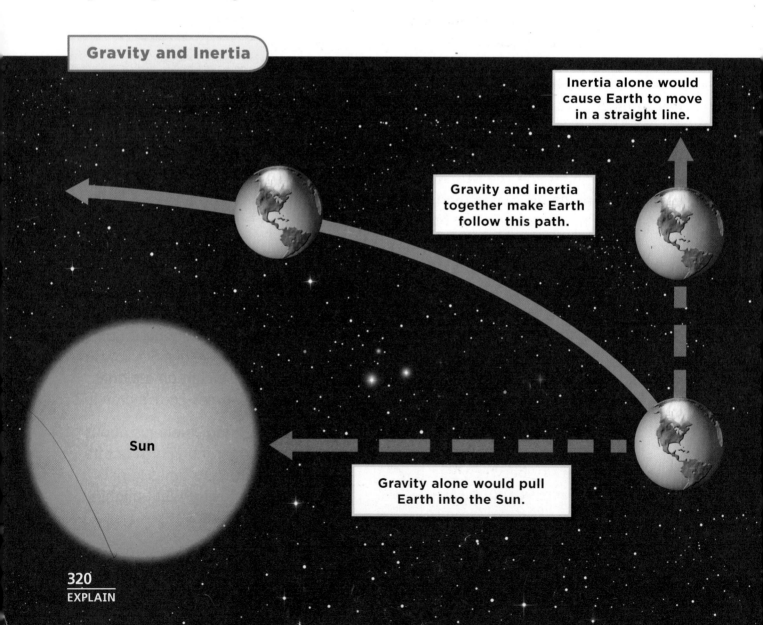

Gravity and Inertia

Inertia alone would cause Earth to move in a straight line.

Gravity and inertia together make Earth follow this path.

Gravity alone would pull Earth into the Sun.

Sun

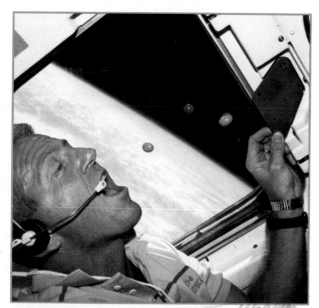

▲ This astronaut catches weightless candy while in a space vehicle orbiting Earth.

Planets in the solar system act very much like the space vehicle. As the planets orbit the Sun, they tend to fall toward it. But at the same time, their forward motion tends to make them move away from it.

The effect of these two motions makes the planets move in a nearly circular orbit called an **ellipse** (uh•LIPS). When the Earth is closest to the Sun, it is 147,098,074 km away. When Earth is furthest from the Sun, it is 152,097,701 km away. This 5 million kilometer difference shows that Earth's orbit is an ellipse and not a perfect circle.

✔ Quick Check

Cause and Effect Why does food float in the space vehicle if the astronauts don't hold on to it?

Critical Thinking What do you think pilots of the space vehicle do to return to Earth?

Quick Lab

Gravity and Inertia

1. Pour beans into a sock. Tie a knot in the top of the sock.

2. Place the pencil on the ground. The pencil will be your target.

3. ⚠ **Be careful.** Start 20 ft from the target. Holding the sock in your hand at waist height, run toward the target.

4. Drop the sock at the moment the sock is above the target. After you drop the sock, you can stop running.

5. **Record Data** Record the distance the sock lands from the target.

6. **Analyze Data** Where did the sock land? Why?

7. Repeat this experiment. Does the sock always land in about the same place?

8. How is what happens to the sock similar to a planet's orbit?

What causes the tides?

The pull of gravity from the Moon and from the Sun both affect Earth. These gravitational pulls cause a bulge or bump in the surface of the Earth. Although the Moon is much smaller than the Sun, it is also much closer to Earth. The Sun is so much farther away that it has less than half the effect on Earth's surface than the pull of the Moon.

On the part of the Earth's surface that is rocky, this pull is so slight we do not notice it. However, the pull can be seen in large bodies of water such as the oceans. This pull causes the **tide**, or the rise and fall of the ocean's surface.

Most oceans have two high tides and two low tides during a 24-hour day. As the Moon orbits around the Earth, its gravity pulls the water on the side nearest to it away from the land. This causes low tide.

About twice a month, the Sun and Moon line up and both pulls are added together. This causes higher high tides and lower low tides, called spring tides. The tides with the smallest range occur between spring tides. These more moderate tides are called neap tides. They are caused when the Sun and Moon pull in different directions and their pulls partly cancel each other.

✓ Quick Check

Cause and Effect Why do stronger tides occur when the Sun and Moon are lined up?

Critical Thinking Why do spring tides and neap tides occur twice a month?

high tide

low tide

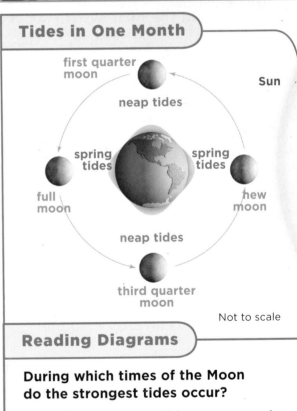

Tides in One Month

first quarter moon

neap tides

Sun

spring tides

spring tides

full moon

new moon

neap tides

third quarter moon

Not to scale

Reading Diagrams

During which times of the Moon do the strongest tides occur?

Clue: The strongest tides are caused when gravity from the Sun and from the Moon pull together on Earth.

LOG ON *Science in Motion* Watch how gravity causes tides @ www.macmillanmh.com

Lesson Review

Summarize the Main Idea

The **pull of gravity** depends on the masses of two objects and the distance between them. (pp. 318–319)

An object stays in **orbit** because the pull of gravity is balanced by its forward motion. (pp. 320–321)

Tides are caused by the gravitational pull of the Sun and the Moon on Earth. (p. 322)

Make a FOLDABLES Study Guide

Make a three-tab book (see p. 481) Use the titles shown. On the inside of each fold, list the causes and effects of that topic related to gravity.

Pull of Gravity

Orbits

Tides

Think, Talk, and Write

1 **Main Idea** How is the gravity between two objects affected by their masses?

2 **Vocabulary** The rise and fall of the ocean's surface is the _____.

3 **Cause and Effect** What would happen to a space vehicle in orbit around Earth if it sped up?

Cause → Effect
→
→
→
→

4 **Critical Thinking** How are mass and weight different?

5 **Test Practice** **Which force keeps Earth in its orbit around the Sun?**
   A lift
   B thrust
   C gravity
   D pressure

6 **Test Practice** **The tide that occurs twice a month when the Sun and Moon pull in different directions is**
   A spring tide.
   B neap tide.
   C low tide.
   D high tide.

Writing Link

Fictional Narrative

Write a story in which the main character is affected in some way by gravity. The gravity may be the same as Earth's, or stronger or weaker.

Math Link

Calculating Weight

If an astronaut weighs 100 lbs on Earth and is now on a planet with a gravity that is 1.325 times the gravity on Earth, what is the astronaut's weight on this planet?

Voyager Discoveries

In 1977, NASA launched the Voyager Interstellar Mission to explore Jupiter, Saturn, Uranus, Neptune, and their moons. The trip had to be very precisely planned. Speeds and distances had to be accurately calculated. The two Voyager spacecraft had to be close enough to each planet to collect data and to get a push from that planet's gravity in order to be propelled toward their next destination. At the same time, the spacecraft had to be far enough away from the planets that they would not go into orbit around them. All of NASA's careful planning worked. The Voyager mission has provided scientists with new and closer looks at our farthest neighbors.

Jupiter - 1979
Images show Jupiter's rings. Volcanic activity is observed on Io, one of Jupiter's moons.

1980

Saturn - 1980-1991
Scientists get a close look at Saturn's rings. They contain structures that look like spokes or braids.

ELA R 5.2.3. Discern main ideas and concepts presented in texts, identifying and assessing evidence that supports those ideas.

After observing these planets, the Voyager spacecraft kept traveling. They are the first human-made objects to go beyond the heliosphere. The heliosphere is the region of space reached by the energy of our Sun. It extends far beyond the most distant planets in the solar system.

Uranus - 1986

Scientists discover dark rings around Uranus. They also see 10 new moons, bringing Uranus's total to 15 moons. Voyager sends back detailed images and data on the planet, its moons, and dark rings.

1990

Neptune - 1989

Large storms are seen on the planet. One of these storms is Neptune's Great Dark Spot. Neptune was originally thought to be too cold to support this kind of weather.

 Write About It

Cause and Effect

1. What caused the Voyager spacecraft to be propelled toward their next destination?
2. What was an effect of the Voyager mission?

LOG ON e-Journal Write about it online @ www.macmillanmh.com

Cause and Effect

▶ Look for the reason why something happens to find a cause.

▶ An effect is what happens as a result of a cause.

AMERICAN MUSEUM OF NATURAL HISTORY

Writing in Science

WHAT WOULD HAPPEN IF GRAVITY WENT AWAY?

A good explanation

▶ describes what happened.

▶ uses time-order words such as *first, second,* and *third.*

▶ lists what happens in an organized and logical way.

The first thing I would do if gravity went away in my room, would be to secure the furniture to keep it from floating around. Then, I would put all my small things into a box so I'd know where to find them. Finally, I would practice somersaults and learn to walk on the ceiling.

Write About It

Explanatory Writing You know that the pull of gravity keeps everything on Earth from floating off into space. Look at the picture. Explain what would happen if gravity suddenly stopped working?

LOG ON e-Journal Write about it online @ **www.macmillanmh.com**

Reaching for the Moon

The Moon is an average of 238,871 miles from Earth. The average fifth grader is 56 inches tall. Susana uses this information to calculate that it would take 270,265,474.3 students lined up head-to-toe to reach the Moon.

Since you cannot have .3 of a student, Susana rounded her calculation to the nearest whole number.

This is how:

270,265,47<u>4</u>.3 = 270,265,474

Rounding Numbers

▶ Once you have the answer to your problem, underline the place to which you want to round.

▶ Look at the digit to the right.

▶ If the digit is 5 or greater, round up. If the digit is less than 5, round down.

 Solve It

1. It would take 420,412,960 yards to reach the Moon. Round this number to the nearest hundred thousand.

2. It would take 1,261,238,880 feet to reach the Moon. Round this number to the nearest thousand.

MA NS 5.1.1. Estimate, round, and manipulate very large (e.g., millions) and very small (e.g., thousandths) numbers.

Summarize the Main Ideas

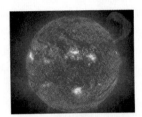

The Sun is a star made of hydrogen and helium. It is located at the center of the solar system and is its largest object. (pp. 296–303)

The solar system is made up of the Sun, the planets and their moons, comets, asteroids, and meteoroids. (pp. 306–313)

The force of gravity keeps the planets in their orbits around the Sun. (pp. 316–323)

Make a **FOLDABLES**™ Study Guide

Take a sheet of paper and tape your lesson study guides as shown.

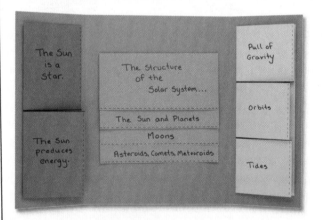

Fill each blank with the best word from the list.

asteroid, p. 312   **satellite**, p. 310

comet, p. 312   **solar system**, p. 308

fusion, p. 302   **star**, p. 299

gravity, p. 318   **tide**, p. 322

1. The force that pulls objects toward one another is called _____.
   5 ES 5.c

2. The Sun, the planets, their moons, and other objects make up the _____.
   5 ES 5.b

3. An object in space that circles around another object is called a(n) _____.   5 ES 5.b

4. A rock that revolves around the Sun is called a(n) _____.   5 ES 5.b

5. A mixture of frozen gases, ice, dust, and rock that circles around the Sun is called a(n) _____.   5 ES 5.b

6. An object in space that produces its own light and heat is called a(n) _____.   5 ES 5.a

7. The gravity of the Moon is mostly responsible for causing a(n) _____ on Earth.   5 ES 5.c

8. The energy of the Sun is produced by _____.   5 ES 5.a

Answer each of the following in complete sentences.

9. Cause and Effect What has to happen to cause an object in orbit to fall toward Earth? 5 ES 5.c

10. Draw Conclusions If the Sun uses up all its hydrogen, what will happen to the Sun? 5 ES 5.a

11. Compare and Contrast Describe at least two objects whose outlines are like an ellipse. 5 ES 5.c

12. Critical Thinking Of all the planets, which is the most different from the others? Explain. 5 ES 5.b

13. Explanatory Writing You have been asked to suggest a site for a new large telescope. Write a short proposal outlining why you think a mountaintop far from a big city should be the site for the new telescope. 5 ES 5.b

 What makes the planets move around the Sun?

CHAPTER 6

Different Looks?

Your objective will be to compare and contrast objects in the night sky.

What to do

1. Obtain an astronomy magazine, newspaper, or material from the Internet that shows the current positions of planets in the night sky.

2. Use your unaided eyes, binoculars, or a small telescope to observe planets and stars.

Analyze your results

▶ Describe the colors of the planets and stars.

▶ Describe the shape of the planets and stars.

▲ astronomical objects

 5 ES 5.b. Students know the solar system includes the planet Earth, the Moon, the Sun, eight other planets and their satellites, and smaller objects, such as asteroids and comets.

329

1 Which planet is closest to the Sun? 5 ES 5.b

A Uranus

B Mercury

C Venus

D Mars

2 Which of the following lists gives the names of the planets in order of their distance from the Sun? 5 ES 5.b

A Mercury, Mars, Venus, Earth

B Jupiter, Saturn, Uranus, Neptune

C Jupiter, Mercury, Venus, Earth

D Mars, Jupiter, Uranus, Saturn

3 Which object's name changes based on its location? 5 ES 5.b

A planet

B moon

C meteoroid

D the Sun

4 What is the *most* significant discovery Galileo made using his telescope? 5 ES 5.a

A The Sun revolves around Earth.

B The Sun revolves around Mars.

C Moons revolve around Jupiter.

D The Moon revolves around Earth.

5 Which of the following processes produces the Sun's energy? 5 ES 5.a

A solar power

B fusion

C winds

D temperature

6 A student collected information about the dwarf planet Pluto.

Pluto Data		
Relative Location	Temperature (°C)	Length of Day (Earth hours)
Beyond Neptune	–230°	153.3

Which of the following inferences could be true? 5 IE 6.g

A On Pluto, water would be a gas.

B On Pluto, water would be liquid.

C On Pluto, water would be liquid and solid.

D On Pluto, water would be solid.

7 Your science teacher suggests that you do an experiment to study how comets form. What is the next step you are likely to take? 5 IE 6.i

A Make a hypothesis.
B Collect data.
C Draw conclusions.
D Write a report.

8 Which of the following *best* describes the effect of the Sun's gravity on the planets? 5 ES 5.c

A Each planet is drawn toward the Sun.
B Each planet is drawn away from the Sun.
C Each planet is drawn closer to each other.
D Each planet is drawn away from each other.

9 What happens to the force of gravity when the distance between two objects decreases? 5 ES 5.c

A no attraction
B stays the same
C decreases
D increases

10 If the Sun increased in size, what would happen to the planets? 5 ES 5.b

A They will be released from their orbits.
B They will move farther away from the Sun.
C They will reverse their orbits.
D They will be drawn closer to the Sun.

11 A student wants to make accurate observations about the path of Mars across the night sky. Which tool should the student use? 5 IE 6.f

A telescope
B microscope
C binoculars
D stethoscope

12 A student plans an experiment to see what effect the distance (the length of a string) has on the length of time it takes a planet (a tennis ball) to revolve. He gathers the following data.

Data collected	
Length of string	Time for one revolution
5 cm	2 seconds
10 cm	4 seconds
15 cm	6 seconds
20 cm	8 seconds

What effect does the length of a string tied to a tennis ball have on the time it takes to complete one revolution? 5 IE 6.h

A The longer the string, the greater the time.
B The longer the string, the shorter the time.
C The longer the string, the time increases and decreases.
D The length of the string has no effect.

THE CASE FOR CLEAN WATER

Calling all water detectives! We have a body of water here that needs investigating. Can you help? People, plants, and animals all need clean water. But how do we know if a pond, lake, river, or stream is healthy? That can be a real mystery.

Clue 1. How does it look?

Begin your investigation with obvious evidence. What does the water look like? How does it smell? Do you notice anything in the water? However, even if water looks clear and clean, it might not be.

Clue 2. What is in it?

If you have special equipment in your detective kit, you may want to do some tests on the water. Finding out about the chemistry of the water is an important way to check its health.

Clue 3. Who lives there?

One of the best ways to find out what is going on is to ask around in the neighborhood. So you will want to observe some of the many insects that spend part or all of their life living in water. Look for them in the water you are investigating. They will tell you a lot about how clean the water is. This is a **dragonfly nymph** (NIMF). One day it will hatch into an adult dragonfly and fly away. It likes to live in clean water, but if it has to, it can live in polluted water. So you cannot know whether or not the water is clean if you see these.

▼ dragonfly and dragonfly nymph

▲ **midge and midge larva**

This **midge larva** does just fine living in polluted water until it hatches into an adult midge. If you notice many of these and not much else, it is a sign that the water is in trouble.

On the other hand, some insects cannot live in polluted water. These insects include ❶ **caddisfly larvae**, ❷ **mayfly nymphs**, and ❸ **stonefly nymphs**. If you find these insects, you know the water must be clean.

We can use these clues to sleuth out the truth about the water we all depend on!

▲ **stonefly and stonefly nymph**

▲ **caddisfly and caddisfly larva**

▼ **mayfly and mayfly nymph**

5 ES 3.d. Students know that the amount of fresh water located in rivers, lakes, underground sources, and glaciers is limited and that its availability can be extended by recycling and decreasing the use of water. • **ELA R 5.2.3** Discuss main ideas and concepts presented in texts, identifying and assessing evidence that supports those ideas.

Careers in Science

Weather Observer

There is an old saying that if you do not like the weather now, wait and it will change. How do people know what the weather will change to? After you finish high school, you might enjoy working as a weather observer. As a weather observer, you would collect information about weather conditions. You would be trained to use instruments that measure temperature, humidity, and air pressure. You would read radar scans and satellite photographs. The weather forecasts made by meteorologists depend on the data collected by weather observers.

▼ weather observers collecting data

▼ astronomer observing stars and planets

Astronomer

Are you interested in looking for planets around distant stars or watching solar systems form? Astronomers study the stars and learn about the other planets and suns in the universe. As an astronomer, you would use telescopes and satellites to gather data about other solar systems. Then you would analyze that data to find out what the stars and planets are made of and how old they are. To be an astronomer, you need to be good at math and physics, have strong computer skills, and obtain a doctoral degree in astronomy. After that, you might say the sky's the limit.

LOG ON **e-Careers** more careers online @ www.macmillanmh.com

Physical Science

Dry ice in water produces physical and chemical changes.

Types of Matter

 What do all types of matter have in common?

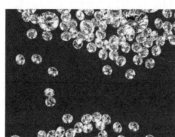

 5 PS 1. Elements and their combinations account for all the varied types of matter in the world.

337

Literature

POETRY

ELA R 5.3.1. Identify and analyze the characteristics of poetry, drama, fiction, and nonfiction and explain the appropriateness of the literary forms chosen by an author for a specific purpose.

ELA W 5.2.2. Write responses to literature:

a. Demonstrate an understanding of a literary work.

338

Metamorphosis

by Carl Sandburg

When water turns ice does it
remember one time it was water?

When ice turns back into water
does it remember it was ice?

Write About It

Response to Literature The famous poet Carl Sandburg is using water and ice to talk about changes in life and our ability to remember them. Why do you think he does this? Now it's your turn. What other changes in matter do you know about? Write about other changes in matter the poet could have used in his poem.

LOG ON **e-Journal** Write about it online
@ **www.macmillanmh.com**

Properties of Matter

Look and Wonder

Air balloons are pretty big, yet they can float in air. How is this possible?

 5 PS 1.g. Students know properties of solid, liquid, and gaseous substances, such as sugar ($C_6H_{12}O_6$), water (H_2O), helium (He), oxygen (O_2), nitrogen (N_2), and carbon dioxide (CO_2).

What makes a large object light?

Make a Prediction

Which is lighter, an inflated balloon or a tennis ball? Which is larger, an inflated balloon or a tennis ball? Why do you think this is? Do you think what they are made of is the reason for this difference? Make a prediction to answer this question.

Test Your Prediction

1. **Measure** Using an equal pan balance, find out which object is heavier. Record your observations.

2. **Measure** Using a bowl of water, find out which object is larger. Record your observations.

3. **Analyze Data** Look at the unfilled balloon and the halved tennis ball. What are the inflated balloon and the tennis ball made of?

Draw Conclusions

4. How can you explain what you observed?

5. Did your observations support your prediction?

Explore More

Predict which is lighter, a box of popped popcorn or a box of unpopped popcorn? Design an experiment to test your prediction. Write a report of your results.

 5 IE 6 i. Write a report of an investigation that includes conducting tests, collecting data or examining evidence, and drawing conclusions.

Materials

- **inflated balloon**
- **tennis ball**
- **equal pan balance**
- **bowl of water**
- **tape**
- **empty balloon**
- **halved tennis ball**

Step 1

Step 2

LOG ON e-Glossary
@ www.macmillanmh.com

▶ Reading Skill

Main Idea

Main Idea	Details

▼ An equal-pan balance can be used to measure mass.

What is matter?

Have you ever noticed how the water level in a glass rises when you add an ice cube? The water level rises because any object placed in water takes up space and pushes water out of the way. When an object sinks into water, it pushes an equal volume (VOL•yewm) of water out of the way. The **volume** of an object is the space it takes up.

You can use a graduated cylinder to measure volume. The unit of volume for liquids is a milliliter (mL). The unit of volume for solids is a cubic centimeter (cc or cm^3). The two units have exactly the same volume.

If you place a marble on a balance, you can find the mass in the marble. **Mass** is the amount of matter in an object. The unit of mass is a gram (g). **Matter** is anything that has mass and volume.

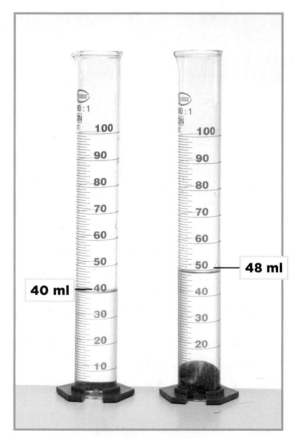

40 ml

48 ml

▲ A graduated cylinder can be used to measure volume.

Weight on Different Planets

	Earth	Venus	Mercury	Saturn	Mars
	0.35 oz	0.32 oz	0.13 oz	0.27 oz	0.13 oz
	30 lbs	27.3 lbs	11.4 lbs	22.8 lbs	11.4 lbs
	2200 lbs	2002 lbs	836 lbs	1672 lbs	836 lbs
	8 oz	7.28 oz	3.04 oz	6.08 oz	3.04 oz

Reading Charts

How much would a car weigh on Mercury?

Clue: Look at the cell where the car row and the Mercury column meet.

What if you held a volleyball in one hand and a bowling ball in the other? You would feel a difference. What you would feel is the weight (WAYT) of each ball. An object's **weight** is how strongly gravity pulls on it. Weight is measured on a scale as a newton (N) or a pound (lb).

Weight and mass are not the same thing. Think about finding the mass and weight of a marble on Earth and then on the Moon. The mass would be the same. The weight, however, would be less on the Moon because the gravity of the Moon is weaker than the gravity of Earth.

Volume, mass, and weight are all examples of physical properties of matter. We can sense these properties with our touch, taste, smell, sight, or hearing. We can also measure them with instruments such as balances, graduated cylinders, and scales.

Quick Check

Main Idea What are matter, volume, and mass?

Critical Thinking What would be different on Saturn, your mass or your weight?

What are the states of matter?

Look at all the matter around you. Books, tables, houses, and trees are made of matter. Milk, oil, and raindrops are made of matter. Tires, balloons, basketballs, and your room are full of matter.

What makes these examples of matter different? One difference between these examples is the state of matter. A **state of matter** is one of the three forms that matter can take—solid, liquid, or gas.

Books, tables, houses, and trees are examples of solids. Milk, oil, and raindrops are examples of liquids. The air that fills tires, balloons, basketballs, and your room is a gas. All matter is made of particles. The behavior of the particles of matter determines the state of matter.

The particles of a solid usually line up in an organized pattern. They vibrate back and forth but do not move past one another. They "wiggle" in relatively fixed positions. Because the particles in a solid are not moving around, their shape and volume does not change.

The diagram of the solid shows how the particles are packed together tightly. You can not compress a solid. This is because it has no room between it's particles.

The particles of a liquid move more than they do in the solid state. They have more freedom of motion and can move past one another. However, they still remain relatively close together.

The diagram of the liquid illustrates the behavior of the basic particles in a liquid. Since the particles of a liquid can flow, the shape of liquid takes on the shape of its container. If there is no container, the liquid spreads out as far as it can. The volume of a liquid remains the same because the particles do not separate from one another.

Gases consist of particles that move very rapidly. The particles are widely spread out and have lots of empty space between them. They are able to take up such a large volume because of their very rapid motion. They move faster when hot and slower when cool.

In the gas diagram, the particles move around freely so their volume and shape fit the shape and volume of the container. If there is no container, gases keep spreading further and further apart.

 Quick Check

Main Idea What do particles in solids, liquids, and gases have in common? How are they different?

Critical Thinking What will happen to the size of an inflated balloon if you put it in a refrigerator? Why?

gas

solid

liquid

Can the state of matter change?

At room temperature, everything has a set state of matter. Rocks are solid, water is liquid, and air is gaseous. However, the state of matter can change at different temperatures. A *phase change* occurs when matter changes from one state to another.

If you've ever held an ice cube on the palm of your hand until it turns into a puddle of water, you've observed matter changing from a solid to a liquid. If you've ever let your wet hands dry in the air, you've observed matter changing from liquid to a gas.

When a solid is heated, its particles vibrate faster and faster. Solids reach their melting point when particles break free and flow past each other.

The **melting point** is the temperature at which a solid changes to liquid. The melting point of water is 0°C (32°F).

The change of state from liquid to gas is called *vaporization* (VAY•purh•righ•zay•shunh).

Vaporization can occur in different ways. When water dries off your hands, it is undergoing evaporation (i•VAP•uh•ray•shuhn). During **evaporation**, the fastest particles on the surface of the liquid escape into the air and become a gas. As temperature increases, liquids evaporate faster.

Another way that vaporization happens is through boiling. When water reaches its boiling point, bubbles of vapor form within the liquid and rise to the surface, which allows the gas to escape to the air. The **boiling point** is the temperature at which a liquid rapidly changes to gas. The boiling point of water is 100°C (212°F).

▼ The melting point of ice is 0°C (32°F). Above 0°C ice changes to liquid water.

▼ The freezing point of water is 0°C (32°F). Below 0°C water becomes ice.

When gases cool, their particles slow down and come closer together. At the *condensing point* (kuhn•DENS•ing POINT) the particles stop flying apart. They form droplets and the gas changes to a liquid. The condensing point of a substance is the same as the boiling point.

When the particles of liquids slow down and stop flowing, they have reached the freezing point. The freezing point is the temperature at which a liquid changes to a solid. The **freezing point** of a substance is the same as the melting point.

Some solids vaporize without melting in a process called sublimation (sub•luh•MAY•shuhn). During **sublimation** a solid changes to a gas. Dry ice is an example of a substance that undergoes sublimation. At room temperature, dry ice changes to gas.

▼ The boiling point of water is 100°C (212°F). Above 100°C water changes to vapor.

Quick Lab

Changes of State

1. **Make a Model** Place enough marbles in a small transparent plastic container to fill half the bottom with a single layer. Leave enough room for the marbles to roll around the bottom. Put a cover on the container.

2. Tilt the container slightly to bring all the marbles together. Shake the container slightly so the marbles settle down. What state of matter have you modeled?

3. Tilt the container in other directions so the marbles roll slowly around but stay together. What state of matter does this model?

4. Shake the container gently so the marbles bounce off the walls in all directions. What state of matter does this model?

✔ Quick Check

Main Idea What are the changes of state of matter?

Critical Thinking Do you think all liquids have the same freezing point?

What is density?

Think about a solid and how its particles are all closely packed together. Since there is so much matter packed into a small space, even a small piece of this solid would have a relatively large mass. The solid, therefore, would have a high density. **Density** (DEN•si•tee) is a measure of how tightly matter is packed in an object.

Have you ever thrown a stick into a pond? How about a stone? You probably wondered why the stick floats but the stone sinks. What makes one object float and the other sink? An object's density provides the answer to this question.

An object that floats in a liquid must be less dense than the liquid. The cork in the diagram is larger than the rock but is floating on the surface.

The cork floats because its density is less than that of water. The rock, on the other hand, sinks in water because its density is greater than the density of water.

You might think that only low-density objects can float. However, any object will float if its density is less than the liquid's density. Even metals can float if they are placed in a very dense liquid.

 Quick Check

Main Idea If you had two equally sized objects in water, how could you tell which one is more dense?

Critical Thinking Why is helium used to fill balloons instead of oxygen or hydrogen? Explain.

Density

Reading Diagrams

How would you represent the density of water?

Clue: Look at the density of the rock that sinks and the cork that floats.

Lesson Review

Summarize the Main Idea

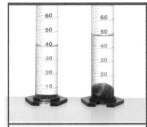
Mass, volume, and weight are physical properties of matter. (pp. 342–343)

The three states of matter are solid, liquid, and gas. (pp. 344–347)

Density determines whether an object will float or sink in a liquid. (p. 348)

Make a FOLDABLES™ Study Guide

Make a three-tab book (see p. 481). Use the titles shown. On the inside of each fold, write the main idea and details.

Think, Talk, and Write

1. **Main Idea** How are solids, liquids, and gases different from one another?

2. **Vocabulary** The amount of matter an object contains is its _____ .

3. **Main Idea** What change of state occurs in freezers if a power failure lasts 24 hours?

Main Idea	Details

4. **Critical Thinking** What is the difference between walking on Earth and on the Moon?

5. **Test Practice** Which of the following is not a physical property of matter?
   - **A** volume
   - **B** mass
   - **C** weight
   - **D** temperature

6. **Test Practice** Changing from solid to gas is called
   - **A** evaporation.
   - **B** contraction.
   - **C** condensation.
   - **D** sublimation.

Writing Link

Fictional Narrative
Write about what life would be like on a planet where everything weighed less.

Math Link

Density and Volume
You have 5 mL of water. How many little hollow cubes that are 1 cm on a side could you fill?

LOG ON e-Review Summaries and quizzes online @ www.macmillanmh.com

Record Data and Infer

You just read that particles in hot liquid move faster than those in cold. Since hot water has more energy to get rid of before it freezes, it shouldn't freeze as fast as cold water.

Well, that's what many people thought. But scientists wanted to know for sure, so they did a series of experiments and recorded their observations. Then they used that data to make an inference: Sometimes hot water freezes faster than cold water, a phenomenon known as *The Mpemba Effect*.

① Learn It

When you **record data**, you accurately arrange and store information collected in science investigations. When you **infer**, you form an opinion after analyzing recorded data.

It's easier to analyze data and form opinions if you organize the information on a chart or in a graph. That way you can quickly see differences between data and **infer** opinions.

▼ Water freezes into ice at 0°C (32°F). Can hot water freeze faster than cold water?

 5 IE 6.g. Record data by using appropriate graphic representations (including charts, graphs, and labeled diagrams) and make inferences based on those data.

❷ Try It

▶ Make a chart like the one shown to **record data** and your observations.

▶ Get one cup and fill it with hot tap water (approximately 70°C) and label it HOT WATER.

▶ Fill another cup with the same amount of cold tap water (approximately 18°C) and label it COLD WATER.

▶ Place both containers in a freezer. **Record** the placement in the freezer, size of freezer, separation between containers, and space from the sides and top of freezer.

▶ Check the freezer every 25 minutes. **Record** how long it takes the water in each container to begin to freeze. **Record** how long it takes the water in each container to completely freeze.

▶ Which froze first, cold water or hot water? Repeat the experiment to confirm your findings.

▶ Scientists inferred that sometimes hot water freezes before cold water. What can you **infer** from the data you recorded?

Time to Freeze		
Temperature	Start time	End time
Hot water 70°C		
Cold water 18°C		

❸ Apply It

What do you think would happen if you repeated this experiment using a smaller container or started with really icy or even hotter water? Try it and **record data** about the investigation. Finally, use that data to help you **infer**, or develop an opinion, about the freezability of hot versus cold water.

Elements

Look and Wonder

You may be surprised to learn that valuable diamonds are made of the same element as the graphite used in your pencil. That element is carbon. The difference lies in the way that carbon is arranged. Where else can you find this element?

 5 PS 1.d. Students know that each element is made of one kind of atom and that the elements are organized in the periodic table by their chemical properties.
5 PS 1.h. Students know living organisms and most materials are composed of just a few elements.

Do living things contain carbon?

Purpose
Carbon is a vital component of all living things. In this activity you will use a blackened spoon to find out if carbon is present in living things.

- **stick of charcoal**
- **hand lens**
- **wax candle**
- **blackened metal spoon**

Procedure

1 **Observe** Examine a stick of charcoal with a hand lens. Charcoal is pure carbon. Draw what you see.

2 Rub the charcoal on a sheet of paper. Examine the result more closely with the hand lens. Note any distinctive color and other properties of carbon.

3 **Experiment** Your teacher will give you a blackened metal spoon. It was held above the tip of a paraffin candle flame for a few seconds. Paraffin is extracted from petroleum which is formed from ancient plants and animals. What substance do you think is on the spoon?

4 Rub the spoon on paper. Examine the result with a hand lens.

Step 2

Draw Conclusions

5 **Infer** What substance did the paraffin candle seem to contain?

Explore More

A wooden toothpick is made of plant tissue. How would you find out if a wooden toothpick contains carbon? Write the procedure and materials you would need to find out. Carry out the procedure with the help of your teacher. What did you find?

Step 4

 5 IE 6.c. Plan and conduct a simple investigation based on a student-developed question and write instructions others can follow to carry out the procedure.

▶ **Main Idea** 5 PS 1.b

Matter is made of elements, which are made of atoms.

▶ **Vocabulary**

element, p. 354

atom, p. 354

 **-Glossary**
@ www.macmillanmh.com

▶ **Reading Skill**

Make Inferences

Clues	What You Know	Inferences

What is an element?

The ancient Greeks thought that every kind of matter was made from combinations of four simple substances they called elements. They had the right idea about elements but they chose the wrong substances: air, fire, earth, and water.

Today we have found about a hundred of the actual elements and we have made some that do not exist naturally. An **element** is a substance that cannot be further simplified. Elements are the simple substances that combine to make all other substances. Some common elements are carbon, aluminum, oxygen, and iron.

Elements are made of tiny invisible particles called atoms. An **atom** is the smallest particle that has the properties of an element. We might obtain one if we could only cut a small piece of aluminum foil in half about 50 times. We would then have a speck of aluminum less than a billionth of an inch in size.

Composition of Aluminum

aluminum foil

Each element is made of one kind of atom. This means all the atoms in an element have the same structure. Some elements are heavy, others are light. Some elements are shiny and some are opaque. A few elements are magnetic, most are not. These and many other properties of elements are determined by the structure of their atoms.

The names of elements may come from various sources. Some names come from ancient words. The element mercury, for instance, was named after the Roman god, Mercury. Elements discovered more recently may be named after scientists, countries, or even states! Germanium, for example, was discovered in Germany. Where do you think the name californium comes from?

Each element is given a symbol of one or two letters. The first is a capital letter, while the second letter is always lowercase. The symbols of many elements match their English names, such as Zn for zinc. Other symbols may not match the English names because the symbols come from Latin, Greek, or other languages. For example, the symbol for gold is Au, after the Latin word *aurum*.

✔ Quick Check

Make Inferences What is matter made of?

Critical Thinking If you were to discover an element, how would you choose to name it? Explain.

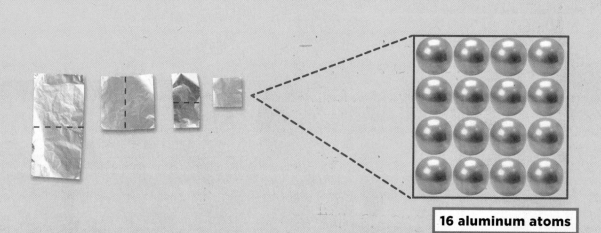

16 aluminum atoms

Reading Photos

How many times would you have to cut this piece of aluminum in half to get a single atom?

Clue: Count the number of whole atoms you see and divide by 2 until you get to 1.

What are the most common elements on Earth?

There are 92 naturally occurring elements on Earth. Surprisingly, only eight elements make up 98% (by weight) of the Earth's crust. In decreasing order, they are oxygen, silicon, aluminum, iron, calcium, sodium, potassium, and magnesium. Where are all the other elements? All together, they are found in the remaining 2% of the soil and rocks of Earth's crust.

The oceans contain mostly water and some dissolved salt. The two most abundant elements in the oceans are oxygen and hydrogen. Together, they make up 96% (by weight) of the oceans. Chlorine and sodium from the salt make up 3% of the oceans. All the other elements dissolved in seawater add up to only 1% of the oceans.

Earth's atmosphere has a much different composition than the crust. Just two elements, nitrogen and oxygen, make up almost 99% of the atmosphere. Argon is a distant third in line at just 1%. All of the remaining gases in the air make up less than 1% of the atmosphere.

How abundant are the elements under Earth's crust? That is a pretty

Composition of Earth

Air
- Oxygen 21%
- Other Elements 1%
- Nitrogen 78%

Water
- Hydrogen 11%
- Other Elements 4%
- Oxygen 85%

deep question to answer. Scientists can't know exactly how much of the elements exist inside Earth, but they can infer based on other data. For example, the lava that erupts from volcanos provides information about Earth's inner secrets.

✔ Quick Check

Make Inferences What three elements are likely to be found in a sample of soil and rocks?

Critical Thinking What are the most common elements found in fresh water?

≡Quick Lab

Map of Elements

1. **Make a Model** Use colored pencils to model the most common elements on Earth. You can trace a map of Earth, with continents and oceans, and draw the atmosphere around it. Use a different color to represent each element.

2. How many different colors did you use on your model?

3. What does each color represent? Identify the elements in your model.

Reading Charts

What element is common in Earth's crust, water, and atmosphere?

Clue: Compare and contrast the three pie charts.

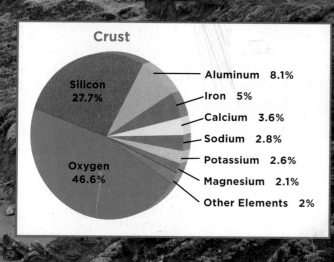

Crust

- Silicon 27.7%
- Oxygen 46.6%
- Aluminum 8.1%
- Iron 5%
- Calcium 3.6%
- Sodium 2.8%
- Potassium 2.6%
- Magnesium 2.1%
- Other Elements 2%

What are the most common elements in living things?

Plants have thick cell walls and many woody structures to provide support. Cell walls and woody tissue are made mainly of carbon, hydrogen, and oxygen, which explains why these three elements are so common in plants.

Like plants, animals are composed mainly of carbon, hydrogen, and oxygen. The amounts of elements typical for animals are shown in the chart. Animal bodies contain a great deal of water. In fact, about 60% of human body weight is water. A lot of our oxygen and hydrogen come from the water in our bodies. Other than bones and teeth, the rest of our tissues are mainly made from carbon, oxygen, hydrogen, nitrogen, phosphorus, and a dash of chlorine and sulfur. So really, carbon, hydrogen, and oxygen are the three main elements shared by all living things.

✔ Quick Check

Make Inferences What happens to the amount of carbon, hydrogen, and oxygen in animals when water is not available?

Critical Thinking Why is it important to animals that plants are made of essentially the same elements?

▼ Plants and animals are mainly made of carbon, hydrogen, and oxygen.

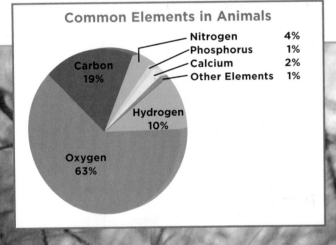

Common Elements in Animals

Element	Percentage
Nitrogen	4%
Phosphorus	1%
Calcium	2%
Other Elements	1%
Carbon	19%
Hydrogen	10%
Oxygen	63%

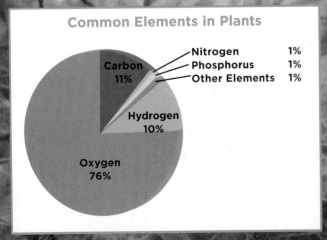

Common Elements in Plants

Element	Percentage
Nitrogen	1%
Phosphorus	1%
Other Elements	1%
Carbon	11%
Hydrogen	10%
Oxygen	76%

Summarize the Main Idea

Matter is made of **elements**. Elements are made of atoms. (pp. 354–355)

Water, air, and Earth's crust are mostly made of eight elements. (pp. 356–357)

Living things are mostly made of oxygen, carbon and hydrogen. (p. 358)

Make a FOLDABLES Study Guide

Make a three-tab book (see p. 481). Use the titles shown. On the inside of each fold, summarize what you learned.

Think, Talk, and Write

1. **Main Idea** What are the basic building blocks of matter?

2. **Vocabulary** The simplest particles of iron are _____ .

3. **Make Inferences** If you were to cut a metal element over and over again, to the point that it is barely visible, would it still be considered that element?

Clues	What You Know	Inferences

4. **Critical Thinking** Which is larger—a living cell or an atom of hydrogen? Explain your answer.

5. **Test Practice** What two elements make up most of the oceans?
   A water and air
   B oxygen and hydrogen
   C sodium and chlorinea
   D silicon and calcium

6. **Test Practice** Which three elements make up most living things?
   A phosphorus, nitrogen, sulfur
   B carbon, hydrogen, oxygen
   C iron, potassium, sodium
   D calcium, chlorine, aluminum

 Math Link

Atomic Geometry

If each aluminum atom was perfectly stacked on another one, a piece of aluminum foil would be about 193,000 atoms thick. If you could cut aluminum until it was a tiny cube, about how many atoms would each side have?

 Social Studies Link

Aristotle

The ancient Greek philosopher Aristotle believed that all matter was made of earth, air, water, and fire. Do research to find out about the reasons he had for this belief. Prepare a presentation with your findings.

Be a Scientist

How can unknown elements be identified?

Materials

6 unknown substances

thermometer

cold and warm water

magnet

Form a Hypothesis

Elements are pure substances that cannot be broken down into any simpler substances. Each element is made up of one kind of atom and the atoms of an element give it a specific set of properties. Scientists can identify elements by observing their properties.

You are going to observe the properties of six unknown substances. These properties include state at room temperature, heat conductivity, and magnetism. The first property you will observe is state at room temperature. What happens to a gas, a liquid, or a solid when you squeeze it? Write the answer as three hypotheses in the form *"If I squeeze a _____ , then…"*

Test Your Hypothesis

1. **Record Data** Prepare a chart to gather your data. Keep in mind you are going to run at least three tests on six unknown substances. Design your chart so that you may add other tests later.

2. Measure the temperature of the six substances to ensure they are all at room temperature.

3. Squeeze substance A. What happens? What is its state at room temperature?

4. Repeat step three for substances B, C, D, E, and F. Record your results.

Step 2

Step 3

 5 IE 6.c. Plan and conduct a simple investigation based on a student-developed question and write instructions others can use to carry out your procedure.

Draw Conclusions

① What is the state of the six substances at room temperature?

② Did the test support your hypotheses?

Inquiry Guided

How can heat conductivity help you identify an element?

Form a Hypothesis

The second property you will observe is heat conductivity. Will raising the temperature help you determine which substance is a good heat conductor? Write your answer as a hypothesis in the form *"If a temperature is raised, then the temperature of good heat conductors…."*

Test Your Hypothesis

Design a plan to test your hypothesis. Write out the materials and resources you will need and the steps you will take. Record your results and observations as you follow your plan.

Draw Conclusions

Did your experiment support your hypothesis? Were you able to use temperature to find out if substances were good or poor conductors of heat? Record your results on your chart.

Inquiry Open

You already know the state at room temperature and if the unknown substances are good heat conductors. What else can you find out about them? What about if they are magnetic? Think of a question to investigate. Then form a hypothesis and carry out the investigation to learn more about the six unknown elements. Record your results in your chart.

Remember to follow the steps of the scientific process.

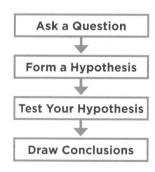

Ask a Question
↓
Form a Hypothesis
↓
Test Your Hypothesis
↓
Draw Conclusions

Lesson 3
Classifying Elements

Look and Wonder

Like these marbles, elements are all different but they have some things in common. How could you organize them according to what they have in common?

 5 PS 1.b. Students know all matter is made of atoms, which may combine to form molecules. • **5 PS 1.d.** Students know that each element is made of one kind of atom and that the elements are organized in the periodic table by their chemical properties. • **5 PS 1.e.** Students know scientists have developed instruments that can create discrete images of atoms and molecules that show that the atoms and molecules often occur in well-ordered arrays.

What patterns can you find?

Materials

Purpose

Classify different shapes into groups to understand how scientists use classisfication.

Procedure

1. **Make a Model** Work in pairs. Draw a small, medium, and large-sized square, circle, and equilateral triangle on each sheet. Make the sides or diameters to be about 2, 3, and 4 cm long (1, 1 1/2, and 2 in. long). Cut out the 18 pieces. Mix them up. Each can represent a different element.

2. How can you bring order out of this? Can you find any patterns?

3. **Classify** Organize pieces that share one characteristic into rows. Place pieces under each other when they share two or more characteristics.

4. **Record Data** Draw a labeled diagram showing your arrangement.

- 2 sheets of differently colored construction paper
- scissors
- ruler
- compass

Step 1

Draw Conclusions

5. Where do you find the most closely related groups in your arrangement? What criteria did you use?

6. **Communicate** Compare your results with the other groups.

Step 2

Explore More

Think about how you would organize and classify a collection that you have or would like to have. Write out instructions that someone else can follow to classify the collection.

5 IE 6.a. Classify objects (e.g. rocks, plants, leaves) in accordance with appropriate criteria.

Main Idea 5 PS 4.d

Each element is made of a different kind of atom. Elements are organized by their properties.

Vocabulary

proton, p.364

neutron, p.364

electron, p.364

atomic number, p.364

molecule, p.365

metals, p.366

nonmetal, p.367

noble gases, p.367

metalloids, p.367

periodic table, p.369

LOG ON e-Glossary
@ www.macmillanmh.com

Reading Skill

Compare and Contrast

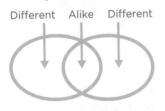

Different   Alike   Different

What are atoms and molecules?

You have learned that elements are made of atoms and that an atom is the smallest unit that has the properties of an element. This means that once you split an atom, you do not get smaller pieces of the element. Instead, what you get is the particles that form all atoms.

The particles that make up all atoms are protons (PROH•tons), neutrons (NEW•trons), and electrons (i•LEK•trons). **Protons** are located in the nucleus (NEW•klee•uhs), at the center of the atom. **Neutrons** are also located in the nucleus. **Electrons** are located outside the nucleus. Scientists have not been able to observe electrons directly because they are too small. However, they have inferred that electrons rotate around the nucleus.

Atoms of different elements have different numbers of protons, neutrons, and electrons. The **atomic number** is the number of protons in an atom. Every element has a different atomic number. This number determines the identity of the atoms of the element. For example, only helium atoms have 2 protons in their nucleus, only magnesium atoms have 12 protons in their nucleus, and only carbon atoms have 6 protons in their nucleus.

▶ This is a model of a beryllium atom. The beryllium atom has 4 protons, 4 electrons, and 4 or 5 neutrons.

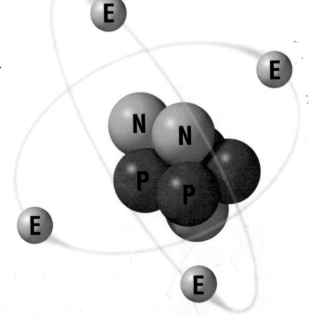

▲ The oxygen atom has 8 protons, 8 electrons, and 8 neutrons.

▲ The oxygen molecule is made of two oxygen atoms that are joined together.

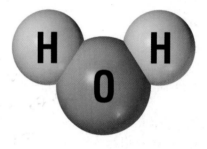

▲ The water molecule is made of 1 oxygen atom and 2 hydrogen atoms.

Another important number is the atomic weight. The atomic weight of an atom is a measure of the mass of its atoms. The atomic weight is calculated by adding the number of protons and the number of neutrons together.

The atoms of some elements are naturally found as molecules (MOL•uh•kyewls). A **molecule** is a particle that contains more than one atom joined together. For example, a molecule of oxygen usually has two oxygen atoms. This is represented by the symbol O_2. Hydrogen is another element which is usually found as a molecule. Hydrogen molecules are usually made of 2 hydrogen atoms.

Molecules can also be made up of atoms from different elements. One common example of this kind of molecule is water. Water molecules are made of 2 hydrogen atoms, and 1 oxygen atom.

Molecules make it possible for there to be many different substances. Remember, 99% of the crust of Earth is made up of 8 elements. How do you account for the huge variety of substances that exist? The elements join together in different combinations to form the substances.

✅ Quick Check

Compare and Contrast What is the difference between an atom and a molecule?

Critical Thinking What is the atomic number of an atom that has 6 protons, 6 neutrons, and 6 electrons?

Helium inflates floating balloons

Carbon atoms are in plants and animals

What are the properties of elements?

The most important property of an element it its atomic number. The atomic number determines which element an atom is. For example, any atom that contains 47 protons in its nucleus is an atom of silver, and an atom that contains 4 protons is an atom of beryllium.

Metals

Metals make up more than 75% of the elements in the periodic table. A **metal** is a substance that conducts heat and electricity well. Metals are usually solid at room temperature. They are shiny when polished. Metals can be bent or flattened into shapes without breaking. Examples of metals include aluminum, iron, copper, gold, and silver. Some metals, such as iron, are magnetic.

Nitrogen/Oxygen make 98 percent of air

Iron in the fence is strong and heavy

Aluminum in the food cart is strong and light

Nonmetals

There are 17 nonmetal elements. A **nonmetal** is an element that is a poor conductor of heat and electricity. Nonmetals that are solid at room temperature will break rather than bend. These elements do not usually shine when polished. Sulfur and carbon are examples of solid nonmetals. However, most nonmetals are gases at room temperature. Some examples of gaseous nonmetals are helium, nitrogen, and oxygen. Only one nonmetal, bromine, is liquid at room temperature.

Fluorine, chlorine, bromine, iodine, and astatine are known as halogens. These nonmetallic elements all have a strong unpleasant odor and they burn flesh. They react with most metals and many nonmetals.

Helium, neon, argon, krypton, xenon, and radon are known as **noble gases**. These nonmetallic elements are considered to be *inert* (in•URT), which means in a state of doing little or nothing. Scientists think this is because these elements rarely react with other elements.

Metalloids

Metalloids (MET•uh•loids) are a very small group of elements that have some properties of the metals and some of the nonmetals. The metalloids are not as good conductors of heat and electricity as the metals, but they are better conductors than the nonmetals. Boron, silicon, and germanium are examples of the metalloids.

 Quick Check

Compare and Contrast Make a Venn diagram to show how metals, nonmetals, and metalloids compare and contrast.

Critical Thinking Why is it useful to know the properties of elements?

What is the periodic table of elements?

Picture having about 60 cards. A different element and its properties are written on each one. How would you organize the cards based on the properties of the elements? This is just what a scientist named Dmitri Mendeleev did in the 1800s. He organized the elements in order of increasing mass. Then, he made a major discovery. He noticed that properties of the elements repeated themselves in cycles! In fact, the word "periodic" (peer•ee•OD•ik) means "occurring in cycles." So, he placed elements with similar properties in columns. The result was the periodic table of elements. Every box in the periodic table represents a different element. Each one includes the element's name, symbol, and atomic number.

The Periodic Table of Elements

1											
1 **H** Hydrogen	2										
3 **Li** Lithium	4 **Be** Beryllium										
11 **Na** Sodium	12 **Mg** Magnesium	3	4	5	6	7	8	9	10	11	12
19 **K** Potassium	20 **Ca** Calcium	21 **Sc** Scandium	22 **Ti** Titanium	23 **V** Vanadium	24 **Cr** Chromium	25 **Mn** Manganese	26 **Fe** Iron	27 **Co** Cobalt	28 **Ni** Nickel	29 **Cu** Copper	30 **Zn** Zinc
37 **Rb** Rubidium	38 **Sr** Strontium	39 **Y** Yttrium	40 **Zr** Zirconium	41 **Nb** Niobium	42 **Mo** Molybdenum	43 **Tc** Technetium	44 **Ru** Ruthenium	45 **Rh** Rhodium	46 **Pd** Palladium	47 **Ag** Silver	48 **Cd** Cadmium
55 **Cs** Cesium	56 **Ba** Barium	57 **La** Lanthanum	72 **Hf** Hafnium	73 **Ta** Tantalum	74 **W** Tungsten	75 **Re** Rhenium	76 **Os** Osmium	77 **Ir** Iridium	78 **Pt** Platinum	79 **Au** Gold	80 **Hg** Mercury
87 **Fr** Francium	88 **Ra** Radium	89 **Ac** Actinium	104 **Rf** Rutherfordium	105 **Db** Dubnium	106 **Sg** Seaborgium	107 **Bh** Bohrium	108 **Hs** Hassium	109 **Mt** Meitnerium	110 **Ds** Darmstadtium	111 **Rg** Roentgenium	

58 **Ce** Cerium	59 **Pr** Praseodymium	60 **Nd** Neodymium	61 **Pm** Promethium	62 **Sm** Samarium	63 **Eu** Europium	64 **Gd** Gadolinium	65 **Tb** Terbium
90 **Th** Thorium	91 **Pa** Protactinium	92 **U** Uranium	93 **Np** Neptunium	94 **Pu** Plutonium	95 **Am** Americium	96 **Cm** Curium	97 **Bk** Berkelium

The **periodic table** arranges all the known elements in a chart of rows and columns of increasing atomic number. Note how different colors are used to show the three different groups of elements. These groups are the metals, the metalloids, and the nonmetals.

The columns in the periodic table are called *groups*, or *families*. The rows are called periods. Families of elements have similar properties. For example, the halogens are found in one column. The noble gases are found in another one. Elements change from metals to nonmetals as you go from left to right across the periodic table. They also develop more metallic properties as you go down any family.

You may have noticed there are two rows separated from the periodic table. These rows include the rare earth elements. Many of these elements are artificial.

✔ Quick Check

Compare and Contrast How is classifying rocks like classifying elements?

Critical Thinking Why aren't aluminum (Al) and silicon (Si) in the same family?

Key

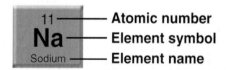

— Atomic number
— Element symbol
— Element name

	Metals
	Metalloids
	Nonmetals

State at Room Temperature:

Black: solid

Purple: liquid

Red: gas

					18
13	14	15	16	17	2 **He** Helium
5 **B** Boron	6 **C** Carbon	7 **N** Nitrogen	8 **O** Oxygen	9 **F** Fluorine	10 **Ne** Neon
13 **Al** Aluminum	14 **Si** Silicon	15 **P** Phosphorus	16 **S** Sulfur	17 **Cl** Chlorine	18 **Ar** Argon
31 **Ga** Gallium	32 **Ge** Germanium	33 **As** Arsenic	34 **Se** Selenium	35 **Br** Bromine	36 **Kr** Krypton
49 **In** Indium	50 **Sn** Tin	51 **Sb** Antimony	52 **Te** Tellurium	53 **I** Iodine	54 **Xe** Xenon
81 **Tl** Thallium	82 **Pb** Lead	83 **Bi** Bismuth	84 **Po** Polonium	85 **At** Astatine	86 **Rn** Radon

66 **Dy** Dysprosium	67 **Ho** Holmium	68 **Er** Erbium	69 **Tm** Thulium	70 **Yb** Ytterbium	71 **Lu** Lutetium
98 **Cf** Californium	99 **Es** Einsteinium	100 **Fm** Fermium	101 **Md** Mendelevium	102 **No** Nobelium	103 **Lr** Lawrencium

Reading Tables

Which elements are gaseous at room temperature?

Clue: Look at the key and list the elements that are indicated.

369
EXPLAIN

Can scientists see atoms?

It is hard to believe just how small atoms are. Suppose you put a pinch of salt in your hand. In that little bit of salt there are more than a billion atoms, half are sodium atoms and half chlorine atoms. So atoms are much too small for us to see with just our eyes.

However, microscopes have allowed scientists to "see" atoms. An electron microscope uses electron beams instead of light to produce images. The electrons are aimed at a sample. When an electron hits an atom and bounces back, an image is formed. The first electron microscope was invented in 1932. It was the first time scientists could see large molecules.

The field ion microscope was invented in 1951. This microscope worked similarly to the electron microscope, but instead of electrons it used ions, which are particles with an electric charge. The field ion microscope was even more powerful than the electron microscope and scientists were able to see atoms for the first time.

Modern versions of the field ion microscope have given scientists an atom-by-atom view of metals. This technology shows that atoms have a spherical shape. Atoms look like "fuzzy balls" through a field ion microscope. The images don't actually show the protons, neutrons, and electrons that you see in atom diagrams. Looking at the behavior of these particles helps scientists determine their shapes and positions inside the atom.

The field ion microscope only shows large atoms and molecules. However, this problem was partially overcome by

Powerful Microscopes

◀ The field ion microscope was invented in 1951. Atoms appear as bright spots.

the invention of the scanning tunneling microscope. The scanning tunneling microscope scans samples using a very fine metallic tip.

The photograph on this page shows one of the most powerful new microscopes, the one-angstrom microscope. These microscopes have confirmed the long-held suspicion that atoms in metals and crystals occur in an orderly fashion and create patterns.

Quick Check

Compare and Contrast What do the scanning tunneling microscope and the one-angstrom microscope allow scientists to see?

Critical Thinking Why do scientists use electrons instead of light to see atoms?

≡Quick Lab

Magnification

1. **Observe** Examine a newspaper photograph with just your eyes. Then examine the same photograph with a magnifying glass.

2. **Communicate** How are your observations similar to what an electron microscope would show? Write out your ideas.

3. **Predict** Suppose you look at the newspaper photo with an electron microscope. At different levels of magnification, what would the views be like? Do research to find your answers.

▲ The one-angstrom microscope shows the pattern made by silicon atoms.

Reading Photos

How is the image of the one-angstrom microscope different from that of the field ion microscope?

Clue: Contrast the images of the two microscopes.

Can scientists grab a single atom?

Scientists can actually "grab" single atoms, or small groups of atoms, with the tip of a scanning tunneling microscope. They can then drag the atoms around on a surface. This allows scientists to place atoms in precise locations. For fun, IBM engineers made "Molecule Man," shown in the photograph. Molecule Man is made of 28 two-atom groups placed on a platinum surface. He is only 5 billionths of a meter tall!

Molecule Man was made to demonstrate the power of the scanning tunneling microscope. However, this technology may lead to amazing advances in building ultra-small devices in the developing field of nanotechnology.

One application of this has been the development of delivery vehicles made of molecules that bring anticancer drugs right to the cancerous cells. What if scientists developed cell-sized memory devices that could be implanted in a person's brain? A student could ace every test!

Nano devices could make every appliance become a smart machine. Imagine what they could do to improve robots from today's clumsy models.

▲ Scanning tunneling microscope

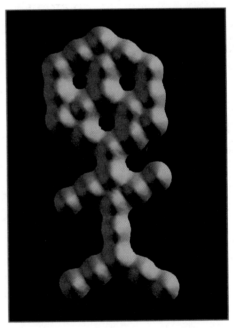
▲ Molecule Man was made with a scanning tunneling microscope.

 Quick Check

Compare and Contrast What are the benefits of a nano device compared to a large device?

Critical Thinking What would you do with a nano device if you had a choice?

Lesson Review

Summarize the Main Idea

Each **element** is made of one kind of atom. Elements are found as atoms or molecules. (pp. 364–365)

Elements are organized in the **periodic table** according to their properties. (pp. 368–369)

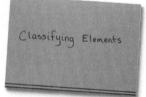

Microscopes allow scientists to "see" and touch atoms. (pp. 370–372)

Make a FOLDABLES™ Study Guide

Make a half book (see p. 479). Use the titles shown. On the inside of each fold, summarize what you've learned.

Classifying Elements

Think, Talk, and Write

1. **Main Idea** How does the periodic table summarize what we know about elements?

2. **Vocabulary** On the periodic table, _____ sit between the metals and nonmetals.

3. **Compare and Contrast** How are lithium and iodine alike and different? Use the periodic table to answer this question.

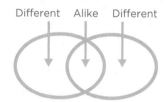

Different   Alike   Different

4. **Critical Thinking** Why are the noble gases called the "inert gases"?

5. **Test Practice** Which one is a nonmetal?
   - **A** bromine
   - **B** copper
   - **C** zinc
   - **D** lead

6. **Test Practice** All of the following are examples of metalloids *EXCEPT*:
   - **A** boron
   - **B** silicon
   - **C** silver
   - **D** arsenic

Writing Link

Expository Writing
Choose an element in the periodic table and research it. Find out what are the properties of the element, where it is found, and how it was discovered.

Math Link

Subtract Particles
Draw the sodium and chlorine atoms. How many protons, neutrons, and electrons are in each? How many more particles are in the chlorine nucleus than the sodium nucleus?

Element Discovery

When Mendeleev laid out the element cards to create the periodic table in 1869, he found gaps in their order. He suspected these were elements that were not yet discovered. Mendeleev predicted they would be discovered and the gaps would eventually be filled.

 1772-74

Oxygen— Scientists Joseph Priestley and Carl Wilhelm Scheele independently discover that when they heat certain compounds, a new kind of "air" or gas is given off. The new gas is named oxygen from the Greek words meaning "acid former." That's because when oxygen combines with other elements, the compounds are usually acidic.

1760   1780   1800   1820   1840   1860

 1766

Hydrogen— In 1766, Henry Cavendish isolates a flammable gas. He calls the new element flammable air. The element later gets its name from the Greek words meaning "water forming," when another scientist discovers that water is made of hydrogen and oxygen.

He **1868-1895**

Helium— Joseph Lockyer discovers helium in 1868 by studying the Sun's spectrum during a solar eclipse. He finds color lines that no element at the time was known to produce. The element is named helium, after Helios, the Greek god of the Sun. In 1895, helium is found on Earth in uranium minerals.

  ELA R 5.2.4. Draw inferences, conclusions, or generalizations about text and support them with textual evidence and prior knowledge.

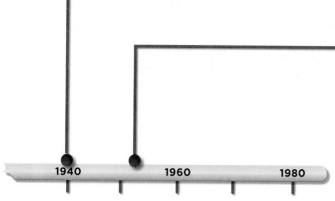

94 Pu **1940**

Plutonium—Scientists in Berkeley, California, create a new element by bombarding uranium with particles of deuterium, a special form of hydrogen. They name the element after the recently discovered planetary body Pluto.

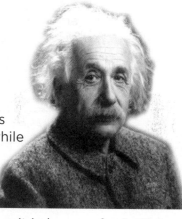

99 Es **1952**

Einsteinium— A team of scientists find this element while studying the radioactive debris created when a hydrogen bomb explodes. They name it in honor of scientist Albert Einstein. Einsteinium exists for a short time before it transforms itself into other elements.

The periodic table isn't finished. Elements are still being added to it. In the past 75 years, 26 new elements have been added to the table. That's about one element every three years! If you found a new element, what would you name it?

Write About It

Make Inferences

Look at the timeline. When was hydrogen discovered? When was oxygen discovered? What can you infer about the discovery of the composition of water? Read about the discoveries of hydrogen and oxygen to find the clues you need to make an inference.

Make Inferences

▶ Review the information to make inferences about information not stated explicitly.

▶ List the details that support the inferences you make.

  -Journal Write about it online @ **www.macmillanmh.com**

AMERICAN MUSEUM OF NATURAL HISTORY

Mixtures

Look and Wonder

When two substances are mixed together, they may seem to become one. Scientific procedures, however, allow people to separate them into their original forms. How is this done?

5 PS 1.f. Students know that differences in chemical and physical properties of substances are used to separate mixtures and identify compounds.

How can you separate mixed substances?

Purpose

The purpose is to mix two substances and then separate them. You can separate mixed substances if they have different properties. Can a magnet help you separate iron filings and sand after they are mixed?

Procedure

① Your teacher will give you sand and iron filings. Write a procedure for mixing and separating them. Have your teacher approve your procedure before you start. Record your observations and results as you follow the procedure.

② **Experiment** Carry out your procedure. You should end up with separated iron filings and sand.

③ **Observe** Examine your samples carefully. Was the separation of the iron and sand complete or partial? Record your observations.

Draw Conclusions

④ **Analyze** How did the properties of iron and sand enable you to separate them?

⑤ **Infer** What kind of changes took place during the separation process?

Explore More

What if salt was added in with the sand and iron filings? Write a procedure for separating the new mix of substances.

 5 IE 6.i. Write a report of an investigation that includes conducting tests, collecting data, or examining evidence and drawing conclusions.

Materials

- sand
- iron filings
- sheet of paper
- spoon
- clear container
- magnet

Step ①

Step ②

Read and Learn

► **Main Idea** 5 PS 1.f

Mixtures are physical combinations of substances.

► **Vocabulary**

mixture, p.378
suspension, p.379
solution, p.379
solvent, p.380
solute, p.380
solubility, p.381
filtration, p.382

 -Glossary
@ **www.macmillanmh.com**

► **Reading Skill**

Draw Conclusions

Text Clues	Conclusions

 Explore mixtures and compounds with Team Earth.

What is a mixture?

The trail mix you see on this page is a mixture (MIKS•chuhr). A **mixture** is a physical combination of two or more substances that do not form new substances. You can add more raisins and it will still be trail mix. You can separate the trail mix into the original ingredients, and these will be unchanged.

Since a mixture contains at least two different substances, no mixture is pure. The properties of a mixture blend the properties of its parts. For example, muddy water—a mixture of clay and water—gets you both dirty and wet. Powdery clay alone can get you dirty, water alone can get you wet, and the mixture can do both.

We classify mixtures according to certain properties. In *heterogeneous mixtures*, separate particles are big enough to see. Trail mix and tossed salad are examples of heterogeneous mixtures. Can you see the separate bits?

Mixtures that look the same throughout are *homogeneous mixtures*. In homogeneous mixtures, the particles are too small to see. Milk, a liquid, and cream cheese, a solid, are examples of homogeneous mixtures. They both look the same throughout because you can't see the individual particles.

▼ Trail mix is an example of a mixture.

Some mixtures separate by themselves when their parts settle out into layers. We call this type of mixture a suspension (suh•SPEN•shuhn). A **suspension** is a mixture whose particles settle and separate within a few hours. In some suspensions, particles settle into layers quickly. Oil and vinegar as a salad dressing, for example, can be shaken into a smooth-looking mixture. However, the oil layers out on top of the vinegar in a matter of minutes.

If the particles in a mixture are the size of atoms or molecules, the mixture is called a **solution** (suh•LEW•shuhn). This happens when one substance dissolves in another, like sugar in water. All solutions are homogeneous, which means they have the same makeup throughout. Solutions may be colored, but if they are liquid or gas they are always transparent, like window cleaner solution or air.

▲ Oil and vinegar are an example of a suspension when mixed together.

✔ Quick Check

Draw Conclusions How is a mixture of water and sand a suspension?

Critical Thinking You have a bottle of salad dressing. Why should you shake it well before using it?

▲ Window cleaner is a solution.

What are the parts of a solution?

Solutions always have a part called the **solvent** (SOL•vuhnt), which does the dissolving, and a part called the **solute** (SOL•yewt), which gets dissolved. For example, we can make a solution by stirring a spoonful of sugar crystals into a glass of water. The crystals seem to disappear, but you could detect their presence by tasting the solution. The water dissolves the sugar, so water is the solvent. The sugar crystals get dissolved, so they are the solute.

In liquid-liquid, gas-gas, and solid-solid solutions, the solvent is the part that is present in the greater amount. Air is a good example of this situation. Air is about 78% nitrogen and 21% oxygen. The solvent in air is nitrogen and oxygen is a solute.

How a Solution Forms

solute — solvent

solution

Reading Photos

What is the solvent?

Clue: Look at the state of the materials that are being mixed.

Have you ever tried to wipe up a wet spill with a sponge and the sponge gets too full of liquid to soak up any more? This principle is also true for solutions. A certain amount of solvent can dissolve only so much solute. For example, only 37 grams of table salt will dissolve into 100 grams of water at room temperature. No matter how much you stir, additional salt crystals will not disappear into the solution. The greatest amount of solute that a given amount of solvent can dissolve is called the **solubility** (SOL•yew•bil•uh•tee) of the solute. So for the table salt, its solubility is 37 grams per 100 grams of water at room temperature.

Water solubility is different for each solute. It also depends on temperature. Most solid solutes get more soluble with increasing temperature, but some get less soluble.

Most gases tend to have a low solubility in water. They also are less soluble at higher temperatures. For example, when water is heated, it often contains less dissolved oxygen because it is less soluble.

Quick Lab

Temperature in Solutions

1. **Predict** Do you think you could dissolve more sugar in hot water or cold water? Why? Write down your reasons.

2. **Observe** Place 7 level teaspoons (25g) of sugar in each of 2 clear cups. Working with a partner, add 25 mL (1 oz) of cold water to one batch of sugar and 25 mL (1 oz) of hot water to the other. Stir the sugar and water in both cups.

3. In which cup does the sugar seem to dissolve most rapidly? How can you tell?

4. **Draw Conclusions** Was your prediction correct? Write out your findings.

✓ Quick Check

Draw Conclusions In a solution made by mixing table salt with water, what is the solute? How do you know?

Critical Thinking Why does a warm soda lose its fizz faster than a cold soda?

▲ The sand particles cannot pass through the pores in the filter, but water particles can. The sand collects on the filter, while the water drips through.

▲ The low density of sawdust lets it float away from the higher-density sand that remains at the bottom.

How can you take mixtures apart?

Mixtures are physical combinations of different substances. They can be separated by physical changes based on their different properties. In some cases this may be easy, whereas in other cases it may be difficult. However, it is always possible in principle. The diagrams on these pages show common methods of physically separating two substances. Study them carefully.

One of the most common methods of separating a liquid and a solid is filtration (fil•TRAY•shuhn). **Filtration** separates substances that have particles of different sizes. A filter is a material with fine holes. Small particles pass through the holes, large particles do not.

If the two substances in a mixture differ in density, it may be possible to use water to separate them by means of flotation. For example, a mixture of sand and sawdust in a container can be separated by pouring in water. The sawdust has a lower density so it floats to the top, while the heavier sand remains at the bottom.

Separating mixtures can also be done by using solubility. For example, suppose you have sugar mixed with sand in a glass. Pouring water into the glass will dissolve the sugar, while the sand remains solid. Filtering the sugar

▲ Dissolving sugar in water separates it from insoluble sand. Filtering and evaporating the water recovers the sugar.

▲ Iron is attracted to a magnet, while sand is nonmagnetic.

solution into another glass separates it from the sand. The sugar is recovered when the water in the glass evaporates.

Magnetism also can be used to separate some mixtures. If you have iron filings mixed with sand, a magnet can be used to separate the iron pieces from the sand. The magnet will only attract the metal pieces, while the sand remains behind.

✔ Quick Check

Draw Conclusions What is there about mixtures that allows them to be separated using physical means?

Critical Thinking What property is used to separate gold from sand when they are swirled in a pan filled with water?

Reading Diagrams

How would you separate a mixture of sand, sawdust, iron filings, and sugar?

Clue: Each diagram shows one separation method.

 Science in Motion Watch how mixtures are separated @ www.macmillanmh.com

▲ Prospectors use density when panning for gold. Swirling water washes the sand out of the pan leaving the gold.

The CN Tower is one of the tallest reinforced concrete buildings in the world.

What is reinforced concrete?

Reinforced concrete is one of the most widely used mixtures in the world. It is a hard, strong, and durable material used in building highways, bridges, and tunnels. America's first concrete street, built in 1891, is still in service today. One of the tallest reinforced concrete buildings in the world is the CN Tower in Toronto, Canada. It soars 553 m (1815 ft) into the air. Not bad for something made from a material that isn't even pure.

Making concrete requires a lot of mixing. Rotating mixers are part of the delivery trucks used to bring the concrete from the cement plant to the job site. The materials for making concrete are put into the mixer in various proportions. They include gravel-sized rocks, fine sand, ultra-fine cement powder, and water. The rocks provide strength and the sand fills any gaps left between the rocks. In the mixer, the cement and water form a pourable mud that fills any remaining spaces.

After mixing is completed, the concrete is poured into forms at the job site. There, it flows over steel wire, rods, or bars used to reinforce it. After the cement hardens, it binds the sand, rocks, and steel reinforcement into a very strong material.

For a modern material, cement has a long history. The ancient Romans used natural cement they found in volcanic rocks. Today the clay and limestone formed in Earth's mantle millions of years ago are being processed inside rotary kilns—giant furnaces at cement factories.

 Quick Check

Draw Conclusions How can a concrete road built in 1891 still be in use today?

Critical Thinking What advantage does an impure mixture have over a pure substance?

Lesson Review

Summarize the Main Idea

Mixtures are physical combinations of substances or materials. (p. 378)

Mixtures can be classified as suspensions or solutions. (p. 379)

Mixtures can be separated by using filtration, magnetism, density, or solubility. (pp. 382–383)

Make a FOLDABLES™ Study Guide

Make a folded book (see p. 479). Use the title shown. On the inside, write what you learned about mixtures.

Mixtures

Think, Talk, and Write

1. **Main Idea** What kind of substance is a physical combination of two or more substances?

2. **Vocabulary** A mixture that settles into layers overnight is a ~~S GS Pensbn~~

3. **Draw Conclusions** Is it easier to clean dishes with hot or cold water? Why?

Text Clues	Conclusions

4. **Critical Thinking** Which passes through filter paper without being separated—a suspension or a solution? Why?

5. **Test Practice** **The part of a solution that is dissolved is called the**
   - **A** solvent.
   - **B** colloid.
   - **C** emulsion.
   - **D** solute.

6. **Test Practice** **If a mixture contains visible particles, it is**
   - **A** a gas.
   - **B** homogenous.
   - **C** heterogenous.
   - **D** an element.

Writing Link

Expository Writing
Write about the different types of foods you eat. Often foods that are mixtures taste better than things eaten by themselves. Write about why you think this is so.

Social Studies Link

Cement in Ancient Times
Research how the ancient Romans used cement. Compare and contrast their use of cement with modern use.

Writing in Science

What's in This Mixture?

Archaeologists study the remains of life from the past. They dig in the ground to find objects from long ago. They examine soil to find clues such as seeds or tiny pieces of bone and stone.

How do archaeologists separate tiny objects in soil? They use a method called water flotation. First, they put dried soil on a fine mesh screen. Then water is bubbled up gently through the soil. Seeds and light objects float off. Stone, bone, and heavy pieces remain.

Archaeologists can also separate mixtures of rock and bone. Soaking the rock in acid for three days, wears it away so the bone can be studied. Separating mixtures enables archeologists to dig out the past!

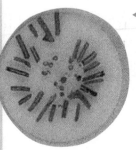

◀ Small objects, such as seeds, are removed from a soil sample using water flotation.

▼ Separating rocks and bone can expose bones of ancient animals.

Write About It

Expository Writing Do some research to write a report about how prospectors panned for gold during the California Gold Rush. What mixtures did prospectors have to separate? How did they do it? Give the steps of the process in order.

 LOG ON e-**Journal** Write about it online @ www.macmillanmh.com

 ELA W 5.1.2. Create multiple-paragraph expository compositions.
a. Establish a topic, important ideas, or events in sequence or chronological order.
b. Provide details and transitional expressions that link one paragraph to another in a clear line of thought. c. Offer a concluding paragraph that summarizes important ideas and details.

Mix It Up!

Have you ever had a tossed salad? Salads are eaten as a mixture. Look at the ingredients for a fruit salad in the chart below. Determine each separate fruit's fractional amount of the whole salad. Then find the percentage of each fruit in the salad.

To determine a fractional part and a percent

▶ use the fruit amount as the numerator and the total number of cups as the denominator.

▶ the amount of apples as a fraction and a percent:
= 2 cups/10 cups
= 2/10
= 20%

FRUIT SALAD

Fruit	Recipe amount	Fraction of whole salad	Percentage of whole salad
apples (chopped)	2 cups	2/10	20%
banana (sliced)	1 cups		
grapes (whole)	3 cups		
strawberries (sliced)	1 cup		
oranges (sliced)	3 cups		
	10 cups total		100% total

 SOLVE IT

Based on the ingredients of the following salad, write the amounts of each type of bean in the mixture as a fraction and a percent.

green beans   6 cups
wax beans   3 cups
red beans   1 cup

 MA NS 5.1.2. Interpret percents as part of a hundred; find decimal and percent equivalents for common fractions and explain why they represent the same value; compute a given percent of a whole number.

Lesson 5

Compounds

Golden Gate Bridge, San Francisco, California

Look and Wonder

Painting the 1.7 mile-long Golden Gate Bridge is a never-ending process. Painters have to constantly touch up the paint to stop the bridge from rusting. Why do you think rust is such a serious threat to the bridge's steel structure?

 5 PS 1.a. Students know that during chemical reactions the atoms in the reactants rearrange to form products with different properties. • **5 PS 1.f.** Students know differences in chemical and physical properties of substances are used to separate mixtures and identify compounds.

What is rust?

Form a Hypothesis

When steel is exposed to air, the iron in it rusts. Does steel become stronger or weaker when it rusts? Think about rust to answer this question. Write your answer as an hypothesis in the form *"If steel is exposed to air, then it becomes . . ."*

Materials

- **small bowl**
- **vinegar**
- **steel wool pad**

Test Your Hypothesis

1. **Experiment** Soak a small piece of steel wool in vinegar for three minutes, remove it and let it sit exposed to air. The vinegar exposes the iron in the steel.

2. Take another small piece of steel wool from the same pad and let it sit in the air near the first piece.

3. **Observe** After 25 minutes, examine both pieces of steel wool. Which piece of steel wool rusted?

4. Look at the properties of rust. Is it the same color as iron? Does it have the same strength?

Step 1

Draw Conclusions

5. Did your results support your hypothesis?

6. **Infer** Did a new material form? Explain.

7. Which element could have caused the change?

8. What would you need to do to find out the specific element that caused the change?

Explore More

Which makes steel rust faster, air or water? How could you determine the answer? Plan and conduct an experiment to find out.

Step 4

5 IE 6.h. Draw conclusions from scientific evidence and indicate whether further information is needed to support a specific conclusion.

What changes produce new and different substances?

When the iron present in nails, cars, or bridges is exposed to air it comes in contact with oxygen. Iron and oxygen combine to make a new powdery, reddish-brown substance called rust. How do we know it is a new substance? Rust is a new substance because it has its own properties.

You have learned that mixtures retain the properties of the substances that make them. Mud retains the properties of water and dirt. However, rust does not have the same properties as oxygen and iron. For example, the color of the iron has changed.

Rust forms as a result of a chemical change. A **chemical change** is a change of matter that

▼ The iron in this ship has been exposed to air. The oxygen in the air reacted with iron to form iron oxide, commonly called rust.

results in a new substance that is different from the original substances.

Turning the reddish-brown powdery rust back into iron takes more than physical changes. Boiling, filtering, or using a magnet on rust won't work. It takes another chemical change to restore the properties of iron. You have to separate the oxygen from its chemical combination with iron. It isn't easy, but it is done every day in the steel mills of the world. It takes huge furnaces, tons of raw materials, and very high temperatures to turn rust back into iron and steel.

Iron atoms can combine with oxygen atoms in different arrangements. There are actually three different compounds of iron oxide. They differ in color; one is magnetic, two are not. Rust is the most common.

Sugar is another example of a compound. A **compound** is formed when the atoms of two or more elements combine. Sugar molecules are formed when the atoms of carbon, hydrogen, and oxygen chemically combine to form a white, sweet substance.

Marshmallows are made of white sugar and taste sweet. What happens when marshmallows are exposed to open fire? The heat rearranges the atoms of sugar into new combinations, and new substances form. When marshmallows are roasted over a campfire, their surface blackens and produces steam. The black material is carbon. The steam is water vapor. Water is composed of hydrogen and oxygen. Sugar contains the atoms of carbon, hydrogen, and oxygen.

Chemical Changes

Reading Photos

Marshmallows contain the compound sucrose ($C_{12}H_{22}O_{11}$). Heat can break this compound down into carbon and water. What other chemical changes can you see in this photo?

Clue: Look at what else the fire is changing.

A chemical change occurs when atoms join to form compounds, and also when they break apart. The atoms might rearrange as elements or they might join atoms of other elements to form new compounds. In either case, atoms are "changing partners."

 Quick Check

Make Inferences Why is the formation of rust a chemical change?

Critical Thinking Why does each compound have only one composition?

How are compounds named?

Many compounds have common names, such as water, sugar, salt, and baking soda. The chemical name for a compound is often the name of the first element plus a modified form of the second element's name.

For example, table salt is the common name for the compound sodium chloride. Table salt is composed of sodium and chlorine. Can you see that the name "chlorine" has been changed to "chlor*ide*" in the chemical name for table salt? You will see that an -*ide* ending is common in compound names when only two elements are present.

Sometimes, prefixes like *mon-*, *di*, or *tri*- are also added to the element names. For example, when carbon combines with one oxygen atom, the new compound is called carbon monoxide. When carbon combines with two oxygen atoms, the new compound is called carbon dioxide.

Chemists also give compounds a chemical formula. A **chemical formula** has symbols to show which elements have combined to form that particular compound. A formula also has numbers to the lower right of the element symbols. These numbers are called subscripts. **Subscripts** indicate the number of atoms that have combined.

Water: H_2O

▲ Two hydrogen atoms and one oxygen atom combine to form a molecule of water.

Sugar: $C_6H_{12}O_6$

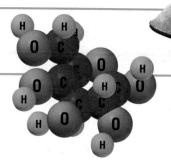

▲ Six carbon atoms, 12 hydrogen atoms, and six oxygen atoms combine to form sugar.

Carbon dioxide: CO_2

▲ One carbon atom and two oxygen atoms combine to form carbon dioxide. CO_2 is present in the smoke.

A common compound is water. The formula for water is H_2O. This means that two atoms of hydrogen combine with one atom of oxygen to make a molecule of water.

Another common compound is sulfur dioxide. The formula for sulfur dioxide is SO_2. This means that one atom of sulfur combines with two atoms of oxygen to make a molecule of sulfur dioxide. If a symbol does not have a subscript that means the chemical formula has one atom of that element.

Certain groups of atoms are given special names in compounds. For example, the chemical name of baking soda ($NaHCO_3$) is sodium bicarbonate. The group of atoms HCO_3 is commonly named "bicarbonate" or "hydrogen carbonate" when it is part of a compound.

✓ Quick Check

Make Inferences Glucose has this formula: $C_6H_{12}O_6$. What information does this formula give you?

Critical Thinking Why don't all compound names end in -ide?

How can you identify compounds?

There are millions of compounds. How can you tell one from another? Every compound has a unique set of properties that identify it. Some properties are physical and others are chemical in nature.

Physical properties include density, freezing, melting and boiling points, and color. For example, what clear liquid freezes at 0°C (32°F) and boils at 100°C (212°F)? There is only one—it's water! What liquid has a density of one gram per mL? Again, it's water.

Carbon dioxide is a colorless gas. The density of carbon dioxide is about 1.5 times that of air. At atmospheric pressure, it passes directly from the gaseous state to the solid state at –78°C (–108°F). When a lighted match comes in contact with CO_2, it is immediately extinguished, as carbon dioxide does not support combustion.

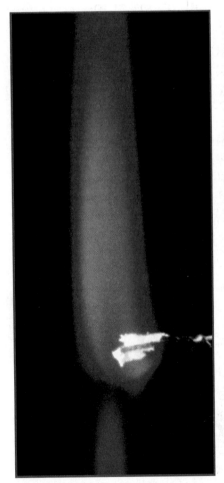

▲ Strontium compounds have red flames.

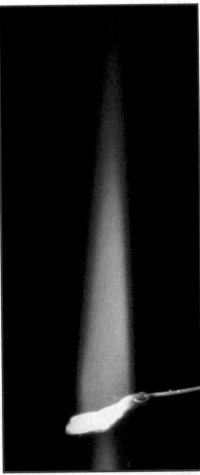

▲ Potassium compounds have violet flames.

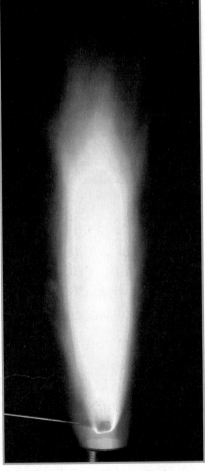

▲ Sodium compounds have bright yellow flames.

Chemical properties are only observed when a chemical change is taking place. Examples of chemical properties include the color that atoms give off when they are reacting.

For example, potassium and compounds that contain potassium will make the flames of a fire turn violet, or purple. Sodium and compounds that contain sodium will color flames bright yellow. Strontium and compounds that contain strontium will color flames red.

Modern scientists use spectrometers and other instruments to identify compounds and elements. Spectrometers can identify the element or compound because it gives off its own set of colors. This shows what elements are in the compound and identifies it.

▲ Spectrometers identify elements and compounds by the light they give off.

Quick Lab

Identify the Compound

Your teacher will give you two mystery compounds. Use the property of density to identify them.

1. Find the mass of an empty container.
2. Pour 100mL of one of the compounds into the container.
3. Calculate the mass of the compound.
4. Repeat step 3 with the second compound.
5. What is the density of the mystery compounds? You can calculate density by dividing mass by volume.
6. The density of water is 1g/mL. Is either of the compounds water? Which one?

✔ Quick Check

Make Inferences Why do you think it is necessary to know both chemical and physical properties to identify a compound?

Critical Thinking A mass spectrometer shows a compound that is made of atoms of iron and oxygen. What is the compound?

How are compounds used?

Chemists and chemical engineers have learned how to produce products from compounds that make our lives much easier. Products from crude oil are an important example. Petroleum engineers can obtain gasoline, kerosene, lubricating oils, diesel fuel, heating oil, and light fuel gases from crude oil. All of these products are **hydrocarbons** (high•druh•KAHR•buhns), which are molecules that are composed of hydrogen and carbon.

Rubber is a flexible material that is formed from long strings of hydrocarbons. Rubber is used to make products such as car tires, erasers, and shoe soles. It is also used to cover electrical wires and make hoses that

▲ Many fibers used in clothing are man-made compounds composed of hydrocarbons and elements such as nitrogen and chlorine.

hold fluids in car engines and in washing machines.

Plastics are made from long strings of carbon with oxygen, nitrogen, chlorine, or sulfur. When heat and pressure are applied, plastics can be formed into different shapes. Plastics are used in many of the products we use every day, including eyeglass lenses, paints, food and drink containers, and carpets. Plastics are used to make boats, automobile bodies, and furniture. Some plastics are also used to make clothes.

Cloth and fabric are made of fibers that are woven together. Some cloths and fabrics are prepared with natural compounds like wool or cotton. Others are made with man-made compounds like nylon or polyester.

Compound Uses

Reading Photos

What uses of compounds can you see in a gas station?

Clue: Look for hydrocarbons and fibers.

✓ *Quick Check*

Make Inferences Why are so many products made from plastic?

Critical Thinking Why are hydrocarbons important in our lives?

Lesson Review

Summarize the Main Idea

Compounds are formed and broken down by chemical changes. (pp. 390–391)

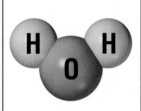

Chemical formulas show the composition of compounds. Compounds can be identified by their properties. (pp. 392–395)

Hydrocarbons are examples of compounds that make our lives easier. (p. 396)

Make a FOLDABLES™ Study Guide

Make a three-tab book (see p. 481). Use the titles shown. On the inside of each tab summarize what you have learned.

Think, Talk, and Write

1. **Main Idea** What happens if you leave a steel shovel outdoors in the rain?

2. **Vocabulary** The composition of a compound is shown by its _____.

3. **Make Inferences** What happens when atoms combine in new arrangements?

Clues	What You Know	Inferences

4. **Critical Thinking** A compound colors flames violet. What could it contain?

5. **Test Practice** **Most compounds used to make plastics and synthetic textiles are**
   A oxide.
   B hydrocarbons.
   C chlorides.
   D bromides.

6. **Test Practice** **Which one is a compound?**
   A iron
   B water
   C chlorine
   D helium

Writing Link

Descriptive Writing
Research the common physical state, the solubility in water, boiling and freezing points, sublimation, and reactivity of sugar and carbon dioxide. Write about your findings.

Math Link

Calculating Atoms
How many atoms are in a molecule of CO_2? How many atoms are needed to make 10 molecules of CO_2?

Be a Scientist

unknown materials A, B, C

filter paper

funnel

beaker

bottled water

Inquiry Structured

How can you tell if a substance is a compound or a mixture?

Form a Hypothesis

Compounds formed by chemical reactions are much more difficult to separate than mixtures formed by physical combinations. You will classify three substances as mixtures or compounds by using physical separation methods. The first separation method will be filtration. The filter allows small particles to pass thought it while trapping larger particles. Observe the three samples. Will filtration separate any of the substances? Write your answer as three hypotheses in the form *"If I pass mixture X through a filter, then…"*

Test Your Hypothesis

Step 1

① Fold the filter paper in half. Then fold it in half again. Press the edges together gently so it opens up into a cone. One side will have one layer of paper, the other side will have three layers. Moisten the cone with your fingers so it does not come apart and put it in the funnel.

② Place the funnel over the beaker. Pour substance A through the filter paper. Did the filter trap anything? Record your results.

Step 2

③ Empty the beaker back into container A. Rinse the beaker and prepare a new piece of filter paper for the funnel.

④ Repeat steps 2 and 3 for unknown substances B and C. Record your results.

5 IE 6.c. Plan and conduct a simple investigation based on a student-developed question and write instructions others can follow to carry out the procedure.

Draw Conclusions

1 **Infer** What can you infer from the results?

2 Did the experiment support your hypotheses? Why or why not?

Inquiry Guided

Can density help determine if it is a mixture or a compound?

Form a Hypothesis

One of the remaining substances is the compound water. Use density to find out which one is water. Remember that density determines what can float in a liquid and how high it can float. Pour water in a jar and find an object that can float in it. Then, write a hypothesis in the form *"If object X floats to _____ , then the substance is water."*

Test Your Hypothesis

Design a plan to test your hypothesis. Then write down the materials, resources, and steps you need to test your hypothesis. Record results and observations as you follow your plan.

Draw Conclusions

Did your test support your hypothesis? Why or why not? Were you able to prove that one of the substances remaining was a compound?

Inquiry Open

Filtration helped you determine that one of the substances was a mixture. Density helped you determine that one of the substances was a compound. You have one substance left. How can you find out if it is a mixture or a compound? How about evaporation? Come up with a question and a hypothesis to find out whether the last substance is a mixture or a compound. Then plan a procedure to test your hypothesis. Present your results to the class.

Remember to follow the steps of the scientific process.

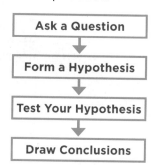

```
Ask a Question
      ↓
Form a Hypothesis
      ↓
Test Your Hypothesis
      ↓
Draw Conclusions
```

Summarize the Main Ideas

Matter can be solid, liquid, or gaseous. The properties of matter include volume, mass, weight, and density. (pp. 342–349)

Matter is made of elements, which are made of atoms. (pp. 352–359)

Each element is made of a different kind of atom. Elements are organized by their properties. (pp. 362–373)

Mixtures are physical combinations of substances. (pp. 376–385)

Chemical combinations produce compounds that can be identified by their properties. (pp. 388–397)

Make a FOLDABLES™ Study Guide

Take a sheet of paper and tape your lesson study guide as shown.

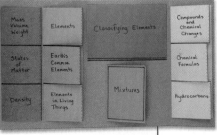

Fill each blank with the best word from the list.

atom, p. 354   **solute**, p. 380

compound, p. 391   **solvent**, p. 380

density, p. 348   **subscript**, p. 392

element, p. 354   **volume**, p. 342

1. A measurement of 5 mL indicates an object's _____. 5 PS 1.g

2. The more closely packed are its particles, the greater an object's _____. 5 PS 1.g

3. Oxygen is an example of a(n) _____. 5 PS 1.d

4. Protons and neutrons are located in the nucleus of a(n) _____. 5 PS 1.d

5. When sugar dissolves in water, the water acts as a(n) _____. 5 PS 1.f

6. The chemical combination of two or more elements produces a(n) _____. 5 PS 1.b

7. In the chemical formula H_2O, the 2 is a(n) _____. 5 PS 1.b

8. Salt in the ocean is a(n) _____. 5 PS 1.f

Answer each of the following in complete sentences.

9. Make Inferences You analyze an unknown substance and discover that it mainly contains the elements carbon, hydrogen, oxygen, and nitrogen. What is the most likely source of the substance? Explain.
5 PS 1.h

10. Record Data and Infer An iron nail is left outdoors as part of an investigation to study rust. How would you record data for this experiment? The nail goes from dull gray to a reddish color. What can you infer from this observation? 5 IE 6.g

11. Compare and Contrast How are mass and weight different? 5 PS 1.g

12. Critical Thinking How can salt be separated from a solution of saltwater? 5 PS 1.f

13. Explanatory Writing Imagine you are Dmitri Mendeleev giving a lecture about his periodic table. Write the part of the speech that describes the characteristics of a column, or family, of elements. 5 PS 1.d

 What do all types of matter have in common? 5 PS 1.b

CHAPTER 7

Now One Thing— Now Another!

Your task is to identify chemical changes that occur in and outside of your home.

What to do

1. Observe objects around you that appear to change over time.

2. Make an illustrated chart that shows how the objects have changed.

Analyze your results

▶ List the changes that you think are chemical.

▶ Describe the evidence that makes you believe a chemical change has occurred.

▲ A layer of paint prevents chemical changes from weakening the bridge.

 5 PS 1.f. Students know differences in chemical and physical properties of substances are used to separate mixtures and identify compounds.

401

1 When a gas reaches its condensation point, it becomes a 5 PS 1.g

A liquid.

B solid.

C crystal.

D gas.

2 A student is trying to determine if an unknown substance is classified as a solid, liquid, or a gas. She can determine that it is a liquid if it 5 PS 1.g

A fills the volume of its container and is able to spread out and be squeezed together.

B takes the shape of its container and has a fixed volume.

C keeps its shape and may even form crystals.

D conducts electricity and is shiny.

3 Which elements combine together to form water? 5 PS 1.b

A hydrogen and nitrogen

B oxygen and helium

C hydrogen and oxygen

D oxygen and nitrogen

4 Which instrument should a scientist use to view single atoms? 5 PS 1.e

A magnifying glass

B laser beam

C seismograph

D electron microscope

5 The periodic table provides useful information about the elements.

28 Ni Nickel	29 Cu Copper	30 Zn Zinc
46 Pd Palladium	47 Ag Silver	48 Cd Cadmium
78 Pt Platinum	79 Au Gold	80 Hg Mercury

What is the element name for the symbol Au? 5 PS 1.d

A palladium

B copper

C silver

D gold

6 A material that can be bent or flattened is a good conductor of heat and electricity. These materials are on the left side of the periodic table. Which of the following belongs to this group? 5 PS 1.d

A metalloid

B gas

C nonmetal

D metal

7 Which of the following can be classified as a solution? 5 PS 1.f

A cinnamon and sugar

B water and sugar

C gold ore

D muddy water

8 A creamy mixture was left out on the kitchen counter overnight. By morning, the mixture settled into layers. This mixture was a(n) 5 PS 1.g

A solution.

B element.

C compound.

D suspension.

9 Paula left her bicycle outside all day and night despite the weather reports.

What is she most likely to find has happened the next morning to her bicycle? 5 PS 1.f

A Physical changes colored it green.

B Chemical changes colored it reddish-brown.

C Physical changes made it shiny.

D No changes have occured.

10 A student conducted an experiment to learn more about compounds. She used baking soda, a simple heating device, and a hand lens. Which of the following would be a testable question for the student to use in the experiment? 5 IE 6.b

A What physical changes can be observed when baking soda is heated?

B How do the atoms in baking soda rearrange when it is heated?

C What electrical forces act internally on baking soda when it is heated?

D How do atoms cluster when baking soda is heated?

11 Which actions will most likely happen after placing a lid on a very full pot of boiling water? 5 PS 1.g

A Condensation will occur on the outside of the pot.

B Slow-moving molecules will contract, creating a vacuum inside the pot.

C Evaporation of the liquid will take place quickly.

D Fast-moving molecules will cause the lid to pop up on the pot.

12 Aluminum is an element because it 5 PS 1.d.

A conducts electricity.

B is made of only one kind of atom.

C does not dissolve in water.

D can be recycled and reused.

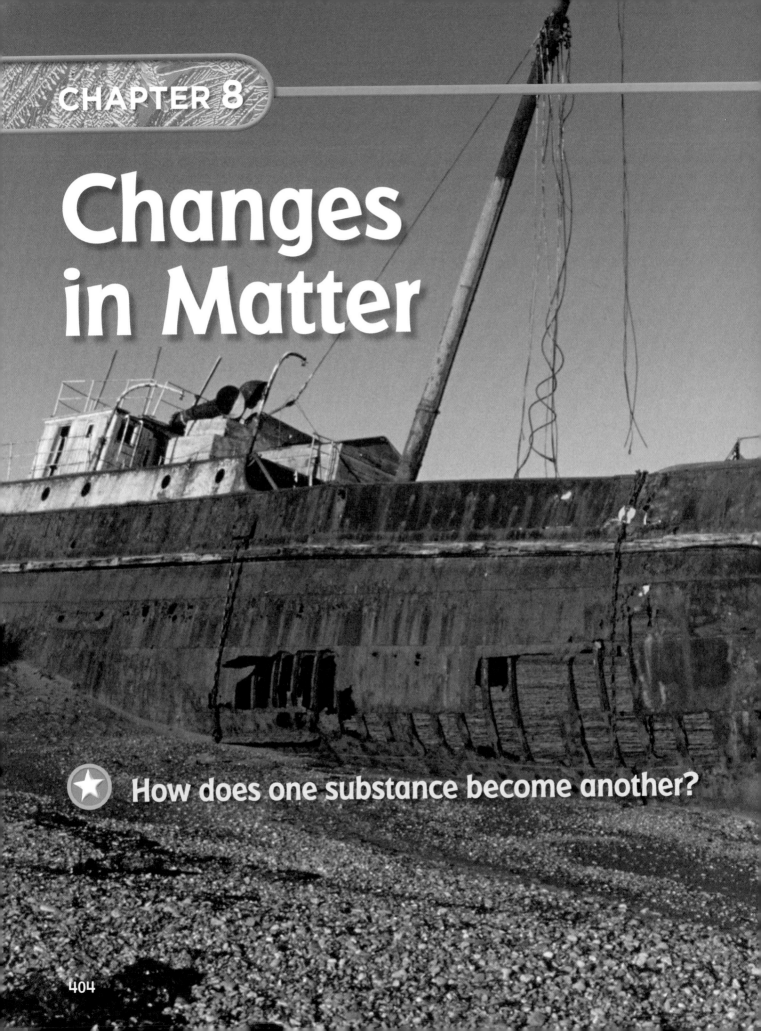

Changes in Matter

⭐ How does one substance become another?

5 PS 1. Elements and their combinations account for all the varied types of matter in the world.

Literature

MAGAZINE ARTICLE

ELA R 5.2.3.
Discern main
ideas and
concepts presented in
texts, identifying and
assessing evidence that
supports those ideas.
ELA W 5.1.1. Create
multiple-paragraph
narrative compositions:
a. Establish and develop
a situation or plot.

The Grizzly Man

from **CURRENT SCIENCE**

How would you like to step off a cliff that's 46 meters (150 feet) high? or get rammed by a pickup truck traveling at 50 kilometers (30 miles) per hour? Troy Hurtubise did all that and not only survived but didn't get a bruise. He built special suits so he could survive attacks by grizzly bears, but his inventions may someday shield firefighters, astronauts, and even kids playing hockey.

Hurtubise has built seven different suits since he had an encounter with a grizzly bear. From then on, Hurtubise had an intense desire to understand grizzlies and even study them up close.

Hurtubise chose titanium as the material to use to construct the suit's outer plates. Titanium is a light, silver-white metal that is stronger than a piece of steel having the same weight. For a helmet, Hurtubise wanted to used an even lighter material than titanium, so he chose an aluminum-titanium alloy. An alloy is a material consisting of a metal plus at least one other element. Unfortunately, the materials in Hurtubise's suit are not quite light enough to move about in.

Hurtubise isn't discouraged, however. "Persistence—that's what every inventor has to have."

 Write About It

Response to Literature The article describes a suit designed to withstand bear attacks. If you were an inventor, what kind of suit would you invent? Write a fictional narrative describing your suit and its uses.

LOG ON **e-Journal** Write about it online @ **www.macmillanmh.com**

Chemical Reactions

Look and Wonder

This massive forest fire began with a bolt of lightning. Now the heat from the flames is turning wood and leaves into new substances. What happens to atoms when substances change?

5 PS 1.a. Students know that during chemical reactions the atoms in the reactants rearrange to form products with different properties.

What happens when substances change?

Form a Hypothesis

Does the total mass of matter change during a chemical change? Think about chemical changes you have observed, such as an egg being cooked, a roasted marshmallow, or wood burning in the fireplace. Write your answer as a hypothesis in the form *"If a chemical reaction occurs, then the total mass of matter . . ."*

Test Your Hypothesis

1. ⚠ **Be careful.** Wear safety goggles! Pour 40 mL of washing soda solution into a bag. Place 40 mL of Epsom salt solution in a paper cup. Put the cup inside the bag so that it rests upright. Seal the bag.

2. **Measure** Place the bag on a balance. Don't mix the solutions! Record the mass.

3. **Observe** Without opening the bag, pour the solution in the cup into the solution in the bag to cause a chemical change.

4. **Measure** Once again, place the bag and its contents on the balance and record the mass.

Draw Conclusions

5. What can you conclude about chemical reactions?

6. Does the data support your hypothesis? If not, how would you change it?

Explore More

What else could you do to test the hypothesis? Plan an experiment that would provide information to support your conclusion.

Materials

- safety goggles
- washing soda solution (sodium carbonate)
- sealable sandwich bag
- Epsom salt solution (hydrated magnesium sulfate)
- small paper cup
- mass balance

Step 2

Step 4

 5 IE 6.h. Draw conclusions from scientific evidence and indicate whether further information is needed to support a specific conclusion.

Read and Learn

Main Idea 5 PS 1.a

In chemical changes, atoms are rearranged into new combinations.

Vocabulary

reactant, p. 410
product, p. 410
chemical reaction, p. 410
reactivity, p. 412
precipitate, p. 414

 e-Glossary
@ www.macmillanmh.com

Reading Skill

Summarize

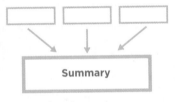

Summary

SCIENCE QUEST Explore chemical reactions with Team Earth.

What are chemical changes?

Matter is constantly changing around you. Water vapor forms clouds, tree leaves fall and rot, and foods in the kitchen are cooked. A starting substance in a chemical reaction is called a **reactant** (ree•AK•tuhnt). The new substance is called a **product**. We say that "reactants yield products" and we write it as:

reactants ⟶ products

When matter undergoes physical changes, no new substances are formed. When matter undergoes chemical changes, a chemical reaction occurs. In a **chemical reaction** substances change into new substances.

Chemical reactions may occur between atoms, molecules, or compounds. A common example of a chemical equation is the formation of carbon dioxide (CO_2). The diagram shows fire causing a chemical reaction between carbon (C) atoms and oxygen (O_2) molecules. The reactants, carbon and oxygen, are chemically changing into a product, carbon dioxide. Fire provides the energy needed for molecules to be rearranged.

Formation of Carbon Dioxide

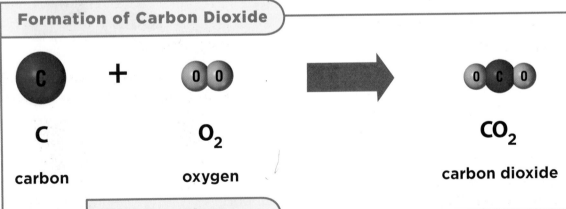

C — carbon

O_2 — oxygen

CO_2 — carbon dioxide

Reading Diagrams

What happens to the atoms during the formation of carbon dioxide?

Clue: Look at the molecules of O_2 and CO_2.

 Science in Motion Watch how atoms rearrange @ www.macmillanmh.com

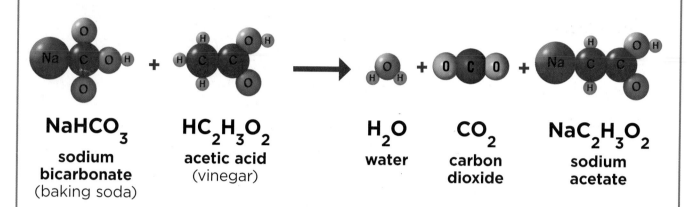

$NaHCO_3$
sodium
bicarbonate
(baking soda)

$HC_2H_3O_2$
acetic acid
(vinegar)

H_2O
water

CO_2
carbon
dioxide

$NaC_2H_3O_2$
sodium
acetate

The reaction between vinegar and baking soda is an example of a chemical change between compounds. When the two reactants are mixed, their atoms rearrange into new patterns that form three new compounds. The signs of the chemical change are the many gas bubbles. These are filled with carbon dioxide, one product of the reaction. A second product is water. The last product is sodium acetate. Sodium acetate is commonly used in the textile, rubber, and paper industries.

The total mass of the reactants always equals the total mass of the products. Since the mass of substances is the mass of their atoms, the total number of atoms remained the same. For instance, the same numbers of atoms are in the reactants and the products shown above.

Atoms simply rearrange into new combinations. The change in combinations of atoms is what gives the products new and different properties. For example, small ethylene molecules are gases at room temperature. The big polyethylene molecules they form,

are solids. Atoms are neither gained nor lost during chemical changes. They are always conserved. Molecular models show you how the atoms are rearranged in the products.

✓ Quick Check

Summarize Why must the total mass of the products equal the total mass of the reactants in a chemical reaction?

Critical Thinking If one gram of hydrogen combines with 16 grams of oxygen, what will be the mass of the products?

▼ Baking soda and vinegar react to produce carbon dioxide, water and sodium acetate.

What are the most reactive elements?

Some metallic elements are much more likely to take part in chemical reactions than others. These elements have a high **reactivity**. This means they react easily. The most reactive family of metals is called the alkali metals. It includes lithium, sodium, potassium, rubidium, cesium, and francium. Metal elements get more reactive as you go down a group in the periodic table. The illustration shows potassium (K) is more reactive than lithium (Li). The most reactive of the alkali metals would be francium (Fr).

least reactive

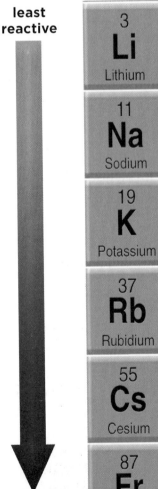

most reactive

◀ Lithium is at the top of this group of elements, called alkali metals, and is the least reactive of the group. When it is combined with water, it takes 30.4 seconds to fizz and bubble.

◀ Cesium is near the bottom of this group of elements and is more reactive than lithium. When it is combined with water, it fizzes wildly and the hydrogen gas released from the water ignites and burns brightly in 7.1 seconds.

▲ The alkali metals

You cannot find reactive metals in the ground in their elemental form. They form compounds too easily. Sodium combines with chlorine to form sodium chloride, or salt. It dissolves in seawater and makes it salty.

The most reactive nonmetals are in the halogen family. The halogens are in the next-to-last column of the periodic table. Fluorine (F) is the most reactive nonmetal. As you go down a column of nonmetals they become less reactive. Chlorine (Cl) is a little less reactive than fluorine. When molten silvery sodium metal meets green chlorine gas, the two elements disappear in a bright flash of light, and are replaced by snowy white salt crystals. Iodine and bromine also react readily with many substances, but not as strongly as fluorine and chlorine.

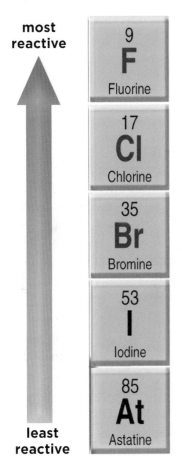

most reactive

least reactive

◀ The halogens

Quick Lab

Compare Reactivities

1. ⚠ **Be careful.** Use a metal file to scratch a tic-tac-toe pattern on both sides of a new penny. You should be able to see silvery zinc in the scratches. Also make several scratches around the penny's edge.

2. **Observe** Put the penny in a cup of vinegar and let it stand for several days. Observe it each day and note what is happening.

3. **Observe** Based on your observations, which metal in the penny is more reactive, the zinc or the copper? How do you know?

Oxygen is another fairly reactive nonmetal. Many metals react with oxygen in the air to form an oxide compound. This reaction causes iron to rust and gradually ruins the metal. A few metals, like aluminum and magnesium, form oxides that actually help protect them from further damage.

✓ Quick Check

Summarize How do the reactivities compare between the alkali metals and the halogens?

Critical Thinking What would happen if a piece of rubidium were dropped in water? Why?

What are signs of a chemical change?

There are several common signs that show that substances have undergone a chemical change. One of these is the formation of a solid when solutions are mixed. The formation of such a solid in the liquid is an example of a **precipitate** (pri•SIP•i•tayt). A precipitate is a solid that forms in solution due to a chemical reaction.

A second sign of a chemical change is when a gas is produced. If you put an antacid tablet containing a mixture of baking soda and citric acid in a glass of water, bubbles of carbon dioxide gas are produced. The formation of a gas upon the mixing of chemicals likely means a chemical change has happened.

Temperature increases are a sign of a chemical change that releases energy. Similarly, a release of energy as light indicates a chemical change. The light from a candle flame is an example. A flame is a burning gas. Heat first melts the candle wax, then turns it to gas, and finally ignites it.

Signs of a Chemical Change

Forms a precipitate	Forms a gas	Temperature changes
When two solutions form a precipitate, a chemical reaction has occured.	When this antacid reacts with water, bubbles of carbon dioxide gas indicate a chemical change is taking place.	When the chemicals in the sealed bag mix, they react and release heat to warm hands or feet.

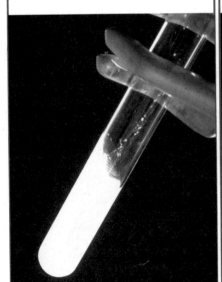

A change in color is another sign of a chemical change. For example, suppose you've spilled food coloring on a white T-shirt. How would you clean it? You could add some bleach to the wash to remove the color. The bleach takes away the color by chemically changing the molecules of the dye. When a drop of red-colored iodine dissolved in alcohol falls on starch, the reddish color turns black. Baking soda turns red cabbage juice to brown or yellow.

Metals change color when they tarnish. Iron turns reddish-brown. Silver turns black. Copper turns black or green depending on the reactant.

 Quick Check

Summarize If mixing two solutions produces a powdery solid, what do you know happened?

Critical Thinking What would tell you that cooking an egg is a chemical change?

Energy is released	Color changes	Tarnish is formed
A release of energy as light indicates a chemical change. The light from a candle flame is an example.	Color change, such as bleach being used to remove color, is another example of a chemical change.	The color change of this spoon is called tarnish. It is caused by the reaction of silver with sulfur.

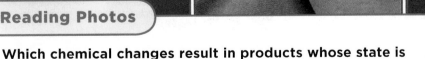

Reading Photos

Which chemical changes result in products whose state is different from the reactants?

Clue: Look at photos that show a change of state.

What are photosynthesis and respiration?

We use chemical reactions in many ways, but the most important ones enable people, animals, and plants to live. In the diagram, you see the chemical reaction known as photosynthesis. Its products provide us with food to eat and oxygen to breathe. The leaves of green plants are the factories where the reaction takes place. The Sun's energy forces the atoms of the reactants to rearrange themselves into the products. The products store the energy from the Sun.

When you eat and breathe, you reverse photosynthesis. The reverse reaction is called respiration. Your body cells force glucose and oxygen to rearrange their atoms back into carbon dioxide and water. This releases the stored energy for you to use so you can run, work, play, learn—live!

Respiration is just as important as photosynthesis. It provides plants with the materials they need to keep the cycle of life going.

✔ Quick Check

Summarize Explain why chemical reactions are important in everyday life.

Critical Thinking What other chemical reactions affect your life? Give three examples.

Photosynthesis and Respiration

Photosynthesis

$$6CO_2 \;+\; 6H_2O \;\longrightarrow\; C_6H_{12}O_6 \;+\; 6O_2$$

| carbon dioxide | water | | glucose | oxygen |

Respiration

$$C_6H_{12}O_6 \;+\; 6O_2 \;\longrightarrow\; 6CO_2 \;+\; 6H_2O$$

| glucose | oxygen | | carbon dioxide | water |

▶ Photosynthesis, the food-making process in green plants, is a chemical reaction. Respiration, the release of energy from food, is also a chemical reaction.

Summarize the Main Idea

In a **chemical reaction** atoms rearrange to form new substances. (pp. 410-411)

The **most reactive** metals are the alkali metals, and the most reactive nonmetals are the halogens. (pp. 412–413)

The **signs of a chemical change** include formation of a precipitate or a gas, the release of energy, and a color change. (pp. 414–416)

Make a **FOLDABLES™** Study Guide

Make a Four-Door book (see p. 482). Use the titles shown. On the inside of each tab, summarize what you have learned.

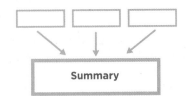

chemical reactions | most reactive metals and nonmetals
chemical reactions in my life | signs of chemical change

Think, Talk, and Write

① **Main Idea** Describe what happens during any chemical reaction.

② **Vocabulary** A solid that forms when two solutions are mixed is a _____.

③ **Summarize** Which nonmetal is more reactive, oxygen or sulfur? Explain.

```
[   ]   [   ]   [   ]
   \      |      /
         ▼
  [    Summary    ]
```

④ **Critical Thinking** A lit candle on a balance loses mass. Explain why.

⑤ **Test Practice** The most reactive metals are in which column of the periodic table?
   A the first
   B the second
   C the next to last
   D the last

⑥ **Test Practice** All of the following are signs of a chemical reaction EXCEPT
   A change of color.
   B change of shape.
   C release of heat or light.
   D formation of a precipitate.

Math Link

Rearranging Atoms
If reactant A (5 grams) chemically reacts with reactant B (8 grams), what will be the total mass of the products?

Social Studies Link

Explanatory Writing
Research how fossil fuels are used to provide energy. What are the advantages and disadvantages of using the different fuels?

LOG ON **e-Review** Summaries and quizzes online @ **www.macmillanmh.com**

Use Variables

If you crush a certain kind of antacid tablet, and then stir it in a large bowl of hot water, the reaction will happen faster than if you put the whole tablet in a cup of cold water. What causes this? Is it the crushing of the tablet? Is it the stirring of the water? Is it the temperature? To answer such questions, scientists experiment by changing one thing at a time. What they change is the controlled (independent) **variable**.

① Learn It

The reaction speed is the dependent **variable**. The reaction speed shows the effect of the controlled (independent) **variable**. Scientists would first observe the reaction speed of a whole antacid tablet in a cup of cold water. This is called a control test. Next, they would place a crushed tablet in a cup of cold water. Then they would observe separately the effects of stirring, the amount of water, and temperature.

5 IE 6.d. Identify the dependent and controlled variables in an investigation. • **5 IE 6.e.** Identify a single independent variable in a scientific investigation and explain how this variable can be used to collect information to answer a question about the results of the experiment.

❷ Try It

Which independent variable has the most effect on the reaction of the antacid and water: using a crushed tablet, a whole tablet that's stirred, or a whole tablet in more water? Test the variables to find the answer. Use a stopwatch to measure the total reaction times. Make a chart like the one shown to record your results.

▶ As a control, place 1 whole antacid tablet in 1/2 cup of cold water.

▶ Crush a tablet in a plastic bag and put it in 1/2 cup of cold water.

▶ Place 1 whole tablet in 1/2 cup of cold water and stir with a spoon.

▶ Place 4 cups of cold water in a pitcher. Then place 1 whole tablet in the pitcher.

▶ Which independent variable increased reaction speed the most?

❸ Apply It

How do you think the results might change if you changed another independent variable? What would happen if you used warm water or stirred with a fork? Pick one of these variables or one of your own to test. Make a chart to record your results.

Time to Dissolve

	Water	Tablet	Time to dissolve
Control	1/2 cup	whole	
Test 1	1/2 cup	crushed	
Test 2	1/2 cup	whole stirred	
Test 3	4 cups	whole	

Metals and Alloys

Look and Wonder

Molten metal is poured into a mold where it will freeze and harden into shapes to make such items as nails and parts of automobiles. What properties make metals such useful materials?

 5 PS 1.c. Students know metals have properties in common, such as high electrical and thermal conductivity. Some metals, such as aluminum (Al), iron (Fe), nickel (Ni), copper (Cu), silver (Ag), and gold (Au) are pure elements; others, such as steel and brass, are composed of a combination of elemental metals.

How can you tell if it is metal?

Purpose

In this activity, you will observe, compare and contrast metal and nonmetal objects.

Procedure

1. Prepare a table to record your observations. Label it as shown.

2. **Experiment** Put on your goggles. Use the conductivity tester to see how well each object or material allows electricity to flow through it. The buzzer will sound, or the bulb will light, for materials that let electricity flow through them.

3. Bend the wire in the paper tie. Bend a toothpick. Which holds its new shape without breaking?

4. Compare the aluminum foil and sheet of paper. Which reflects light better?

Draw Conclusions

5. **Classify** Use your observations to place the materials and objects you've tested into groups.

6. **Summarize** Based on your observations, summarize the properties of metals and nonmetals.

Explore More

Are the properties of all metals the same? Plan and conduct an experiment to find out.

5 IE 6.a. Classify objects (e.g., rocks, plants, leaves) in accordance with appropriate criteria. • **5 IE 6.g.** Record data by using appropriate graphic representations (including charts, graphs, and labeled diagrams) and make inferences based on those data.

Materials

- safety goggles
- conductivity tester
- plastic, metal, and glass rods
- paper ties with steel wire
- wood toothpicks
- aluminum foil
- paper

Step 1

Properties of Metals and Nonmetals		
Property Tested	Metal Results	Nonmetal Results
electrical conductivity		
thermal conductivity		
ductility		
luster/shine		

Step 2

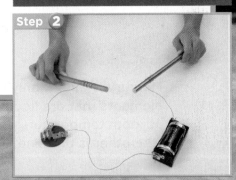

Main Idea 5 PS 1.c

Metals share some properties. Some metals are pure elements, some are mixtures.

Vocabulary

metal, p. 422

conductivity, p. 424

insulator, p. 424

superconductor, p. 424

malleable, p. 426

ductile, p. 426

corrosion, p. 428

alloy, p. 428

LOG ON e-Glossary
@ www.macmillanmh.com

Reading Skill

Problem and Solution

Problem
↓
Steps to Solution
↓
Solution

What are metals?

About three-fourths, or 75%, of the elements on the periodic table are metals. The metals fill the left and center of the periodic table. Among these you may be familiar with are metals such as gold (Au), copper (Cu), silver (Ag), zinc (Zn), aluminum (Al), iron (Fe), lead (Pb), mercury (Hg), magnesium (Mg), and chromium (Cr). A **metal** is a substance that is a good conductor of heat and electricity. When metals are polished, they reflect most of the light that strikes them. This gives metals a shiny appearance or luster.

The melting points of metals are spread over a wide range of temperatures. This makes them useful for many purposes. Mercury, for example, has a melting point of −39°C (−38.2°F) and is a liquid at room temperature 25°C (77°F). A column of liquid mercury about 760 mm (30 in.) high is used in barometers. The air pressure is measured by the height of the mercury column in millimeters.

▲ Copper nuggets like this may be the earliest metals used by humans.

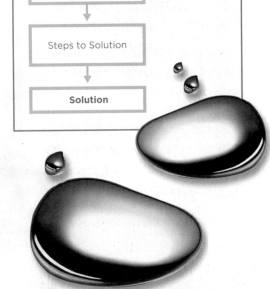

▲ Mercury is one of only two elements that are liquid at room temperature (the other is bromine).

▼ Iron is the second-most abundant metal in Earth's crust.

Mercury also expands very evenly with increasing temperature, which is why the element was used in glass thermometers. Unfortunately, mercury is harmful to the environment and to people. So if the glass of a thermometer broke and the mercury accidentally spilled, it could be dangerous.

Gallium (Ga) melts at 30°C (86°F) and boils at 2403°C (4357°F). Because of its large liquid temperature range, it is used in high temperature thermometers. When it is a liquid, gallium is reflective. It can be painted on glass to make mirrors or used to focus beams of light.

Metals with high melting points are useful because they can withstand high temperatures. Aircraft and spacecraft, for instance, often have metal parts that are made of titanium (Ti). This element can take the heat—titanium melts at 1668°C (3034°F)! It is also lightweight and strong, an added plus for a flying craft.

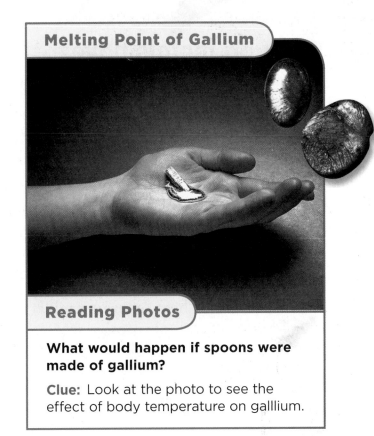

The aerospace industry uses another metal to stop the space shuttle as it lands: beryllium. This element is used to make the disks of the wheel brakes in the shuttle. Beryllium's high melting point of 1287°C (2349°F) allows the disks to withstand the heat from the friction that happens when the pilots apply the brakes.

✓ Quick Check

Problem and Solution Why is the use of mercury in thermometers being discontinued?

Critical Thinking Why would titanium be a good metal to use for firefighters' ladders?

▲ Titanium's high melting point makes it a good choice to make parts in aircraft jet engines.

What do metals have in common?

Metals have good electrical **conductivity** (kon•duk•TIV•i•tee), which means that they let electricity flow through them easily. Nonmetallic materials, however, resist the flow of electricity through them. For this reason, nonmetals are good insulators (IN•suh•lay•tuhrs). An **insulator** is something that can help prevent the movement of heat, energy, and even sound. Wood, plastics, glass, and ceramics are examples of electrical insulators.

When power companies send electricity to customers, the wires must be very good conductors. However, these power line wires strung on

▲ Power cords are used to transmit electricity. The wires are copper or aluminum, which allow electricity to flow.

high towers are not insulated. They are very dangerous to touch! Wires that conduct electricity into offices and homes are coated with plastic or rubber insulation. It prevents an electric shock if the wire is touched.

Electrical wires are made of copper or aluminum because these elements are some of the best electrical conductors of all metals. In addition, they are plentiful in nature, so their cost is affordable. Silver and gold are excellent conductors. However, they are much too expensive to use in power lines.

At temperatures way below freezing, some materials become **superconductors** because they lose all resistance to electrical flow. If materials could superconduct at room temperature, then electrical power could be transferred without a loss of energy from the power plants to users thousands of miles away. Superconductors are being used today in maglev trains that

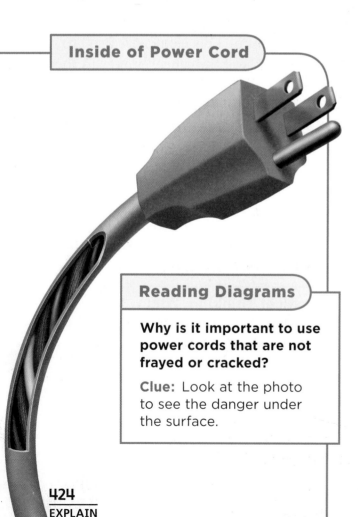

Inside of Power Cord

Reading Diagrams

Why is it important to use power cords that are not frayed or cracked?

Clue: Look at the photo to see the danger under the surface.

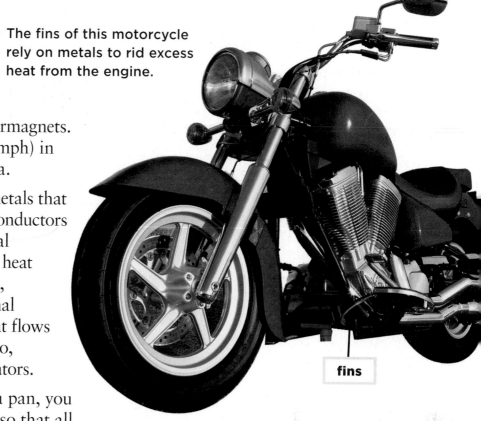

The fins of this motorcycle rely on metals to rid excess heat from the engine.

float above the rails on supermagnets. They "fly" at 500 kph (300mph) in Germany, Japan, and China.

The same properties of metals that make them good electrical conductors also make them good thermal conductors. This means that heat flows readily through metals, which gives them high thermal conductivity. In contrast, heat flows poorly through nonmetals. So, nonmetals are thermal insulators.

When you cook food in a pan, you want the pan to heat evenly so that all the food gets cooked. However, you don't want the handle to become hot. If it did, you'd burn your fingers picking up the pan! For these reasons, cookware is often made of metal bodies with handles of wood, plastic, or ceramic. For pots with metal handles, pot holders or oven mitts will keep you safe.

fins

Internal combustion engines also rely on the ability of metals to conduct heat. For example, the air-cooled motorcycle engine in the photograph has heat fins. The fins conduct heat from the engine. Their large surface area helps them to radiate, or pull, the heat away. This keeps the engine from overheating. Heat fins are also used in baseboard heating units.

 Quick Check

Problem and Solution Would you select silver or copper wire for the wiring in your house? Explain.

Critical Thinking How can firefighters protect themselves from the heat of a fire?

◀ The metal in this cookware spreads heat well. The insulating gloves protect the cook.

How hard are metals?

If you try to bend a glass rod it will break. If you try to pound a ceramic plate into a thin sheet with a hammer, it will shatter. If you bend a wooden stick too far, it will splinter and tear apart. If you do all these things to most metals, though, something different happens.

You can bend a metal rod without breaking it. You can pound a number of metals into flat sheets. If you pull on certain metals, they will stretch into strands of wire. The ability to be pressed or pulled into shape without shattering or breaking is something many metals share.

Any metal that can be rolled or pounded into flat sheets is said to be **malleable** (MAL•ee•uh•buhl). Any metal that can be drawn out into strands of wire is said to be **ductile** (DUK•tuhl). Copper and gold, for example, are among the most malleable and ductile metals. Copper is made into wires or is rolled like dough into sheets.

Gold is very often used for decorative objects. Sometimes the gold is pounded into very thin sheets called gold leaf. The gold leaf can be applied to an object, giving it a beautiful, shiny look.

You might think that metals are always very hard. After all, you've seen people pounding nails into wood with hammers. However, not all metals are as hard as the head of a hammer. Sodium metal can be cut with a butter knife!

▲ The malleability of silver has made it a favorite of metalsmiths.

The hardness of metals is measured by denting them. The size of the dent indicates the hardness. The softer the metal, the deeper or wider the dent. Chromium is the hardest metal in pure elemental form. It's almost as hard as diamonds. Cesium (Cs) is the softest metal.

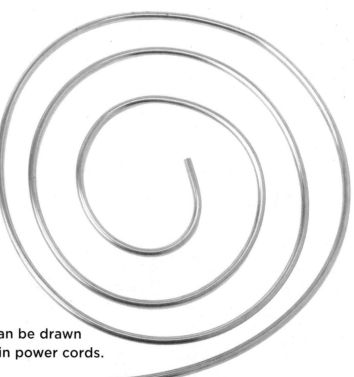

▼ Due to its ductility, copper can be drawn into thin wires that are used in power cords.

▲ Sodium metal being sliced with a butter knife. Sodium metal is an example of a soft metal.

You might be surprised to see that pure copper, silver, and gold are fairly soft. Jewelry and other objects made with these as pure metals would not wear very well. Over time, the metal would tend to get rubbed or scratched away. For this reason, copper, silver, and gold are usually mixed with smaller amounts of other metals to improve their strength and hardness. In a similar way, chromium is mixed with iron to make steel harder. As metals are made harder, they get stiffer and more brittle. As a result, hard metals are more likely to break.

Quick Lab

Hardness vs. Flexibility

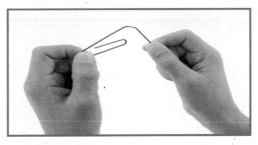

1. ⚠ **Be careful.** Wear goggles to protect your eyes. Bend one end of a steel paperclip 90° and then bend it back to its original position.

2. **Predict** How many times can you repeat this step before the paper clip breaks? Record how many bends were required to break the steel.

3. Repeat the experiment with a steel bobby pin. Note any differences in the bobby pin compared to the paper clip. Make your prediction. Record the actual results.

4. Which steel product was harder? Explain your reasoning.

✔ Quick Check

Problem and Solution Which metal would be easier to form into thin sheets, iron or gold?

Critical Thinking How could you show that chromium is harder than iron?

▲ Gold is both malleable and ductile. This nugget of gold can be hammered into gold leaf or decorative objects.

What are metal compounds and mixtures?

What happens if iron rusts? Or when silver and copper form a blackish tarnish? In each of these cases, the atoms of a metal have combined with atoms of a nonmetal. Rust is iron oxide, silver tarnish is silver sulfide, and copper tarnish is copper oxide. The process is called corrosion (kuh•ROH•zhuhn). **Corrosion** is the gradual "eating away" of a metal because it reacts chemically to form a compound that weakens it.

The most reactive metals are the quickest to corrode. Sodium metal, for example, must be stored under oil to keep it from reacting in seconds with oxygen in the air. Aluminum and magnesium also react quickly with oxygen in the air. However, the oxide, or oxygen-based, compound formed by these metals coats the metal tightly. The coating protects the metal from further corrosion. If salt and moisture are present, though, the protective coating can be dissolved. The metals may be damaged just like rusting iron, only without the red color.

Most of the time, metals are not used in their pure form. While still molten, or melted, other metals and nonmetals are added to form an alloy (AL•oy). An **alloy** is a mixture of two or more metals and

▲ Rust has turned this machine from a useful object into junk.

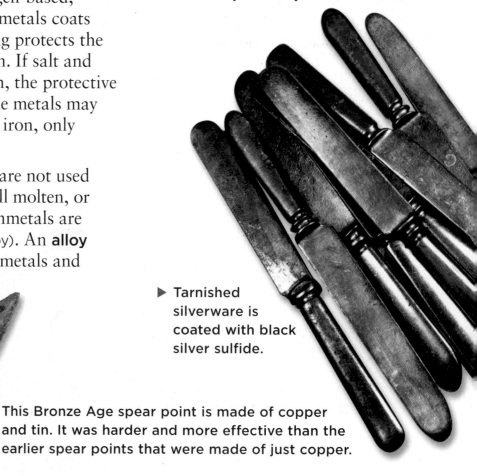

▶ Tarnished silverware is coated with black silver sulfide.

◀ This Bronze Age spear point is made of copper and tin. It was harder and more effective than the earlier spear points that were made of just copper.

nonmetals. People make alloys with the properties they need. For example, pure gold is too soft to make durable jewelry. Mixing gold with copper, silver, nickel, or palladium makes it harder. Alloying gold can also color it white, pink, rose, or green. Other precious metals are also mixed with common metals. Sterling silver is an alloy of silver and copper.

Iron is soft and weak until carbon, manganese, chromium, nickel, and tungsten are added. They make increasingly stronger and harder steel alloys. There are hundreds of alloy steel recipes, each designed for particular products.

Pure copper is only used for wires to conduct electricity. For applications needing strength and hardness, people use copper alloys. The main ones are: brass, made of copper and zinc; and bronze, a very durable material made of copper and tin. When ancient civilizations discovered how to make bronze, they learned that they could use this tough copper alloy to create long-lasting tools and weapons. Civilizations that could make bronze had a distinct advantage over earlier peoples. The use of bronze helped these civilizations grow in size and power, and this time in history is called the Bronze Age.

✅ Quick Check

Problem and Solution What is one way in which bronze differs from pure copper?

Critical Thinking Why does rust fail to protect iron from more corrosion?

▼ The strength of steel supports the tallest buildings.

What other ways are alloys used?

Chromium and nickel can be added to steel to harden it, and they also fight corrosion. If steel is made with 18% chromium and 8% nickel, it rusts hardly at all. The chromium and nickel oxides form a protective coating over the steel. Since this type of alloy doesn't "stain" with rust, it is called stainless steel. Stainless steel kitchen utensils and surgical instruments are durable and are easily sterilized to be germ-free.

Tungsten carbide is another alloy commonly used to make surgical tools because surgeons need the cutting edges of these tools to be extra sharp. The cutting edges of tungsten carbide scissors are preferred over stainless steel because they cut better and need less frequent sharpening.

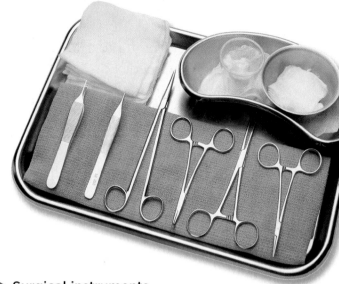

▶ Surgical instruments are made with alloys.

Musical instruments made of hard brass alloys have a bright sound quality. If they were made of soft copper, the sound vibrations would be deadened and dull. The sound of a few brass instruments can be heard easily over the rest of an orchestra. When you have a full brass band, the sound is loud and exciting.

✔ Quick Check

Problem and Solution Why is it good to have kitchen utensils made of stainless steel?

Critical Thinking Why do you think musical instruments are not made of pure titanium?

◀ Many musical instruments are made of alloys, such as this brass horn.

Summarize the Main Idea

Metals have a broad range of useful properties. (pp. 422–427)

Pure metals are generally soft, malleable and ductile. (pp. 426–427)

Corrosion turns metals into **compounds**. Metal mixtures are alloys. (pp. 428–429)

Make a FOLDABLES™ Study Guide

Make a three-tab book (see p. 481). Use the titles shown. On the inside of each tab, summarize what you have learned.

properties of metals | pure metals | metal compounds and mixtures

Think, Talk, and Write

1. **Main Idea** What are two properties common to all metals?

2. **Vocabulary** A material that resists the flow of electricity is a(n) _____.

3. **Problem and Solution** What problems might your friend have wearing a pure gold ring?

Problem

↓

Steps to Solution

↓

Solution

4. **Critical Thinking** How do some reactive metals avoid serious corrosion damage?

5. **Test Practice** Metals that are shaped using pressure have high
   A hardness.
   B melting points.
   C ductility.
   D corrosion.

6. **Test Practice** A metal will not break when pounded because of its
   A hardness.
   B strength.
   C malleability.
   D corrosion.

Math Link

Calculate Area
A cube of gold 2.5 in. on one side can form enough gold leaf to cover a football field (300 ft x 180 ft). What is the area of the field?

Social Studies Link

Research the Bronze Age
Write an essay to describe some of the metal objects used during the Bronze Age. Explain how the properties of the metal made it useful for each purpose.

Be a Scientist

battery

battery holder

6 alligator clips

wire

miniature bulb

bulb holder

copper, aluminum, iron and tin electrodes

Inquiry Structured

How can you compare the electrical conductivity of metals?

Form a Hypothesis

Are some metals better conductors than others? What would happen if you used a poor conductor in an electrical circuit? Would the brightness of a light bulb connected to the circuit change? Write your answer as a hypothesis in the form *"If a poor conductor is used in an electrical circuit, then the brightness of the light bulb will…"*

Test Your Hypothesis

1. Place the battery in the battery holder. Connect one alligator clip and wire to one end of the battery holder. Connect another alligator clip and wire to the other end of the battery holder.

2. Connect one of the wires from the battery to the miniature bulb in the socket using an alligator clip. Use separate wire to attach the light socket to one end of a copper electrode. You still have an open circuit. Draw your setup.

3. **Experiment** Connect the second wire from the battery to the other end of the electrode to close the circuit. Observe how brightly the light bulb glows and record the results.

4. **Observe** Replace the copper electrode with the aluminum, iron, and tin electrodes. Observe and record your results for each.

5. **Compare** Rank the metals from highest to lowest conductivity.

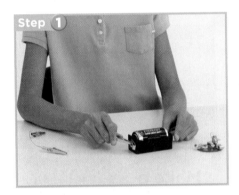

Step **1**

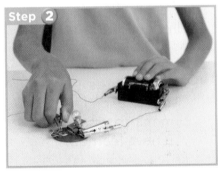

Step **2**

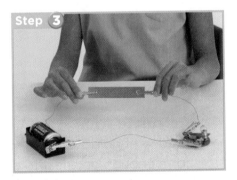

Step **3**

 5 IE 6.b. Develop a testable question.

Draw Conclusions

1. **Explain** Did the light bulb act as a conductivity tester?

2. **Infer** Why is copper used to make wire?

3. Do your results support your hypothesis? Explain why or why not.

Inquiry Guided

How does alloying metals affect their electrical conductivity?

Form a Hypothesis

You have already used a light bulb to discover how conductive some metals are. If an alloy is made of two highly conductive pure metals, will the alloy's conductivity be higher or lower than either or both of the pure metals? Answer your prediction to the question as a hypothesis in the form *"If an alloy is made from two metals with high conductivity, then the alloy's conductivity will be…"*

Test Your Hypothesis

Design an experiment to determine if a metal alloy has higher or lower conductivity than the pure metals that were mixed to form it using the materials provided. Then write out the resources and steps you will follow. Record your results and observations as you follow your plan.

Draw Conclusions

Did your experiment support your hypothesis? Why or why not?

Inquiry Open

For example, do metals conduct heat energy as well as they conduct electrical energy? Design an experiment to answer your question. Your experiment must be organized to test only one variable. Your experiment must be written so that someone else can complete the experiment by following your instructions.

Remember to follow the steps of the scientific process.

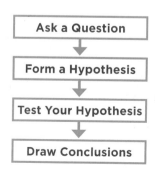

Ask a Question

↓

Form a Hypothesis

↓

Test Your Hypothesis

↓

Draw Conclusions

Lesson 3

Salts

Look and Wonder

The salt crystals you see here were once so valuable they were used as money in the Roman Empire. What exactly is salt? What properties make it so useful?

 5 PS 1.i. Students know the common properties of salts, such as sodium chloride (NaCl).

What are salts made of?

Make a Prediction

Metals conduct electricity, but nonmetals do not. What do you think salt is made of? Do you think a solution with salt will conduct electricity?

Test your Prediction

1. Fill three cups halfway with distilled water. Stir one teaspoon of table salt in one of the cups. Stir one teaspoon of Epsom salt into another cup. Label your cups.

2. Make a chart like the one shown to record your results.

3. **Observe** Put the wires of your conductivity tester into each liquid. Rinse the wires with water between tests! If the light is lit, the conductivity is good. If the light is out, the conductivity is poor. After testing, fill in your data table with "good" or "poor."

Draw Conclusions

4. **Infer** What did you observe? Did any of your samples conduct electricity? Based on what you have learned, why do you think that was?

Explore More

A student has developed this hypothesis: *If the amount of salt dissolved increases, then the conductivity of a salt solution will increase.* How could you use a conductivity tester to test the student's hypothesis? Explain your ideas.

 5 IE 6.g. Record data by using appropriate graphic representations (including charts, graphs, and labeled diagrams) and make inferences based on those data.

Materials

- 3 plastic cups
- distilled water
- measuring spoon (teaspoon)
- table salt
- conductivity tester
- Epsom salt

Step 1

Step 2

Conductivity Test

substance	rating
distilled water	
Epsom salts	
table salt	

Main Idea 5 PS 1.i

Salts are compounds made of metallic and nonmetallic elements. A salt may be formed by an acid reacting with a base.

Vocabulary

salt, p.436

acid, p.438

indicator, p.438

base, p.439

neutralization reaction, p.439

acidity, p.440

alkalinity, p.440

pH scale, p.440

LOG ON e-Glossary
@ www.macmillanmh.com

Reading Skill

Draw Conclusions

Text Clues	Conclusions

What is a salt?

A compound made of a metal and a nonmetal is usually called a **salt**. Common table salt, or sodium chloride, is made by combining sodium and chlorine. The metals of the first two columns of the periodic table very often combine with the elements in fluorine's column to form salts.

Another way to make a salt is to combine an acid with a base to form a salt plus water. The diagrams below show both salt-making reactions.

The particles of a salt strongly attract each other into an orderly arrangement. Salts are usually hard and brittle. It takes lots of heat energy to pull them apart. Thus, salts have high melting points: 801°C (1,474°F) for sodium chloride, 996°C (1,825°F) for sodium fluoride.

Crystals of Salt

Reading Photos

What evidence indicates that particles in salt crystals are lined up in orderly rows?

Clue: Look at the shapes of the crystals that the particles form.

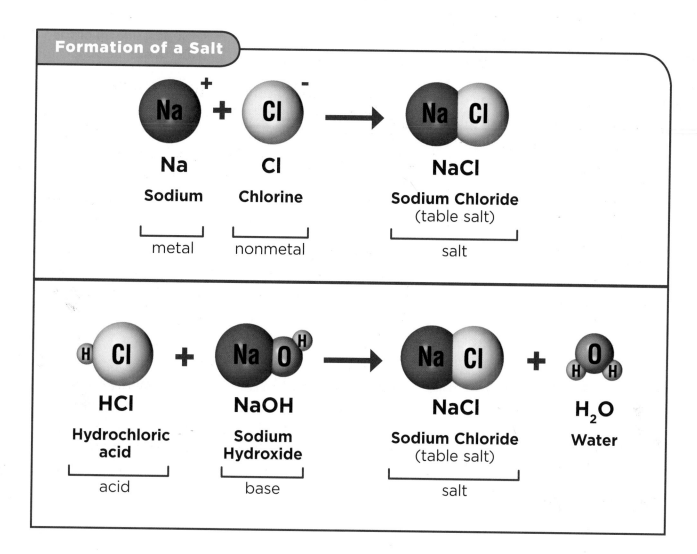

A dissolved compound made of a metal and a nonmetal conducts electricity well. This is generally true for all salt solutions. The reason is that in salts the metal and nonmetal particles are electrically charged. When a salt dissolves, these electrically charged particles can flow through the water. The flow of the charged metal and nonmetal particles is one way to conduct electricity.

If a salt does not dissolve well in water, it cannot produce many freely moving charged particles. Solutions of this type of salt will not be good electrical conductors. For example, the salt barium sulfate is poisonous.

Yet it dissolves so little in water that doctors have patients drink barium sulfate suspensions. As the barium sulfate moves through a patient's digestive system, it makes X-rays of the organs appear much sharper. The low solubility of the barium sulfate salt keeps it from being absorbed into the body.

✔ Quick Check

Draw Conclusions Why couldn't nitrogen dioxide, NO_2 be a salt?

Critical Thinking Why would ocean water conduct electricity well?

What are acids and bases?

Vinegar, lemons, and oranges taste sour because each contains an acid. An **acid** (AH•sed) is a substance that tastes sour and turns blue litmus paper red. Blue litmus paper is an indicator. An **indicator** changes color in ways that let you identify a substance. This is a common test to see if a solution is acidic. △ **Be careful.** Never taste unfamiliar substances to see if they are acids. Many acids can badly burn your skin.

Acids usually have hydrogen atoms combined with other nonmetal atoms in their molecules. Their formulas usually start with H for hydrogen. When acids dissolve in water, their molecules separate into charged particles just like salts do. This enables an acid solution to conduct electricity. Acidic solutions always contain charged hydrogen particles and have a chemical formula of H^+.

Acids can be used to form salts. Do you recall that a salt is made of a metal combined with a nonmetal? Which half of the salt is supplied by part of the acid? If you said the nonmetal part, you are correct. However, half a salt is not enough. You need another reactant to supply the missing part.

▼ Charged hydrogen particles in acids turn blue litmus paper red.

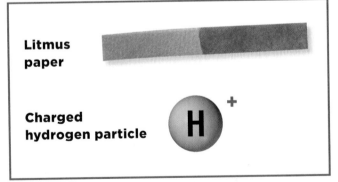

Litmus paper

Charged hydrogen particle

▼ Oranges, like all citrus fruit, contain acids.

Cleaning products like soap and ammonia contain bases. A **base** is a substance that tastes bitter and turns red litmus paper blue. Red litmus paper is a common indicator used to identify a base. Bases feel slippery, very much like soap. △ **Be careful.** Never taste or feel an unfamiliar base. Just like acids, many of them can badly burn your skin.

Bases contain a metal atom joined to a negatively charged particle called hydroxide. The hydroxide particle is composed of an atom of oxygen tightly stuck to an atom of hydrogen. The hydroxide formula is OH^-. When bases dissolve in water, their molecules separate into charged particles that allow the solution to conduct electricity like acids and salts.

When bases react chemically with acids, they form salts and water. This is called a **neutralization** (noo•truh•luh•ZAY•shuhn) **reaction** because the acid changes to water. Did you ever have a "sour" stomach, or indigestion, caused by excess stomach acids? Indigestion is treated by taking antacids. These are mild bases that are safe to eat. They neutralize the excess acid in your stomach. This helps you feel better.

Bases also form salts when they neutralize acids. The base supplies the metal atoms that join the nonmetal atoms from the acids. These then rearrange themselves to form the salt, a compound of a metal and a nonmetal.

▼ Charged hydroxide particles in bases turn red litmus paper blue.

Litmus paper

Charged hydroxide particle

O **H**⁻

▲ Soaps contain a base.

✔ *Quick Check*

Draw Conclusions What particles are present in a solution of hydrochloric acid?

Critical Thinking Why is milk of magnesia a base?

Are all acids and bases equally strong?

There are strong acids and bases and weak acids and bases. Molecules of strong acids in solution separate into charged particles almost completely. Molecules of weak acids separate only partially into charged particles. As a result, strong acids produce a large number of charged hydrogen particles in solution. Weak acids produce smaller numbers of such charged particles. The same applies to bases, except their strength depends on the number of charged hydroxide particles.

The strength of an acidic solution is called its **acidity** (uh•SID•i•tee). The strength of a basic solution is called its **alkalinity** (al•kuh•LIN•i•tee). The strength of acids and bases is measured on the pH scale. The **pH scale** measures the amount of charged hydrogen particles. The scale runs from 0, which represents the largest amount of hydrogen particles, to 14, which represents the smallest amount of hydrogen particles. Thus a pH of 0 is the most acidic and least basic. A pH of 14 is the least acidic and most basic.

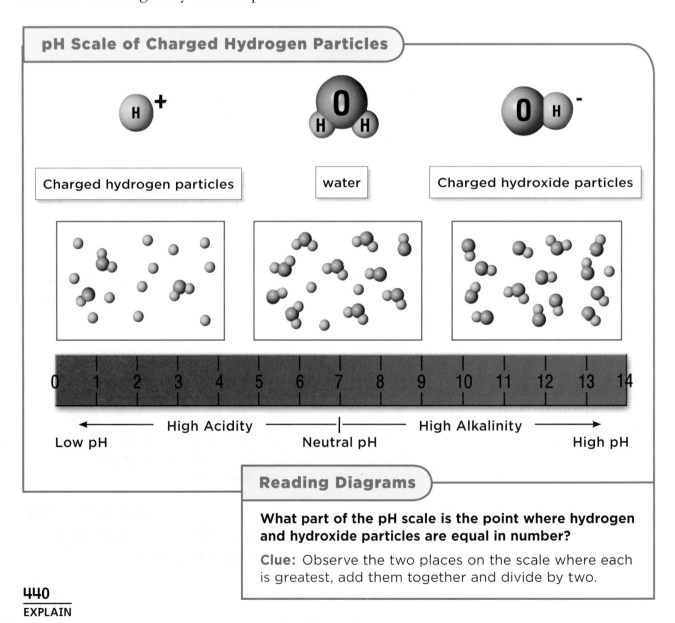

pH Scale of Charged Hydrogen Particles

Charged hydrogen particles

water

Charged hydroxide particles

0 1 2 3 4 5 6 7 8 9 10 11 12 13 14

← High Acidity ——————— High Alkalinity →

Low pH   Neutral pH   High pH

Reading Diagrams

What part of the pH scale is the point where hydrogen and hydroxide particles are equal in number?

Clue: Observe the two places on the scale where each is greatest, add them together and divide by two.

▲ Hydrangeas grown in acidic soil have blue flowers, but in basic soil they are pink.

Acids have a pH from 0, the strongest acids, to just under 7. In acidic solutions, hydrogen particles outnumber hydroxide particles. Water has a neutral pH of 7. At pH 7, the amounts of hydrogen and hydroxide particles are equal. Bases have a pH over 7 up to 14, the strongest bases. In basic solutions, hydroxide particles outnumber hydrogen particles.

Scientists have developed indicator papers and electric meters that measure pH. Measuring pH is necessary in many laboratory, industrial, farming, and environmental activities.

Most plants grow best in slightly acidic soil. Acid rain caused by fossil fuels raises the acidity of lakes and rivers. This harms the growth of forests and wildlife. Environmental scientists often measure the pH of lakes and rivers to see if they are successfully reducing acid rain.

Red Cabbage Juice Is an Indicator

1. Fill a cup halfway with vinegar. Repeat with water and clear ammonia solution for a total of three cups.

2. **Observe** Put one tablespoon of red cabbage juice into each cup. Record the color you see in each case.

3. **Infer** Based on your observations, what cabbage juice color indicates an acid? What cabbage juice color indicates a base?

4. Soak a paper towel or coffee filter in red cabbage juice and allow it to dry overnight. The next day, cut the paper into test strips.

5. **Communicate** Suppose that you are going to sell your paper strips to scientists as an acid-base indicator. Write a set of instructions for the use of your product.

✔ *Quick Check*

Draw Conclusions Why does sulfuric acid (battery acid) eat away zinc faster than acetic acid (vinegar)?

Critical Thinking What tests would you make if you were looking for evidence of acid rain?

How do we use salts?

Salt was precious in ancient times. Ancient Egyptians used salt to dry the bodies of their kings to turn them into mummies. Paintings on the walls of the tombs often showed the mining of salt with innovative tools. Salt was considered so precious that it was often used as money and traded for gold. Roman soldiers were paid in salt. It was their *salary*, a word derived from the Latin word for salt.

What made salt so valuable? It was the best way to preserve foods in a time when refrigeration was unavailable. Salt preserves food by removing water from the food. Bacteria can't survive in a dry environment, so foods dried with salt won't spoil as quickly. Fishermen of ancient times who spent days at sea

▲ Mummies dried in salt remain preserved for over 2,000 years.

packed their catch in salt to keep it from spoiling. Today, salted codfish are still a prized ingredient in Hispanic and Portuguese cooking.

Salt is used to season foods to give them more flavor. The best chefs prefer using sea salt in their dishes. It is a mixture of different salts and provides a richer flavor. Common table salt is usually used for regular cooking. Flavorings like onion or garlic are often added to salt to give many dishes a special taste.

Table salt is sodium chloride, but it often includes other compounds that are added to improve its usefulness for curing meats and baking. Plain, pure sodium chloride salt is used for canning and pickling. It is fine for ordinary seasoning, too, provided you can get it out of the shaker.

Compounds, such as magnesium carbonate, hydrated calcium silicate, or

▼ Salted codfish resists spoiling for many months.

Moisture absorbing minerals added to salt let it pour easily.

tricalcium phosphate, are added to the salt to prevent it from clumping when it's damp. These compounds absorb the water that could cake the salt.

Iodized salt contains tiny amounts of potassium iodide, a compound that contains essential iodine. This provides users with enough iodine mineral to prevent goiter, an illness of the thyroid gland that often makes the neck swell. Too much sodium can make people who have high blood pressure ill. "Light" salt substitutes some potassium chloride for half of the sodium chloride.

Salt is used in cold climates as **deicers** (dee•IGHS•uhr). Deicers work by dissolving into the ice and lowering the freezing point. The ice turns into slush and is easier to remove. Calcium chloride works best, but is expensive. Rock salt (sodium chloride) has a lower cost and is used most often. Spreading deicers helps prevent slipping on

▶ Salt spreaders ease the removal of ice and snow from the road.

pavements and skidding on roads. Bags of deicing salt are sold in hardware stores and supermarkets in places that get snow during the winter.

While some salts are beneficial in small amounts, other salts are poisonous, even at low levels. These salts are compounds of heavy metals such as cadmium, lead, and mercury. Contact with these dangerous salts should be avoided.

 Quick Check

Draw Conclusions What are two useful properties of salt?

Critical Thinking What kind of salt should never be used for making cookware?

Where is salt found?

Salt was formed early in Earth's history as a solid. When water formed, much of the salt was dissolved by rain and ended up in the oceans. Today, salt makes up 3.5% of the oceans by weight. That means there are 3.5 kg (7.7 lb) of salt in 100 kg (220 lb) of ocean water.

In many places in the world, salt is extracted from sea water by drawing it into shallow ponds. Sunlight and warm air slowly evaporate the water. The salt concentration increases until the solution becomes saturated. As more water turns to vapor, the dissolved particles of salt form solid crystals of salt. When all the water has escaped, the pond is a solid mass of crystals of sea salt. These are then collected, further refined, and packed for use.

Salt is also mined from underground deposits that may have formed when inland seas became trapped by rising land masses. The evaporated water left a thick layer of salt which ended up underground when covered up by sediments. Mining the salt is done by pumping water through holes drilled down to the deposit. The salt dissolves in the water and rises through other drilled holes to the surface. The salt is separated from the water and refined.

▲ Salt is obtained from seawater in these shallow seaside pools by letting the sun evaporate the liquid, which leaves the salt.

▲ Salt obtained from underground salt deposits is piled high, waiting to be distributed to major users.

✓ Quick Check

Draw Conclusions What are two sources of salt?

Critical Thinking Where would be the hardest places to make salt from the sea? Explain your answer.

Lesson Review

Summarize the Main Idea

 **Salts** have high melting points, are hard and brittle, and conduct electricity when dissolved. (pp. 436–437)

 **Salts are made** when a metal and a nonmetal combine, or when acids react with bases. (pp. 436–439)

 The acidity of a solution is measured using the **pH scale**. (pp. 440–441)

Make a FOLDABLES™ Study Guide

Make a three-tab book (see p. 481). Use the titles shown. On the inside of each tab, summarize what you have learned.

properties of salt

making salts

pH scale

Think, Talk, and Write

1. **Main Idea** What reactants would you select to make a salt?

2. **Vocabulary** The strength of acids and bases is measured on the _____.

3. **Draw Conclusions** What are three uses of salts?

Text Clues	Conclusions

4. **Critical Thinking** Explain why molten salts conduct electricity well.

5. **Test Practice** A substance has a pH of 4. It is a
   A salt.
   B acid.
   C metal.
   D base.

6. **Test Practice** All of the following contain an acid EXCEPT
   A vinegar.
   B orange.
   C soap.
   D lemon.

Writing Link

Fictional Narrative

Pretend you are a soldier in the Roman army and are paid in salt. What would you spend your salary on? Do research on things you might buy with salt in the days of the Roman Empire.

Math Link

Calculating De-icer Usage

A 10-lb bag of salt can de-ice 240 ft of sidewalk. How much of the bag will be used if the sidewalk is 60 ft long?

Meet CHRISTINA ELSON

▲ Christina Elson is studying Aztec artifacts.

Christina Elson is a scientist at the American Museum of Natural History. She studies how salt was used by the ancient Aztec culture.

From the 12th to 16th centuries, the Aztecs lived in the area that is now Mexico. This area was very rich in salt, which is a natural mineral resource that is mined from the ground. Christina studies a region in Mexico where salt was obtained from deposits around a dried lake bed. The Aztecs turned these deposits into different kinds of salt. First, they collected the salty soils by scraping and digging them out of the ground. Then they filtered water through the soils to dissolve out the salts into big pots. The final step required boiling the salt solution so the water evaporated away. The salt remained behind in the form of crystals.

AMERICAN
MUSEUM of
NATURAL
HISTORY

ELA R 5.2.4 Draw inferences, conclusions, or generalizations about text and support them with textual evidence and prior knowledge.

Aztecs used salt for much more than a cooking spice. In one Aztec town, Christina found thousands of ceramic fragments, pieces of clay pots that were used to transport salt for sale or trade.

She also found that salt was used to dye cloth. Colorfully dyed cotton cloth was a valuable product because it was greatly desired by the Aztec nobles. Aztec women learned to spin cloth at an early age. The cloth was dyed with pigment in a hot watery dye-bath. When salt was added to the dye-bath, it helped the pigment "stick" to the cloth. The salt combined with the color pigment to make a compound that could not be dissolved in water.

Salt was important to many other ancient cultures, and continues to be important today. Salt can be used to preserve food so it can be stored for a long time without refrigeration; to prepare and preserve animal skins for clothing; and to make soap. Salt's value stems from its usefulness, durability, and portability.

▲ Christina Elson records data at an archeological "dig" site in Mexico.

Write About It

Draw Conclusions

1. How did the Aztecs change a mineral resource into a finished product?
2. What would happen to the colors in Aztec cloth when washed if salt was not part of the dye-bath?

LOG ON **e-Journal** Write about it online
@ www.macmillanmh.com

Draw Conclusions

▶ Use information in the text and background knowledge.

▶ Support your conclusions with information found in the text.

Writing in Science

A good explanation

▶ tells what you want to do or make.

▶ tells what materials will be needed.

▶ presents step-by-step instructions organized in a time-ordered sequence using words such as "first" and "then."

▶ gives clear details that are easy to follow.

Cleaning Solution

64 FL. OZ. (2 QTS.) 1.89L

Clean Up!

A lot of advertisements on television talk about special cleaners that keep your house sparkling and smelling great. Here's a way you can get the same results by making a cleaner yourself. This all-purpose cleaner will be safer for you, your family, and the environment. It doesn't contain any harmful chemicals and it doesn't smell bad. It is also cheaper than most store-bought cleaners.

To make the cleaner, first mix 1 teaspoon borax, 1/2 teaspoon washing soda, 2 tablespoons vinegar, 1/2 teaspoon liquid soap, and 2 cups of very hot water. Then put the ingredients in a spray bottle. Use it to clean everything but wood and glass.

The chemical reaction that makes this product comes from the acid (vinegar) reacting with the base (in borax and washing soda).

If you want a great smell, use lemon juice in the cleaner instead of vinegar. Who knows? You may be able to market this product someday, and really "clean up"!

Write About It

Explanatory Writing Do research online to find other products that come from the reaction of an acid and a base. Choose one of those products and write out instructions to make it. Explain clearly what the finished product will look like and do.

LOG ON e-Journal Write about it online @ www.macmillanmh.com

 ELA W 5.1.2. Create multiple-paragraph expository compositions:
a. Establish a topic, important ideas, or events in sequence or chronological order.

What is the pH?

Many foods and household products you use every day are either acidic or basic. We can tell how acidic or basic they are by using the pH scale. The scale ranges from 0 to 14, with 0 being very acidic and 14 being very basic or alkaline. Water is neutral and has a pH value of 7. The acidity decreases by a factor of ten with each number up the pH scale as the basic strength increases. The pH values do not have units.

Look at the data below and how it is organized and displayed in a number line.

To Make a Number Line

▶ arrange numbers from least to greatest.

▶ look at the range of values you need to organize. This will tell you the range of your number line.

▶ place all values on the number line.

pH of Products

Product	pH
hand soap	9.5
lemon juice	2
watermelon	5.4
eggs	7.8
oven cleaner	13
celery	6

pH of common substances

0   2   5.4 6   7.8   9.5   13   14

lemon juice   watermelon   celery   eggs   hand soap   oven cleaner

 Solve It

1. Do research to find the pH of six foods or household products.

2. Display the data on a number line.

 MA NS 1.5. Identify and represent on a number line decimals, fractions, mixed numbers, and positive and negative integers.

Summarize the Main Ideas

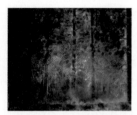

In chemical changes, atoms are rearranged into new combinations. (pp. 408–417)

Metals share some properties. Some metals are pure elements, some are mixtures. (pp. 420–431)

Salts are compounds made of metallic and nonmetallic elements. A salt may be formed by an acid reacting with a base. (pp. 434–445)

Make a **FOLDABLES**™ Study Guide

Take a sheet of paper and tape your lesson study guide as shown.

Fill each blank with the best word from the list.

acid, p. 438   **pH scale**, p. 440

alloy, p. 428   **products**, p. 410

base, p. 439   **reactants**, p. 410

insulator, p. 424   **salt**, p. 436

1. In a chemical reaction, the starting substances are _____. 5 PS 1.a

2. Sodium chloride, which is a combination of a metal and nonmetal, is a typical _____. 5 PS 1.i

3. Litmus paper turns red in _____. 5 PS 1.i

4. A mixture of two metals is a(n) _____. 5 PS 1.c

5. Nonmetallic substances are generally good _____. 5 PS 1.c

6. In the reaction $6CO_2 + 6H_2O \rightarrow C_6H_{12}O_6 + 6O_2$, $6O_2$ and $C_6H_{12}O_6$ are the _____. 5 PS 1.a

7. Red litmus paper turns blue in a(n) _____. 5 PS 1.i

8. A strong acid has a value of 0 or 1 on the _____. 5 PS 1.i

Skills and Concepts

Answer each of the following in complete sentences.

9. Summarize In general, how is a neutralization reaction produced?
5 PS 1.i

10. Draw Conclusions If two clear liquids are mixed and a precipitate forms, what has probably happened? 5 PS 1.a

11. Use Variables How could you determine the effect of temperature on the rate of the chemical reaction between baking soda and vinegar?
5 IE 6.e

12. Critical Thinking What could you do to find evidence to support the idea that mass is conserved during a chemical change? 5 PS 1.a

13. Persuasive Writing Write an article persuading people that the use of heavy metals endangers the environment. Provide an example.
5 PS 1.c

 How does one substance become another? 5 PS 1.a

CHAPTER 8

Performance Assessment

Fizzy Evidence?

Your goal is to determine whether lemon juice or apple juice is more acidic when they react with baking soda, a weak base, to form water and a salt.

What to do

1. Add a 1/4 teaspoon of baking soda to each of two small glasses.

2. Add a tablespoon of lemon juice to one glass and repeat with the other using clear apple juice.

3. Evaporate the liquid to recover the salt that formed.

Analyze your results

▶ What evidence supports the idea that a chemical reaction occurred in the glasses?

▶ What evidence suggests that lemon juice contains a stronger acid?

Lemon Juice   Apple Juice

5 PS 1.i. Students know the common properties of salts, such as sodium chloride (NaCl).

451

1 What happens when iron and oxygen combine to form rust? 5 PS 1.a

  A A mixture is formed.
  B A chemical reaction occurs.
  C A solution is formed.
  D A physical reaction occurs.

2 Students mix clear, colorless solutions of Epsom salt and washing soda. They immediately notice a white powdery substance appears in the liquid and settles to the bottom. What happened? 5 PS 1.a

  A a physical change, because the products cannot be easily separated from each other
  B a physical change, because the experiment will be easy to reverse
  C a chemical change, because the products have different properties than the reactants
  D a chemical change, because the solution did not get hot

3 What are the properties of all metals? 5 PS 1.c

  A Metals have luster and low melting points.
  B Metals have luster, are malleable, and do not conduct electricity.
  C Metals are dull, soft, and are insulators.
  D Metals have luster, are malleable, and conduct electricity.

4 Scientists use instruments to measure properties and obtain data.

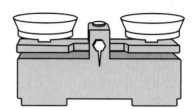

Which of the following questions is testable using the instrument shown in the diagram? 5 PS 1.b

  A When substances are dissolved, will the mass of the substances be smaller?
  B How many atoms are lost when you mix hydrogen and oxygen to make water?
  C Is silver a better conductor than aluminum?
  D Can oxygen be tested easier than hydrogen?

5 Juan removes a pan from the stove. Why isn't the plastic handle hot? 5 PS 1.c

  A Heat leaves with the water vapor.
  B Plastic conducts heat.
  C Heat stays in the liquid.
  D Plastic is an insulator.

6 In an experiment, students added 50 grams of baking soda to 1 liter of vinegar. Which tool should they use to measure the volume of the vinegar? 5 PS 1.f

  A a scale
  B a tablespoon
  C a balance
  D a graduated cylinder

7 Which process will produce a salt?
5 PS 1.i

A Strong acids are mixed together.
B Strong acids react with strong bases.
C Two bases are mixed together.
D Strong acids evaporate into the air.

8 The chemical formula for table salt is NaCl. Which of the following best describes salt? 5 PS 1.i

A an element
B a mixture
C a compound
D an atom

9 Indicators are used to determine if solutions are acidic or basic.

Which statement is correct? 5 IE 6.h

A The solution is acidic.
B The solution is basic.
C The solution is water.
D More information is needed.

10 Students are working on an experiment. They have been asked to find out if adding salt to a solution will increase conductivity. One student is having trouble dissolving the salt and suggests that his team boil the water as he adds the salt. Why is this wrong? 5 PS 1.e

A He is changing more than two variables.
B Salt will not dissolve in hot water.
C He is changing more than one variable.
D The salt will crystallize and break the beaker.

11 Which of the following best describes metals? 5 PS 1.c

A Metals cannot be combined.
B Metals are safe for humans.
C Metals are often mixed.
D Metals will not melt.

12 Which of the following best describes acids? 5 PS 1.i

A Vinegar and orange juice are weak acids.
B Red litmus paper turns blue when put in acid.
C All acids are the same strength.
D Acid solutions do not conduct electricity.

National Wildlife Federation

Ranger Rick

Green and Clean:

Plants as Pollution Control

Plants give us food. They provide materials for our clothes and houses. They even produce the oxygen we breathe. As if that weren't enough, plants can also clean up the environment!

Too Much Heavy Metal

The matter around us is made of elements and combinations of elements. We can't live even a short time without some of them, such as oxygen (O_2) and water (H_2O). Yet other elements—for example, lead (Pb), mercury (Hg), cadmium (Cd), and arsenic (As)—are toxic. They can make people and animals sick. Sometimes known as "heavy metals," these elements occur in small quantities in the Earth's crust. They become a problem only when they build up in larger amounts. This often happens when people use them to make products or dump them as waste. For example, arsenic was once used in insecticides. Lead used to be added to gasoline and paint. Over time, these toxic elements have accumulated in our soil and water.

▷ Runoff has carried heavy metals from an iron and copper mine to this creek in California.

Double Trouble

Cleaning up heavy metals isn't easy. One way is to dig up all the contaminated soil and put it in a landfill. But that's a lot of work and very expensive. It leaves a big hole in the ground and only moves the problem to another place.

◀ **Alpine pennycress thrives on soils contaminated with zinc and cadmium. It cleans the soil by removing the excess metals.**

Plants to the Rescue!

Scientists have discovered that certain plants can remove toxic elements from the soil or water. They take up heavy metals through their roots and store them in leaves. Then people can collect the contaminated plant parts, leaving behind soil that is cleaner and safer. They might even be able to remove the metals from the plants and reuse them!

Some kinds of bacteria also help clean up pollution. They actually digest toxic materials, changing them into harmless waste products. We still do not fully understand how plants and bacteria do this. We do know that we need help from other living things to keep our planet healthy for us all. So have you thanked a plant today?

△ **Brake fern soaks up toxic arsenic, safely cleaning polluted soils.**

▼ **Sunflowers have an unusual appetite for toxic metals, such as uranium.**

5 PS 1.h. Students know living organisms and most materials are composed of just a few elements. ● **ELA R 5.2.3.** Discern main ideas and concepts presented in texts, identifying and assessing evidence that supports those ideas.

Careers in Science

Food Science Technician

For many students, the most interesting and fun part of science class is doing laboratory experiments. Do you enjoy handling lab equipment and learning new things while working in a lab? Have you ever thought about how to keep foods from spoiling? Food science technicians operate laboratory instruments. You might do tests on chemicals that are added to foods to make them taste better or keep them fresh. These tests are needed to make sure that the color, texture, and nutrients in foods meet government standards. The best way to get started in this career is to get an associate degree in a two-year college program.

▼ Food science technicians study corn and other foods.

▼ Green chemists keep the benefits of chemistry from harming the environment.

Green Chemist

More than 150 years ago, chemists first started creating useful materials in the laboratory. These materials included dyes, plastics, medicines, food products, and building materials. In the past, the manufacture of many of these materials has resulted in chemical waste that polluted the environment. Green chemists work to create reactions that produce safe, useful products without harmful side effects. If you like chemistry, you might want to become a green chemist. You will need a college degree in chemistry followed by graduate studies. Then you can work on finding or improving processes that produce materials that people use in their everyday lives in ways that do not harm the environment.

LOG ON e-Careers More careers online @ www.macmillanmh.com

Reference

▶ **A ruler can help you make a scale.**

Science Content Standards

Physical Sciences

1. **Elements and their combinations account for all the varied types of matter in the world. As a basis for understanding this concept:**

   a. *Students know* that during chemical reactions the atoms in the reactants rearrange to form products with different properties.

   b. *Students know* all matter is made of atoms, which may combine to form molecules.

   c. *Students know* metals have properties in common, such as high electrical and thermal conductivity. Some metals, such as aluminum (Al), iron (Fe), nickel (Ni), copper (Cu), silver (Ag), and gold (Au), are pure elements; others, such as steel and brass, are composed of a combination of elemental metals.

   d. *Students know* that each element is made of one kind of atom and that the elements are organized in the periodic table by their chemical properties.

   e. *Students know* scientists have developed instruments that can create discrete images of atoms and molecules that show that the atoms and molecules often occur in well-ordered arrays.

   f. *Students know* differences in chemical and physical properties of substances are used to separate mixtures and identify compounds.

   g. *Students know* properties of solid, liquid, and gaseous substances, such as sugar ($C_6H_{12}O_6$), water (H_2O), helium (He), oxygen (O_2), nitrogen (N_2), and carbon dioxide (CO_2).

   h. *Students know* living organisms and most materials are composed of just a few elements.

   i. *Students know* the common properties of salts, such as sodium chloride (NaCl).

Life Sciences

2. **Plants and animals have structures for respiration, digestion, waste disposal, and transport of materials. As a basis for understanding this concept:**

   a. *Students know* many multicellular organisms have specialized structures to support the transport of materials.

   b. *Students know* how blood circulates through the heart chambers, lungs, and body and how carbon dioxide (CO_2) and oxygen (O_2) are exchanged in the lungs and tissues.

   c. *Students know* the sequential steps of digestion and the roles of teeth and the mouth, esophagus, stomach, small intestine, large intestine, and colon in the function of the digestive system.

   d. *Students know* the role of the kidney in removing cellular waste from blood and converting it into urine, which is stored in the bladder.

   e. *Students know* how sugar, water, and minerals are transported in a vascular plant.

   f. *Students know* plants use carbon dioxide (CO_2) and energy from sunlight to build molecules of sugar and release oxygen.

   g. *Students know* plant and animal cells break down sugar to obtain energy, a process resulting in carbon dioxide (CO_2) and water (respiration).

Earth Sciences

3. **Water on Earth moves between the oceans and land through the processes of evaporation and condensation. As a basis for understanding this concept:**

   a. *Students know* most of Earth's water is present as salt water in the oceans, which cover most of Earth's surface.

   b. *Students know* when liquid water evaporates, it turns into water vapor in the air and can reappear as a liquid when cooled or as a solid if cooled below the freezing point of water.

c. *Students know* water vapor in the air moves from one place to another and can form fog or clouds, which are tiny droplets of water or ice, and can fall to Earth as rain, hail, sleet, or snow.

d. *Students know* that the amount of fresh water located in rivers, lakes, underground sources, and glaciers is limited and that its availability can be extended by recycling and decreasing the use of water.

e. *Students know* the origin of the water used by their local communities.

4. **Energy from the Sun heats Earth unevenly, causing air movements that result in changing weather patterns. As a basis for understanding this concept:**

a. *Students know* uneven heating of Earth causes air movements (convection currents).

b. *Students know* the influence that the ocean has on the weather and the role that the water cycle plays in weather patterns.

c. *Students know* the causes and effects of different types of severe weather.

d. *Students know* how to use weather maps and data to predict local weather and know that weather forecasts depend on many variables.

e. *Students know* that the Earth's atmosphere exerts a pressure that decreases with distance above Earth's surface and that at any point it exerts this pressure equally in all directions.

5. **The solar system consists of planets and other bodies that orbit the Sun in predictable paths. As a basis for understanding this concept:**

a. *Students know* the Sun, an average star, is the central and largest body in the solar system and is composed primarily of hydrogen and helium.

b. *Students know* the solar system includes the planet Earth, the Moon, the Sun, eight other planets and their satellites, and smaller objects, such as asteroids and comets.

c. *Students know* the path of a planet around the Sun is due to the gravitational attraction between the Sun and the planet.

Investigation and Experimentation

6. **Scientific progress is made by asking meaningful questions and conducting careful investigations. As a basis for understanding this concept and addressing the content in the other three strands, students should develop their own questions and perform investigations. Students will:**

a. Classify objects (e.g., rocks, plants, leaves) in accordance with appropriate criteria.

b. Develop a testable question.

c. Plan and conduct a simple investigation based on a student-developed question and write instructions others can follow to carry out the procedure.

d. Identify the dependent and controlled variables in an investigation.

e. Identify a single independent variable in a scientific investigation and explain how this variable can be used to collect information to answer a question about the results of the experiment.

f. Select appropriate tools (e.g., thermometers, meter sticks, balances, and graduated cylinders) and make quantitative observations.

g. Record data by using appropriate graphic representations (including charts, graphs, and labeled diagrams) and make inferences based on those data.

h. Draw conclusions from scientific evidence and indicate whether further information is needed to support a specific conclusion.

i. Write a report of an investigation that includes conducting tests, collecting data or examining evidence, and drawing conclusions.

Measurement

Units of Measurement

Temperature

▶ The temperature is 77 degrees Fahrenheit. That is the same as 25 degrees Celsius.

▶ Water boils at 212 degrees Fahrenheit.

▶ Water freezes at 0 degrees Celsius.

Weight and Mass

▶ This baseball bat weighs 32 ounces. 32 ounces is the same as 2 pounds. The mass of the bat is 907 grams.

Length and Area

▶ A classroom is 10 meters wide and 20 meters long. That means the area is 200 square meters.

Volume of Fluids

▶ This bottle of juice has a volume of 1 liter. That is a little more than 1 quart.

Weight/Force

▶ A student weighs 85 pounds. That is a force of 380.8 newtons.

Table of Measurements	
International System of Units (SI)	**English System of Units**
Temperature Water freezes at 0° C (degrees Celsius) and boils at 100°C.	**Temperature** Water freezes at 32°F (degrees Fahrenheit) and boils at 212°F.
Length and Distance 1,000 meters (m) = 1 kilometer (km) 100 centimeters (cm) = 1 meter (m) 10 millimeters (mm) = 1 centimeter (cm)	**Length and Distance** 5,280 feet (ft) = 1 mile (mi) 3 feet (ft) = 1 yard (yd) 12 inches (in.) = 1 foot (ft)
Volume 1,000 milliliters (mL) = 1 liter (L) 1 cubic centimeter (cm^3) = 1 milliliter (mL)	**Volume of Fluids** 4 quarts (qt) = 1 gallon (gal) 2 pints (pt) = 1 quart (qt) 2 cups (c) = 1 pint (pt) 8 fluid ounces (oz) = 1 cup (c)
Mass 1,000 grams (g) = 1 kilogram (kg)	**Weight** 2,000 pounds (lb) = 1 ton (T) 16 ounces (oz) = 1 pound (lb)

Measurement

Measure Time

You use timing devices to measure how long something takes to happen. Some timing devices you use in science are a clock with a second hand and a stopwatch. Which one is more accurate?

Comparing a Clock and Stopwatch

1. Look at a clock with a second hand. The second hand is the hand that you can see moving. It measures seconds.

2. Get an egg timer with falling sand or some device like a wind-up toy that runs down after a certain length of time. When the second hand of the clock points to 12, tell your partner to start the egg timer. Watch the clock while the sand in the egg timer is falling.

3. When the sand stops falling, count how many seconds it took. Record this measurement. Repeat the activity, and compare the two measurements.

4. Switch roles with your partner.

5. Look at a stopwatch. Click the button on the top right. This starts the time. Click the button again. This stops the time. Click the button on the top left. This sets the stopwatch back to zero. Notice that the stopwatch tells time in minutes, seconds, and hundredths of a second.

6. Repeat the activity in steps 2–4, using the stopwatch instead of a clock. Make sure the stopwatch is set to zero. Click the top right button to start timing the reading. Click it again when the sand stops falling.

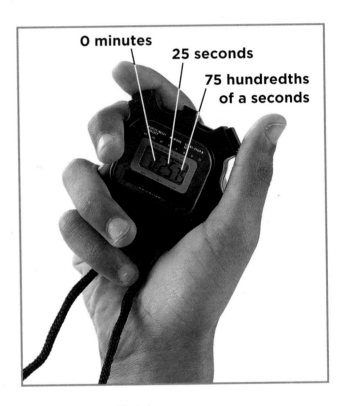

0 minutes

25 seconds

75 hundredths of a seconds

More About Time

1. Use the stopwatch to time how long it takes an ice cube to melt under cold running water. How long does an ice cube take to melt under warm running water?

2. Match each of these times with the action you think took that amount of time.

   a. 00:14:55   1. Taking a shower

   b. 44:39:45   2. Saying the Pledge of Allegiance

   c. 10:23:00   3. Recess

Measure Length

Find Length with a Ruler

1 Look at the ruler below. Each centimeter is divided into 10 millimeters. How long is the paper clip?

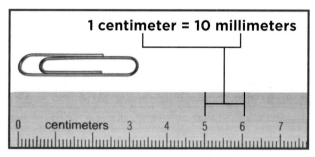

1 centimeter = 10 millimeters

2 The length of the paper clip is 3 centimeters plus 2 millimeters. You can write this length as 3.2 centimeters.

3 Place a ruler on your desk. Lay a pencil against the ruler so that one end of the pencil lines up with the left edge of the ruler. Record the length of the pencil.

Find Length with a Meterstick

1 Line up the meterstick with the left edge of the chalkboard. Make a chalk mark on the board at the right end of the meterstick.

2 Move the meterstick so that the left edge lines up with the chalk mark. Keep the stick level. Make another mark on the board at the right end of the meterstick.

3 Continue to move the meterstick and make chalk marks until the meterstick meets or overlaps the right edge of the board.

4 Record the length of the chalkboard in centimeters by adding all the measurements you've made. Remember, a meterstick has 100 centimeters.

Estimating Length

Try estimating the length of objects in the room. Then measure the length, and compare the estimation with the measurement.

Measuring Area

Area is the amount of surface something covers. To find the area of a rectangle, multiply the rectangle's length by its width. For example, the rectangle here is 3 centimeters long and 2 centimeters wide. Its area is 3 cm x 2 cm = 6 square centimeters. You write the area as 6 cm^2.

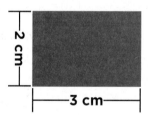

2 cm

—3 cm—

To find the area of a parallelogram you multiply the base times the height. Two triangles can fit together to form a parallelogram. You can use the formula for finding the area of a parallelogram to find the area of a triangle. You multiply the base of the triangle times the height of the triangle and then multiply it by 1/2.

Measurement

Measure Mass

Mass is the amount of matter an object has. You use a balance to measure mass. To find the mass of an object, you balance it by using objects with masses you know. Let's find the mass of a box of crayons.

Measure the Mass of a Box of Crayons

1. Place the balance on a flat, level surface. Check that the two pans are empty and clean.

2. Make sure the empty pans are balanced with each other. The pointer should point to the middle mark. If it does not, move the slider a little to the right or left to balance the pans.

3. Gently place a box of crayons on the left pan. This pan will drop lower.

4. Add masses to the right pan until the pans are balanced.

5. Add the numbers on the masses that are in the right pan. The total is the mass of the box of crayons in grams. Record this number. After the number write a *g* for "grams."

More About Mass

The mass of your crayons was probably less than 100 g. You may not have enough masses to balance a pineapple. It has a mass of about 1,000 g. That's the same as 1 kg, because *kilo* means "1,000."

Estimating Mass

Once you become familiar with the mass of objects, you can try estimating the masses of objects. Then you can compare the estimation with the actual mass.

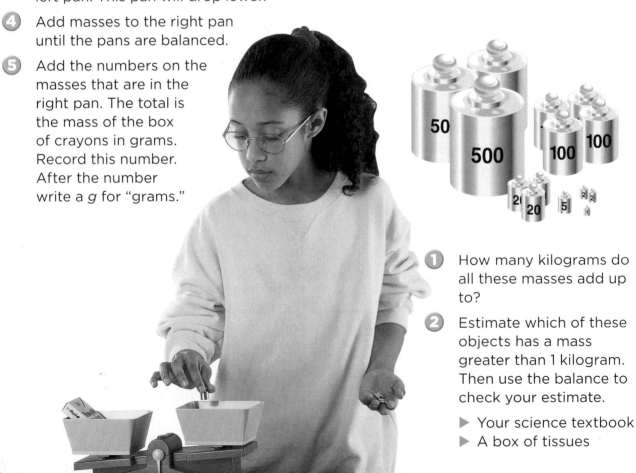

1. How many kilograms do all these masses add up to?

2. Estimate which of these objects has a mass greater than 1 kilogram. Then use the balance to check your estimate.
   ▸ Your science textbook
   ▸ A box of tissues

Measure Volume

Volume is the amount of space something takes up. In science you usually measure the volume of liquids by using beakers and graduated cylinders. These containers are marked in milliliters (mL).

Measure the Volume of a Liquid

1. Look at the beaker and at the graduated cylinder. The beaker has marks for each 25 mL up to 300 mL. The graduated cylinder has marks for each 1 mL up to 100 mL.

2. The surface of the water in the graduated cylinder curves up at the sides. You measure the volume by reading the height of the water at the flat part. What is the volume of water in the graduated cylinder? How much water is in the beaker? They both contain 75 mL of water.

3. Pour 50 mL of water from a pitcher into a beaker.

4. Now pour the 50 mL of water into a graduated cylinder.

Find the Volume of a Solid

1. Start with 50 mL of water in a graduated cylinder.

2. Place a small rock in the water. The water level rises.

3. Measure the new water level. Subtract 50 mL from the new reading. The difference is the volume of the rock. Record the volume in cm^3.

Estimating Volume

Once you become familiar with the volumes of liquids and solids, you can estimate volumes. Estimate the amount of liquid in a glass or can. Estimate the volume of an eraser.

Measurement

Measure Weight/Force

You use a spring scale to measure weight. An object has weight because the force of gravity pulls down on the object. Therefore, weight is a force. Weight is measured in newtons (N) like all forces.

Measure the Weight of an Object

1 Look at a spring scale like the one the students are holding. See how many newtons it measures. See how the measurements are divided. The spring scale shown here measures up to 5 N. It has a mark for every 0.1 N.

2 Hold the spring scale by the top loop. Put the object to be measured on the bottom hook. If the object will not stay on the hook, place it in a net bag. Then hang the bag from the hook.

3 Let go of the object slowly. It will pull down on a spring inside the scale. The spring is connected to a pointer. The pointer on the spring scale shown here is a small bar.

4 Wait for the pointer to stop moving. Read the number of newtons next to the pointer. This is the object's weight. The mug in the picture weighs 4 N.

More About Spring Scales

You probably weigh yourself by standing on a bathroom scale. This is a spring scale too. The force of your body stretches a spring inside the scale. The dial on the scale is probably marked in pounds—the English unit of weight. One pound is equal to about 4.5 newtons.

◀ A bathroom scale, a grocery scale, and a kitchen scale are some spring scales you may have seen.

Measure Temperature

You use a thermometer to measure temperature—how hot or cold something is. A thermometer is made of a thin tube with colored liquid inside. When the liquid gets warmer, it expands and moves up the tube. When the liquid gets cooler, it contracts and moves down the tube. You may have seen most temperatures measured in degrees Fahrenheit (°F). Scientists measure temperature in degrees Celsius (°C).

Read a Thermometer

1. Look at the thermometer shown here. It has two scales—a Fahrenheit scale and a Celsius scale.

2. What is the temperature shown on the thermometer? At what temperature does water freeze?

4. Carefully place the beaker on a hot plate. A hot plate is a small electric stove. Plug in the hot plate, and turn the control knob to a middle setting.

5. After 1 minute measure the temperature of water near the bottom of the beaker. At the same time, a classmate should measure the temperature of water near the top of the beaker. Record these temperatures. Is water near the bottom of the beaker heating up faster than near the top?

6. As the water heats up, notice what happens to the fish food. How do you know that warmer water at the bottom of the beaker rises and cooler water at the top sinks?

What Is Convection?

1. Fill a large beaker about two-thirds full of cool water. Find the temperature of the water by holding a thermometer in the water. Do not let the bulb at the bottom of the thermometer touch the sides or bottom of the beaker.

2. Keep the thermometer in the water until the liquid in the tube stops moving—about 1 minute. Read and record the temperature in °C.

3. Sprinkle a little fish food on the surface of the water in the beaker. Do not knock the beaker, and most of the food will stay on top.

Collect Data

Use a Hand Lens

You use a hand lens to magnify an object, or make the object look larger. With a hand lens, you can see details that would be hard to see without the hand lens.

Magnify a Coin

1. Place a coin on a flat surface. Look at the coin carefully. Draw a picture of it.

2. Look at the coin through the large lens of a hand lens. Move the lens toward or away from the coin until it looks larger and in focus. Draw a picture of the coin as you see it through the hand lens. Fill in details that you did not see before.

3. Look at the coin through the smaller lens, which will magnify the coin even more. If you notice more details, add them to your drawing.

4. Repeat this activity using objects you are studying in science. It might be a rock, some soil, or a seed.

Observe Seeds in a Petri Dish

Can you observe a seed as it sprouts? You can if it's in a petri dish. A petri dish is a shallow, clear, round dish with a cover.

1. Line the sides and bottom of a petri dish with a double layer of filter paper or paper towel. You may have to cut the paper to make it fit.

2. Sprinkle water on the paper to wet it.

3. Place three or four radish seeds on the wet paper in different areas of the dish. Put the lid on the dish, and keep it in a warm place.

4. Observe the seeds every day for a week. Use a hand lens to look for a tiny root pushing through the seed. Record how long it takes each seed to sprout.

Use a Microscope

Hand lenses make objects look several times larger. A microscope, however, can magnify an object to look hundreds of times larger.

Examine Salt Grains

1. Look at the photograph to learn the different parts of your microscope.

2. Place the microscope on a flat surface. Always carry a microscope with both hands. Hold the arm with one hand, and put your other hand beneath the base.

3. Move the mirror so that it reflects light up toward the stage. Never point the mirror directly at the Sun or a bright light. Bright light can cause permanent eye damage.

4. Place a few grains of salt on a slide. Put the slide under the stage clips. Be sure that the salt grains you are going to examine are over the hole in the stage.

5. Look through the eyepiece. Turn the focusing knob slowly until the salt grains come into focus.

6. Draw what the grains look like through the microscope.

7. Look at other objects through the microscope. Try a piece of leaf, a human hair, or a pencil mark.

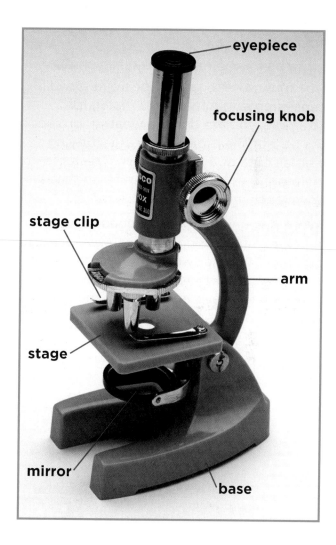

eyepiece

focusing knob

stage clip

arm

stage

mirror

base

Use Technology

Use Calculators

Sometimes after you make measurements, you have to analyze your data to see what it means. This might involve doing calculations with your data. A calculator helps you do time-consuming calculations.

Find an Average

After you collect a set of measurements, you may want to get an idea of a typical measurement in that set. What if, for example, you are doing a weather project? As part of the project, you are studying rainfall data of a nearby town. The table below shows how much rain fell in that town each week during the summer.

What if you want to get an idea of how much rain fell during a typical week in the summer? In other words, you want to find the average for the set of data. There are three kinds of averages—mean, median, and mode. Does it matter which one you use?

Rainfall Data	
Week	Rain (cm)
1	2.0
2	1.4
3	0.0
4	0.5
5	1.2
6	2.5
7	1.8
8	1.4
9	2.4
10	8.6
11	7.5

Find the Mean The mean is what most people think of when they hear the word *average*. You can use a calculator to find the mean.

1. Make sure the calculator is on.

2. Add the numbers. To add a series of numbers, enter the first number and press ⊞. Repeat until you enter the last number. See the hints below. After your last number, press ⊟. Your total should be 29.3.

HINTS If the only number to the right of the decimal point is 0, you don't have to enter it into the calculator. To enter 2.0, just press ②. If the only number to the left of the decimal point is 0, you don't have to enter it into the calculator. To enter 0.5, just press ．⑤.

3. While entering so many numbers, it's easy to make a mistake and hit the wrong key. If you make a mistake, correct it by pressing the clear entry key, CE. Then continue entering the rest of the numbers.

4. Find the mean by dividing your total by the number of weeks. If 29.3 is displayed, press ÷ ① ① ⊟. Rounded up to one decimal point, your mean should be 2.7.

Find the Median The median is the middle number when the numbers are arranged in order of size. When the rainfall measurements are arranged in order of size, they look like this.

0.0
0.5
1.2
1.4
1.4
1.8 ——————— The median is 1.8. This is in the middle; there are five numbers above it and five numbers below it.
2.0
2.4
2.5
7.5
8.6

Find the Mode The mode is the number that occurs most frequently. From the ranked set of data above, you can see that the most frequent number is 1.4. It occurs twice.

Here are your three different averages from the same set of data.

Average Weekly Rainfall (cm)

Mean	2.7
Median	1.8
Mode	1.4

Why is the mean so much higher than the median or mode? The mean is affected greatly by the last two weeks when it rained a lot. A typical week for that summer was much drier than either of those last two weeks. The median or mode gives a better idea of rainfall for a typical week.

Find the Percent

Sometimes numbers are given as percents (%). Percent literally means "per hundred." For example, 28% means 28 out of 100.

What if there are about 14,000 trees in the forest and 28% are over 50 years old? How many of them are over 50 years old?

Use your calculator. You want to find 28% of 14,000. Press 1 4 0 0 0 × 2 8 %. The answer should be 3,920.

Mathematical Operations

Addition and subtraction are reverse operations, or inverses of each other. For example:
2 + 3 = 5
5 - 3 = 2
5 - 2 = 3
Similarly, multiplication and division are also inverses of each other. For example:
6 x 3 = 18
18 ÷ 6 = 3
18 ÷ 3 = 6

Mathematical Statements

Mathematical statements using symbols may be true only when the symbols are replaced by certain numbers. For example:
A < B
If A = 2 and B = 3, the statement is true.
If A = 3 and B = 2, the statement is false.

Use Technology

Use Computers

A computer has many uses. The Internet connects your computer to many other computers around the world, so you can collect all kinds of information. You can use a computer to access this information and write reports. Best of all, you can use a computer to explore, discover, and learn.

You can also get information from CD-ROMs. They are computer disks that can hold large amounts of information. You can fit a whole encyclopedia on one CD-ROM.

Use Computers for a Project

Here is how one group of students uses computers as they work on a weather project.

1. The students use instruments to measure temperature, wind speed, wind direction, and other weather variables. They input this information, or data, into the computer. The students keep the data in a table. This helps them compare the data from one day to the next.

2 The teacher finds out that another group of students in a town 200 km to the west is also doing a weather project. The two groups use the Internet to talk and share data. When a storm happens in the town to the west, that group tells the other group that it's coming their way.

3 The students want to find out more. They decide to stay on the Internet and send questions to a local television weather forecaster. She has a Web site and answers questions from students every day.

4 Meanwhile some students go to the library to gather more information from a CD-ROM. The CD-ROM has an encyclopedia that includes movie clips. The clips give examples of different kinds of storms.

5 The students have kept all their information in a folder called Weather Project. Now they use that information to write a report about the weather. On the computer they can move around paragraphs, add words, take out words, put in diagrams, and draw weather maps. Then they print the report in color.

473

Represent Data

Make Graphs to Organize Data

When you do an experiment in science, you collect information. To find out what your information means, you can organize it into graphs. There are many kinds of graphs.

Bar Graphs

A bar graph uses bars to show information. For example, what if you do an experiment by wrapping wire around a nail and connecting the ends of the wire to a battery? The nail then becomes a magnet that can pick up paper clips. The graph shows that the more you wrap the wire around the nail, the more paper clips it picks up. How many paper clips did the nail with 20 coils pick up? With 50 coils?

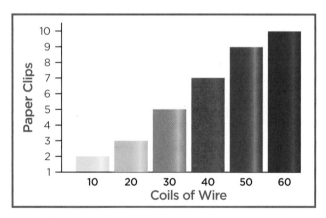

Pictographs

A pictograph uses symbols, or pictures, to show information. What if you collect information about how much water your family uses each day?

You can organize this information into a pictograph like the one shown below. The pictograph has to explain what the symbol on the graph means. In this case each bottle means 20 L of water. A half bottle means half of 20, or 10 L of water.

1 Which activity uses the most water?

2 Which activity uses the least water?

A Family's Daily Use of Water

Drinking
Showering
Bathing
Brushing teeth
Washing dishes
Washing hands
Washing clothes
Flushing toilet

= 20 liters of water

Circle Graphs

A circle graph is helpful to show how a complete set of data is divided into parts. The circle graph here shows how water is used in the United States. What is the single largest use of water?

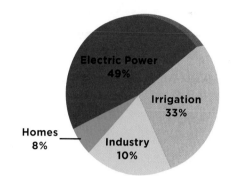

Electric Power 49%

Irrigation 33%

Homes 8%

Industry 10%

Line Graphs

A line graph shows information by connecting dots plotted on the graph. It shows change over time. For example, what if you measure the temperature outside every hour starting at 6 A.M.? The table shows what you find.

Time	Temperature (°C)
6 A.M.	4
7 A.M.	6
8 A.M.	8
9 A.M.	10
10 A.M.	12
11 A.M.	14

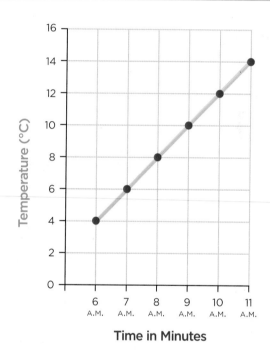

Time in Minutes

You can organize this information into a line graph. Follow these steps.

1 Make a scale along the bottom and side of the graph. The scales should include all the numbers in the chart. Label the scales.

2 Plot points on the graph.

3 Connect the points with a line.

The line graph at right organizes measurements of a plant's growth.

1 Between which two weeks did the plant grow most?

2 When did plant growth begin to level off?

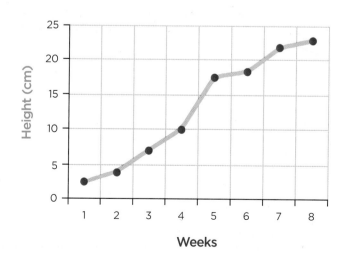

Weeks

Represent Data

Make Tables to Organize Information

Tables help you organize data during experiments. Most tables have columns that run up and down, and rows that run across. The columns and rows have headings that tell you what kind of data goes in each part of the table.

A Sample Table

What if you are going to do an experiment to find out how long different kinds of seeds take to sprout? Before you begin the experiment, you should set up your table. Follow these steps.

1. In this experiment you will plant 20 radish seeds, 20 bean seeds, and 20 corn seeds. Your table must show how many radish seeds, bean seeds, and corn seeds sprouted on days 1, 2, 3, 4, and 5.

Number of Seeds that Sprout					
	Day 1	Day 2	Day 3	Day 4	Day 5
Radish Seeds					
Bean Seeds					
Corn Seeds					

2. Make your table with columns, rows, and headings. You might use a computer to make a table. Some computer programs let you build a table with just the click of a mouse. You can delete or add columns and rows if you need to.

3. Give your table a title. Your table could look like the one shown above.

Make a Table

What if you are going to do an experiment to find out how temperature affects the sprouting of seeds? You will plant 20 bean seeds in each of two trays. You will keep each tray at a different temperature, as shown below, and observe the trays for seven days. Make a table you can use for this experiment.

Make Charts to Organize Information

Charts can help you show information that is best shown by a picture. A chart can be a table with pictures as well as words to label the rows and columns. Charts do not always have rows and columns. They can also be in other forms.

A Sample Chart

Suppose you need to collect information about the food choices you are making. You could make a chart like the one below and record the kinds of foods you eat during one day. Then you can compare the results with the recommended amounts in MyPyramid and see if you should make changes to your diet. MyPyramid is a food guidance system developed by the Center for Nutrition Policy and Promotion, that gives people ideas on how to eat better.

Make a Chart

What if you want to find out if your food choices during a whole week are close to those recommended by MyPyramid? Make a chart you can use to collect this information.

MyPyramid Chart		
Food	**MyPyramid recommends**	**My food choices**
Grains	6 ounces	
Vegetables	2 1/2 cup	
Fruits	1 1/2 cup	
Milk	3 cups	
Meat and Beans	5 ounces	

Use Technology

Make Maps to Show Information

Locate Places

A map is a drawing that shows an area from above. Most maps have coordinates—numbers and letters along the top and side. Coordinates help you find places. What if you wanted to find the library on the map below? It is located at B4. Place a finger on the letter B and another finger on the number 4. Then move your fingers straight across and down the map until they meet. The library is located where the coordinates B and 4 meet.

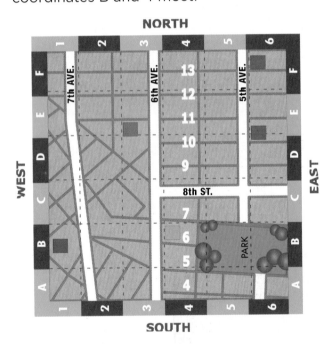

Idea Maps

Idea maps show how ideas are connected to each other. Idea maps help you organize information about a topic.

The idea map below connects ideas about rocks. This map shows that there are three major types of rock: igneous, sedimentary, and metamorphic. Connections to each rock type provide further information. For example, this map reminds you that igneous rocks are classified into those that form at Earth's surface and far beneath it.

Make an idea map about a topic you are learning in science. Your map can include words, phrases, or even sentences. Arrange your map in a way that makes sense to you and helps you understand the ideas.

1. What color building is located at F6?

2. The hospital is located three blocks north and two blocks east of the library. What are its coordinates?

3. Make a map of an area in your community. Include coordinates. Use a compass to find north, and mark north on your map. Exchange maps with classmates, and answer each other's questions.

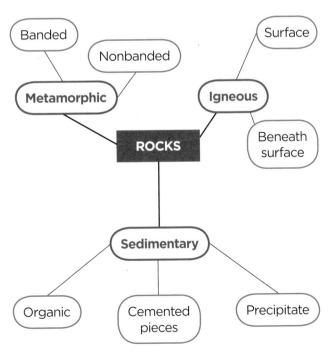

by Dinah Zike

Folding Instructions

So how do you make a Foldables study guide? The following pages offer step-by-step instructions—where and when to fold, where to cut—for making 11 basic Foldables study guides. The instructions begin with the basic shapes, such as the hot dog fold.

Half-Book

Fold a sheet of paper ($8\frac{1}{2}$" x 11") in half.
1. This book can be folded vertically like a hot dog or …
2. … it can be folded horizontally like a hamburger.

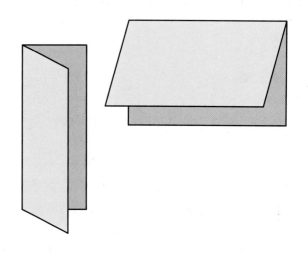

Folded Book

1. Make a Half-Book.
2. Fold in half again like a hamburger. This makes a ready-made cover and two small pages inside for recording information.

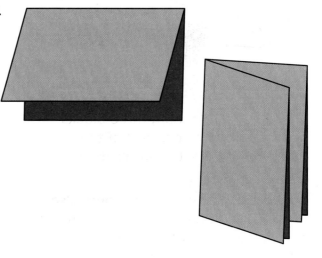

Trifold Book

1. Fold a sheet of paper ($8\frac{1}{2}$" x 11") into thirds.
2. Use this book as is, or cut into shapes.

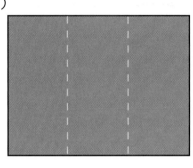
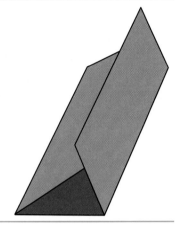

Shutter Fold

1. Begin as if you were going to make a hamburger, but instead of creasing the paper, pinch it to show the midpoint.
2. Fold the outer edges of the paper to meet at the pinch, or midpoint, forming a Shutter Fold.

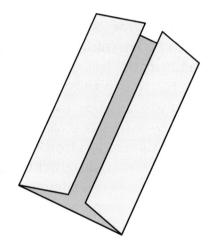

Pocket Book

1. Fold a sheet of paper ($8\frac{1}{2}$" x 11") in half like a hamburger.
2. Open the folded paper and fold one of the long sides up two inches to form a pocket. Refold along the hamburger fold so that the newly formed pockets are on the inside.
3. Glue the outer edges of the two-inch fold with a small amount of glue.

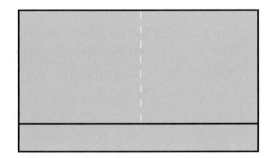

Two-Tab Book

Take a Folded Book and cut up the valley of the inside fold toward the mountain top. This cut forms two large tabs that can be used on the front and back for writing and illustrations.

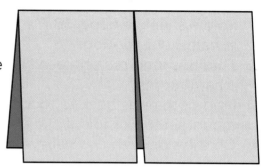

Three-Tab Book

1. Fold a sheet of paper like a hot dog.
2. With the paper horizontal and the fold of the hot dog up, fold the right side toward the center, trying to cover one half of the paper.
3. Fold the left side over the right side to make a book with three folds.
4. Open the folded book. Place one hand between the two thicknesses of paper and cut up the two valleys on one side only. This will create three tabs.

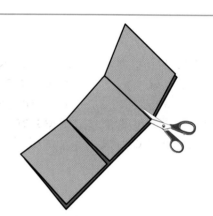

Layered-Look Book

1. Stack two sheets of paper ($8\frac{1}{2}''$ x 11") so that the back sheet is one inch higher than the front sheet.
2. Bring the bottoms of both sheets upward and align the edges so that all of the layers or tabs are the same distance apart.
3. When all the tabs are an equal distance apart, fold the papers and crease well.
4. Open the papers and glue them together along the valley, or inner center fold, or staple them along the mountain.

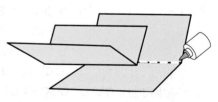

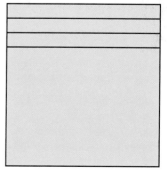

Four-Tab Book

1. Fold a sheet of paper ($8\frac{1}{2}''$ x 11'') in half like a hot dog.
2. Fold this long rectangle in half like a hamburger.
3. Fold both ends back to touch the mountain top or fold it like an accordion.
4. On the side with two valleys and one mountain top, make vertical cuts through one thickness of paper, forming four tabs.

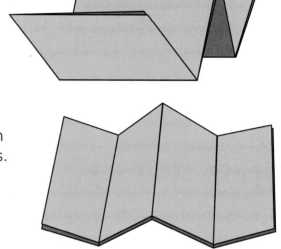

Four-Door Book

1. Make a Shutter Fold using 11'' x 17'' or 12'' x 18'' paper.
2. Fold the Shutter Fold in half like a hamburger. Crease well.
3. Open the project and cut along the two inside valley folds. These cuts will form four doors on the inside of the project.

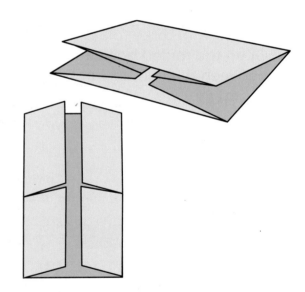

Folded Table or Chart

1. Fold the number of vertical columns needed to make the table or chart.
2. Fold the horizontal rows needed to make the table or chart.
3. Label the rows and columns.

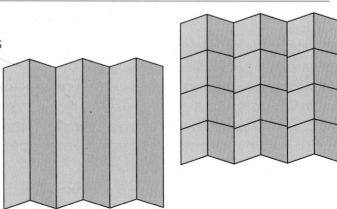

Glossary

Use this glossary to learn how to pronounce and understand the meanings of Science Words used in this book. The page number at the end of each definition tells you where to find that word in the book.

absorption (əb sôrp′shən) A process in which something is taken in and used, as by a cell. (p. 127) *The absorption of nutrients into the body takes place in the small intestine.*

acid (aśid) A substance that tastes sour, sharp or biting. (p.438)

acidity (əsid′) The strength of a acidic solution (p.440)

aerobic (er′ō′bik) Having to do with the use of oxygen. (p. 109) *Aerobic exercise, such as running or swimming, strengthens the lungs and heart.*

aerial root (âr′ē əl rüt) A root that never touches the ground. (p. 86) *Aerial roots take in moisture from the air.*

air mass (âr mas) A large region of air that has a similar temperature and humidity. (p. 265) *Air masses can be cold, warm, dry, or moist.*

air pressure (âr presh′ər) The force put on a given area by the weight of the air above it. (p. 235) *Air pressure, also called atmospheric pressure, pushes in all directions at once.*

algae (al′jē) A plant-like protist that lives in a water environment. (p. 56) *Algae produce their food using chlorophyll and other similar chemicals.*

alkali metal (al′kə lī met′əl) An element in the most reactive family of metals. (p. 412) *Lithium, sodium, and potassium are all alkali metals.*

alkalinity (al′kə līn ī tē) The strength of a base solution (p. 440)

alloy (al′oi) A mixture of two or more elements, usually metals. (p. 428) *Bronze is a durable alloy made from copper and tin.*

Pronunciation Key
The following symbols are used throughout the Macmillan McGraw-Hill Science Glossaries.

a	**at**	e	**e**nd	o	h**o**t	u	**u**p	hw	**wh**ite	ə	**a**bout
ā	**a**pe	ē	m**a**	ō	**o**ld	ū	**u**se	ng	so**ng**		tak**e**n
ä	f**a**r	i	**i**t	ôr	f**or**k	ü	r**u**le	th	**th**in		penc**i**l
âr	c**are**	ī	**i**ce	oi	**oi**l	ù	p**u**ll	th	**th**is		lem**o**n
ô	l**aw**	îr	p**ier**ce	ou	**ou**t	ûr	t**ur**n	zh	mea**s**ure		circ**u**s

′ = primary accent; shows which syllable takes the main stress, such as **kil** in **kilogram** (kil′ e gram′).

′ = secondary accent; shows which syllables take lighter stresses, such as **gram** in **kilogram**.

altitude (al'tə tüd') How high something is above Earth's surface. (p. 236) *As altitude increases, air pressure decreases.*

alveoli (al vē'ə lī) Thin-walled air sacs within the lungs. (p. 136) *The bronchi eventually empty air into the alveoli during respiration.*

amoeba (əmē' bə) A common animal-like protist that changes shape to catch food. (p. 56) *Amoeba move by shifting cytoplasm in their cells.*

amphibian (am fib'ē ən) A vertebrate animal that spends part of its life in water and part on land. (p. 50) *Frogs and salamanders are amphibians.*

anaerobic (an' rō'bik) Energy production without oxygen. (p. 109) *Anaerobic exercise, such as lifting weights, helps to build muscles.*

angiosperm (an'jē ə spûrm') A seed plant that produces flowers. (p. 74) *Fruits, vegetables, grains, and almost all nuts come from angiosperms.*

anus (ā'nəs) The opening through which solid waste leaves the body. (p. 128) *The strong muscles of the anus are located just below the rectum.*

aorta (āôr'tə) The large artery that carries blood away from the heart and to the rest of the body. (p. 147) *The left ventricle pumps oxygen-rich blood out through the aorta.*

aqueduct (a'kwə dəkt') A structure that carries large amounts of water from one place to another. (p. 218) *California has many aqueducts.*

aquifer (a'kwə fər) An underground layer of rock, sand, or gravel that contains water. (p. 205)

artery (är'tə rē) A blood vessel that carries blood away from the heart. (p. 144) *Arteries circulate oxygen-rich blood.*

arthropod (är'thrə päd') An invertebrate animal with a hard outer skeleton, a segmented body, and jointed legs. (p. 51) *Insects, spiders, and crabs are arthropods.*

artificial (är'tə fi'shəl) Made by man but working like the natural thing. (p. 164) *Doctors have created artificial organs and limbs to help their patients.*

asteroid (as' tə roid') A large piece of rock or metal in space. (p. 312) *Many asteroids orbit the Sun.*

astronomer (ə strä'nə mər) A person who studies stars, planets, and other objects in outer space. (p. 334) *Many astronomers rely on telescopes to get their data.*

astronomical unit (as'trə nä'mi kəl ù'nit) The distance between the Earth and the Sun. (p. 299) *One astronomical unit (AU) equals about 150 million kilometers.*

atmosphere (at'məs fîr) All of the air surrounding the Earth. (p. 234) *The atmosphere can be divided into several distinct layers.*

atom (at'əm) The smallest particle of an element that has the properties of that element. (p. 354) *The atoms in each element are unique and determine its properties.*

atomic number (ə tä'mik num'bər) The number of protons in a single atom of an element. (p. 364) *Every element has a different atomic number.*

atomic weight (ə tä'mik wāt) A measure of the mass of a single atom of an element. (p. 364) *Hydrogen has the smallest atomic weight.*

atrium (ā'trē əm) An upper chamber of the human heart. (p. 146) *A valve connects the atrium to the ventricle below it.*

aurora borealis (ə rôr'ə bôr'ē a'ləs) Colored lights seen in the upper atmosphere of the northern hemisphere. (p. 301) *Solar flares can cause the aurora borealis, or nothern lights.*

bacteria (bak tîr'ē ə) Unicellular organisms that have cell membranes but no distinct nuclei. (p. 55) *Ancient bacteria are the oldest living organisms on Earth.*

bark (bärk) The tough outer covering of a tree trunk. (p. 85) *The characteristics of a tree's bark can be used to identify the type of tree.*

base (bās) A compound that reacts with an acid to form a salt. (p. 439) *Soap is a base.*

barometer (bə rom'i tər) An instrument that measures air pressure. (p. 238) *There are two kinds of barometers: mercury and aneroid.*

bile (bīl) A digestive juice that breaks down fats in the small intestine. (p. 127) *Bile is produced by the liver.*

bird (bûrd) A vertebrate animal that has both feathers and wings. (p. 50) *Turkeys, hawks, and ducks are birds.*

bladder (bla'dər) An organ of the excretory system that temporarily stores urine. (p. 160) *The human bladder can increase in size to hold one and a half pints.*

boiling point (boil'ing point) The particular temperature at which a substance changes state from liquid to gas. (p. 346) *The boiling point of water is 100°C, or 212°F.*

bolus (bō'ləs) A ball of chewed food. (p. 124) *Food taken into the mouth is turned into a bolus before being swallowed.*

bronchi (bräng'kī) Small branchlike tubes in the lungs. (p. 136) *The bronchi lead back to the trachea.*

cambium (cam′bē əm) A layer of cells in plants that separates the xylem and the phloem. (p. 84) *The cambium also produces new xylem and phloem cells.*

cancer (kan′sər) A disease in which harmful cells multiply without stopping. (p. 23) *Different types of cancer attack different parts of the body, such as bones or specific organs.*

canines (kā′nīnz) The long, pointy teeth next to the front teeth. (p. 124) *Canines are useful for cutting and tearing into food.*

capillary (ka′pəler′ē) A tiny blood vessel. (p. 134) *The many capillaries in the lungs help blood to absorb oxygen from the air.*

carbohydrate (kär′bō hī′drāt) A group of chemical compounds made from carbon, oxygen, and hydrogen. (p. 95) *Carbohydrates are the major source of food energy for plants and animals.*

cardiovascular system (kär′dē ō vas′kyələr sis′təm) Another name for the circulatory system, which transports materials throughout the body. (p. 144) *The heart, blood vessels, and blood are all parts of the cardiovascular system.*

cecum (sē′kəm) The first, shortest part of the large intestine. (p. 128) *The cecum connects the large intestine to the small intestine.*

cell (sel) The smallest unit of living matter that can carry out the basic processes of life. (p. 26) *Your body is made up of trillions of cells.*

cell membrane (sel mem′brān) The layer around the outside of a cell. (p. 29) *The cell membrane gives the cell its shape and controls what goes in and out.*

cellular respiration (sel′yə lər res′pə rā′shən) The life process in which energy is released from food (sugar) inside a cell. (p. 95) *During cellular respiration, animals take in oxygen and release water and carbon dioxide.*

cell wall (sel wol) An additional layer around the outside of plant cells. (p. 31) *Cell walls provide extra support and help plants stand tall.*

chemical (kem′i kəl) A substance obtained by or used in a chemical process. (p. 31) *Cleaning products are made from chemicals.*

chemical change (kem′i kəl chānj) A change that causes a new kind of matter to form with different properties. (p. 390) *When food burns, the chemical change makes it look, feel, and taste different.*

chemical formula (kem′i kəl fôr′myə lə) A way to write a compound's name using symbols (p. 392) *The chemical formula tells what elements are in the compound, and the subscripts tell the number of particles in the compound.*

chemical reaction (kem′i kəl rē′ak′shən) A change or reaction that creates a new kind of matter (product) with different properties from the original matter (reactant). (p. 410) *Wood yields charcoal in the chemical reaction caused by fire.*

chlorophyll (klôr′ə fil) A green chemical that plants use for photosynthesis. (p. 31) *Chlorophyll allows plants to turn sunlight into food.*

chloroplast (klôr′ə plast) Green structures inside plant cells that turn sunlight into food. (pp. 31, 92) *Chloroplasts contain the chemical chlorophyll.*

Chordata (kôr′dā tə) A phylum of animals that have a supporting rod that runs most of the length of the body for at least part of their lives. (p. 50) *Dogs, cats, and humans are all in the phylum Chordata.*

class (klas) A smaller group within a phylum of similar organisms. (p. 48) *Classes are made up of even smaller groups called orders.*

circulatory system (sûr′kyə lə tôr′ē sis′ təm) The organ system that moves blood through the body. (p. 115) *The circulatory system aids in the transport of oxygen, carbon dioxide, and nutrients.*

classify (klas′ə fī) To place similar materials together in a group. (p. 78) *You can classify materials by comparing and contrasting their properties.*

climate (klī′mit) The average weather patterns of a region. (p. 255) *Climate includes average temperature, rainfall, humidity, and wind conditions.*

collecting duct (kə lek′ting dəkt) A tube connected to nephrons within the kidney. (p. 159) *The collecting duct holds waste material filtered out by the nephron.*

colon (kō′lən) The widest and longest part of the large intestine. (p. 128) *Some absorption of water and minerals takes place in the colon.*

comet (kom′it) A piece of ice mixed with rocks, dust, and gases moving through space. (p. 312) *A comet may have a glowing tail as it approaches the Sun.*

communicate (kə mū′ni kāt) To share information. (p. 240) *Some scientists communicate their results by writing books and making presentations.*

compound (kom′pound) A substance formed by the chemical combination of two or more elements held together by chemical bonds that cannot be separated by physical means. (p. 391) *A compound has properties unlike those of the elements that make up the compound.*

condensation (kon′den sā′shən) The process in which matter changes state from gas to liquid. (p. 190) *When water vapor in the air condenses, it can form dew on cool surfaces.*

condensing point (kən dens′ing point) The particular temperature at which a substance changes state from gas to liquid. (p. 346) *The condensing point of water is 100°C, or 212°F.*

conduct (kən dukt′) To transfer heat or electricity from one place to another. (p. 367) *Metals, such as iron and copper, are good conductors.*

conductivity (kən′dukt i′və tē) The degree to which heat or electricity flows through a substance. (p. 424) *Electrical wiring is made from metals with high conductivity.*

conservation (kän′sərv ā′shən) The act or policy of saving or protecting something. (p. 220) *Conservation leads people to use less of the planet's resources to help preserve them for the future.*

contaminate (kən ta′mə nāt′) To make dirty or impure. (p. 208, 455) *Litter and other kinds of pollution can contaminate fresh water.*

convection (kən′vek′shən) The transfer of heat through the movement of a gas or liquid. (p. 247) *When convention occurs in the air, winds are formed.*

Coriolis effect (kôr′ē ō′lis i fekt′) In the Northern Hemisphere, counterclockwise movement caused by Earth's rotation. (p. 271) *The spiral of a hurricane shows how ths storm is shaped by the Coriolis effect.*

corrosion (kə rō′zhən) The gradual weakening and wearing away of something, usually due to a chemical reaction. (p. 428) *Corrosion occurs when the metal iron reacts with water and forms rust.*

current (kûr′ənt) An ongoing movement in one direction. (p. 256) *An ocean current is a large stream of water that flows through the ocean. Electrical current describes the flow of charged particles through a wire.*

cyclone (sī′klōn) A storm with a low pressure closure and a circular pattern of winds. (p. 271) *Tornadoes and hurricanes are both types of cyclones.*

cytoplasm (sī′tə pla′zəm) The gel-like substance that fills a cell. (p. 29) *The cytoplasm supports all of the other cell structures.*

dam (dam) A barrier that prevents or restricts the normal flow of water. (p. 205) *Reservoirs are usually made by constructing a dam across a stream or river.*

density (den′si tē) A measure of how tightly matter is packed in a given amount of space. (p. 348) *Density can tell you whether an object will float or sink in a liquid.*

desalination (dē sa′lə nā′shən) To remove salt from a substance. (p. 223) *At a desalination plant, salt and other impurities are removed from ocean water to create fresh water.*

dialysis (dī a′lə səs) A medical treatment that carries out the same processes as the human kidney. (p. 162) *A dialysis machine filters the blood to remove waste and excess water.*

diaphragm (dī′ə′fram) A flat muscle that controls breathing. (p. 134) *Your diaphragm is beneath your lungs near the bottom of the rib cage.*

diffusion (di fyü′zhən) The movement of particles from areas with high concentrations to areas with low concentration. (p. 137) *Oxygen passes from the lungs into the blood by diffusion.*

digestion (di jes′chən) The process by which food is broken down into usable substances. (p. 122) *Digestion begins the moment you start to chew something.*

digestive system (di jes′tiv sis′təm) The organ system that breaks down food into nutrients that cells need. (p. 115) *The mouth and stomach are parts of the digestive system.*

disperse (di spərs′) To scatter or spread. (p. 76) *Plant seeds are dispersed in many ways, including by animals and the wind.*

draw conclusions (drô kən klü′zhənz) To arrive at possible answers based on information you have gathered. (p. 304) *After you analyze the data from an experiment, you can draw conclusions about what you observed.*

drought (drout) A long period of dry weather. (p. 216) *A drought can destroy crops and lead to water shortages.*

ductile (duk′təl) Capable of being drawn out into wire or thread. (p. 426) *Copper and gold are both ductile metals.*

ecology (ē kol′ə jē) The study of how all things in an environment interact with one another. (p. 172) *A plant ecologist may study the ecology of plants in specific environments, such as wetlands or farms.*

electron (i lek′tron) A particle in the space outside the nucleus of an atom that carries one unit of negative electric charge. (p. 364) *Atoms have the same number of protons and electrons.*

electron microscope (i lek′tron mī′krə skōp′) A magnifying tool that uses electron beams instead of light to "see" small objects. (p. 370) *Atoms can only be seen using an electron microscope.*

element (el′ə mənt) A pure substance that cannot be broken down into any simpler substances. (p. 354) *Oxygen, carbon, and iron are all elements.*

elimination (i li′mə nā′shən) The process of removing or getting rid of something. (p. 128) *In the body, elimination takes place through many pores and openings, such as the anus.*

ellipse (i lips′) A flattened circle. (p. 321) *Planets move through space in ellipses.*

endocrine system (en′də krin sis′təm) The organ system that produces chemicals to regulate and control body functions. (p. 115) *The chemicals of the endocrine system also affect the reproductive system.*

epidermis (ep′i dûr′mis) The outermost layer. In plants, the epidermis is the outermost layer of a leaf. (p. 92) *In humans, it is the surface layer of the skin.*

epiglottis (e′pə glä′təs) The flap of tissue in the back of the throat that protects you from choking. (p. 135) *The epiglottis closes when you swallow food.*

equator (i kwā′tər) The imaginary line that runs around the middle of Earth. (p. 244) *Sunlight strikes Earth most directly at the equator.*

esophagus (i sä′fə gəs) A long muscular tube leading to the stomach. (p. 125) *Your esophagus is lined with mucus that helps food slide along.*

evaporation (i vap′ə rā′shən) The slow changing of a liquid into a gas. (p. 183, 346) *Evaporation is slower than boiling and can occur at lower temperatures.*

evergreen (ev′ər grēn′) A type of gymnosperm that replaces leaves that are lost. (p. 75) *The leaves of evergreens, such as pine, spruce, and firs, are sometimes called needles.*

excretory system (ek′skri tôr′ ē sis′təm) The organ system that removes waste materials from the body. (p. 115) *The kidneys are part of the excretory system.*

exhale (eks hāl′) To breathe out. (p. 134) *When you exhale, your body expels carbon dioxide.*

family (fa′mə lē) A group of things that are related in some way. In the classification of living things, families fall between orders and genera. (pp. 48, 369) *In the periodic table, families of elements have similar chemical properties.*

feces (fē′sēs) Solid animal waste. (p. 128) *In humans, feces are stored in the rectum until they can be expelled.*

fertilization (fûr′tə lī zā′shən) The joining of a male sex cell with a female sex cell to make one new cell. (p. 76) *Fertilization in plants occurs when pollen transfers to the egg cell.*

fibrous root (fī′brəs rüt) One of the many thin, hairy, fibrous roots that characterize some plants. (p. 86) *Grasses have fibrous roots.*

filtration (fil trā′shən) The passing of a mixture through a system that can separate small particles from larger particles. (p. 382) *A mixture of dirt and water can be separated by filtration.*

fish (fish) A vertebrate animal that lives its entire life in the water. (p. 50) *The bodies of fish are covered with scales.*

flood (flŭd) The flow of water over the banks of a body of water and across land. (p. 207) *Large amounts of rainfall can cause floods along rivers.*

fog (fog) A cloud that forms near the ground. (p. 194, 272) *Dense fog is considered to be a severe form of weather.*

forecast (fôr′cast) To predict; a prediction. (p. 278) *A weather forecast makes the best guess at what the weather will be in the near future.*

freezing point (frēz′ing point) The particular temperature at which a substance changes state from liquid to solid. (p. 347) *The freezing point of water is 0°C, or 32°F.*

freshwater (fresh′wô′tər) Characterized by water that is not salty. (p. 182) *Most ponds and most rivers are freshwater environments.*

front (frunt) The place where two air masses meet. (p. 265) *A change in weather usually occurs when a front passes over an area.*

fungus (fung′gəs) n. sing., **fungi** (fun′jē), pl. Members of a kingdom that cannot make their own food and must absorb it from their environment. (p. 54) *Mold, mildew, and mushrooms are all examples of fungi.*

fusion (fū′shən) The smashing together of particles to create new particles. (p. 302) *Fusion can create energy and produces the light and heat of the Sun.*

gallbladder (gôl′bla′dər) A small structure in the body's digestive system that stores bile. (p. 127) *The gallbladder looks like a small sack.*

gas (gas) Matter in a state that has no definite shape or volume. (p. 344) *The particles in a gas are moving very rapidly and are widely spread out.*

genera (jen′ər ə) n. pl., **genus** (jē′nəs) sing. A group made up of two or more very similar species. (p. 48) *Genera fall between families and species in the classification of living things.*

glacier (glā′shər) A large body of ice that moves slowly over land. (p. 184) *Glaciers are capable of creating deep valleys.*

gland (gland) A group of cells that can filter blood and/or produce substances that assist in various bodily processes. (p. 122) *The salivary glands in the mouth and throat assist with digestion.*

global wind (glō'bəl wind) A wind that blows in a predictable direction. (p. 248) *Global winds blow because of differences in air pressure between Earth's poles and the equator.*

gravity (gra'vi tē) The force of attraction between two masses. (p. 318) *The gravity between your body and Earth prevents you from floating into space.*

groundwater (ground'wô'tər) Precipitation that seeps below the surface of Earth. (p. 205) *People drill wells to tap into Earth's groundwater.*

gymnosperm (jim'nə spûrm') A seed plant that does not produce a flower. (p. 75) *Most gymnosperms are evergreens that have seeds inside their cones.*

hardness (härd'nis) How well a mineral resists scratching or a metal resists denting. (p. 427) *Gold has a low hardness.*

halogen (ha'lə jən) An element in the most reactive family of nonmetals. (pp. 367, 413) *Fluorine and chlorine are both halogens.*

heart (härt) The muscular organ that pumps blood throughout the body. (p. 144) *The human heart beats about 70 to 90 times a minute in the chest.*

heavy metals (he'vē met'əlz) Certain toxic elements, such as lead and mercury. (p. 454) *Heavy metals in drinking water can make a person sick.*

heterogeneous (het'ər ə jē'nē əs) Made up of things that differ in kind and/or nature. (p. 378) *In a heterogeneous mixture you can see the particles of different substances.*

high pressure system (hī pre'shər sis'təm) A large mass of air with high atmospheric pressure at the center. (p. 282) *The wind in a high pressure system turns in a clockwise direction.*

homogenous (hō'mō jē'nē əs) Made up of things that either look the same or are the same. (p. 378) *In a homogeneous mixture, the individual particles are too small to distinguish and look the same throughout.*

humidity (hū mid'i tē) The amount of water vapor in the air. (p. 237) *As humidity increases, air pressure decreases.*

hurricane (hûr'i kān') A very large, swirling storm with very low pressure at its center and wind speeds higher than 73 miles per hour. (p. 270) *Hurricanes have an "eye" that forms at the center.*

hydrocarbon (hī'drō kär'bən) A compound made only of hydrogen and carbon atoms. (p. 396)

hypothesis (hī poth′ə sis) A testable statement about what someone thinks is logically true. (p. 44) *A hypothesis is tested using an experiment that may either support or disprove it.*

ice sheet (īs shēt) A large covering of ice and snow that lasts a long time. (p. 184) *Antarctica is covered in an ice sheet.*

immune system (im ūn′ sis′təm) The organ system that fights disease and helps heal injuries. (p. 115) *The immune system includes cells that attack harmful organisms in the body.*

incisors (in sī′zərz) The teeth in the front of the mouth. (p. 124) *Incisors are used for biting into food.*

indicator (in′di kā′tər) A person or thing that indicates. (p.438)

inertia (i nər′shə) The tendency of a moving object to continue moving in a straight line. (p. 320) *Gravity and friction affect an object's inertia.*

infer (in fûr′) To come up with an idea based on facts or observations. (p. 350) *The data from an experiment can help you infer what happened.*

inhale (in hāl′) To breathe in. (p. 134) *When you inhale, air enters the body through the nose and mouth.*

insulator (in′sə lā tər) Something that resists the flow of energy, such as heat, electricity, or sound. (p. 424) *Most nonmetals, such as wood and rubber, are good insulators.*

integumentary system (in te′gyə men′tə rē sis′təm) The organ system that covers and protects the body from injury and infection. (p. 115) *The integumentary system includes hair, skin, and nails.*

invertebrate (in′vûr′tə brit) An animal that does not have a backbone. (p. 50) *Mollusks, sponges, and arthropods are all invertebrates.*

jet stream (jet strēm) Powerful high altitude global winds above high and low pressure systems. (p. 283) *Jet stream winds can move faster than 150 miles per hour.*

kidney (kid′nē) A bean-shaped organ that filters waste out of the blood. (p. 156) *The kidneys produce urine.*

kingdom (king'dəm) The broadest group into which organisms are classified. (p. 48) *The animal kingdom and the plant kingdom are two of the six kingdoms.*

land breeze (land brēz) The movement of air from land to water. (p. 192)

large intestine (lärj in tes'tən) A thick, tubelike organ that removes waste from the body. (p. 128) *The large intestine is shorter and thicker than the small intestine.*

latitude (la'ti tüd) A measure of how far north or south something is from the equator. (p. 248) *You can describe an object's location on Earth in terms of its latitude and longitude.*

leaf (lēf) The part of a plant that collects light from the Sun and makes sugar. (p. 82) *The leaves also take in carbon dioxide and release oxygen.*

lightning (līt'ning) A large spark caused by the discharge of electricity in a thunderhead. (p. 267) *Lightning can jump from one cloud to another or from a cloud to the ground.*

liquid (lik'wid) Matter in a state that has a definite volume but not a definite shape. (p. 344) *The particles in a liquid move faster than in a solid but remain relatively close together.*

liver (li'vər) A large glandular organ that produces digestive juices and breaks down harmful substances in the blood. (pp. 127, 158) *The liver is part of both the digestive and the excretory systems.*

low pressure closure (lō pre'shər clō'zhər) An area of low pressure surrounded by an area of high pressure. (p. 268) *A low pressure closure can lead to the creation of a tornado.*

low pressure system (lō pre'shər sis'təm) A large mass of air with low atmospheric pressure at the center. (p. 282) *The wind in a low pressure system turns in a counterclockwise direction.*

lungs (ləngz) The main organs of the respiratory system. (p. 134) *The lungs fill with air and allow gases to enter and leave the blood.*

malleable (ma'lē ə bəl) Capable of being rolled or pounded into flat sheets. (p. 426) *Tin, copper, and aluminum are malleable metals.*

mammal (ma'məl) A vertebrate animal with hair that feeds its young milk. (p. 51) *Some mammals, such as horses, live on land while others, such as whales, live in water.*

mass (mas) The amount of matter in an object. (pp. 299, 342) *Mass is measured in units called grams (g),*

matter (ma'tər) Anything that has mass and takes up space. (p. 342) *Scientists think that mass is made up of particles.*

measure (mezh'ər) To find the size, volume, area, mass, weight, or temperature of an object, or to find how long an event occurs. (p. 186) *When you measure something, you gather data or information about it.*

melting point (melt'ing point) The particular temperature at which a substance changes state from solid to liquid. (p. 346) *The melting point of water is 0°C, or 32°F.*

metal (met'əl) A substance that conducts heat and electricity. (pp. 366, 422) *Metals, such as gold and iron, are shiny when polished and can be bent or flattened into shapes without breaking.*

metalloid (met'ə loid) A small group of elements with some properties of both metals and nonmetals. (p. 367) *Boron and silicon are metalloids.*

metamorphosis (met'ə môr fə sis) A process in which something changes form from one thing into another thing. (p. 339) *Caterpillars undergo metamorphosis to change into moths.*

meteor (mē'tē ər) A small piece of ice, rock, or metal that enters Earth's atmosphere. (p. 312) *Most shooting stars are also meteors.*

meteorologist (mē tē ə rä'lə jist) A scientist who studies Earth's atmosphere and weather. (p. 278) *Meteorologists try to predict the weather.*

microscope (mī'krə skōp') A tool that magnifies objects. (p. 32) *A microscope allows us to see and study very small objects like cells.*

mitochondria (mī'tə kon'drē ə) Structures within a cell that break down food and turn it into energy. (p. 29) *The more energy a cell needs, the more mitochondria it will have.*

mixture (miks'chər) A physical combination of two or more substances that does not form a new substance. (p. 378) *A bowl of raisins, nuts, and pretzels is a mixture.*

molars (mō'lərz) The flat teeth in the back of the mouth. (p. 124) *Molars are useful for crushing and grinding food.*

molecule (mol'ə kūl') A particle that contains two or more atoms joined together. (p. 365) *Oxygen molecules are made up of two oxygen atoms.*

mollusk (mä'ləsk) Invertebrate animals with an external or internal shell. (p. 51) *Snails, clams, and octopuses are mollusks.*

monsoon (män sün') A seasonal wind usually associated with heavy rains. (p. 272) *Monsoon winds occur in southern Asia and the southwestern U.S.*

moon (mün) An object that circles around a planet. (p. 310) *Some planets have many moons of different shapes and sizes.*

mucus (myü'kəs) A slippery liquid inside the body. (p. 125) *Mucus in the esophagus keeps food from getting stuck.*

multicellular (mul'tē sel'ū lər) Made up of more than one cell. (p. 39) *Animals and plants are multicellular organisms.*

muscular system (mus'kyə lər sis'təm) The organ system made up of muscles attached to bones. (p. 115) *The muscular system helps you move.*

nanotechnology (na'nō tek nä'lə jē) Science that works with materials at the atomic or molecular level. (p. 372) *Nanotechnology refers to devices and procedures that are very, very small in size.*

nephron (ne'frän') Small individual filters within the kidneys. (p. 158) *Nephrons separate waste from useful substances in the blood.*

nervous system (nûr'vəs sis'təm) The organ system that controls all other body systems. (p. 115) *The nervous system includes the brain, the spinal chord, and nerves.*

neutralization reaction (nü'trēl ī zā'shən rē ak shən) The reaction that occurs when an acid and a base react to form water and salt. (p. 439)

newton (nü'tən) A basic unit that measures a force, such as gravity. (p. 343) *A person's weight can be expressed in newtons.*

noble gases (nō'bəl gas'əz) The nonmetallic elements helium, neon, argon, krypton, xenon, and radon. (p. 367) *Noble gases rarely react with other elements.*

nonmetals (non'met əlz) A group of elements that are poor conductors of heat and electricity. (p. 367) *Many nonmetals, such as oxygen and helium, are gases at room temperature.*

nonvascular (non vas'kyə lər) Containing no plant tissue through which food or water moves. (p. 53) *Mosses are nonvascular plants that get water and food directly from the ground.*

nucleus (nü'klē əs) An object positioned at the center; in cells, the structure that controls all activity within a cell. (p. 29, 364) *The nucleus is the central command center of the cell.*

nutrient (nü'trē ənt) Any substance that is useful to an organism. (p. 122) *Cells draw their energy from nutrients.*

observe (əb zûrv′) To use one or more of your senses to identify or learn about an object or event. (p. 186) *You conduct an experiment to observe what happens in a particular situation.*

ocean (ō′shən) A large body of salt water. (p. 180) *The Atlantic and the Pacific are both oceans.*

orbit (ôr′bit) The path an object takes as it travels around another object. (p. 320) *Earth's orbit requires about 365 days to complete.*

order (ôr′dər) A smaller group within a class of similar organisms. (p. 48) *Orders are made up of even smaller groups called families.*

organ (ôr′gə n) A group of tissues that work together to perform a specific bodily function. (p. 41) *The lungs, heart, and stomach are all organs.*

organism (ôr′gə niz′əm) An individual living thing. (p. 28) *All organisms carry out five basic life functions.*

organ system (ôr′gə n sis′təm) A group of organs that work together to perform a specific bodily function. (p. 41) *The digestive system and the respiratory system are examples of animal organ systems.*

oscillation (ä′sə lā′shən) Movement back and forth. (p. 258) *Shifting wind patterns can lead to an oscillation in weather conditions.*

pancreas (pang′krē əs) A gland that produces digestive fluids and other helpful chemicals. (p. 127) *The pancreas is located on top of the small intestine.*

paramecium (pa′rə mē′shē əm) A common animal-like protist that cannot produce its own food. (p. 56) *A paramecium moves using hairlike structures that stick out of its cell membrane.*

pericardium (per′ə kär′dē əm) The sac of tissue around the heart. (p. 146) *The pericardium protects the heart.*

periodic table (pîr′ē od′ik tā′bəl) A chart that shows all of the known elements and their properties. (p. 368) *The periodic table places elements with similar chemical properties in groups or families.*

petiole (pet′ē ōl) The part of a plant that connects the leaf to the stalk. (p. 82) *Veins in a leaf usually branch out from the petiole.*

pharynx (fa′ringks) The part of the throat that connects the mouth to the digestive tube. (p. 125) *The pharynx is located just above the esophagus.*

pH scale (pē'aitch') The scale that measures the acidity or alkalinity of a solution. (p. 440) *Fourteen on the pH scale is basic.*

phloem (flō'əm) The tissue in a plant that moves food down from the leaves to other parts of the plant. (p. 84) *The location of phloem depends on the type of stem.*

photosynthesis (fō'tō sin'thə sis) The process by which plants turn sunlight, water, and carbon dioxide into food. (p. 92) *Most photosynthesis takes place in the chloroplasts of a plant.*

phylum (fī'ləm), n. sing., **phyla** (fī'lə), pl. The level of classification of living things below kingdom and above class. (p. 48) *The two phyla in the animal kingdom are vertebrates and invertebrates.*

pistil (pis'təl) The part of a plant that produce the female sex cells. (p. 76) *The ovary is part of the plant's pistil.*

plasma (plaz'mə) A fluid in which other materials are suspended, as with blood cells in blood. (p. 148) *Blood plasma is made up of water and proteins.*

platelet (plāt'lət) Small cell fragments that help the body heal. (p. 148) *Platelets clump together to form patches that stop bleeding.*

pollen (pol'ən) The powder-like grains in a flower that contain the male sex cells. (p. 76) *During pollination, pollen is transferred from stamen to pistil.*

pollination (pol'ə nā'shən) The process in which the male and female cells of plants come together. (p. 76) *After pollination a seed develops that lets the plant reproduce.*

pollute (pə lüt') To make dirty, unclean, or contaminated. (p. 208) *Litter pollutes the landscape.*

pore (pôr) A small opening. (p. 161) *Pores in the skin are connected to sweat glands and assist in waste elimination.*

precipitate (prē sip'ə tət) The solid product of a chemical reaction in a solution. (p. 414) *Magnesium carbonate is the precipitate formed when Epsom salts react with washing soda.*

precipitation (prē sip'i tā'shən) Water droplets that form in the atmosphere and fall to the ground. (p. 196) *Precipitation can take the form of rain, snow, sleet, or hail.*

product (prod'ukt) A new substance resulting from a chemical change. (p. 410) *Glass is the product of heated sand.*

property (prop'ər tē) A trait of something that can be observed and measured. (p. 343) *The physical properties of matter include volume, mass, and weight.*

prop root (prop rüt) Roots that grow like fingers out of the stem of a plant. (p. 86) *Corn plants and mangroves have prop roots.*

protist (prō'tist) A member of the kingdom Protista, which contains mostly unicellular organisms with distinct nuclei. (p. 56) *Protists can be like animals, plants, or fungi in terms of how they get food.*

proton (prō'ton) A particle in the nucleus of an atom that carries one unit of positive electric charge.(p. 364) *Atoms have the same number of protons and electrons.*

pulmonary (pùl'mə ner'ē) Having to do with the lungs. (p. 146) *A pulmonary artery brings oxygen-poor blood from the heart to the lungs; a pulmonary vein brings oxygen-rich blood from the lungs to the heart.*

reactant (rē ak'tənt) An original substance at the beginning of a chemical reaction. (p. 410) *Carbon and oxygen atoms are reactants that yield the product carbon dioxide when carbon is burned.*

reactivity (rē ak'ti'və tē)The ability of elements to take part in chemical reactions. (p. 412) *Most metals have high reactivity, while the noble gases do not.*

reclamation (re'klə mā'shən) The act of recycling or restoring something to a usable state. (p. 217) *Land reclamation efforts can convert poor soil back into fertile farmland.*

record data (rē côrd da'tə) To make note of an observation in a permanent way, as in writing. (p. 350) *When you record data on a chart, you organize your observations.*

rectum (rek'təm) The last part of the large intestine. (p. 128) *Solid waste is stored in the rectum until it can be expelled.*

renal (rē'nəl) Having to do with the kidneys. (p. 158) *The renal artery brings blood into the kidneys.*

reproduction (rē'prə duk'shən) The process of creating more of the same kind of organism. (p. 39) *Reproduction is one of the basic life processes of all living things.*

reproductive system (rē'prə duk'tiv sis'təm) The organ system that produces offspring. (p. 115) *The reproductive system differs between males and females.*

reptile (rep'tīl) A land vertebrate with thick, dry, scaly skin. (p. 50) *Snakes, lizards, and turtles are reptiles.*

reservoir (re'zə vwär') A man-made lake that stores water for later use. (p. 205) *Most reservoirs are created by damming a stream or river.*

respiration (res'pə rā'shən) The life process in which energy is released from food (sugar). (p. 39, 140) *Plants and animals take in oxygen during respiration.*

respiratory system (res'pə r ə tôr'ē sis'təm) The organ system that brings oxygen to body cells and removes waste gas. (p. 115) *The lungs are part of the respiratory system.*

root (rüt) The part of a plant that absorbs water and mineral, stores food, and anchors the plant. (p. 82) *The roots usually spread out and down into the soil.*

saliva (sə'lī'və) A watery fluid that moistens and softens food. (p. 124) *Saliva helps digestion by chemically breaking down food.*

salt (sôlt) A white substance that is found in sea water and in the earth. (p.436)

salivary glands (sa'lə ver'ē) Glands that produce a watery fluid that aids in digestion. (p. 124) *You have salivary glands in your mouth and throat.*

satellite (sa'tə līt) An object in space that circles around another object. (p. 310) *Earth's moon is a satellite.*

sea breeze (sē brēz) The movement of air from water to land. (p. 192) *You feel sea breezes on beaches.*

seed (sēd) An undeveloped plant with stored food in a protective covering. (p. 74) *Seeds are formed when a male and a female cell join.*

skeletal system (skel'i təl sis'təm) The organ system made up of bones that support the body. (p. 115) *The skeletal and muscular systems work together to help you move.*

small intestine (smôl in'tes'tən) A coiled, tubelike digestive organ connected to the stomach. (p. 127) *Partially digested food is broken down into nutrients inside the small intestine.*

solar flare (sō'lər flār) A huge burst of heat and energy from the surface of the Sun. (p. 301) *Solar flares can affect electronic equipment even on Earth.*

solar system (sō'lər sis'təm) The Sun and the objects in orbit around it. (p. 308) *Our solar system is in the Milky Way galaxy.*

solid (sol'id) Matter in a state that has a definite shape and volume. (p. 344) *The particles in a solid are not moving around.*

solubility (sol'yə bil'i tē) The greatest amount of a solute that can be dissolved by a given amount of solvent. (p. 381) *The solubility of table salt is 37 grams per 100 grams of water at room temperature.*

solute (sol'ūt) The substance in a solution that dissolves. (p. 380) *In salt water, salt is the solute.*

solution (sə lü'shən) A mixture that is blended so completely that it looks the same everywhere. (p. 379) *When sugar dissolves in water, it forms a solution.*

solvent (sol'vənt) The substance in a solution into which other substances dissolve. (p. 380) *In salt water, water is the solvent.*

species (spē'sēz) The narrowest group in the classification system of living things. (p. 48) *Organisms in the same species are very closely related.*

spore (spôr) A single cell that can develop into a plant exactly like the one that produced it. (p. 74) *Spores will not grow and produce plants unless they are near water.*

stamen (stā'mən) The part of the plant that holds the male cells for reproduction. (p. 76) *The stamen is part of the plant's anther.*

star (stär) An object in space that produces its own light and heat. (p. 299) *The nearest star to the Earth is the Sun.*

starch (stärch) A complex carbohydrate made of thousands of sugar units. (p. 95) *Plants store sugar in the form of starch.*

state of matter (stāt uv mat'ər) One of three forms that matter can take. (p. 344) *The states of matter are solids, liquids, and gases.*

stem (stem) The main stalk of a plant. (p. 82) *A plant's stem holds it uprights and carries food and water.*

sternum (stər'nəm) The vertical bone in the center of the chest. (p. 146) *The sternum helps to protect the heart from injury.*

stomach (stə'mək) The main digestive organ in most animals. (p. 126) *The human stomach has three layers of muscles and glands that produce chemicals for breaking down food.*

stomata (stō'mə tə) n. pl., **stoma** (stō'mə) sing. Small pores on plants, usually on the bottoms of leaves, through which air and water pass. (p. 93) *Stomata open and close to let in and give off gases.*

storm surge (stôrm sûrj) A bulge of water created by an area of very low pressure in the ocean. (p. 271) *The storm surge can be the most destructive part of a hurricane along the coast.*

sublimation (sə'blə mā'shən) The process in which matter changes state from a solid directly into a gas. (p. 347) *When dry ice is exposed to room temperature, the crystals sublime rapidly into a vapor.*

subscript (sub'skript) A number in a chemical formula that tells how many atoms of a particular element are in the compound. (p. 392) *The subscript is usually a small number written to the right and lower than the symbol for the element.*

sunspot (sun'spät) A dark spot that occurs on the Sun's surface. (p. 304) *The number of sunspots changes over time.*

superconductor (sü'pər kən dək'tər) A material that loses all resistance to electrical flow at extremely low temperatures. (p. 424) *Superconductors are used today in some fast-moving trains in Germany, Japan, and China.*

suspension (sə spen'shən) A mixture whose visible particles settle and separate over time. (p. 379) *Oil and vinegar shaken together create a suspension.*

sweat (swet) Fluid that helps the body eliminate excess water and waste materials through pores in the skin. (p. 161) *Sweat also helps the body to cool off.*

taproot (tap'rüt') A root that grows deep into the ground and has few hairy branches. (p. 86) *Dandelion, carrot, and beet plants have taproots.*

telescope (tel'ə skōp') A tool that makes distant objects appear closer and larger. (p.308) *The Hubble telescope allows us to see distant planets and stars more clearly.*

temper (tem'pər) To warm up something cold, or cool down something hot. (p. 254) *Cold air that comes in contact with warm water is tempered.*

thunder (thun'dər) The noise caused by rapidly expanding air heated by lightning. (p. 267) *Thunder can sound like a big bang or a low rumble.*

thunderhead (thun'dər hed') A cloud in which a thunderstorm forms. (p. 266) *Most thunderheads are cumulonimbus clouds.*

thunderstorm (thun'dər stôrm') A rainstorm that includes thunder and lightning. (p. 266) *Thunderstorms are the most common types of severe weather.*

tide (tīd) The rise and fall of the ocean's surface. (p. 322) *The Moon's gravitational pull affects tides on Earth.*

tissue (tish'ü) A group of similar cells that work together to do the same job. (p. 40) *The cells in muscle tissue all work to move parts of the body.*

tornado (tôr nā'dō) A rotating, funnel-shaped cloud with extremely high winds. (p. 268) *Tornados are also called "twisters" because they often twist as they move.*

toxin (täk'sən) A poisonous substance within the body. (p. 158) *The liver and kidneys both help to remove toxins from blood.*

trachea (trā'kē ə) The strong tube that connects the throat to the bronchi of the lungs. (p. 136) *The trachea, or windpipe, is a major part of the respiratory system.*

trade winds (trād windz) Winds that blow between 30°N latitude and 30°S latitude. (p. 248) *Sailors relied on trade winds to transport items for sale around the globe.*

tropical storm (trop'i kəl stôrm) A large storm near the equator with low pressure at its center and rotating winds. (p. 270) *A tropical storm becomes a hurricane when its winds reach a certain speed.*

troposphere (trop′ə sfîr) The layer of Earth's atmosphere that is closest to the surface. (p. 234) *All of the organisms on Earth exist in the troposphere.*

unicellular (ū′nə sel′ū lər) Made up of only one cell. (p. 38) *A unicellular organism can carry out all the basic life processes in one cell.*

ureter (yùr′ə tər) A tube that carries urine from the kidney to the bladder. (p. 157) *Ureters are part of the body's excretory system.*

urethra (yù rē′thrə) A tube that carries urine from the bladder to the outside of the body. (p. 160) *The urethra is part of the excretory system.*

urinary system (yər′ə ner′ē sis′təm) The part of the excretory system that handles most liquid wastes. (p. 156) *The kidneys, bladder, and urinary tract are parts of the urinary system.*

urination (yər′i nā′shən) The process of releasing urine from the bladder and out of the body through the urethra. (p. 160) *Urination may become more frequent shortly after a person drinks more fluids.*

urine (yər′ən) A fluid consisting of body waste and excess water. (p. 156) *The kidneys produce urine by filtering the blood.*

vacuole (vak′ū ōl) A cell structure used for storage. (p. 29) *Vacuoles can hold water, food, and waste products.*

valve (valv) A flap that allows fluids to flow in only one direction. (p. 146) *In the heart, valves allow blood to pass from the atrium into the ventricle and not the other way.*

variable (vâr′ē ə bəl) Something that can be changed or controlled. (p. 418) *When measuring solubility, temperature is a significant variable.*

vascular (vas′kyə lər) Containing vessels that transport water and food. (p. 52) *Vascular plants have tissue that allows them to grow tall and still move food and water throughout the organism.*

vein (vān) A blood vessel that transports blood back to the heart. (p. 144) *Veins, such as the vena cava, connect to the heart's atriums.*

vena cava (vē′nə kā′və) The main vein leading from the body back to the heart. (p. 146) *The vena cava enters the right atrium of the heart.*

ventricle (ven′tri kəl) A lower chamber of the human heart. (p. 146) *In the heart, blood flows from an atrium into a ventricle and is then pushed out into the body.*

vertebrate (vûr'tə brit) An animal that has a backbone. (p. 50) *Fish, amphibians, reptiles, birds, and mammals are all vertebrates.*

villi (vi'lī') Small hairlike structures that protrude from a surface. (p. 127) *Villi in the small intestine increase absorption by providing more surface area.*

volume (vol'ūm) The amount of space that an object takes up. (p. 236) *The unit measure of volume for liquids is the liter (L); for solids it is the cubic meter (m³).*

water cycle (wô'tər sī'kəl) The continuous movement of water from a liquid state on the ground to a vapor state in the air and back again. (p. 198) *Cloud formation and rainfall are two parts of the water cycle.*

watershed (wô'tər shed) An area of land that drains into a specific river. (p. 206) *There are ten watersheds in California.*

water vapor (wô'tər vā'pər) The gas state of water. (p. 183) *You cannot see water vapor in the air.*

weight (wāt) A measure of how strongly gravity pulls on an object. (p. 343) *Weight can be measured in newtons or in pounds and ounces.*

weather map (weth'ər map) A model or representation of one or more weather variables. (p. 279) *A weather map might show temperatures, precipitation amounts, or wind speeds.*

xylem (zī'ləm) Plant tissue that moves water and minerals up from the roots. (p. 84) *Most of the layers in a tree trunk are made of xylem.*

Index

Note: Page references followed by an asterisk (*) indicate activities.

P

Credits

Illustration Credits: 28: John Megahan. 30: John Megahan. 40-41: John Megahan. 42: John Megahan. 60: Terry Kovalcik. 65: John Megahan. 76: Sam Tomaselo. 82-83: Paul Mirocha. 84: John Megahan. 92: John Megahan. 93: John Megahan. 96: John Megahan. 94: Sam Tomaselo. 105: John Megahan. 114: Jennifer Fairman. 123: Bart Vallecoccia. 124: Bart Vallecoccia. 127: Bart Vallecoccia. 128: Bart Vallecoccia. 135: Jennifer Fairman. 136: Bart Vallecoccia. 138: John Megahan. 145: Linda Nye. 147: Laurie O'Keefe. 148: Linda Nye. 149: Linda Nye. 150: Linda Nye. 157: Laurie O'Keefe. 158: Linda Nye. 161: Laurie O'Keefe. 168: Bart Vallecoccia. 169: Bart Vallecoccia. 176: Lou Pappas. 182-183: John Kaufman. 191: John Edwards. 192: Jeff Grunewald. 193: Jeff Grunewald. 194: John Kaufman. 196: John Kaufman. 197: John Kaufman. 198: John Kaufman. 204-205: John Kaufman. 210: Jeff Grunewald. 220: David Coulson. 235: John Kocon. 235: Jeff Grunewald. 236: John Edwards. 237: Jeff Grunewald. 238: John Kocon. 244-245: John Edwards. 245: Jeff Grunewald. 246-247: Jeff Grunewald. 258: John Kaufman. 265: John Kaufman. 266: John Kaufman. 294-295: Stan Maddock for Prcision Graphics. 300-301: John Kaufman. 302: Jeff Grunewald. 309: John Kaufman. 316: John Kaufman. 319: Jeff Grunewald. 320: Jeff Grunewald. 322: Jeff Grunewald. 326: David Coulson. 327: David Coulson. 344: Jeff Grunewald. 345: Jeff Grunewald. 348: Jeff Grunewald. 364: Jeff Grunewald. 365: Jeff Grunewald. 366-367: Jeffrey Mangiat. 368-369: Jeff Grunewald. 393: Jeff Grunewald. 403: David Coulson. 410: Jeff Grunewald. 411: Jeff Grunewald. 424: Rainey Kirk. 436: Jeff Grunewald. 437: Jeff Grunewald. 438: Jeff Grunewald. 439: Jeff Grunewald. 440: Jeff Grunewald. 452: Bart Vallecoccia. 453: Bart Vallecoccia.

Photography Credits: All photographs are by Macmillan/McGraw Hill (MMH) except as noted below:

24: Kevin & Betty Collins/Visuals Unlimited. 26: Jim Zuckerman/Corbis. 27: (tl) Michael Gabridge/Visuals Unlimited; (bcl) Visuals Unlimited. 32: (tl) The Granger Collection; (cr) Dr. Gopal Murti/Visuals Unlimited; (bl) The Granger Collection. 33: (tl) Visuals Unlimited; (tc) Michael Gabridge/Visuals Unlimited; (tc) Dr. Gopal Murti/Visuals Unlimited. 38: Science Photo Library. 39: Rich Kirchner/NHPA. 41: (c) Geoff Brightling/Dorling Kindersley; (c) Grant Heilman. 48: Carol Walker/nature.pl. 49: (l) Brent Huffman/NHPA; (tr) George McCarthy/nature.pl; (tcr) Ernie James/NHPA; (cl) Getty; (cl) Martin Harvey/NHPA; (r) Photo Researchers. 50: (r) Jim Zuckerman/Corbis; (bl) John Serrao / Photo Researchers, Inc. 51: (tr) Steve Harkin/Ardea.com; (tcr) James Carmichael/NHPA; (tcr) Wolcott Henry/National Geographic Image Collection; (tcr) Ken Lucas/Animals/Animals; (tcl) Corbis (tl); DIL_BXP_47990.jpg. 52: Darrell Gulin/Getty Images. 53: (tl) David Sieren / Visuals Unlimited; (tc) Bonnie Sue Rauch / Photo Researchers, Inc.; (tc) The Image Works; (tcr) Photo Researchers; (tr) Gary Moss/Botanica 54: (c) Phil Degginger/Getty Images; (cr) Alamy; (tr) DIL. 55: (cl) Agricultural Science Department of Canada; (bc) Alamy; (bc) Dr. David Phillips/Visuals Unlimited; (bcr) Stem Jems / Photo Researchers, Inc. 56: (c) Alamy; (cl) Win van Egmong Getty Images (cr) Eye of Science / Photo Researchers, Inc. 110: James Cavalleni/Photo Researchers. 113: Getty Images. 116: Ron Chapple/Getty Images. 120: Susumu Nishinaga/Photo Researchers. 122: Alamy Images. 124: (c) Philip Dowell /Dorling Kindersley; (tr) Ralph Hutchings/Visuals Unlimited. 125: Mediscan/Visuals Unlimited. 127: Dr. Richard Kessel and Dr.Gene Shih Visuals Unlimited. 132: Anatomical Travelogue/Photo Researchers. 134: Jackie Chapman/Alamy. 142: Photo Researchers. 144: Megapress/Alamy. 145: (tl) BSIP / Photo Researchers, Inc; (cl) SPL / Photo Researchers, Inc; (cr) David Bassett / Photo Researchers, Inc. 146: (tcr) Science Photo Library; (tr) Biophoto Associates / Photo Researchers, Inc1. 148: (tcr) Eye of Science / Photo Researchers, Inc; (bl) Science Photo

Library. 154: Dr. Dennis Kunkel/Visuals Unlimited. 159: Dr. Dennis Kunkel/ Visuals Unlimited. 160: (cl) Science Photo Library; (cr) Science Photo Library. 180: Andrew McKinney/Dorling Kindersley. 184: (tr) Getty Images. 184-185: (b) Getty Images. 188-189: (inset) Corbis. 188-189: (l) Ernie James/NHPA. 192-193: Corbis. 195: (tl) Brian Cosgrove/Dorling Kindersley; (tl) Photo Researchers. 195: (bl) Alamy. 195: 196: (cl) Corbis. 196: (bl) Visuals Unlimited; (bc) Visuals Unlimited; (br) Corbis. 202: ML Sinibaldi/Corbis. 206: NASA/GOES. 207: (tr) Alamy; (r) Getty Images. 208: (bkgd) Getty Images; (inset) Jack Kelly Clark/University of California. 210: Lawrence Migdale/Photo Researchers. 214: Getty Images. 217: Lancaster California Department of Water. 218: (c) Peter Arnold; (tl) Corbis. 219: Corbis. 232: Chris Beall. 234: Science Photo Library/Photo Researchers. 235: Alamy. 242-243: Corbis. 245: (br) Bill Ross/Corbis; (br) Tim McGuire/Corbis. 252: Science Photo Library. 257: Curt Ebbesmeyer. 262: Digitalvision. 264: Corbis. 267: National Geographic. 268: Weatherpix. 270: Alamy. 271: NASA/JPL. 272: Alamy. 276: Alamy. 278: Index Stock. 282: NOAO. 284: (br) Alamy cr) Ray Nelsonn/ Phototake; (tr) Alamy. 296-297: NASA/JPL/Caltech/Corbis. 298: NASA/JPL/SOHO/Photo Researchers. 306-307: Astronomy Picture of the Day. 308: The Granger Collection. 310: (tc) NASA/JPL; (tr) NASA/JPL;(tr) NASA/JPL. (tl) NASA/JPL; (br) Corbis. 311: (tl) NASA/JPL; (tr) NASA/JPL. 312: DIL. 316-317: Picture Quest. 318: NASA/Corbis. 321: NASA/Corbis. 322: (tr) Ken Lucas / Visuals Unlimited; (tr) Ken Lucas / Visuals Unlimited. 340: Alamy. 344: NHPA. 370: (br) Oak Ridge National laboratory. 371: (tl) University of California Berkeley; (tr) National Center Electron Microscope(bl) Oak Ridge National Laboratory. 372: (cr) IBM; (tr) Peter Arnold. 381: Dorling Kindersley. 388-389: Getty Images. 390: Visuals Unlimited. 391: Getty Images. 392: Corbis. 393: (tr) Getty Images. 393: (cl) Alamy. 394: (cl) Visuals Unlimited. (c) Visuals Unlimited. (cry) Visuals Unlimited. 396: Corbis. 408-409: Getty/Image Bank. 410: (c) Visuals Unlimited. 412: (CT) Chemistry Comes Alive. 412: (CB) Chemistry Comes Alive. 414: (CL) Photo Researchers. 414: (C) Photo Researchers. 415: (CL) Corbis. 415: (CR) Peter Arnold. 416: (TR) Alamy. 420-421: Corbis. 422: (BL) Photo Researchers. 422: (C) Visual Unlimited. 423: (B) Peter Arnold. 423: (TL) Alamy. 423: (TR) Getty Images. 423: (TR) Peter Arnold. 424: (TR) Getty Images. 425: (TR) Getty Images. 426: (TR) Getty Images. 426: (TR) Corbis. 427: (TL) Photo Researchers. 427: (BL) Bridgeman Art Gallery. 427: (BL) Royalty Free/Corbis. 428: (BL) National Geographic Society. 428: (BR) IPN Stock. 429: (R) Alamy. 430: (BR) Alamy. 430: (TR) Corbis. 434-435: Photo Researchers. 436: (BL) Corbis. 437: (T) Photo Researchers. 438: (R) Getty Images. 439: (BR) Getty Images/Image Bank. 441: (TL) Getty Images. 442: (BR) Corbis. 442: (TR) Corbis. 443: (TL) Getty Images. 443: (BR) Alamy. 444: (TR) Alamy. 444: (C) Alamy.

Acknowledgments

"Astronaut Stopping by a Planet on a Snowy Evening" from Science Verse by Jon Scieszka. Text copyright © 2004 by Jon Scieszka. Published by The Penguin Group. All rights reserved.

"Bigger Muscles or a Stronger Heart" from Current Health. Copyright © 2005 by Current Health. Published by Weekly Reader Corporation.

"Branches" from Echoes for the Eye by Barbara Juster Esbensen. Text copyright © 1996 by Barbara Juster Esbensen. Published by HarperCollins Children's Books. All rights reserved.

"Cancer-Catching Canines" from Scholastic SuperScience. Copyright © 2005 by Scholastic SuperScience. Published by Scholastic, Inc.

"Metamorphosis" from Honey and Salt by Carl Sandburg. Copyright © 1963 by Carl Sandburg and renewed 1991 by Margaret Sandburg, Helga Sandburg Crile, and Janet Sandburg.

Credits